THE SECOND EDITION
RACING-
CRUISER

THE RACING-CRUISER

SECOND EDITION

RICHARD HENDERSON

Illustrations by the author

INTERNATIONAL MARINE PUBLISHING COMPANY
Camden, Maine

Dedicated to my father
William L. Henderson

OTHER BOOKS BY RICHARD HENDERSON

First Sail for Skipper
Hand, Reef and Steer
Dangerous Voyages of Captain William Andrews (ed.)
Sail and Power (with B.S. Dunbar)
The Racing-Cruiser
The Cruiser's Compendium
Sea Sense
Singlehanded Sailing
Better Sailing
East to the Azores
Choice Yacht Designs
Philip L. Rhodes and His Yacht Designs
John G. Alden and His Yacht Designs
  (with Robert W. Carrick)

© 1983 by International Marine Publishing Company
Typeset by Journal Publications, Camden, Maine
Printed and bound by The Alpine Press, Stoughton, Massachusetts

Published by International Marine Publishing Company
21 Elm Street, Camden, Maine 04843
(207) 236-4342

Library of Congress Cataloging in Publication Data

Henderson, Richard, 1924-
   The racing cruiser.
   Includes index.
   1. Sailboat racing.   I. Title.
GV826.5.H46   1983   797.1'4   82-25858
ISBN 0-87742-169-2

Contents

Preface to Second Edition

About 15 years have elapsed since the first edition of this book appeared. Not long after it was published, the International Offshore Rule (IOR) came into full flower, altering the complexion of racing. Existing boats soon became outmoded for serious competition, and new ones designed especially for IOR racing became increasingly specialized, sophisticated, and expensive; often in major races they were manned by "factory teams" of semiprofessional sailors. This led to the development of so-called Grand Prix racing, and it left out in the cold a great many part-time racing yachtsmen who owned dual-purpose racing-cruisers.

Happily, this situation has changed over the past few years, and dual-purpose boats now have a place (actually, at least two places) to race. Today the vast majority of sizable sailing yachts are competing against each other under two different handicap rules, which are reasonably fair to all types of racing-cruisers. These rules are the MHS (Measurement Handicap System) and the popular PHRF (Performance Handicap Racing Fleet); both of these systems are explained in Chapter 7. There is still a real need for IOR racing for international competition (since many different countries use this rule) and for speed development. I am glad, however, that, with the MHS and PHRF systems, there is ample opportunity to enjoy keen competition in boats that are not only fast but comfortable, seakindly, and easily handled as well. This book covers the IOR, but it does not concentrate on the Grand Prix style of racing. Rather, it is directed at the beginning racer and the numerous owners of multipurpose boats who wish to spend only part of their time racing.

Preface to First Edition

Many fine books have been written on the subject of yacht racing. The vast majority of these books have concentrated on small racing sailboats of a particular kind — the *one-design classes* or boats of as nearly as possible identical hulls and rigs that race boat for boat (one boat of a certain class competing against sisters of the same class).

In general, this book deals with the subject of yacht racing, but it focuses on selecting and racing fairly large boats that have some cruising accommodations — those sailing yachts sometimes described as *racing-cruisers*. These boats usually race against each other on a handicap basis. I have chosen to concentrate on racing-cruisers for several reasons. First, this is the area of racing in which I feel most at home and have the most experience. Second, it is the area least covered by other books — especially the area of handicap racing *on soundings* (near shore). And third, it is an area of rapid growth and increasing popularity.

Several factors account for the increasing interest in racing-cruisers. New materials and methods of production have brought the price of moderate-size boats within the grasp of many dedicated sailors. In recent years boat designers have developed a great variety of high-performance craft that incorporate surprisingly comfortable accommodations at very little sacrifice to speed. In fact, it is not uncommon to see racing-cruisers overtake out-and-out racing boats of comparable size when they are sailing over the same race course. Many skippers of small one-design boats are finding that they can enjoy high-performance sailing in larger racing-cruisers and the same keen competition that is found in small-boat classes. Indeed, many small-boat-class champions who have moved up to big boats have been surprised to find that the "pickin's" are not so easy, that the newfound competition is more than bargained for. Of course, much of this competition is due to the accumulation over the years of top talent from the many competitive small-boat classes. At any rate, many small-boat sailors are coming to realize that they can enjoy fairly economical racing of high quality in versatile boats that can also serve as comfortable family day-sailers and overnighters or even offshore cruisers.

Other newcomers to the racing-cruisers are first-boat

owners who have improved their sailing skills to the point where they wish to begin racing, crewmembers who have acquired a great deal of racing knowledge and wish to try their hand at being skippers, and devotees of cruising who want fast cruising boats that will be competitive for occasional racing.

This book is directed primarily to the following: (1) sailors in general who wish to begin racing, (2) experienced small-boat racers who wish to race bigger boats, (3) all prospective buyers of racing-cruisers, especially those for whom racing is a prime objective, (4) those who wish to crew on racing-cruisers, and (5) experienced racing-cruiser sailors who want a handy compendium of reference material. The book attempts to cover boat selection, equipping, safety, and accommodation features; hull and rig tuning; sails; and basic tactics, strategy, and sailing techniques. It discusses in simple terms such semitechnical subjects as yacht design, aerodynamics, and handicap measurement rules. In addition, the book strives continually to point out differences between racing large and small boats.

I assume that the reader already knows the basic principles and terminology of sailing. In this book, therefore, only those words pertaining to racing or those that are unusual or semitechnical are defined. When a word that needs explaining or defining appears, it is italicized and accompanied by an explanation when first used in the text.

Here's wishing the reader satisfaction in selecting, tuning, and racing his racing-cruiser. May he have his fair share of challenging windward legs, steady winds, and well-set starting lines.

Acknowledgments

Many knowledgeable people have been helpful and generous in expressing their opinions and supplying me with specific information for this book. The following list includes sailors, designers, sailmakers, riggers, yacht yard workers and managers, race committee officials, and yacht measurers to whom I am indebted. Many thanks to: James F. Allsopp, Robert S. Blumenstock, Richard D. Carlson, Thomas H. Closs, Sr., Thomas H. Closs, Jr., Reid A. Dunn, Clayton Ewing, Paul F. Fitzgerald, Frederick C. Grell, Irving Groupp, Robert G. Henry, Jr., Richard F. Jablin, Edward Karkow, A. Preston Kelly, Sr., A. Preston Kelly, Jr., Karl L. Kirkman, A.E. Luders, Jr., Allan Mackenzie, James A. Potter, Frederick A. Potts, John F. Quinn, Wallace C. Ross, Bruce Smart, Charles F. Stein, Jr., Roger C. Taylor, Owen C. Torrey, Charles R. Ulmer, Dwight Webb, Harold R. White, John White, and John W. Wright.

1/ An Introduction to Racing

WHY RACE?

Sailboat racing may be considered as both a means to an end and an end in itself. In the latter case, it is racing for the love of the sport; for the competition, excitement, and stimulation; for the mastery of sailing skills; for the team spirit and crew camaraderie; and even for the almost unparalleled visual beauty of racing boats in action. In addition, there is the great satisfaction gained by acquiring and applying a wide variety of knowledge that includes boat behavior, sails, wind, weather, tide, and much more.

As a means to an end, racing rounds out the sailor's life and exposes him to many fine points of the art that, without competition, he might never come to know. Admittedly, formal racing is not everyone's cup of tea. There are those who like to cruise, whether they be the offshore passagemakers or the gunkholers, those who quietly push from one shallow creek to another. Cruising is a wonderful way of life, but for those who want to get the most from a balanced sailing life and to live sail-

ing to the hilt, racing is a must, even if it is only occasional. Racing does not merely broaden the sailor's range of experience, it sharpens his awareness, develops efficiency, and improves his seamanship. For example, after a lengthy period of leisurely cruising, many sailors are satisfied with complacent and lethargic sailing, seldom bothering to improve a sheet lead or to set a light sail when there is a need for it. An occasional diet of racing will shake him from such lethargy, make him more aware of the need for rigging adjustments or sail trim, make him alert to changing conditions of the wind or tide, give him confidence to set the spinnaker or drive the boat in heavy weather. Thus is racing a means to an end: it will give the sailor more pleasure and a better sense of values in all forms of sailing.

There are some sailors who profess a distaste for formal racing, but when these people own fast boats, they seldom shy away from a subtle brush or informal race. Although they may not care to admit it, most boat owners take pride in their skill as sailors and especially in the performance of their boats. Even the rare sailor who openly decries every form of racing can often be seen slyly changing course or improving sail trim when he finds his boat alongside another of similar size. Occasionally he can be caught casting a furtive glance in the direction of the other boat to judge the relative performance of his own craft. This is almost irresistible for a devoted sailor who owns a smart sailing boat. Chances are that any true sailing buff who never can be tempted to race owns a sluggish tub of a boat (but, of course, he'll claim his boat is wonderfully comfortable or seaworthy).

With formal racing, a proper mental attitude has a marked effect on full enjoyment of the sport. First of all, newcomers to yacht racing must accept certain responsibilities. They must learn and abide by the rules of the game. They must familiarize themselves with the measurement rules and the racing rules, principally those that have to do with right-of-way situations. Impeccable honesty and sportsmanship are important in any sport, of course, but especially so in yacht racing, where there are no umpires or referees.

In boat racing there should be a happy medium between levity and seriousness. There is no doubt that the top racing skippers have a determined and earnest desire to win, but when racing becomes grim, it ceases to be fun. Then there is no point in doing it. However, a certain degree of calm seriousness from both skipper and crew during a race is essential for concentration and attention to details.

Racing sailors need never feel humiliated for simply losing a race. The main considerations should be to avoid unnecessary mistakes and to learn something from the mistakes they do make. After all, the object is complete enjoyment of the sport, and the greatest rewards come from gradual improvement and the challenge of trying to approach perfection in sailing skills and seamanship.

KINDS OF RACES

Although there are several variations in the way that sailboats can race, the two basic forms of competition are boat-for-boat and handicap racing. In the first case, identical boats or boats of similar speed potential race over the same course. With this form of competition, the boat that finishes first, or has the least *elapsed time* (the actual time from start to finish), is the winner.

Handicap racing, however, involves the competition of boats of different sizes and different speed potentials against each other; therefore, the first boat to finish is not necessarily the winner. Performance of handicap racers is predicted by observing performance or by measuring various features of each boat and applying these measurements to a *rating formula.* As a result of this, each boat is given a *rating* or *rated length* that is assigned a *time allowance* in seconds per mile. The allowance one boat receives from another in a given race is the difference between their time allowances, as shown in standard tables, multiplied by the race distance in miles. The elapsed time of each boat is taken, and time allowances are applied to give each boat a *corrected time.* The boat with the lowest corrected time is the winner.

Rating measurements are the principal dimensions and characteristics of a boat that have a direct bearing on her potential speed or performance. These include length, beam, draft, *displacement* (or weight), sail area, and certain propeller measurements. Measurement rules are rather complex, so most of Chapter 7 is devoted to them.

Most racing-cruisers compete under handicap systems, but if there are enough boats of the same stock class (identical boats of the same design), they may race each other as a class on a boat-for-boat basis. Examples in the United States are the Alberg 30 and Cal 40 classes. These boats may and usually do participate in handicap racing as well.

Under the International Offshore Rule (IOR) there has evolved the concept of *level racing,* whereby boats of similar handicap ratings compete against each other boat-for-boat. The various rating levels are referred to as *Ton Cup* classes (named after an historic trophy awarded for international racing). The Ton Cuppers may be entirely different designs, but they must have ratings at or below a designated rating level. The levels in order of size are the fairly large Two-Ton class (to be discontinued in 1984) and the progressively smaller One-Ton, Three-Quarter-Ton, Half-Ton, Quarter-Ton, and Mini-Ton classes.

What we have been talking about thus far might be termed *fleet racing,* where individuals in a fleet of boats race against every other boat in the group. This is the usual form of racing, but on certain occasions boats *match race* or *team race.* Match racing is limited to a pair of boats, one against the other. Although this type of competition is relatively infrequent, it has been brought to the public's attention through the America's Cup races, where, in recent times, one 12-meter boat has been matched against another.

Team racing matches a team of boats, usually a small group of four or five boats, against another team or, in rare instances, several teams having the same number of boats. This kind of competition is most often seen when one yacht club challenges another to race in identical or nearly identical boats. Sometimes an interclub competition involving many clubs will use class boats to fleet race in a *round-robin series,* with one club using one boat. In this case, there is an exchange of boats, with each crew sailing a different boat in each race.

Both match racing and team racing involve special tactics or subtle variations of standard tactics. Chapter 10 is devoted to boat-vs.-boat tactics and general course strategy, with an occasional mention of match racing, but, for the most part, the chapter concentrates on the tactics of the most common form of competition, fleet racing.

RACE COURSES

All race courses belong to one of two broad classifications: the *closed course* and the *point-to-point course.* The latter involves racing from one geographic location to another. The race distance may be great or small as long as the start and finish are not in the same general locality. Points of sailing during this kind of race depend to a large extent upon the vagaries of wind direction, but many courses include intermediate turning marks to give legs of varying directions, thereby increasing the chances that there will be at least some windward work and/or downwind sailing suitable for carrying spinnakers. Most distance and ocean races are point to point.

Closed courses have their starts and finishes in the same or nearly the same general locality. The usual day race over a fairly short closed course is often referred to as a round-the-buoys race. In this kind of race, the courses are laid out to vary the points of sailing, to give reaches, runs, and especially beats to windward. Courses are usually planned to keep beam reaches and close reaches to a minimum, because boats are least likely to change positions on these points of sailing. A race composed of reaching legs that are too close to the wind for effective spinnaker sailing is very likely to end up as a "parade," with each boat being unable to pass the next boat ahead of her. Most closed courses are laid out to give long windward legs, because working to windward provides the greatest test of ability in helmsmanship and tactics, in nonplaning boats at least. Whenever possible, the course should be planned so that the first turning mark lies dead to windward.

Short closed courses are nearly always planned to be *windward-leeward, triangular,* or some combination of both. The most common forms of these courses are illustrated in Figures 1-1 through 1-5. These figures show typical windward-leeward, triangular, *Gold Cup, modified Gold Cup,* and *Olympic* courses.

Figure 1-1 shows three windward-leeward variations, with A being the simplest form of an acceptable course. Variation B involves an extra turning mark and places the starting line in the middle of the beating leg to give an initial short beat, followed by a long run and another short beat to the finish. C is similar to A, except that there is an extra windward leg that puts the finish line at the first turning mark. Figure 1-2 shows a typical triangular course, with a right angle, but such a course may have an equilateral or any other triangular shape as long as it gives the desirable points of sailing. The Gold Cup course, Figure 1-3, has a windward-leeward round followed by a triangular round, while the modified Gold Cup, Figure 1-4, puts the triangular round first and the windward-leeward second. The Olympic course in Figure 1-5 is similar to the modified Gold Cup with an extra windward leg.

All turning marks should be left on the same *hand* (side) unless participants are instructed to the contrary. Port turns, as shown in Figures 1-1 through 1-5, are preferable, since they allow boats to round the windward mark on the starboard tack, which gives them the right-of-way. However, when the course is laid out so that boats have to cross their own tracks soon after rounding a mark, there may be a mixture of rounding designations, in the interest of safety, with some marks being left to port and others to starboard. Turning marks may be government marks, such as channel markers, buoys, beacons, or lighthouses, or they may be partially or entirely privately owned club marks. The latter type may be large, inflatable, orange-colored buoys or brightly painted Styrofoam buoys on pylons. Often these markers will be fitted with pieces of shiny metal to increase visibility.

Very often locales are restricted geographically so that perfect windward-leeward and triangular courses cannot be laid out. In such cases it becomes necessary to sail irregular courses, but these usually are oriented to the prevailing winds, and they can nearly always be planned to give at least one good windward leg per race, with some variety in points of sailing on the other legs.

STARTING AND FINISHING LINES

Figure 1-6 shows three types of starting or finishing lines. For racing-cruisers, A is the most usual type. Each line is imaginary and runs between two marks, or between a mark and a yellow or orange flag on a *committee boat.* This boat, usually displaying a flag marked RC

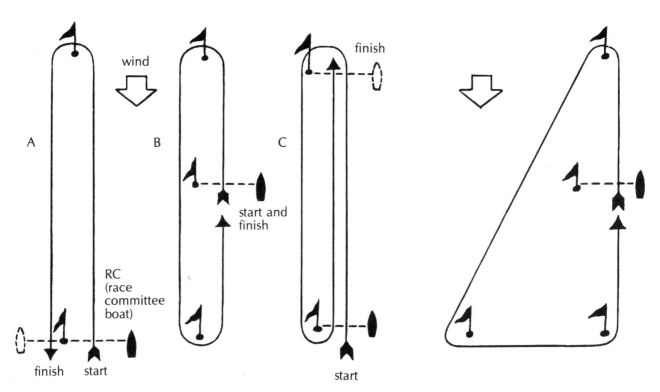

Figure 1-1. WINDWARD-LEEWARD COURSES   **Figure 1-2. TRIANGULAR COURSE**

(race committee), may be of any kind large enough to accommodate several of the sponsoring club's committeemen, but not so large that she blocks the starting boats or interferes with their wind. She needs a rig for hoisting signals. Each contestant attempts to cross the starting line headed toward the first turning mark with full way on, exactly when the starting signal is given.

As shown in Figures 1-1 through 1-6(A), it is customary to set up the starting line so that the starting mark is left on the same hand as the other marks of the course. If marks are left to port, as shown in the diagrams, then the starting mark is on the port-hand end of the line when heading toward the first turning mark, and the committee boat is to starboard. Although this practice is customary, it is by no means invariable. Some race committees prefer to place the committee boat at the port-hand end of the line, because boats tend to jam up on the starboard side of the line. This crowding occurs because many skippers like to start at the windward end of the line on the starboard tack. However, a port-side committee boat can be dangerous on a windward start, because it can create a trap, often called *coffin corner,* for starboard-tack boats on the extreme port side of the line when there is a last-minute heading wind shift. This is explained in Figure 1-7. If boat A sails into the shaded area, she is trapped because she cannot bear off suffi-

ciently to clear the committee boat, and she cannot tack because of the proximity of boat B, A must bear off, as shown by the curved arrow, before she reaches the shaded area.

It is also customary (but optional) to set the finish line so that the finishing mark is passed on the same hand as the other marks. In Figures 1-1, 1-3, and 1-4 the committee boats have changed positions relative to their accompanying markers for the sake of mark-passing uniformity. Of course, this method requires moving the committee boat, but often she must be moved anyway if the line's mark is a fixed buoy, because in most cases the finish line should be no more than half the length of the starting line. Of course, a finish line in the middle of the windward leg, as in Figures 1-1(B) and 1-2, makes it unnecessary to move the committee boat, unless shortening the finish line is the consideration. The finish line is usually set at right angles to the last leg, as shown in Figures 1-1 through 1-5.

Most competent race committees try to set the starting line in such a way that the first turning mark lies dead to windward and the line lies nearly at right angles to the wind. Of course, this is often impossible. On many point-to-point races, for example, reaching and running starts are necessary, but whenever possible, the start should be to windward. Even if the course cannot

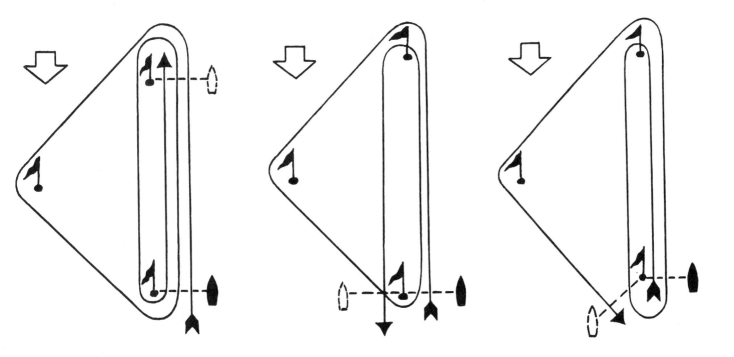

Figure 1-3. GOLD CUP COURSE **Figure 1-4. MODIFIED GOLD CUP COURSE** **Figure 1-5. OLYMPIC COURSE**

be planned so that the first turning mark is dead to windward, *the line should be set nearly square to the wind.* The reason for this is that such a setting tends to spread contestants fairly evenly along the line. The object of such a line is to avoid bunching or jams near the line's mark or the committee boat. Theoretically, every point on the perfectly set line should be equally attractive. An argument in favor of windward starts is that beating tends to spread the distance between contestants so that boats do not arrive simultaneously at the first turning mark.

In attempting to achieve the ideal windward starting line, some race committees slant the line slightly away from the right angle by about 5 or even 10 degrees, with the port end slightly closer to the first turning mark (see Figure 1-8). The reason for this is that, given a line exactly 90 degrees to the wind, many starboard-tack starters will crowd the starboard end of the line, trying to get to windward of their adversaries. Also, with a perfectly square line, those starboard-tack starters to leeward will lack the right-of-way after tacking and thus will be unable to tack if they so desire immediately after the start. This tends to make the starboard end of the line slightly more attractive. Slanting the line away from the perpendicular makes the end that is closest to the first mark more favorable (see Figure 1-8). This is ex-

plained in greater detail in the discussion of starting tactics in Chapter 8. Line slanting on windward starts should be very slight because overdoing it would overly favor the port end and cause boats to crowd at that end.

It is interesting to note that in old editions of the *Race Committee Handbook,* published by the North American Yacht Racing Union (now the United States Yacht Racing Union), a 10-degree slant is recommended, while later editions suggest only a 2-to-5-degree slant. Actually the degree of slant should be determined by a judgment of all factors that would favor either end of the line, such as tide, wind, and anticipated courses of most boats.

With reaching starts, line slanting is (or should be) much more drastic when the line is cocked as much as 15 to 30 degrees away from a perpendicular to the course to the first turning mark, with the leeward end considerably closer than the windward end to the first mark. This increases the attractiveness of the leeward end and prevents crowding at the windward end. With running starts, however, the line is approximately square to the course to the first mark.

The length of the starting line is determined by the size and number of boats participating. A general rule of thumb is that for windward starts, the line should be slightly more than the product of the number of boats

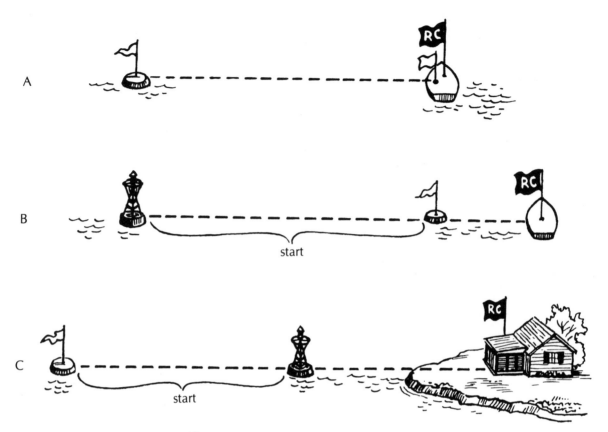

Figure 1-6. TYPICAL STARTING LINES

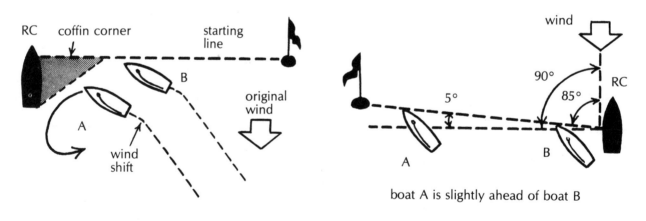

Figure 1-7. COFFIN CORNER

boat A is slightly ahead of boat B

Figure 1-8. RECOMMENDED LINE FOR WINDWARD STARTS

times the overall length of the largest boat. For example, if there are 20 boats racing, with the largest being 40 feet, the line should be at least 800 to perhaps 1,000 feet long.

STARTING SYSTEM

Races are started with both visual and audible signals. The audible signals are traditionally made with guns or signal cannons, but nowadays the extremely loud freon horns are often used. Visual signals are in the form of flags or various geometric shapes, usually cylinders or cones, that are raised or hoisted a short distance off the committee boat's deck.

The following starting system is customary: At 10 minutes before the start, a warning signal is made, audibly and visibly at the same instant. Four minutes later, the visual warning signal is lowered, and one minute later a preparatory signal is given audibly and visibly. Four minutes later, the preparatory signal is lowered, and one minute after this, the starting signal is made, again by sight and sound. Because guns can misfire and horns can fail, the visual signals govern, and the exact time of the start is judged by the raising of the flag or shape. The customary visual signals (especially for racing-cruisers) are a white flag or shape for the 10-minute warning signal, a blue flag or shape for the five-minute preparatory signal, and a red flag or shape for the start.

Frequently, many different classes of boats use the same starting line. A large fleet of racing-cruisers is often divided into classes designated as A, B, C, etc., according to number and size or measurement ratings. Class A is generally made up of the largest boats. In such cases, one class usually starts after another, and very often the starting signal for class A will be the warning signal for class B, the start of B will be the warning signal for C, and so forth. Most race committees explain their exact system in race instructions that are mailed or otherwise distributed before the race.

Other signals used frequently by the race committee are shown in Figure 1-9. These include postponement, abandonment, missing mark, reverse course, shortened course, and recall signals. When code flag P is used for a preparatory signal, the warning signal is usually the class flag or another distinctive signal, and the start is indicated by lowering both the warning and the preparatory signals. All these signals are explained in greater detail in the USYRU (United States Yacht Racing Union) Racing Rules. The usual reasons for the postponement or abandonment of a race have to do

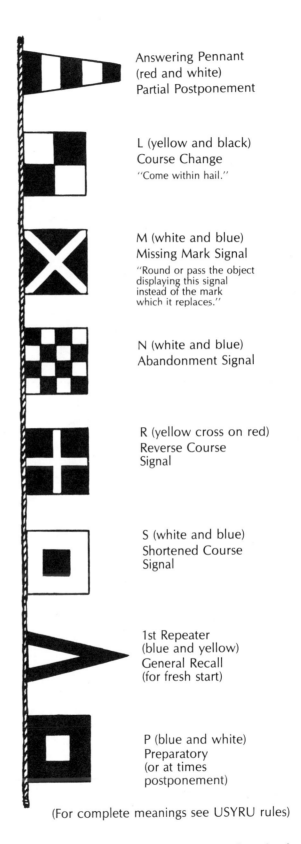

Answering Pennant
(red and white)
Partial Postponement

L (yellow and black)
Course Change
"Come within hail."

M (white and blue)
Missing Mark Signal
"Round or pass the object displaying this signal instead of the mark which it replaces."

N (white and blue)
Abandonment Signal

R (yellow cross on red)
Reverse Course Signal

S (white and blue)
Shortened Course Signal

1st Repeater
(blue and yellow)
General Recall
(for fresh start)

P (blue and white)
Preparatory
(or at times postponement)

(For complete meanings see USYRU rules)

Figure 1-9. RACE SIGNALS (International Code Flags)

C·B·Y·R·A

STANDARD ENTRY FORM
(Print Legibly)

CLASS: _____

EVENT TITLE: _____

SANCTIONED EVENT NO.: | | | |

Sail Number	Name of Yacht	Competitor's Name.	CBYRA Membership No.	Affiliate Yacht Club	Club Code No.

Competitor's Name _____

Address: _____
           (Number and Street)   (City)   (State)   (Zip)

Telephone Numbers: Home (_____)_____-_____ Office (_____)_____-_____

HANDICAP CLASSES	This yacht conforms in every way to her Class Rules and Measurements. Handicap rating (if applicable) is on file with Class Representative, Host Club, or attached her:to.	ONE DESIGN CLASSES
Class Rating _____		Hull Color _____
Yacht Type _____		Crew _____
Hull Color _____		_____
Score in Region _____	YES_____ NO_____	_____

    I agree to abide by the regulations and sailing instructions for this event. In consideration of being permitted to enter this event, being knowledgeable of the risks of competitive sailing and knowing that it is my sole responsibility to decide whether to enter or continue any race, I voluntarily assume the risk of participation in this event and release the Host Club _____ and the people conducting the event from all liability in connection with any injury or damage that may occur.

Signature of Competitor _____ Date _____

NOTE: **Membership in CBYRA, Class Association, and an affiliate Yacht Club are required PRIOR to earning any points toward CBYRA High Point Trophies.**   (Failure to complete all pertinent blanks may cause rejection of entry.)

---

with the weather — too much wind, too little wind, or fog. The general recall signal is given when many boats have crossed the line before the starting signal and all boats are recalled for a fresh start on the next gun. When only one or a few boats cross the line early, only these boats are recalled and there is no new starting signal. Usually the committee boat will give one horn blast for each early starter, then the committee will endeavor to notify each yacht recalled by signaling or hailing, but it is the responsibility of each yacht to make a proper start. An early starter must recross the line and start over again. In order that they command attention, flag signals (except for R and S before the warning signal) are accompanied by sound signals.

RACE INSTRUCTIONS, REQUIREMENTS, AND EQUIPMENT

Race instructions usually come in the form of circulars, mailed or handed to contestants before the race. Collec-

tions of circulars in book form, published annually, are often sold in local yacht chandleries. Sometimes these written instructions are accompanied by oral instructions given from the committee boat or at a skippers' meeting held prior to a race or series. The race circular contains vital information such as the race date, racing rules under which the race is being sailed (nearly always the USYRU rules in the United States), the course, marks, signals, time and location of the start, the location of the finish line, scoring system, method of breaking ties, any special instructions or exceptions to standard USYRU procedures, length of course, time limit if any, protest procedure, prizes, postponement or abandonment procedure. Many race circulars even include a rough chart of the area showing location of marks and the course.

Most race committees require that participants fill out entry forms before entering a race. This is especially important for handicap races so that the committee has all the proper rating information. Reproduced on this page is a typical entry blank, in this case a form used by the Chesapeake Bay Yacht Racing Association (CBYRA). The racing number required in the form is the large identification number sewn on the sails of each participating boat. These numbers should be on both sides of mainsails and spinnakers, and on overlapping jibs. Numbers are assigned according to area location by the USYRU directly or often by the USYRU through the local yacht-racing association.

The word *class* on the entry form means any particular group (one-design or handicap) to which the entering boat belongs and for which there is a race scheduled, as shown in the race circular. The sanctioned event number is given in a book of sailing instructions published annually by the CBYRA, while the "club code number" is given in the *CBYRA Yearbook,* which is available to members. "Class rating" refers to the boat's handicap number, given on her rating certificate either in feet of rated length or seconds per mile, depending on the rule under which her class races. Details and explanations of the most frequently used measurement rating rules appear in Chapter 7.

Following is a partial checklist of recommended racing equipment to be carried aboard: (1) race circular, (2) USYRU Racing Rules, (3) stopwatch and clock, (4) detailed charts of the area, (5) compass, (6) binoculars,

(7) current tables, (8) class rules or handbook of local racing organization containing local regulations and list of competitors with their ratings, (9) parallel rulers or course protractor, (10) dividers, (11) protest flag, code flag B or a solid red flag, (12) spare parts and extras such as battens, sail tape, assortment of shackles, pins, turnbuckles, blocks, line, sail stops, sewing gear, marline, ribbon and thread for telltales, (13) masthead windsock or indicator, (14) small anchor and line, (15) leadline, (16) basic tools: screwdriver, pliers, etc., and (17) safety equipment.

The last item requires extensive comment, so it is considered in Chapter 4, where there are equipment lists for both short on-soundings races and offshore races. Many items in the preceding list should be carried on board at all times, but all are listed with the prime consideration of usefulness during a race. For example, the extra items are to replace gear that may be carried away, so that the boat can continue racing. The small anchor is of great importance in light air when sailing against a strong foul current. The protest flag is flown when a boat has been fouled in a right-of-way situation, or when the skipper wants to protest any racing-rule infringement or violation of the race instructions. Racing rules are discussed in Chapter 7.

2/ *Thoughts on Hull Design*

Some sailors seem to have the attitude that, since hulls are the way they are and existing hulls can't be changed drastically, they might as well leave hull design to the naval architect and not bother to investigate the subject. This kind of thinking falls short for several reasons. First of all, hull design is a fascinating subject and should be of real interest to sailors, especially those who race or sail offshore. The study of hull shape teaches us about the performance and behavior characteristics of boats, and this is important not only in getting to know your own new boat but also in understanding the boats of competitors. This latter point is also important in handicap racing, when boats of various designs are competing (more about this later when we discuss competition tactics).

As for your own boat, a little understanding of hull design will help guide you in such important matters as determining the best angle of heel, best fore-and-aft trim, and amount and distribution of ballast; obtaining favorable measurement ratings; managing your boat in heavy weather; helm balance; selection of propeller; centerboard adjustment; optimum sailing angles; fair-

ing and minor hull modifications; steering control; amount of gear to be carried and stowage of same; placement of tanks. As a new boat buyer, you will have a great variety of hulls to choose from, and often you will have to make many design judgments after simply looking at boats, plans, dimensions, advertising information, and written data. These judgments will include such vital characteristics as stability, seaworthiness, speed in various winds, behavior in head seas, performance to windward, steering tendencies, and general racing competitiveness.

As a final argument for knowing some of the principles of hull design, it seems logical that the more you learn about all aspects of sailing, the more successful you will be and the more fun you will get from it.

THE MODERN CONCEPT OF THE RACING-CRUISER

Today, sailing-yacht design has reached a high degree of scientific sophistication. A great deal of theoretical research is being done, and much use is being made of computers, wind tunnels, and model-testing tanks. Most stock hulls are tested thoroughly in the tank before they are produced. Despite advanced technology, however, sailboat design remains an art as well as a science. In fact, several of the most successful designers are men who have had little if any formal training as naval architects. Tank tests may yield useful information, but the designer produces the original concept. The designer still must make use of his "eye" for form, his intuition, and empirical knowledge developed through observation and sailing experience.

The tank cannot, at present at least, "design" a boat or give the naval architect all the answers. Imagine the complexity of forces and resistances working on a yacht offshore, beating against a head sea. The hull is being pushed through the water in a forward direction while yawed, or turned askew, at varying angles of heel, and it is simultaneously swaying (being moved bodily sideways), heaving (rising and falling), rolling, and pitching. Meanwhile, the helmsman is constantly changing the rudder angle to vary the effects of lift and drag forces acting on the hull.

There is very little radically new in sailing-yacht design. Many of the fads and trends of today were tried and used in only slightly different ways by such designers as Nathanael Herreshoff, Starling Burgess, F.D. Lawley, William Gardner, and Clinton Crane. To be convinced of this, leaf through the design sections of the yachting books and periodicals of the turn of the century. Of course, many gradual improvements in boat design have been made through slow evolution and step-by-step refinements.

The greatest changes influencing yacht design in recent years are new construction materials, changes in rating rules, and the yachtsman's and designer's concepts of what constitutes a cruising or racing type. Let me elaborate on this last point. Around 40 years ago, a cruising boat was usually thought of as a heavy, rugged, seakindly, not especially weatherly (close-winded) craft. These boats were built for comfortable cruising, and they were intended to be raced only rarely, and then only in a relatively informal way, against boats of similar type. By comparison, many of the modern, so-called cruising boats that are racing today, especially those light-displacement types with dinghy-shaped hulls and fin keels, are out-and-out racing machines. Those boats certainly would have been considered as such if they had been put into the cruising divisions of the past. With most popular cruisers racing today, there is great emphasis on racing ability. Although this type of boat is often designated as a "cruising" class boat in contemporary race circulars, perhaps the more accurate appellation is racing-cruiser, because she has been designed at least as much for racing as for cruising. (This name should not be confused with the European *International Cruising-Racer classes,* which are divided into 7-, 8-, 9-, 10.5-, and 12-meter classes. These boats race each other on a boat-for-boat basis.)

Boat design nearly always involves some compromises that require accentuating some important qualities at the expense of others. Compared with racing-cruising boats of the past, modern boats designed to the IOR are definitely faster, at least when running and beating to windward, but they almost always give up a certain amount of comfort, ease of handling, and seakindliness. The last characteristic has to do with steering control and especially ease of motion. It has little to do with seaworthiness, or the ability of the boat to hold together in heavy weather regardless of her crew's comfort. Many of the more conservative modern hulls could be considered reasonably seaworthy with proper handling, even if they are not seakindly. However, there are a number of recent designs, usually the smaller extreme IOR types, that should never be exposed to heavy weather offshore. These are the extremely beamy, flat-bottomed, ultralight boats with very fine bows, very short keels, high center of gravity, vulnerable rudders, and wide open sterns. Skippers of these boats may be willing to take some extra chances for the sake of a bit more speed, but there is little advantage in such a boat even for the fanatical racer, because any gain in speed is paid for with an increase in handicap rating. I would strongly recommend, especially for the beginner, a fairly conservative boat with moderate proportions. Such a boat can be reasonably fast but also safe and easy to manage.

PRELIMINARY TERMS AND DEFINITIONS

Before discussing the basic principles of hull design, let us review some descriptive terms and definitions. Figure 2-1 illustrates many basic dimensional terms, most of which are self-explanatory.

Strictly speaking, *garboard* means the plank, or *strake,* next to the keel, but the word is also used to refer to that part of the hull next to the keel on metal or molded boats. The word *rocker* is used to describe the fore-and-aft upward curvature, from amidships toward each end, of the bottom of the keel, but it may also refer to the fore-and-aft curvature of a boat's bottom or bilge. *Fairbody draft* refers to the depth below the water's surface of the deepest part of the hull's actual body (not including the keel). The *turn of the bilge* is the

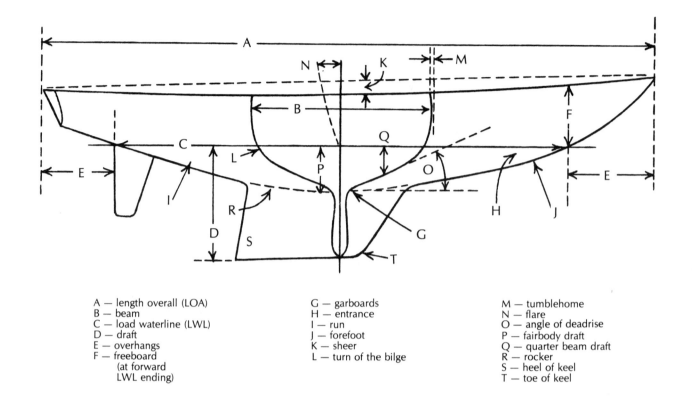

A — length overall (LOA)
B — beam
C — load waterline (LWL)
D — draft
E — overhangs
F — freeboard
    (at forward
    LWL ending)

G — garboards
H — entrance
I — run
J — forefoot
K — sheer
L — turn of the bilge

M — tumblehome
N — flare
O — angle of deadrise
P — fairbody draft
Q — quarter beam draft
R — rocker
S — heel of keel
T — toe of keel

Figure 2-1. HULL DESCRIPTIVE AND DIMENSIONAL NOMENCLATURE

athwartships curve where the boat's bottom turns into her topsides. A *slack bilge* makes a slow, gradual turn, while a *hard bilge* makes a sharper, tighter turn. The *angle of deadrise* refers to the upward slanting of the bottom from the keel to the turn of the bilge. A boat with a very low angle of deadrise would have a nearly flat bottom. *Flare* is the outward slanting of the topsides, while *tumblehome* refers to the inward curve of the topsides near the rail. *Sheerlines* are of several types, concave or conventional (shown in Figure 2-1), straight, *reversed* or *hogged* (having a humpbacked appearance), and *powderhorn sheer* (concave aft and reversed forward).

Figure 2-2 is a perspective sketch of a hull to show her lines. *Waterlines* are the horizontal lines representing planes passing through the hull parallel to the water's surface. The *load waterline* (LWL) is the actual contact line of the water's surface and the hull when the boat is floating upright. *Sections* are the lines formed by vertical planes passing through the hull at right angles to the fore-and-aft centerline. They usually divide the LWL into 10 equal parts. The *midship section* is at the midpoint of the LWL and is usually numbered station 5. *Buttocks* are the lines formed by vertical planes slicing

the hull parallel to the fore-and-aft centerline. The *diagonals* (not shown in Figure 2-2) are lines formed by oblique, longitudinal planes, which, from the fore-and-aft view, run from the centerline downward and outward and cut the sections approximately at right angles.

Plans are shown in three views. The side view, called the *sheer plan,* or *profile,* shows the sections as straight vertical lines, the waterlines as horizontal straight lines, and the buttocks as curved fore-and-aft lines. The fore-and-aft view, called the *body plan,* shows the buttocks as straight vertical lines, the waterlines as horizontal straight lines, and the sections as curves (usually S-curves in a round-bottomed keel boat). The view looking down on the hull, by convention usually showing half its width, is the *half-breadth plan,* and this shows the sections as straight lines at right angles to the centerline, the buttocks as straight lines parallel to the centerline, and the waterlines as curves running fore and aft.

Most of the following definitions are short and simple. In some cases, they may not be entirely adequate for complete understanding, but elaborations follow later in the chapter.

Displacement. Actual weight. As Archimedes discovered, a floating object displaces its own weight.

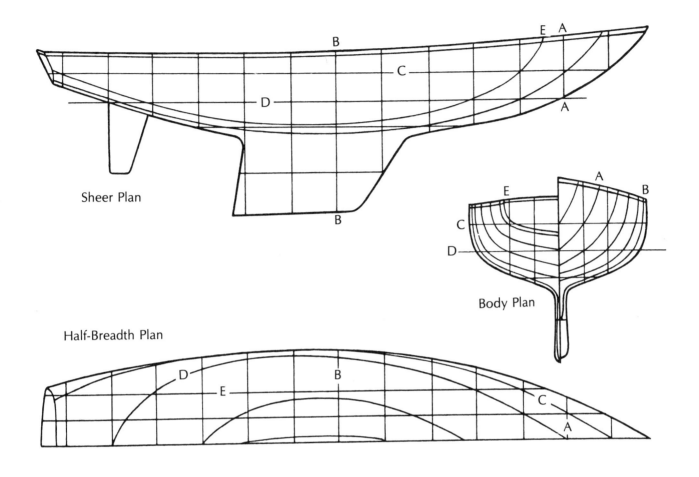

Sheer Plan

Body Plan

Half-Breadth Plan

A — sections
B — midship section
C — waterlines
D — load waterline
E — buttocks

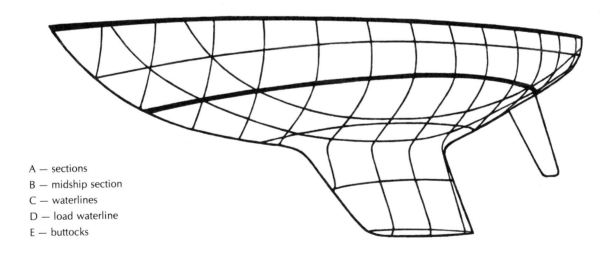

Figure 2-2. LINES AND PERSPECTIVE SKETCH (Author's Design)

Center of gravity (CG). The point at which the entire weight of the hull may be considered as concentrated.

Buoyancy. Upward pressure of the water exerted on the hull equal to the hull's displacement.

Center of buoyancy (CB). Center of gravity of the volume of water displaced by the hull. When the hull is upright, the CB and CG will lie on the same vertical line both laterally and longitudinally (fore and aft).

Metacenter (transverse metacenter). The point of intersection of a vertical line through the hull's CB when it is floating upright, with a vertical line through the new CB when the hull is heeled at a small angle (see Figure 2-25).

Stability. Tendency of a boat to return to an upright position after being heeled. A *stiff* boat is very stable, while a *crank,* or *tender,* boat heels easily.

Directional stability. Tendency to hold a straight course or not yaw (swing from side to side around the vertical axis).

Yaw angle (also *angle of leeway*). The angular difference between a boat's centerline and her actual course made good owing to her making leeway or crabbing, but not including any effects of current. Yaw angle is not a constant factor for a given hull design, of course; it varies for any hull according to conditions of wind and sea.

Helm balance. Relating to *weather helm,* when a boat turns into the wind, or *lee helm,* when a boat turns away from the wind, with the helm unattended in both cases.

Lateral plane. The immersed profile area or underwater, fore-and-aft, vertical plane.

Center of lateral resistance (CLR). The geometric center of the lateral plane or the theoretical point at which the hull could be pushed sideways without turning.

Center of effort (CE). The geometric center of a sail's silhouette or that of the entire sailplan where the wind's side force theoretically is concentrated. Helm balance has to do with the relationship of the CE of the sails that are set to the CLR.

Wave-making resistance. Waves caused by the hull's forward movement that become increasingly harmful to speed as a heavy boat moves faster. In general, designers try to shape the hull so that as little propulsion power as possible will be wasted in forming waves. Wave-making resistance depends on hull shape, displacement, and length.

Form resistance. Additional resistance, apart from wave making, due to the formation of eddies.

Induced drag. Increased resistance arising from heeling and making leeway.

Wetted-surface resistance. The skin friction between the *wetted surface,* or immersed surface area of the hull, and the water. Designers often lump wave, form, and induced resistance into one category called *residual resistance.* Residual resistance can be found from tank testing by measuring total resistance after model towing, then calculating skin friction, and subtracting this from the total resistance.

Planing. High-speed sailing when the hull rides up on its bow wave and partially escapes from its own wave system. Planing requires a planing hull, one that is fairly flat and of light displacement, in conjunction with good winds. Following seas are definitely helpful. The opposite of a planing hull is a *displacement hull,* which cannot plane and is limited in speed by its own wave system.

Speed-length ratio. The speed of a boat is relative to her length. The speed-length ratio compares a boat's speed to her length and is expressed in the formula

$$R = \frac{V}{\sqrt{L}}$$

R is the speed-length ratio, V is velocity in knots (nautical miles per hour), and L is the load waterline length in feet. For example, a boat making 4 knots with an LWL of 16 feet has a speed-length ratio of 1.0, the same as a 25-foot boat making 5 knots. Most racing-cruisers have a maximum speed-length ratio of about 1.35.

Displacement-length ratio

$$\frac{D}{(.01L)^3}$$

D is the displacement in tons and L is load waterline length. This ratio is useful for estimating resistance and for determining a boat's proper weight for her length, or vice versa.

Sail area–displacement ratio. Comparing sail area (SA) in square feet to displacement in cubic feet is expressed as

$$\frac{SA}{d^{2/3}}$$

This is a guide in determining amount of sail for a hull of given weight.

Sail area–wetted surface ratio

$$\frac{SA}{WS}$$

This gives a good indication of light-weather performance.

Ballast-displacement ratio

$$\frac{B}{D}$$

Comparing weight of keel to displacement gives some indication of stability.

Lift-drag ratio

$$\frac{L}{D}$$

Although this usually is associated with aerodynamics, the same principle is involved in hydrodynamics. The keel is a hydrofoil that alters the direction of water flow to create a *lift* force at right angles to the direction of flow, and *drag,* or resistance, in the direction of flow. The price for obtaining lift is drag, and the lift-drag ratio measures the efficiency of the hydrofoil.

Aspect ratio. A comparison of height and width of an airfoil or hydrofoil expressed by the formula

$$AR = \frac{height^2}{area}$$

Often, luff length is divided by foot length for sails.

Moment. Tendency to produce motion, especially about an axis. Examples are: heeling moment; its opposite, righting moment; and moment of inertia — all of which relate to a hull turning on its axis. The moment of a force is the force times the lever arm, or distance from the axis.

Scantlings. Specifications for construction; minimal sizes and weights of structural parts such as frames, beams, and planking for various types and sizes of vessels.

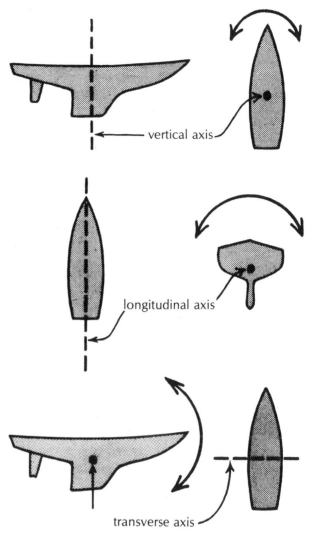

Figure 2-3. AXIAL TURNING

BASIC DESIGN CONSIDERATIONS

At the risk of great oversimplification, it might be said that the designer of a sailboat's hull is concerned primarily with two major factors — axial turning and resistance.

The hull turns around three axes: the vertical, the longitudinal, and the transverse, as shown in Figure 2-3. Turning on the vertical axis relates to steering control, yawing, and helm balance. Longitudinal axial turning relates to rolling, heeling, and righting, or transverse stability. Transverse axial turning relates to such matters as pitching and hull trim.

The second major factor, resistance, can be divided into two categories — lateral and forward. Lateral resistance, of course, is concerned with reduction of leeway and includes such considerations as draft, shape of the underwater lateral plane, and hydrodynamic lift. Forward resistance affects the speed of the hull through the water, and this is concerned with wetted-surface resistance, wave-making resistance, form resistance, induced drag, and windage, the last of which may help or hinder, depending on the point of sailing. A hull's axial turning characteristics and its forward and lateral resistance will depend on its dimensions, sailplan, form, and displacement.

DISPLACEMENT

In the United States, the gradual trend has been toward

light or moderately light displacement racing-cruisers. Some of the principal advantages of lighter over heavier boats are good performance over a wide range of conditions, generally lower cost, racing competitiveness over the most frequently sailed short- and middle-distance courses, and certain special qualities for cruising and offshore racing. These qualities are: (1) relatively great space in length and breadth because a light-displacement boat gives more usable space for a given weight, (2) relatively great buoyancy, which is essential to seaworthiness and dryness, and (3) the fact that only a relatively small rig, light gear, and consequently a smaller crew are required. A good-quality, light-displacement boat is somewhat less expensive to build than one of heavy displacement because cost is roughly proportional to weight. The light boat generally is also cheaper to maintain. In races that are not extremely long, most light-displacement boats are quite competitive, provided their ratings are reasonably good, because their hulls are easily driven and they are capable of especially high speeds in good winds on the frequently encountered reaching and running points of sailing. However, these boats may be at a disadvantage in long-distance races, when they are deeply loaded with gear and supplies.

As an argument for moderately heavy displacement, there have been some high-performance, moderately heavy boats, and these do not seem to suffer as much from heavy loading. Some sailors mistakenly assume that light boats are better than heavy ones in light airs, but quite often the opposite is true, because the heavy boat has the larger rig. The height of the rig is especially important in light going. In addition, the heavy boat has more momentum to carry her from one patch of breeze to the next. The light boat will pick up faster in puffs, but she will be stopped more quickly by seas when the breeze is light. Actually, a great criterion of light-weather performance is the sail area – wetted surface ratio, which will be discussed briefly when we consider sail area.

Compared to her heavy sister, a light-displacement boat usually performs best when it blows, because she has less form resistance. One performance criterion for moderate to heavy winds, when the hull moves at high speeds, is the displacement-length ratio, which varies according to boat size but gives figures generally ranging from 150 to 400 for moderate-size, conservative racing-cruisers. Those on the low side, the lighter boats, will probably have less resistance at high speeds. However, in heavy-weather sailing there are other important factors, such as stability and the ability to carry sail.

The United States initiated the trend toward light-displacement offshore cruising boats when young Olin Stephens designed the *Dorade* back in 1930. She has been hailed as the first truly modern ocean-racer, and she was quite light by the standards of those times. Immediately after World War II, however, the British took over leadership in this design trend when certain loopholes in the RORC (Royal Ocean Racing Club) rating rule were exploited. First and most famous of these new, light racing-cruisers was the Laurent Giles–designed *Myth of Malham,* a superior performer, especially in strong winds.

With the exception of a few ultralight types developed by enlarging dinghies or small racing hulls, the United States produced racing-cruisers of medium displacement during the late 1940s and the 1950s. In fact, the trend toward lighter boats received a slight setback in 1954 with the appearance of *Finisterre,* an Olin Stephens–designed keel-centerboarder of moderately heavy displacement. *Finisterre*'s success in ocean racing is well known, and she exerted a great influence on the design of racing-cruisers in subsequent years. Reasons for her success, besides the obvious one that she was very well sailed, were that she could be deeply loaded at little sacrifice to speed; she had a deep, fairly efficient centerboard that gave her good performance to windward but reduced wetted surface downwind when the board was retracted; she had above-normal beam and unrated ballast, such as heavy bronze floors, to give her great sail-carrying power in strong winds; and, perhaps most important, early in her career she had a very low handicap rating for her performance under the weather conditions to which she usually was exposed. Later the rating rule caught up with her, and no matter who sailed her, she was much less competitive, at least in round-the-buoys racing. This decline could also be attributed to the fact that her later competition included many high-performance boats of moderately light displacement.

In the United States, light racing-cruisers were pioneered by such designers as Farnham Butler, William Tripp, and particularly William Lapworth, who first got a lot of attention when a controversial boat of his design, the *Flying Scotchman,* entered the 1950 Bermuda Race from Newport, Rhode Island, to Bermuda. Lapworth boats have been very successful racers, particularly the Cal classes and especially the moderately light-displacement Cal 40s, which dominated ocean racing in the late 1960s and early 1970s. For many years these boats were considered the design "target," or boat to beat, when new cruisers were built for racing.

The object of this brief discussion of displacement has not been necessarily to advocate either light or heavy boats, but to give a little background on displacement considerations in racing-cruiser design, and to

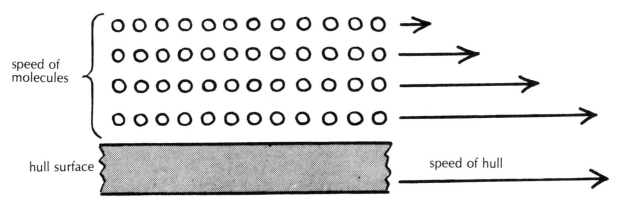

Figure 2-4. BOUNDARY LAYER

show a few of the ways in which displacement affects performance. At the present time, especially in Grand Prix–style racing, there are more than a few ULDBs (ultralight displacement boats) with displacement-length ratios of well under 150. These craft can have exceptional speed downwind, but they are apt to pound in head seas and they seldom perform very well on a beat.

Another important factor in the consideration of displacement is strength of the hull. Light hulls must be lightly built, yet they take strains greater than those to which cruisers of the past were exposed. This is due to the greatly increased popularity of offshore racing today and the facts that modern sails do not readily blow out and modern rigging does not stretch easily. The solution to this problem is construction that is light but very strong. To achieve this end, new construction methods and techniques have been developed, and some of these are mentioned very briefly later.

FORWARD RESISTANCE

A hull's total forward resistance may be divided into various kinds of drag forces. For the sake of this nontechnical discussion, I prefer the system of division mentioned earlier: (1) resistance due to wetted surface, (2) wave making, (3) form, (4) induced resistance due to leeway and heeling, and (5) windage, or wind resistance. Total windage comes from the rig and the part of the hull above the water, so this is discussed briefly in Chapter 5, which deals with rigging.

Wetted Surface

When designing a modern racing-cruiser, the naval architect puts a great deal of thought into the nonsacrificial reduction of wetted surface. He does this because wetted surface area causes most of the forward resistance at low to medium speeds, those speeds at which most boats in most localities travel the majority of the time. Nonsacrificial means that there is little sacrifice of characteristics associated with good performance to achieve a low wetted-surface area.

Wetted surface causes skin friction between the hull's surface and the water, or, to be more accurate, friction between water molecules that cling to the hull surface and molecules a slight distance from the hull surface. The molecules that cling or partly cling to the surface and move along with the hull are referred to as the *boundary layer.* This layer varies in thickness, and it is considerably thinner forward than aft. Figure 2-4 shows, in a simple way, how the boundary layer is built up of rows of molecules, with the inner rows next to the hull moving along at the same speed as the hull and the rows out from the surface moving progressively slower the farther away they are from the hull. To be convinced of the boundary layer's existence, one need only drop a small floating object, such as a wooden match, in the water next to a moving hull and watch the object be pulled along with the boat for a brief period of time.

Obviously, the way to reduce skin friction is to reduce wetted area, but this is not easy to do without increasing some other form of resistance or detracting from some desirable characteristic. Some sailors seem to judge wetted area entirely by the shape of the lateral plane, but the fore-and-aft view gives as much or more indication of wetted surface. Figure 2-5 shows four types of midship sections. The triangular form shown in section A was used frequently over a century ago. In fact, the section is typical of the yacht *America,* which beat the British yachts in 1851. The champagne glass, section C, is typical of some of the light-displacement racing-cruisers of today, such as the *Myth of Malham* or, in a very general way, some of the Cal classes, C&C designs, and Rangers. As can be seen in the illustration, the

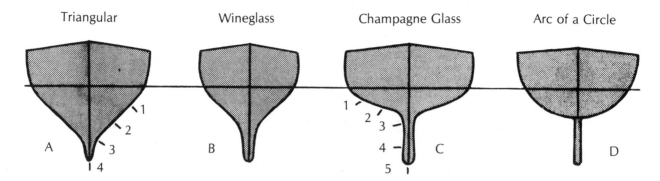

Figure 2-5. MIDSHIP SECTIONS

wetted surface of the triangular section is much less than that of the champagne-glass section. The scale drawn on the bilge and keel of each section shows the same unit of measurement.

In order to compensate for the unfavorable wetted area in section C, it is necessary to reduce drastically the area of its lateral plane. Figure 2-6 shows in section A the lateral plane of a hull similar to the *America*'s, and in sections C and D two drastic reductions of lateral-plane wetted surface that could be used for the champagne-glass section. As a net result, C and D might have slightly less total wetted area than A, and at the same time, C and D will have keels that are more efficient for windward sailing, but this consideration of the lateral plane is discussed later. In choosing between C and D, the latter is preferable, in one very important respect at least: the rudder, separated from the keel and moved aft, gives the longest possible distance from a completely submerged rudder to the boat's vertical turning axis. This increases the length of the lever arm, as shown in the diagram, for easier steering. More is said about this in the specific discussion of rudders.

Sections D in Figure 2-5 and E in Figure 2-6 show another approach to the wetted-surface problem. These sections are arcs of circles, and the bottom of the immersed hull profile in Figure 2-6(E) is an arc also. This hull shape is based upon the fact that the sphere has the smallest area for a given volume; thus, by making the hull conform to arcs of circles, wetted surface is reduced. This type of section often works well for fin-type keels or short keels (having little distance from the leading to trailing edges), where the hull is considered the main body and the keel a separate appendage. If the keel were long, running the entire length of the hull, the total wetted area would be high, because we would have to consider the girth of the hull and keel together over the whole waterline length. This is the same kind of

problem faced with the champagne-glass section. Examples of the arc-of-a-circle section are the Charles Hunt–designed Melody 34 class and some of Richard Carter's designs. Also, some of Britton Chance's IOR racers approach this shape. At least one of Ted Hood's designs comes close to the profile shown in Figure 2-6(E).

The wineglass section shown in Figure 2-5(B) might be considered a compromise between the triangular and arc sections. This section is not appropriate for a fin keel because of the fullness at the garboards. The keel for this type, which we might call an *integral keel,* should be considered as an integral part of the hull. The lateral plane often associated with this section is shown in Figure 2-6(B). Reduction of wetted area has been accomplished by trimming down the forefoot and raking the rudder. Until quite recently, this kind of profile was used very successfully on the majority of Sparkman & Stephens racing-cruising keel boats. The rudders on some of these boats are raked as much as 45 degrees. As can be seen, the wetted area is not large on the lateral plane; also see the sectional view shown in Figure 2-5(B).

Another very important aspect of skin friction is the fairness and smoothness of the hull. Rough seams, paint, and especially any indentations or protuberances, cause resistance. However, this aspect is considered in Chapter 4, in the discussion of tuning the hull.

Wave Making

Next to wetted-surface friction, the most significant resistance is that caused by wave making. This is the dominating drag at high speeds, whereas wetted-surface drag dominates at low speeds. Figure 2-7 gives the approximate curves of the two kinds of resistances for a displacement hull. Of course, exact curves would depend on the form and dimensions of the particular hull. However, these curves show the general character of resistances for a racing-cruiser. Notice that the skin friction curve is almost straight and slopes up slowly as speed is increased, whereas the wave-making curve starts very low on the resistance scale and curves up with increasing rapidity until, at high speed, it constitutes most of the total resistance.

As a displacement hull moves forward, it pushes up a mound of water at the bow and sets up complicated pressures that propagate several wave systems. These are transverse bow-wave and stern-wave systems and divergent-wave systems, as shown in Figure 2-8, but we are concerned primarily with the transverse waves, which have their crest lines almost at right angles to the boat's centerline. These waves move in the direction of the boat and at the same speed. The faster the boat moves, the faster her transverse waves will be and the longer they will become, because the speed of a wave is in proportion to its length from crest to crest.

Wave making takes energy and thus causes resistance. When a hull travels at so great a speed that the transverse wavelength corresponds to the load waterline length, there is such resistance that the hull theoretically can go no faster. This is the maximum speed for a displacement hull, and the only way it can overcome this natural speed barrier is to lift up and partially plane. This would require enormous power for a heavy-displacement boat, and it could be accomplished only momentarily, running before strong winds with long following seas. The maximum speed-length ratio for an average fast racing-cruiser would be approximately 1.35, and beating to windward in ideal conditions, it would be about 1.0. A 25-foot-LWL boat, for example, could make just under 7 knots reaching and about 5 knots to windward.

Of course, some of the small, light-displacement racing-cruisers, such as J-24s, can exceed a speed-length ratio of 1.35 because they can partially plane under ideal conditions. Even large yachts of good hull form and light displacement can, for brief periods, partially plane down long ocean waves. This is often called surfing, and it is one of the most exciting and demanding forms of sailing. However, it is rare that a displacement boat can exceed her hull speed or speed-length ratio of 1.35, and the most critical factor in high-speed sailing is effective length of the LWL.

A heavy boat, displacing more water than a light one, has a fuller, deeper underbody that depresses the water into a deeper wave system. Even though the heavy boat's LWL is similar to the light one's, and the waves

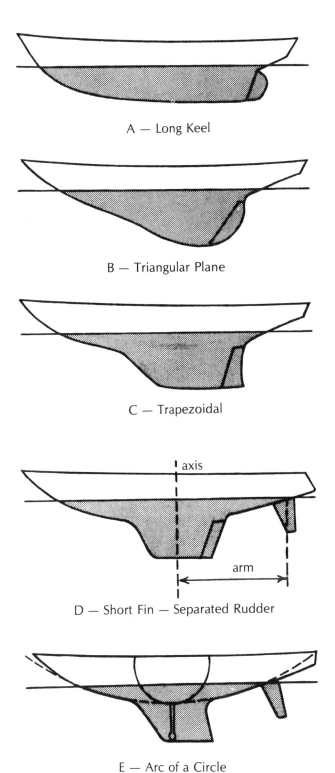

A — Long Keel

B — Triangular Plane

C — Trapezoidal

D — Short Fin — Separated Rudder

E — Arc of a Circle

Figure 2-6. LATERAL PLANES

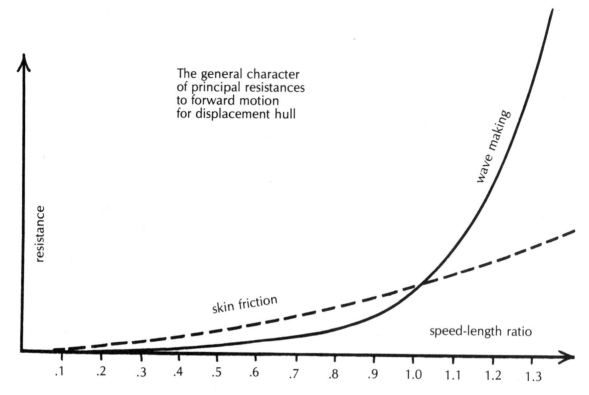

The general character
of principal resistances
to forward motion
for displacement hull

resistance

wave making

skin friction

speed-length ratio

.1   .2   .3   .4   .5   .6   .7   .8   .9   1.0   1.1   1.2   1.3

Figure 2-7. RESISTANCE CURVES

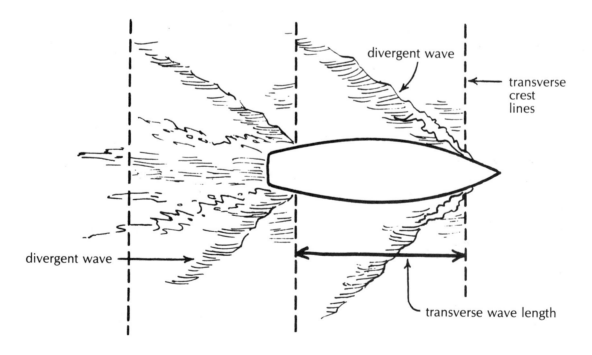

divergent wave

transverse
crest
lines

divergent wave

transverse wave length

Figure 2-8. WAVE SYSTEMS

of each are the same length, the deeper hull causes more resistance. This is shown in Figure 2-9.

One of the reasons that a nonplaning hull has such difficulty exceeding the speed of a wave equal in length to its LWL is the correspondence or superimposing of the bow wave upon the stern wave. As the hull speed increases, the second transverse wave abaft the bow wave moves aft. When it reaches the stern, at hull speed, it is reinforced by the independently formed stern wave (often called quarter wave). This is explained in Figure 2-10. Notice in boat A that the second bow wave has not reached the stern, and it partly negates or cancels out the effect of the quarter wave, but when the two waves reinforce each other, there is enormous resistance.

Another consideration in hull-made wavelength is bow and, particularly, stern overhang. A boat with long overhangs can increase her waterline length at good speeds, often considerably, when heeled in a good breeze. She then has a new load waterline, which is often called her *sailing length*. See Figure 2-11.

Form Resistance (Hull Shape, Balance, and Appendage Drag)

Although form resistance is often considered under the wave-making category and there is interaction among all underwater resistances, it seems convenient to think of the drag caused by the form or shape of the hull as a distinct and separate kind of resistance. A submarine moving deep below the surface makes no waves and thus has no resistance from this source; and if wetted-surface friction were the only consideration, the submarine would be ball-shaped. However, a submerged spherical submarine could not move very fast because of the existence of another type of drag caused by the form of the hull.

The search for the ideal hull form has been going on for some time. Even the multitalented Leonardo da Vinci tried towing models to determine optimum hull form. The da Vinci ideal was the so-called cod's head and mackerel tail, or *fish form*. Some designers feel that da Vinci's conclusions retarded the progress of naval architecture because of improper use of the fish form on so many vessels for so many years. However, this form, with its greatest body fullness forward of amidships, is not always bad. It is often effective at low, or ghosting, speeds in light airs. Captain J.H. Illingworth's successful, light-displacement *Mouse of Malham* has a slightly fish-shaped hull.

The fish form exerted a strong influence on the design of sailing vessels until the middle 1800s, but after this,

wave length A = wave length B
depth C is greater than D

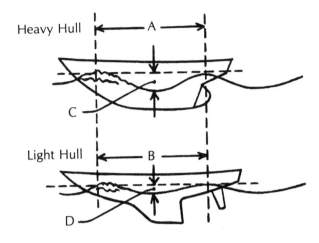

Figure 2-9. DISPLACEMENT AND WAVES

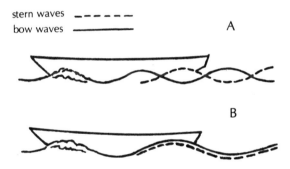

Figure 2-10. WAVE CORRESPONDENCE

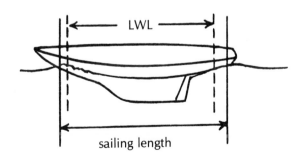

Figure 2-11. SAILING LENGTH

yachts began to take a different shape. Scott Russell had developed his *wave-line theory,* which proposed that a hull should fit or conform to the outline of a wave, and this produced a hull with a fine bow and maximum fullness abaft amidships, the so-called *wedge form.* The yacht *America,* designed by George Steers, had this form, and she had a great influence on designs of that period. Another promoter of the wedge form was Norwegian designer Colin Archer. He developed a waveform theory differing from Russell's in that the *curve of areas,* or the distribution of displacement, should conform to the wave (as opposed to the actual curve of the hull's body conforming to the wave).

One of the main problems with either a fish or a wedge form is improper balance. As every sailor knows, a rudder turned hard to one side to correct for poor balance causes great drag. When heeled, the wedge form tends to round up into the wind, while the fish form may tend to fall off or bear away from the wind, as shown in Figure 2-12. As a result of trying to achieve good balance, most modern yachts are a compromise form having somewhat similar ends.

The hull often has been shaped, very roughly, to be in accord with the *metacentric shelf theory,* developed in 1931 by Rear Admiral Alfred Turner. This rather complex analysis estimates how the immersed volume of a heeled hull is disposed symmetrically with respect to a vertical fore-and-aft plane passing through the metacenter. This theory predicts that a *symmetrical hull* will not trim down by the bow or stern on heeling and will be well balanced.

Another balance analysis was made by D.A. Rayner. This compares the increase and decrease of immersed and emersed sectional areas for a given angle of heel as seen on the body plan. Figure 2-13 shows the immersions or emersions of a heeled hull at three different sections. In the Rayner analysis, a curve is plotted from the differences between the areas of immersed and emersed wedges at all sections on the waterline. This curve can then be interpreted by a designer or experienced observer to predict hull balance. Usually, when wedge differences in the bow and stern are similar, the plotted curve is quite symmetrical, and this indicates that the boat will have good balance. In other words, a boat with symmetrical ends (or with her displacement distributed somewhat the same way in the hull's forward half as in the after half) should balance reasonably well when heeled.

In practice, it is not that simple, because a symmetrical hull sometimes has bad qualities. Often such a hull is either not sharp enough at the entrance or lacks buoyancy in her after sections. This latter point is par-

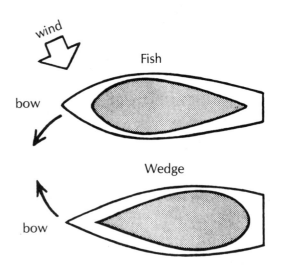

Figure 2-12. BALANCE OF FISH AND WEDGE FORMS

ticularly important with a small racing-cruiser, because crew weight is largely concentrated around the cockpit. This is just the area where fullness and buoyancy are needed. Also, many light-displacement boats capable of semiplaning need a slightly hollow entrance and a wide, flat run — a partial dinghy shape. This form helps reduce pitching in head seas, because the sharp bow is not easily thrown upward by a wave, while the full stern also helps prevent the bow from lifting. Such a hull, therefore, must sacrifice a certain amount of balance and she must be sailed on her feet, at low angles of heel. In sailing-yacht design, compromises nearly always have to be made. The hulls of most modern racing-cruisers are, in varying degrees, compromises between wedge and symmetrical forms. Examples are shown in Figure 2-14. Slightly wedge-shaped forms often have a little less resistance than symmetrical forms between the speed-length ratios of 0.5 and 1.0.

Beam, fairbody depth, displacement, and shape of the ends all contribute to wave making and form resistance. As the hull moves ahead, the water must be moved aside and divided, and this takes energy. The flows on either side of the hull reunite, and this action — together with disturbances caused by various appendages in the form of the rudder, keel or centerboard, and propeller — can cause turbulence and harmful eddies. This type of drag is significant at all speeds, but it might be said that surface friction dominates at low speeds, wave making at high speeds, and form resistance at the middle to high speeds.

In the interest of reducing turbulence and eddies, appendages should be streamlined, sharp angles and

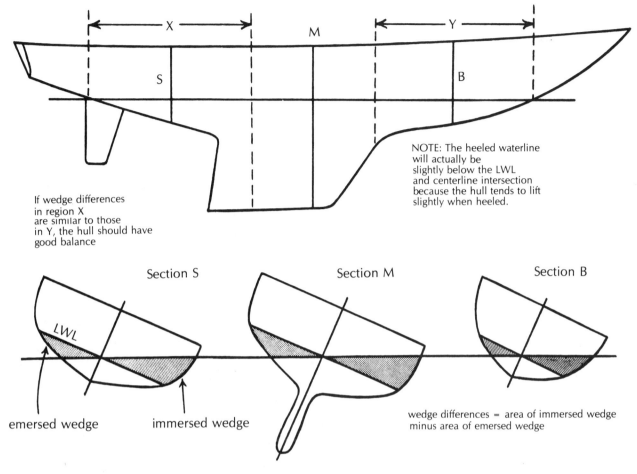

NOTE: The heeled waterline will actually be slightly below the LWL and centerline intersection because the hull tends to lift slightly when heeled.

If wedge differences in region X are similar to those in Y, the hull should have good balance

Section S

Section M

Section B

emersed wedge   immersed wedge

wedge differences = area of immersed wedge minus area of emersed wedge

Figure 2-13. BALANCE WHEN HEELED

corners should be avoided, waterlines should not be excessively full or blunt at the ends, nor should entrance angles be too sharp, and buttocks should have an easy sweep and not be too steep. It is usually better to have the garboards faired smoothly into the keel (as in sections B and C of Figure 2-15), although the garboard area would have to be very small and tight in a fin-keeler.

A fairly recent design development is the *bustle,* which might be described simply as an added fullness or filling-out of a boat's underwater afterbody, especially where the hull joins with a skeg. This shape is illustrated by the buttocks lines at the skeg shown in Figure 2-15. Bustles afford a means of placing some buoyancy and displacement aft in boats with fairly narrow sterns. This fullness and merging of the hull lines into the skeg seem to help the water move in smooth streamlines past the afterbody, and in effect they may extend the boat's sailing length. As designer Olin Stephens explained, "It [the bustle] is an effort to get a greater spread between

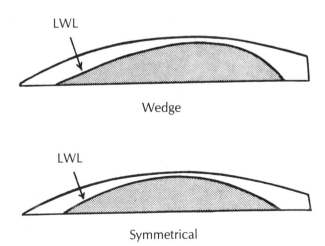

Wedge

Symmetrical

Figure 2-14. MODERATE WEDGE AND NEARLY SYMMETRICAL HULLS

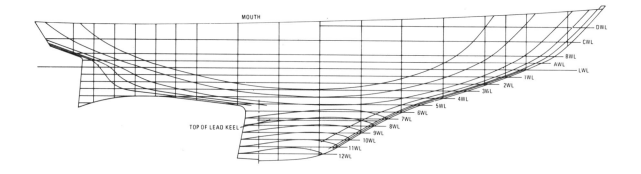

Figure 2-15. INTEGRAL STREAMLINING SKEG SHOWING BUSTLE

(From *Yachting World Annual 1973* edited by Guy Cole and Bernard Hayman. St. Martin's Press, New York, NY. First published 1972. All rights reserved)

This stern view of an Ohlson 38 shows a slight bustle, the swollen area just forward of the rudder and skeg. (Bob Cochran photo)

bow and stern waves and get the boat up to higher speed before these waves come together." Bustles are not seen on all the latest racing-cruisers, because current handicap rules do not discourage wide sterns, and many afterbodies are dinghy shaped. For these types of hulls, a bustle could add too much fullness aft. Boats with narrower sterns, however, can benefit from the extra fullness of the bustle, while the kind of skeg shown in Figure 2-15 may help prevent any turbulence caused by water flowing under the afterbody from the leeward to the windward side as the hull makes leeway.

Propeller drag is a great problem for sailboats with auxiliary engines. Some of the small racing-cruisers use outboard motors that either attach to the transom or protrude through a motor well in the boat's counter. In these cases, the outboard may be removed when under sail in order to eliminate the drag. A boat with an outboard well is usually equipped with a flush-fitting hatch that closes the opening through the counter and virtually eliminates any resistance from water entering and sloshing around in the well.

On racing-cruisers with inboard power, there always will be at least some prop drag, but this can be minimized. Ways of doing so include the use of two-bladed props with movable, folding, or *feathering* blades. A three-bladed prop causes tremendous drag and is almost unthinkable for any racing boat. The feathering prop has blades that twist, so that, in effect, the blade width can be reduced. On the folding type, which has the least resistance by far, the blades are hinged and fold back against each other (see Figure 4-5). More is said of this in Chapter 4, in the discussion of tuning the hull.

Figure 2-16 shows several propeller installation arrangements. Type A is probably the most common on boats with keel-attached rudders, but each arrangement has advantages and disadvantages. A and B have apertures, or holes, cut out of the lateral plane, and these in themselves cause a great deal of drag. Type A will probably have the best steering control under power because the prop wash is directed onto the rudder. However, a rudder with an aperture loses efficiency when under sail, because it loses area and the aperture allows some water flow to leeward of the keel to escape to windward. Installation B, seen on many William Tripp–designed boats, has an advantage in that the aperture is forward in the thick area of the keel, where the prop, when vertical, may hide behind the deadwood to reduce drag. Installations C, D, E, and F are without apertures, and each can be fitted with a solid prop (having nonmovable blades) or one with movable blades. The boat owner will have to weigh the advantages of a low-drag prop against the increase of measurement rating it gives him.

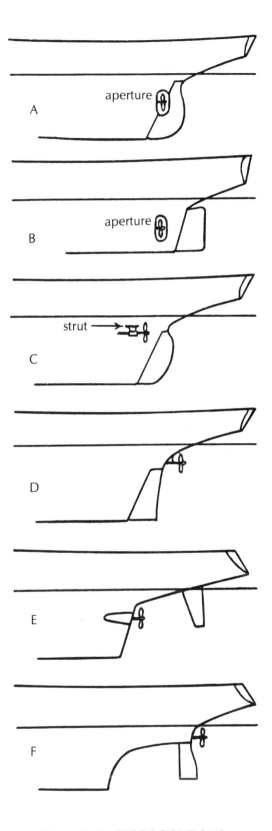

Figure 2-16. PROP LOCATIONS

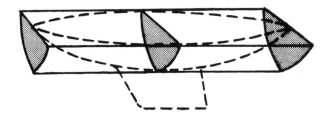

Figure 2-17. PRISMATIC COEFFICIENT

The off-center propeller, C, is usually put on the port side to offset the *torque* (tendency for a propeller to move the stern sideways and thus turn the boat) of the normal right-hand prop's forward motion. Despite the torque, however, it is often necessary to angle the shaft so that it does not run exactly fore and aft, in order to counteract the off-center propeller push that would ordinarily make the boat turn to starboard. A shaft angled to the direction of water flow adds to the making of eddies. Then, considering the drag of the shaft strut and the fact that there is no way to hide the prop behind the deadwood, it is evident that the offset propeller creates a large amount of drag, especially if the prop is solid.

Propellers D, E, and F are on center and therefore may partly hide behind the keels, but even when vertical, the props are partially exposed to the water flow, because at these locations the keels are relatively thin. The arrangement of E, as in a Cal 40 and others, has the prop forward of the rudder, which may assist in steering under power. In arrangement D, as in a Cal 30, and especially in E, like some of Bruce King's designs, the propeller is very near the water surface, which makes for some inefficiency under power but low resistance under sail.

More is said about propeller drag, streamlining, and fairing appendages in the discussion of tuning the hull in Chapter 4. Keels and rudders are discussed later in this chapter.

Prismatic Coefficient

Although this is a nontechnical discussion of yacht design, it seems unavoidable in the interest of thoroughness to introduce occasionally a frightening term from the jargon of naval architects. The *prismatic coefficient* (often called simply the prismatic) tells how displacement is distributed longitudinally. It is a measure of how fine or full the ends are in comparison to the midship section. Technically, the prismatic coefficient (Cp) is defined as the ratio of displaced volume to

that of a prism equal in length to the LWL and having a cross-section area equal to the immersed midship section. This definition is illustrated in Figure 2-17. The immersed hull is shown by dotted lines, the immersed midship sections are shaded, and the prism is shown by the solid lines. The Cp is a comparison of the volume of the dotted hull with the volume of the area defined by the solid lines.

The prismatic has a significant effect on form resistance and especially wave making. For displacement racing-cruisers, the Cp may vary from .51 to .58, with the lower coefficients indicating that the yacht has relatively fine ends, while the higher figures indicate full ends. A very full-ended craft was Captain Joshua Slocum's *Spray,* with a prismatic of .65. It is generally agreed that the higher coefficients indicate good performance at high speeds, whereas low coefficients are better at low speeds in light winds. Optimum prismatics might be .52 or .53 for speed-length ratios of below 0.8, but .56 or higher for speed-length ratios of over 1.0. At the highest planing or semiplaning hull speeds, .60 or higher coefficients would be more suitable. Selection of a suitable Cp depends to some extent on where the boat will be sailed and whether heavy winds or light airs will predominate in her locality.

Induced Drag

The additional resistance due to a boat's angle of yaw (or angle of leeway) and her angle of heel is called induced drag. Both yaw angle and heeling cause drag, but there seems to be a tendency for some sailors to underrate the former and overrate the latter, at least insofar as racing-cruisers are concerned. The yaw angle causes far more drag than moderate heeling in most well-balanced displacement yachts. Admittedly, under actual sailing conditions, drag from each of these two sources is combined, and it is difficult to differentiate and determine exactly what percentage is due to leeway or heeling alone.

In evaluating the resistance from heeling only, tests have shown that there is some additional drag at very low angles of heel, but beyond this, until medium angles are reached, there is very little increase in resistance. Tests on the yacht *Gimcrack,* made in 1936, showed that increased resistance from heeling was significant up to 5 degrees of heel, but then there was little more increased drag until nearly 25 degrees, at which time the *Gimcrack* immersed her rail. These results have largely been verified by later tests, which include computer experiments at the Massachusetts Institute of Technology and tests on a full-size 5.5.-meter boat at the David Taylor Model Basin near Washington, D.C.

Of course, heeling causes some drag in most boats because the heeled waterline is usually asymmetrical; thus, it is puzzling that many tests show so little additional drag with heeling. The English designer-author D. Phillips-Birt offers the explanation that the increased sailing length from overhangs gives additional speed, which partially cancels out the increased drag due to heeling. Then, too, many of the experiments have been performed on narrow, displacement racing hulls with rather symmetrical ends and heeled waterlines. Nevertheless, many dinghy sailors moving into racing-cruisers who have been brought up on the dictum "keep your boat flat," don't always realize that there are times when it may pay to sail certain boats that are not dinghy shaped at a definite angle of heel. Heeling affects the set of the sails, helm balance, waterline length, airflow loss at the foot of sails, stability, and wetted surface; if some heeling proved beneficial in these areas, it might more than compensate for the slight drag it caused.

Figure 2-18 shows two entirely different types of hulls. A is a displacement, symmetrical type with a deep fairbody and round bilges. B is a light-displacement dinghy type with flattish shallow bilges. The heeled waterline plane of each is shown by the shaded areas. A will probably have good balance and little heeled resistance because her ends are quite symmetrical and also because the windward side (the emersed side) of the waterline plane is not too dissimilar from the leeward side. On the other hand, B will undoubtedly have considerable weather helm and considerable heeled resistance because of her wedge-shaped waterline plane and the fact that the windward waterline is entirely dissimilar to the leeward waterline. We can see, therefore, that A can be sailed at moderate angles of heel at very little cost in drag, and that she may benefit by (1) increasing her waterline length, (2) possibly decreasing her wetted area slightly, (3) increasing weather helm slightly for effective steering in light airs, (4) probably increasing stability because of hull shape and the effect of keel ballast, and (5) increasing effectiveness of sails in light air at slight angles of heel. Points 3, 4, and 5 are discussed in the consideration of sailplan balance, stability, and sail trim. Boat B, on the other hand, should be sailed very flat in most winds on account of her high resistance when heeled. However, even she could be given a slight angle of heel in light airs to improve the set of her sails and to reduce wetted surface, which might be considerable in this case.

There are further discussions of heeling in the sections on lateral resistance and stability, but it should be

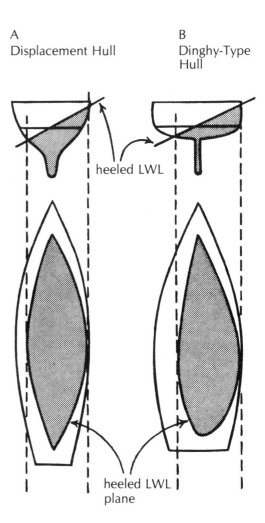

A
Displacement Hull

B
Dinghy-Type Hull

heeled LWL

heeled LWL plane

Figure 2-18. HEELED RESISTANCE

stressed here that any time the lee rail becomes submerged (usually just before or after 30 degrees of heel), resistance increases tremendously. This is due not only to greater hull resistance and sail inefficiency at the higher angles of heel but also to the fact that the rail, shroud turnbuckles, jibsheets, blocks, winch bases, cleats, and the like, become submerged and obviously cause great drag.

Drag caused by a wide yaw angle can be considerable — up to perhaps 40 percent more than upright unyawed resistance — because the hull is crabbing or moving forward while being turned askew. Of course, a certain amount of leeway is essential for windward performance in order that the keel or centerboard can act as a hydrofoil and exert transverse lift to windward and thus counteract the side force in the opposite direction exerted by the sails. The lift and drag forces acting on the keel of a boat beating to windward are diagrammed in

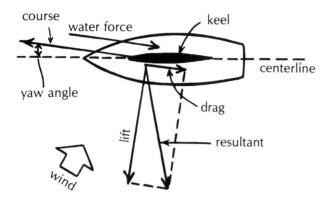

Figure 2-19. KEEL-WATER FORCE

Figure 2-19. Increasing the angle of yaw will increase the lift but will also increase the drag. Yaw angles will vary between 2 and 5½ degrees on racing-cruisers, but angles over 5 degrees will usually produce excessive drag in proportion to lift.

LATERAL RESISTANCE

Up to this point, for the most part, we have been talking about resistance to forward movement, but in the sailing yacht, consideration of lateral resistance is of equal importance. This is especially true for a displacement racer, because it is probably still the case that the more weatherly boats of this type win the majority of races over the average closed course.

Leeway and the Hull

Lateral resistance is supplied by the keel or centerboard, but the hull itself may have considerable influence on leeway. The amount of influence depends on whether the keel is an integral part of the hull or a separate fin. It also depends on the shape of the hull and the angle of heel. There is a great deal of interaction between heeling and leeway. One of the obvious interactions is the relationship between angle of heel and draft. A hull draws less when she heels, for two reasons. First, the angle away from the perpendicular reduces the vertical distance from the water surface to the keel's bottom. Second, the hull has a tendency to float higher when the immersed volume begins to exceed the emersed volume.

Another, less obvious interaction between heeling and leeway can be seen by comparing the hull forms shown in Figure 2-20. The hull itself (not including the keel) can act as a hydrofoil. The arrows on the hulls in the diagrams show the direction the hulls tend to move due to the hydrofoil shape of their heeled waterlines. On hull B in Figure 2-20, the heeled waterline on the leeward or low side is a pronounced curve, while the windward waterline has very little curvature. This causes the water flow on the leeward side to move faster than the flow on the windward side, and therefore (in accordance with the physical law known as Bernoulli's principle, which states that the higher the velocity of a moving fluid the lower will be its pressure) there is less pressure on the boat's leeward side than on her windward side. Naturally, this imbalance of pressures will tend to force the hull to leeward.

Hull A has a very unusual form. She is a scow with straight sides and a very pronounced rocker at the bottom. A friend of mine learned the basics of sailing in the

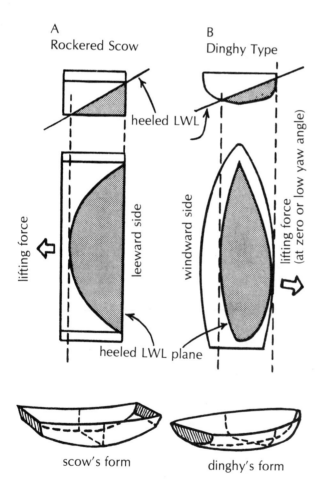

Figure 2-20. HULL LIFT

same type of boat, which had neither rudder nor keel nor centerboard. Steering was accomplished by the movement of crew weight fore and aft in order to relocate the center of lateral resistance. Lateral resistance for windward performance was supplied by the immersion of the leeward chine. But there was probably another reason the boat could be sailed to windward without a keel or centerboard. In hull B, the heeled waterline plane has the opposite shape of hull A. The scow (her owner prefers to call her a punt) has her waterline curve on the windward side, and this lowers the pressure on that side, which tends to pull the boat to windward. Actually, this force cannot counteract the opposite lateral force from the wind on the sails, but the net result is a slight reduction of leeway.

Also, compare these two hulls with the normal displacement hull A in Figure 2-18 and observe how the low-pressure force works on the three hulls. The scow with straight sides and rocker bottom has the force to windward. The dinghy with curved sides and flattish bottom is forced to leeward, and the displacement hull with curved sides and rocker bottom is pulled slightly to leeward, but it is affected little by the force. This substantiates my conviction that there is little harm done (and there may be some benefits) in sailing the well-balanced displacement boat at moderate angles of heel. On the other hand, it is often very harmful to sail the dinghy type, or wedge-shaped hull with little deadrise, at pronounced angles of heel to leeward. In moderate winds it may even pay to sail a true dinghy with a slight heel to windward.

Keels

Although the hydrofoil action of the hull is part of the picture, the keel or centerboard has the far greater effect on lateral resistance. The efficiency of a keel depends on its area, aspect ratio, sectional form, profile shape, depth, and location on the hull. The latter two considerations are more closely related to stability and balance, which are discussed separately later.

Area, together with aspect ratio, has the greatest effect on leeway. The area is determined primarily by the draft, LWL length, displacement, wetted surface, and hull form. Draft in a keel boat is usually fixed by certain practical considerations, such as rating rule penalties and the depth of water in the sailing locality. Also, the draft is roughly in proportion to the LWL length. The normal, medium-size racing-cruiser with keel is about five times as long on the waterline as she is deep. Smaller boats are slightly deeper, but large boats have proportionally less draft.

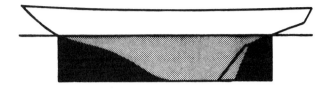

C_{lp} = grey area/black + grey area

Figure 2-21. LATERAL PLANE COEFFICIENT (C_{lp})

The grey area in Figure 2-21 shows a moderately heavy displacement racing-cruiser's immersed lateral plane. The ratio of a boat's lateral plane to a rectangle formed by her LWL length and draft, as indicated by the black-and-grey area in the diagram, is called her *lateral plane coefficient*. This usually varies from about .40 to .65 for moderate-draft keel boats of the kind we have been discussing. A light-displacement type might have the lower figure and a heavy boat the higher one. Hull form and beam as well as displacement will make a difference in the coefficient, partly because the lateral plane might be composed mostly of an efficient, thin keel in a light boat, although it might be composed mostly of an inefficient (for lateral resistance) full, fat hull on a heavy, integral-keel boat. However, these coefficient figures can serve as a rough guide to the amount of lateral area needed. To put it very simply, the lateral plane area of a normal keel boat with modest draft should be roughly 50 percent of the rectangle under the waterline, but the area should be less for a light-displacement boat and perhaps even slightly greater for a heavy seagoing boat.

A very important consideration concerning keel area and aspect ratio is wetted surface. The optimum is the least wetted area for the most lateral plane efficiency. Referring back to Figure 2-5, we can see that a triangular midships section, A, with an integral keel will lower wetted surface, but this will give a thick, angular-sided hydrofoil that will not be as efficient as a fin-type keel, which more nearly resembles a vertical airplane wing. However, if we use a champagne-glass section, which gives a more efficient keel, we increase wetted surface. One answer to this dilemma is use of the latter section with a very short fore-and-aft length. This gives us a high-aspect-ratio keel, deep in proportion to its length. This is by far the most effective type of keel for a given area.

Of course, a high-aspect-ratio keel is not the most suitable type for every boat. If draft is limited, the high aspect ratio must be achieved by reducing the keel's length, and this has its point of diminishing returns on some racing-cruisers. An overly short keel reduces the lateral plane and may very well increase the yaw angle. On a light-displacement fin-keeler, a slight increase in yaw angle might be tolerated, because the lower friction of the short keel could more than compensate for a slightly greater induced resistance caused by the additional yaw. However, on a full-bodied heavy-displacement boat, the yaw angle should be kept low, because any yawed resistance will probably be high, and it is doubtful that this could be compensated for by the reduction in wetted surface of a short keel. In other words, heavy boats of limited draft should generally have longer keels than light boats. Directional stability is a related consideration discussed later.

The profile shape of the keel is determined not only by the area and aspect ratio but also by certain practical considerations. For instance, the leading edge of the keel should be raked, as shown in the various keel configurations in Figure 2-6. This is a very important antifouling measure to prevent the snagging of various kinds of flotsam, floating seaweed, and the lines from lobster pots or crab traps. In many areas boats are especially troubled with eelgrass and kelp. In fact, some skippers of one-design-class boats having nearly vertical keels have found it necessary to install glass windows in their boats' bottoms to aid in the detection of keel fouling.

Of course, the keel's after edge need not be raked for antifouling reasons, but it is sometimes raked in the opposite direction (as shown in Figure 2-6(B)). This moves the rudder's center of pressure farther aft for better steering leverage at a minimum cost in wetted-surface area when the rudder is attached to the keel. When the rudder is separated from the keel, it may pay to have the after keel edge fairly vertical.

Tank tests have shown that a straight trailing edge and a sharp angle at the heel of the keel give good lateral plane efficiency. Of course, other considerations affect the shape of the keel's trailing edge, such as the distribution of keel area to produce maximum length for directional stability at a minimum cost in the wetted area when the draft is fixed. Thus, the keel could have a trapezoidal shape with the fore-and-aft edges raked the opposite way, like a Cal 40's keel. See Figure 2-6(D). A further advantage of this keel shape is that the opposite raking edges tend to raise the CLR, which minimizes heeling (see Figure 5-1). In addition, such a shape shortens the bottom of the keel, and this may reduce head resistance by lessening turbulence at the keel's bottom.

Another factor that affects the keel's profile and sectional shape is the amount and location of ballast. On most boats, the ballast must be placed far forward on the keel in order that the boat be trimmed properly fore and aft. Of course, this will depend on the fore-and-aft location of the keel, which in turn will depend on the position of the sailplan's center of effort. However, most modern racing-cruisers must have their keel ballast well forward to float on their designed waterlines. This is especially true with small boats, which are easily affected by the concentration of crew weight in the cockpit. If such is the case, when the keel is triangular without a toe (Figure 2-6(B)), the ballast must be moved up to a higher position, where it will contribute less to the boat's stability than if it were at the keel's bottom. This is one advantage of a keel with a toe (Figure 2-6(C)). In this case the ballast can be kept low.

Induced drag caused by the yaw angle creates a kind of turbulence at the bottom of the keel often referred to as tip, or end, *vortices*. These are similar to the vortices at the ends of airplane wings occasionally visible at high altitudes. When a boat reaches or sails to windward, some of the high-pressure flow on the keel's leeward side escapes under the keel's bottom to its low-pressure, windward side. This creates the swirling eddies somewhat similar to those shown in Figure 2-22. Not only do these vortices detract slightly from the keel's lateral resistance, but they can cause a considerable increase in forward resistance. In recent years there has been a good deal of experimentation with variations in the shape of keel bottoms in an effort to minimize this type of turbulence. The V'd bottom has been used with apparent success in helping to reduce cross flow under the keel, while at the same time it has a favorable shape for low forward resistance. This shape may also have some advantages when pitching while sailing into head seas. V'd keels have been used on the 12-meter cup defenders, as well as on some Olin Stephens and Charles Morgan racing-cruiser designs. On the other hand, the designer A.E. (Bill) Luders recently wrote: "In regard to V'd keels, I never agreed that they were any good, and we made quite a few model tests and could never see any improvement."

Some recent designs, usually those used more for cruising than racing, have made use of the *end plate fin*, which has a flaring section or semibulb at the keel's bottom. The best-known version of this type is the Scheel Keel, devised by yacht designer Henry A. Scheel. Its section is shown in Figure 2-22. This shape is designed to minimize the end vortices and allow shallow draft with little loss in lateral resistance. The Scheel Keel has been somewhat controversial (many designers like it, others don't), but one indisputable advantage is that it allows the ballast to be placed at the lowest point for a given draft, and this is helpful to stability.

A debate could probably be started between pro-

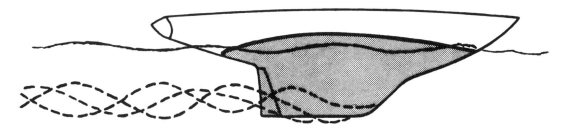

Figure 2-22. KEEL-END VORTICES

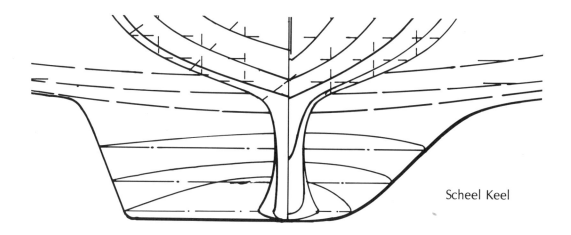

Scheel Keel

ponents of the thin, all-metal fin bolted to a boat's bottom and advocates of the thicker integral fin that is blended into the hull. However, for moderately light racing-cruisers, above the smallest sizes at least, the latter type of keel has many more advantages. To begin with, a flat keel causes more resistance to yawed forward motion than a streamlined keel with a certain amount of thickness. Tank tests have shown that a practical, high-lift, streamlined keel should be roughly 12 times as long (or slightly longer) as it is thick, with maximum thickness about 25 to 40 percent abaft the leading edge. The trailing edge should be quite fine, while the leading edge should be slightly thicker and rounded. A sharp leading edge often causes turbulence at certain yaw angles.

Other arguments for the integral fin would include greater strength at the junction of hull and keel, less maintenance on account of the corrosion associated with many flat metal keels, space in the keel for a water tank and bilgewater sump, and a sectional shape permitting the use of curved garboards to mitigate turbulence. In addition, part of the boat's displacement could be

put into her keel in order to allow a less full, bulky, and deep hull to reduce form resistances.

Centerboards

Most of the basic principles discussed in regard to keels apply also to centerboards, but there are differences. With centerboards, draft, aspect ratio, and area are not fixed. We may choose a very efficient, high-aspect-ratio board with little consideration for depth of water in the sailing locality or concern over wetted surface area. Upwind, we can lower the board for great draft and efficiency and downwind pull it up for a great reduction of wetted area. By raising or lowering the board, we can move the center of lateral resistance to improve balance. However, with all the advantages that centerboarders have, they also have disadvantages. There are maintenance problems, which include difficulties in cleaning and painting the board, worn pins, and broken pendants (see Figure 2-23). In addition, the centerboard often thumps in its well in rough seas. Furthermore,

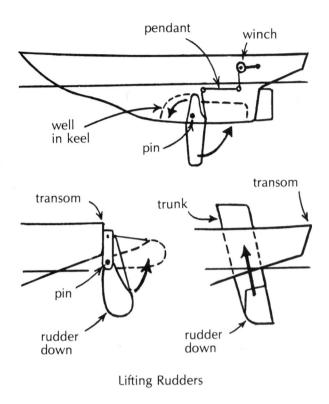

well
in keel

pendant   winch

pin

transom   trunk   transom

pin

rudder
down

rudder
down

Lifting Rudders

Figure 2-23. CENTERBOARDER AND ITS RUDDER

metal centerboards can be bent after a hard grounding while heeled with the board fully down. For this reason, it is advisable to keep the board partly housed when sailing in shoal waters.

Centerboard boats require ample beam for stability, and it is nearly always necessary that their rudders be shallow. Unless a boat is fitted with a *lifting rudder* (one that pivots up or retracts as shown in Figure 2-23), which is very rare for a large boat, her rudder cannot extend below her keel, because it could be broken or damaged by grounding. This means that centerboarders can have steering problems when running before fresh winds and following seas. Furthermore, the broad beam can compound the problem if there is excessive heeling, because balance is disturbed by the asymmetrical heeled waterlines due to the beam, and the lee side supplies buoyancy that tends to lift the shallow rudder farther from the water.

Disregarding helm balance and susceptibility to snagging seaweed, there might be an advantage in a centerboard that can be lowered to rake forward of the vertical (with the bottom of the leading edge ahead of the top of the leading edge). Such a rake will cause lift to act in a more lateral (rather than an upward) direction

when heeled. If the board should twist from water pressure, added lift will force the hull to windward. Twist or bending of an after-raking board will be harmful to lift. This is one reason that it seldom pays to raise the board when beating, except possibly in very light airs, to reduce wetted surface, or in heavy winds to improve helm balance or to reduce heeling.

It is not my intention to sound discouraging about centerboards but merely to point out some of the potential problems. There have been some outstanding centerboarders such as *Finisterre,* the Philip L. Rhodes–designed *Carina,* and the Charles Morgan-designed *Paper Tiger,* to name a few, but boats of this type can be very demanding under certain conditions. Perhaps the most important characteristic needed by any keel-centerboard offshore racer is sufficient depth of ballasted keel. She should have: (1) sufficient ultimate stability to prevent capsizing at sea, (2) a sufficiently long, deep keel to prevent yawing and steering problems, and (3) enough lateral plane so that she can be sailed to windward fairly well with the board fully housed. A very general rule of thumb is that the draft of a small to medium-size yacht with board up should be no less than one-seventh of the LWL length.

Twin Keels

Before leaving the subject of keels and centerboards, mention should be made of twin keels. These are side-by-side fins, each being attached to the hull approximately halfway between the boat's centerline and her LWL, as shown in Figure 2-24. Notice that on this fore-and-aft view the keels are angled away from the LWL vertical. The obvious advantage of the design is that the upright hull gives minimal draft, but heeling gives maximum draft to prevent leeway. Twin-keelers have enjoyed some popularity in England, and they are beginning to catch on in the United States in the smallest sizes of racing-cruisers. A desirable feature is that a twin-keel boat can be beached and easily put on a boat trailer, because she can stand upright on her two fins.

Advocates of this design claim that, despite the low aspect ratio of the usual twin keel, the fin can be made very efficient by means that are not possible with a conventional single keel. For instance, a twin keel can be angled to the hull's centerline in order to give it an angle of yaw without the hull's being yawed. The keel on one side can be yawed for one tack while the opposite keel can be yawed for the other tack. Then, too, the keels can be made asymmetrical if this is deemed an advantage. Twin-keelers are said to have great directional stability and resistance to pitching when the boat is heeled, at which time the forces created by the weather keel act in a more up-and-down rather than lateral direction.

Despite the claims of twin-keel enthusiasts, however, this kind of underwater configuration is by no means a panacea, and important trade-offs are necessary. Twin keels increase the wetted surface considerably, and excellent performance to windward is seldom possible. Furthermore, there is some loss in stability range as compared with a deep-draft boat with a single keel.

AXIAL TURNING

The main considerations relating to axial turning are transverse stability, turning about the longitudinal axis; steering and directional stability, the turning related to the vertical axis; and pitching, turning on the transverse axis.

Stability

There are several kinds of stability — longitudinal, which has to do with turning on the transverse axis, and directional, which is concerned with turning on the vertical axis, but when we speak of "stability" alone, we are talking about transverse stability, the tendency of a vessel to return from a heeled position to an upright position. Of course, all sailboats must have sufficient stability for sail-carrying power. They need stiffness to stand up to their rigs and sail at low or optimum angles of heel in fresh winds. Furthermore, racing-cruisers need the reserved or ultimate stability for safety, to prevent capsizing or rolling over at very high angles of heel.

The characteristics that affect a boat's stiffness are the area and height of her sails, sectional form of the hull, draft, displacement, beam, and ballast. The latter two are the most significant for hull stability. Figure 2-25 illustrates the importance of beam and ballast and shows the righting forces at work. The center of gravity (CG) is fixed on the boat's centerline, but the center of buoyancy (CB), also on the centerline when the boat is upright (at CB1), moves to the side (to CB2) when the boat is heeled. The distance between the upward force acting through the heeled center of buoyancy (CB2) and the downward force acting through the center of gravity is the righting arm. This arm changes in length as the angle of heel changes and as the CB moves toward or away from the boat's centerline. The longer the righting arm, the more righting force is exerted on the hull. You

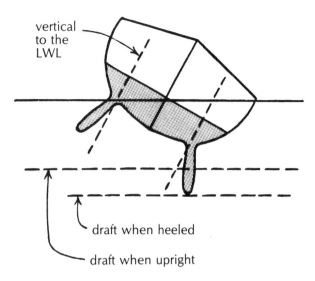

Figure 2-24. TWIN KEELS

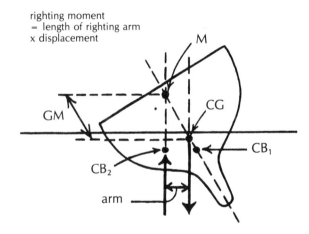

Figure 2-25. HULL STABILITY

can see by studying the diagram that there are two ways that the arm can be lengthened: (1) by increasing the beam or changing the hull shape to make the CB move outboard, because the CB is the geometric center of the immersed hull, or (2) by lowering or increasing the keel ballast to lower the center of gravity.

The actual measure of stability is the *righting moment,* which is the length of the righting arm times the displacement of the boat. Thus, it is possible for a light-displacement boat with a slightly longer lever arm than that of a heavy boat to be more tender than the heavy boat. The *metacentric height* (GM), shown in the illustration, varies according to the height of the CG and the lateral location of the CB. The GM on most racing-

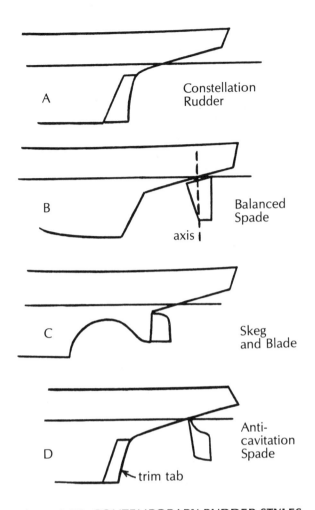

A — Constellation Rudder

B — Balanced Spade
axis

C — Skeg and Blade

D — Anti-cavitation Spade
trim tab

Figure 2-26. CONTEMPORARY RUDDER STYLES

because those forces act in a downward as well as a lateral direction when the boat is heeled. High freeboard and flaring topsides give good reserve stability at the higher sailing angles of heel, and a slight tumblehome near the rail will often delay dragging the rail.

Stability due to beam is most effective at normal sailing angles of heel, but stability from keel ballast is what is needed for ultimate stability. A boat designed for offshore sailing should be able to recover from a 120-degree knockdown *at the very minimum*. Ballast-displacement ratios on most racing-cruisers vary from about 33 to 50 percent, meaning that that percentage of their total weight has been consigned to ballast.

The relationship of stability to the sail area is considered in Chapter 6.

Rudders and Steering

Innovations in the refinements of yacht design often seem to develop into fads. Most innovations have real merit, but they are not always suitable for every type of boat.

Several years ago, there was a vogue for *Constellation rudders* (named for the 12-meter cup defender). Tank tests have shown that rudders of this kind, with concavely curved or straight after edges, wide bottoms, narrow tops, and angular heels (see Figure 2-26(A)), are very effective for steering and reducing leeway at a minimum cost in area. Then came the rage for the so-called *spade rudders*. These are separated from the keel, underhung, and moved to the extreme after end of the LWL (see Figure 2-26(B, D)).

The chief advantage of a rudder separated from the keel is that its location far aft gives the maximum distance between the boat's vertical turning axis and the rudder's center of pressure, and this distance means a long lever arm for effective rudder power and control. Any separated rudder seems most appropriate for: (1) a boat having a short keel in a forward location, (2) a boat that will spend a large percentage of her time running or broad reaching in high winds and seas, especially with a spinnaker set, and (3) a fairly large boat that steers with a tiller. As to the first point, many sloops that concentrate their sail area forward, in conformance with another modern trend of large headsails and short main booms, need a forward keel location for proper balance. If these boats have short keels or fins with rudders attached, they could have serious steering problems under certain conditions; thus, the rudder should be separated from the keel and moved aft.

As to the second and third points concerning the ap-

cruisers measures between less than 2.5 feet to more than 3.5 feet. The CG is slightly above, on, or slightly below the LWL on most racing-cruisers.

Hull form also has its effects on stability. Hard bilges and low angles of deadrise usually contribute to stiffness when such a form extends the beam at the waterline, while slack bilges with higher angles of deadrise are often associated with moderate waterline beam, causing some initial tenderness at low angles of heel. Boats with high prismatic coefficients are usually relatively stiff in good breezes, partly because their full ends allow support by the bow and stern waves when there is little support amidships at the hollow between the waves. The hull form also has some effect on dynamic stability (meaning, in this nontechnical discussion, stability or lack of it due to the boat's forward motion) at high speeds. The asymmetrical heeled waterlines have an influence on heeling as well as on the lateral forces that were mentioned in the discussion of lateral resistance,

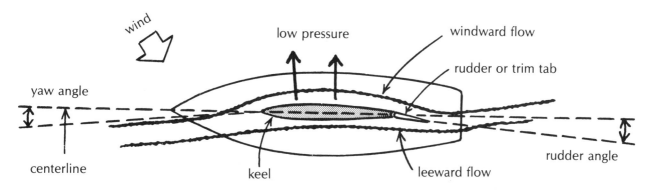

Figure 2-27. KEEL-RUDDER OR TRIM-TAB HYDROFOIL ACTION

propriateness of separated rudders, running or broad reaching at top speeds under the spinnaker puts heavy demands on steering. Under these conditions, instant helm response and immediate power are required. For boats that participate in offshore, downwind races (the Transpacific Race is an example), the spade rudder or skeg-attached rudder located well aft certainly fills the bill. For instant helm response, tiller steering is hard to beat, but with large boats this requires great physical effort. One solution offered by the spade rudder is that it is often *semibalanced,* that is, the turning axis lies slightly abaft the leading edge, so that water force will assist in the turning (Figure 2-26(B)).

On the other side of the coin, there are often problems with spade rudders, and for some boats there are advantages in having conventional rudders attached to the keel. Some of the advantages of a keel-hung rudder are: (1) it can contribute considerably to keel lift, (2) it requires less area than a spade rudder for a given length of lever arm because the keel directs water flow against the rudder, (3) it causes less drag when yawed, and it *stalls* (causes turbulence and a sudden loss of lift) at a wider angle than a spade, (4) there is less chance of fouling seaweed or other flotsam, and (5) there may be greater inherent strength in a properly hung keel rudder compared with a free-standing spade rudder.

To elaborate on the first point, a slight amount of weather helm is a definite asset to a boat with a keel-hung rudder, because the helm gives extra side force and the effect of *camber,* or curvature, to the keel-rudder combination (see Figure 2-27). The water flow on the keel's windward side moves faster than the flow on the leeward side, so the relative pressure is lower on the windward side, resulting in a force to windward. The slightly turned rudder thus contributes to the lift caused by the yawed keel. Optimum helm angles vary between three and five degrees. Angles beyond this cause too much drag in proportion to lift.

A trim tab at the after end of a keel. The tab acts like a wing flap on an airplane to increase lift. (Sally Henderson photo)

Free-standing spade rudders should have very little weather helm. They must be almost perfectly balanced, because their drag contributes nothing to keel hydrofoil shape. Furthermore, a semibalanced rudder, with its leading edge turned away from the centerline, causes more drag than if the edge were on the centerline. With the edge being separated from the keel or skeg, there is some danger of early stalling and *flow separation*. This means that the flow cannot make the abrupt turn without breaking away into turbulence. Many spade rudders are especially subject to stalling and loss of control when heeled, reaching in a blow. Under these conditions it is often necessary to reef the main and slack the mainsheet during puffs. Another point that should be mentioned is that perfectly balanced helms often make windward sailing difficult, because the helmsman has no consistent pressure, or helm "feel." This may not be a serious point when one is accustomed to such helms, but it's necessary to get used to it.

A questionable practice, seen occasionally, is the positioning of a spade rudder well abaft the end of the LWL. The stern wave usually will cover the rudder's top at high speeds, but if its top should emerge, the rudder could *ventilate*, or suck air down from the surface, which would hurt its effectiveness. This might happen on a reach in a strong wind when the boat is heeled and has a strong weather helm. Improvements were made to early models of a certain class of boat with this problem by adding *cavitation plates* — thin horizontal plates on the rudder similar to those found on some outboard motors. These form a barricade to help prevent bubbles from being pulled down from the surface. Of course, the best solution is to have the rudder positioned where it is well submerged in nonturbulent water, usually little if any distance abaft the after end of the LWL, or else to have the rudder type shown in Figure 2-26(D).

Some of the problems connected with a spade rudder can be avoided with the use of a skeg ahead of the rudder (Figure 2-26(C)). In this case, the rudder can be aft, the rudder can be smaller than if it were free-standing, and there is often not as much eddy-making resistance. Also, the skeg may add considerably to the boat's directional stability, and stalling is delayed. On the other hand, the skeg adds to the wetted-surface area, and the rudder does not augment keel lift.

One solution to the problem of no keel lift with a separated rudder is the installation of a trim tab on the trailing edge of the keel. This concept received a lot of publicity after the 1967 America's Cup races in which the *Intrepid* used a trim tab. The Dutch designer E.G. Van de Stadt began using this device many years ago, and American designers such as Richard Carter and Olin Stephens have used keel tabs with success on some of their racing-cruiser designs. A keel receives extra lift when the tab is turned a few degrees to leeward, thereby providing some camber and a higher angle of attack at the trailing edge. Like the wing flap on an airplane, the keel tab gives lift but at a high cost in drag. For this reason and because the device is penalized under most measurement rules, the trim tab is not often used on today's racing-cruisers. For pure cruising boats, tabs do offer the advantage of being able to tune out weather helm, and they can serve as spare rudders if the main rudder is damaged. However, these benefits hardly seem worth the expense and complication of a tab.

Rudders attached to keels are often sharply raked, up to 45 degrees, for the primary purpose of reducing wetted lateral plane area, but there may be a beneficial side effect on certain points of sailing. Figure 2-28 shows the principal forces at work on a rudder. Notice that when the raked rudder is turned there is a downward force component, which makes the helm feel heavy, but when the boat carries weather helm while heeling, the resultant of the downward force and upright side force is converted to mostly side force. On boat B, which has a vertical rudder, the side force is directed upward when she carries weather helm when heeled. This force could be harmful to a shoal-draft centerboarder because it could lift the stern, decrease rudder draft, and add to the rudder's ineffectiveness. The upward force due to heeling can also add to spade-rudder control problems. It should be said, however, that when the boat is upright, a vertical rudder is more effective than one that is raked, because it is acting in one plane only. One reason for the control problems with some spade rudders is that their turning axes are raked in the direction opposite to that of the rudder shown in Figure 2-28(A). This causes the rudder side force to act sharply upward even at moderate heeling angles.

Directional stability is related to the length of keel as well as the length of the lever arm between the rudder and the boat's turning axis. It is generally conceded that boats with long keels are steadier on the helm and do not yaw back and forth as much as boats with short keels do. However, on modern racing-cruisers, reasonably short keels are needed not only to reduce wetted surface but also to achieve quick turning and good helm response. Although a short-keeled boat may have a tendency to start yawing fairly quickly in a following sea with a spinnaker set, she needs a short keel combined with a correctly positioned rudder of the proper size and shape to counteract the yawing and to prevent broaching-to. As Phillips-Birt has pointed out, the inertia of a yaw is overcome more easily in a boat having a moderately short keel. Long keels are probably more suited to

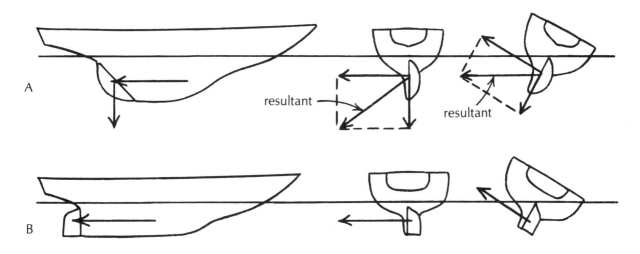

Figure 2-28. RAKED VERSUS VERTICAL RUDDERS

offshore cruisers having special steering devices or twin headsails especially designed for shorthanded cruising or easy downwind sailing.

When the hull is heeled, directional stability is largely a problem of helm balance as a result of the hull's form relating to the rig and sailplan. Much more is said about this in Chapter 5.

Pitching

A vessel is pitching when she moves up and down, turning around her transverse axis. If the pitching becomes very severe, she is said to be *hobbyhorsing.* Some racing yachtsmen have been accused of making a fetish of gear stowage and ballasting in the interest of minimizing pitching, but these yachtsmen know the disastrous effect that hobbyhorsing can have on speed to windward in a head sea.

Pitching is minimized when weights are concentrated amidships. This means that the keel ballast, tanks, inside ballast, and all major weights should be located as close as possible to the boat's longitudinal center of gravity, when doing so has no adverse effect on trim, balance, or any other important aspects of the hull's behavior. Most designers are very conscious of weight placement. A number of modern racing-cruisers by Olin Stephens and other leading designers have their engines placed in the main cabin in an effort to concentrate major weight components amidships.

The boat's resistance to turning about its axis, described as the *moment of inertia,* is its weight times the square of its distance from the axis. Thus, the spread of weights can be critical. This is true not only in the

fore-and-aft direction but also in the vertical direction. Excessive weight up the mast and even excessive keel ballast in a very deep location can contribute to hobbyhorsing. Richard Carter has written that he prefers low ballast-displacement ratios on some of his designs for this reason. Of course, his designs have good form stability to compensate for any lack of ballast.

Spreading the weights from a boat's center can adversely affect her motion by increasing the pitching period to the point where it nearly corresponds to the period of the waves, the time period between the passing of two successive crests. A short pitching period can help keep the bow from burying in the seas, and if this happens, the light-ended boat has a relatively quick recovery.

Of course, there are other factors that affect pitching, perhaps the most important being the shape of the bow sections. The bow must have enough buoyancy to prevent burying but not so much as to cause excessive quickness. V'd and flaring sections forward can cut through the seas clearly and throw them aside. Slightly rounded bow sections are often good in light airs but not when pounding into head seas. There are indications that for heeled resistance, it is important for the bow to be fine in the general region just under the forefoot where the hull joins the keel. Stern sections should generally be fuller, with more U-shaped sections, to damp pitching, but the designer has to be sure that the ends are reasonably matched for good balance. A boat with flat bilges, having little deadrise, will tend to pound in head seas, but if pitching is not excessive, this may not have much effect on speed. The main question becomes whether the boat and crew can take it for a lengthy period.

For the best performance in these conditions, racing-cruisers should not have excessive overhangs. This seems especially true for small light-displacement boats, as they usually have enough buoyancy in the ends. With long overhangs, they would tend to pound and hobby-horse. However, some heavy boats might need moderate overhangs for pitch damping and reserve buoyancy.

Rolling is not an especially important point for a racing-cruiser. An out-and-out cruising boat might need a short metacentric height for seakindliness, but a boat that will be raced needs power to stand up to large sails, so she needs all the stability she can get without paying too large a price in rating. Another consideration is that large racing sails are often effective roll dampers.

3/ Hull Selection

In choosing a racing-cruiser, the prospective buyer must give careful thought to both primary and secondary purposes for which the boat is intended. This is a subjective matter, of course, that will vary with individuals. However, if the boat will be raced, the buyer might list the main considerations in the following order of importance: (1) price and upkeep, (2) seaworthiness and safety, (3) racing potential, (4) versatility and accommodations, and (5) aesthetics.

PRICE AND UPKEEP

Boat costs are listed first because this is the foremost concern for most buyers. Obviously, the first step before shopping for the boat is to figure out how much can be spent on the initial purchase. The boat buyer should realize that most advertised or listed prices represent a fairly bare or stripped boat. A few are advertised as completely equipped, with the basic price including everything down to the eating utensils. However, the buyer usually will find he needs more, and often that he would prefer different equipment. Standard fittings and sails are not always the best, and in some cases they are not even adequate. The buyer of an average new racing-cruiser should be prepared to pay at least 20 percent more than the basic boat price to equip his boat adequately for racing.

Extras and optional equipment often include such desirable or necessary items as working sails, racing sails, spinnaker gear, compass, winches of ample number and size, lifelines, pulpits (metal railings) at bow and stern, a gimbaled stove, extra sheets and blocks for racing sails, awning, sail covers, spreader lights, and much more. Usually all Coast Guard safety equipment, such as fire extinguishers, foghorn, life preservers, proper ventilation, and the like, are standard. Extras and options vary with individual boats.

New boat prices change rapidly, so there is no point in quoting exact current prices. There are, however, a few general rules of thumb for relative pricing. The cost of a stock boat is roughly in proportion to her displacement (unless one is buying an ultralight racing machine, which would be very expensive). Also, the larger a boat, the greater will be her cost per foot of overall length. For instance, an average new 20-foot boat might cost $500 per foot of LOA, a 25-foot boat $750 per foot, a 30-foot boat $1,000 per foot, and a 35-foot boat $2,000 per foot. Generally speaking, stock molded fiberglass boats are the least expensive. It is very expensive to mold a single boat by standard methods, but when many boats are made from the same mold, costs go down. Conventional wood construction in the United States is quite high, but in many countries where labor is cheap, prices of wooden boats are competitive with those for molded boats, and often the quality of work is excellent. However, the buyer should be wary of some foreign fittings and fixtures, such as electrical systems, rigging, and so forth. Some of these items are very good, but others are definitely not.

Frequently, bargains can be found in the used-boat market. Sound, fully equipped boats only a few years old often can be bought very inexpensively because their design has been slightly outmoded for racing. Also, many boat owners buy a new boat before the old one is sold, and this often results in a desperation sale. Sound, beautiful boats of wood can be bought at bargain prices because of the demand for boats of fiberglass or other low-maintenance materials. It can pay to shop for a used boat at the end, or even just before the beginning, of the sailing season rather than in midseason.

The old rule of thumb concerning annual costs and maintenance was 10 percent of the initial cost per year. On first impression, this figure seems a little high, but it is based on all costs, including insurance, yacht club, and storage fees. Annual costs today may be somewhat less than 10 percent, because many modern boats require substantially less upkeep than those of former times. Of course, there is a direct relation between upkeep and appearance. The more brightwork, areas that need varnish or metals that need polishing, the greater will be the upkeep. Boats with fiberglass, or even painted, cabin trunks with a minimum of varnished wood trim, or with teak trim that is allowed to weather, will be relatively maintenance-free above the water, but these boats can suffer in appearance. Anodized aluminum spars do not need paint or varnish, and in some localities where boats are left afloat, masts can be left in the boat the year round. In fact, where this is possible, it is often preferable, because it saves the spars from getting scratched or bent from improper storage. Yearly maintenance for a fiberglass boat with aluminum spars might now be less than 10 percent of initial cost, but perhaps not a great deal less, as maintenance costs have climbed considerably in recent years.

SEAWORTHINESS AND SAFETY

After the prospective buyer has decided what size of boat he can afford to buy and maintain, his next consideration should be for seaworthiness and safety. This is especially true if the boat is to be raced, because in the heat of competition, boats are often driven beyond the point when sails would ordinarily be reefed or other precautionary measures would be taken.

The Midget Ocean Racing Club (MORC) has a minimal set of safety rules for racing-cruisers under 30 feet LOA, and, of course, if the new boat will be raced under MORC rules, she must meet those safety requirements. These rules state that a boat must be self-righting; in some cases where a boat's stability is questionable, a self-righting test is performed. This consists of heaving the boat down on her beam ends after all hatches and openings have been closed. From this position, the boat must be able to right herself with the mast weighted with her bagged mainsail and largest genoa jib tied to the masthead.

The International Offshore Rule also requires boats to have enough stability to recover from a knockdown. Under the IOR, the probability of any yacht's having inadequate reserve stability at 90-degree heel is determined by a rather complicated formula that considers the boat's length, beam, depth of hull, and righting moment. When a boat's ability to self-right is questionable, she must pass a heaving-down test similar to that of the MORC before she is allowed to race under the IOR.

Hatches, companionways, and ports must be watertight, and companionways that extend below the level of the main deck must be capable of being blocked off (with a slide) to the main deck level. After the Fastnet Race disaster in 1979, when 15 sailors died and numerous boats capsized, it was found that companionway slides, especially those that are tapered (wide at the top and narrow at the bottom), can fall out easily during a severe knockdown. Thus, many offshore events require latches, operable from inside or outside of the cabin, for companionway slides.

The cockpit should be watertight and self-bailing, and it should not be of excessive volume. There is always the possibility that a sea will break into and fill the cockpit, and the larger the cockpit volume, the more the stern will be sunk down by the weight of water before it can drain or be cleared. MORC requirements state: "The maximum cockpit volume below lowest coamings shall not exceed 12 percent length times beam times freeboard aft." A further requirement is for "cockpit drains adequate to drain cockpit quickly but not less in combined area (after allowance for screens, if attached) than the equivalent of two 1-inch (2.5-cm) diameter drains.'' The Offshore Racing Council (ORC), which sets the safety regulations for IOR boats, states that for offshore events the maximum cockpit volume below lowest coamings shall not exceed 6 percent L (rated length shown on the rating certificate) times beam times freeboard aft. Furthermore, it is required that the cockpit sole be at least 2 percent of L above the LWL. The requirement for drains is the same as that for MORC.

Some small keel boats with open or nonwatertight cockpits lack flotation. This is positively dangerous. A capsizable centerboard boat with flotation is far safer. All small keel boats should be fitted with flotation, but this is especially important for boats with open cockpits.

The MORC Category A Requirements (recommended for offshore and night races) state that: ''A rigid, non-sinkable dinghy or raft or inflatable raft with bottle inflation must be carried, the combined capacities of such being sufficient to support the maximum crew to be shipped. All such must be carried secured above decks or accessible from companionway. As an alternative to the above, the yacht may be provided with means for positive flotation in the event of being filled, capable of flotating the hull, ballast, crew, stores, and a 250-pound reserve. Use of plastic foam for this purpose is encouraged. If inflated or inflatable bags or tanks or similar devices are used, they must, in the opinion of the measurer, be adequately secured and protected against puncture.''

Grabrails on cabinhouse tops and lifelines are also important safety features. In regard to lifelines, MORC Category A Requirements state: ''For yachts 24 feet LOA and over, 24-inch lifelines and bow pulpits are required. For yachts under 24 feet LOA, 18-inch minimum height lifelines and bow pulpit are required provided that they are adequate for the yacht so equipped.'' The Offshore Racing Council also requires a stern pulpit ''unless lifelines are arranged so as to adequately substitute for a stern pulpit.''

Both the ORC and the MORC require (except for short races in relatively protected waters) ''seacocks or valves on all through-hull openings below LWL, except integral deck scuppers, shaft log, speed indicators, depth finders, and the like; however, a means of closing such openings, when necessary to do so, shall be provided.''

There are other design features not especially required by the MORC or the ORC that can be nonetheless important for rugged offshore racing. For small seagoing boats, it is best that freeboard be more than 12 percent of the LWL at its forward end. Large boats need proportionally less freeboard than small boats. Overhangs

are often needed for reserve buoyancy on heavy boats, but the ends should not be too long. Ocean-racing instructions have limited combined overhangs to one-third of LOA. Extremely beamy boats, especially those with very fine bows, are subject to burying their bows and capsizing in the very heaviest weather. Ultralight-displacement boats are sometimes barred from certain distance ocean races. The most important criterion, however, is constructional strength and sufficient hull thickness to resist puncture from flotsam.

For standard methods of construction, aluminum and fiberglass are among the lightest-weight hulls, and these hulls are immensely strong in most respects. However, after hearing reports of failures and damages to these hulls as a result of several rugged ocean races, one might wonder why they are not reinforced in certain vulnerable areas. Aluminum bows have been dented by head seas, and fiberglass hulls have flexed and prevented taut adjustment of the rigging. Some of the late-model fiberglass boats are being strengthened and made more rigid with greater use of constructional bulkheads, metal backbones, stringers, and web frames, and also by making lockers, stowage shelves, and integral tanks serve double duty as constructional stiffeners.

Many steel hulls are being built today, and some of these are covered with fiberglass. In theory, this sounds very satisfactory, because the steel gives the hull rigid strength, while the fiberglass checks corrosion, but the construction is relatively heavy, and only time will tell how successful the method is in coping with the problem of rust.

Another construction material is *ferrocement* (a type of reinforced-concrete construction), in which thin layers of cement are applied to both sides of a wire-mesh-and-metal-pipe skeleton of the hull. Ferrocement has some advantages in cost, upkeep, strength, and durability, but this material thus far has proved too heavy for small racing-cruisers.

Wood as a hull material is very satisfactory, especially the strip-plank and edge-glued construction. This gives a smooth, strong, bottle-tight hull that can be completely free of rough, leaky seams caused from alternate drying out and swelling of the wood. However, this type of construction is probably best in cool climates and regions where there are no great extremes of temperature. Molded plywood construction gives excellent strength and rigidity for light-displacement hulls. In recent years a number of racing boats have been built by the so-called WEST (wood epoxy saturation technique) System. By this method, wood veneers and strips are sealed, preserved, strengthened, and bonded together with coatings of epoxy resin. The technique seems most appropriate for very light displacement boats or when

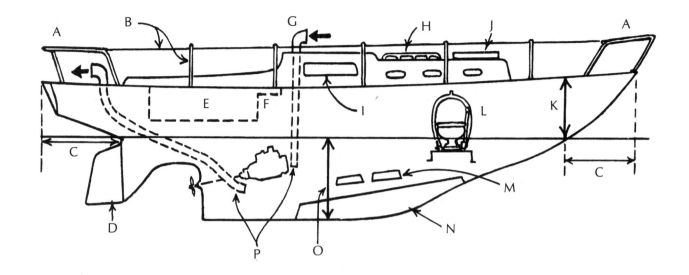

A—bow and stern pulpits. B—lifelines above knee level and bolted stanchions. C—moderate overhangs (less than ⅓ LWL). D—rudder of ample depth and located well aft. E—draining cockpit fairly deep but of small volume. F—bridge deck (or raised companionway. G—removable or watertight vents. H—strong grabrails. I—small, unbreakable, doghouse windows. J—latching hatches permitting exit. K—freeboard at least 12% of LWL length. L—head above LWL and discharge hose with vented loop above LWL at greatest angle of heel. M—inside ballast secured or well wedged. N—sufficient keel ballast to at least right boat from 120° heel (at least 30% displacement). O—draft at least ½ LWL length. P—Coast Guard–approved gas engine installation and ventilation.

Figure 3-1. HULL SAFETY SUGGESTIONS FOR RACING-CRUISERS

one wants a varnished hull that shows off the beauty of natural wood. Sunlight, however, can have a degrading effect on the epoxy, so the varnish should have an ultraviolet filter.

Some highly recommended safety features in addition to what has already been discussed are:

• *dogs,* or latches, for all opening ports, hatches, and cockpit seat lockers;

• a means of closing all ventilators in stormy weather;

• proper gas-tank installation, with the features shown in Figure 3-2;

• head (WC) bowl located above the LWL so that the boat will not flood in the event of a stuck or faulty valve, and the discharge hoses (on the WC and fixed bilge pump) looped and vented to prevent back-siphoning (see Figure 3-1);

• approved Coast Guard ventilating system for the engine compartment, which requires a large vent and duct bringing air into the bottom of the compartment and a large vent and duct taking the air out (see Figures 3-1 and 3-2);

• small doghouse or cabin windows of safety glass, heavy Plexiglas, or Lexan (except for protected-

water events, the MORC and the ORC require storm coverings for all windows more than two square feet in area);

• mast, chainplates, stemhead, and permanent backstay, if possible, electrically grounded to the keel ballast or a ground plate for lightning protection (see Figure 3-2);

• a strong rudder of ample size at an after location for good steering control;

• skidproof decks of either teak or fiberglass having a molded pattern, or a smooth surface painted with abrasive paint;

• bow and stern pulpits;

• lifelines higher than knee level with through-bolted stanchions spaced no farther than seven feet apart (see Figure 3-2);

• all fittings through-bolted whenever possible;

• a forward hatch large enough for an alternate exit;

• through-bolted grabrails below as well as on deck.

The question often arises about the seaworthiness for offshore sailing of centerboarders as compared with deep-keel boats. This is a controversial question — it depends on the individual design. There have been very unseaworthy keel boats and some very seaworthy cen-

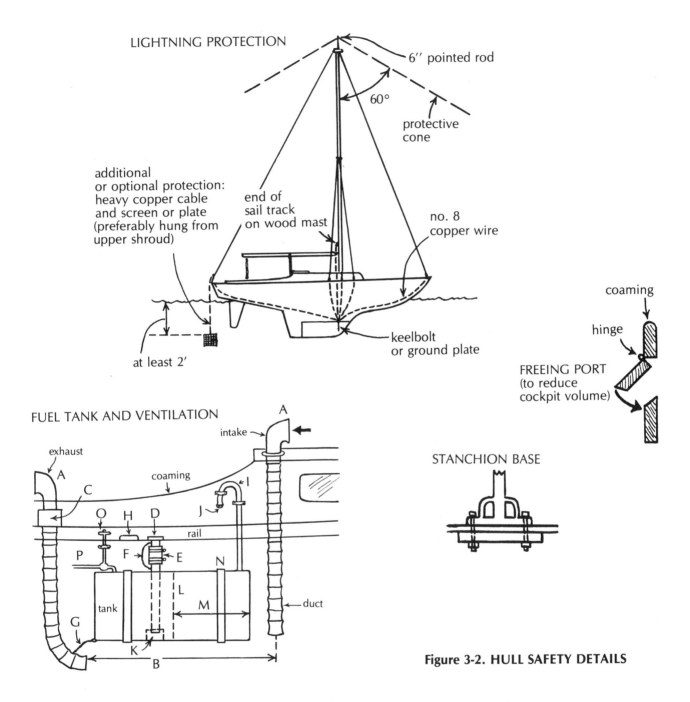

LIGHTNING PROTECTION

6'' pointed rod

60°

protective cone

additional or optional protection: heavy copper cable and screen or plate (preferably hung from upper shroud)

end of sail track on wood mast

no. 8 copper wire

keelbolt or ground plate

at least 2'

coaming

hinge

FREEING PORT (to reduce cockpit volume)

FUEL TANK AND VENTILATION

intake

exhaust

coaming

rail

tank

duct

STANCHION BASE

Figure 3-2. HULL SAFETY DETAILS

A—cowl ventilators, intake higher. B—ducts sufficiently far apart for thorough purging. C—blower location. D—fill pipe connected to deckplate. E—flexible hose with stainless steel clamps (Coast Guard standards now call for "two adjacent metallic hose clamps.") F—jumper wire for grounding. G—tank grounded. H—deck scupper at low point to discharge fumes or spilled gas. I—air vent outside coaming securely attached and protected and with swan neck facing aft (powerboat vent may go through upper topsides if there is a high loop in the line). J—removable flame screen. K—Coast Guard recommends fill pipe extend to bottom of tank in well to form liquid seal. L—tank baffle. M—baffle's distance to end of tank not over 30''. N—secure holding straps insulated from tank. O—shutoff valve. P—fuel line at top of tank. (A pickup tube, not shown, extends from the fuel line at the tank's top to a strainer at the tank's bottom.)

terboarders. The important point with the safety of a centerboarder's design is that its stability should not be overly dependent on beam, because beam contributes little to and may detract from stability at extremely high angles of heel.

For ultimate stability, to prevent a capsizing or rollover, a boat needs ample and deeply located keel ballast. A keel-centerboarder can meet this requirement if she has sufficient depth of keel and keel ballast. As said in the last chapter, a general rule of thumb for draft is that it should be at least one-seventh of the LWL for the smaller racing-cruisers. This ratio is also important for sufficient rudder depth (because the rudder usually cannot extend below the keel) and also for sufficient lateral plane for windward sailing in the event the centerboard is put out of service due to jamming or a broken pin or pendant. As a general rule, the ballast-displacement ratio should be at least 30 percent. If there is any doubt about a centerboarder's ultimate stability, and if she will be sailed at night and/or offshore, then a heaving-down test, as described earlier, should be performed. On a large boat, the stability can be calculated by a naval architect.

In one respect, a keel-centerboarder may have a safety advantage over a deep-keel boat. In extremely heavy weather at sea, the shoal-draft boat will be less subject to being knocked down as a result of tripping on her keel (having excessive lateral resistance) when she is *lying ahull* (lying nearly beam to the seas while stripped of sail). She will make considerable leeway and give to the seas, but she must have a reasonable range of stability.

In the first edition of this book I set 110 degrees as the lowest heeling angle at which a racing-cruiser should be able to recover from a knockdown. As a result of the 1979 Fastnet Race disaster, however, when 77 boats were knocked down to substantially beyond the horizontal, I think the stability range should be raised to at least 120 degrees. Following the Fastnet affair, the stability of a "representative" keel half-tonner was investigated, and it was found that she only had positive stability to 117 degrees of heel. It seems obvious that this range is too low for the most rugged conditions in open waters.

A brief summary of safety features for racing-cruiser hulls that will be used in unprotected waters is as follows:

• Hull self-righting from a position on her beam ends with the weight of the sails on her mast. It is preferable that a boat have recovery from at least a 120-degree angle of heel.

• Strong construction with ample frames, strapping, and stiffening bulkheads.

• A watertight, or preferably self-bailing, cockpit having minimal volume. If the volume exceeds the limit specified in the formulas given in this chapter, it might be reduced by means of rigid flotation bodies securely fastened in the cockpit or by putting scuppers or clearing ports in the cockpit coamings. (See Figure 3-2.)

• Flotation to prevent the hull from sinking in the event of a capsizing or swamping. This is essential if the boat has an open cockpit. If she has a watertight or self-bailing cockpit but no flotation, carry a nonsinkable dinghy or an inflatable liferaft with bottle inflation capable of supporting the entire crew.

• All hatches, ports, vents, and seat lockers capable of being closed and secured. Don't put ventilating holes in the sides of seat lockers unless the vents can be closed, or unless the lockers are an integral part of the watertight cockpit.

• Bottom of companionway hatch raised high off cockpit floor or a bridge deck at forward end of cockpit.

• Adequate freeboard (over 12 percent of LWL at forward end of LWL for small boats).

• Overhangs not excessive (perhaps no more than one-third of LOA).

• Sufficient draft (perhaps no less than one-seventh of the LWL for small boats).

• Seacocks installed on all through-hull openings below or near the LWL.

• Proper gas-tank installation and ventilation. Exact requirements appear in the Coast Guard publication *Federal Requirements for Recreational Boats.*

• Head above the LWL, and discharge hoses looped and vented.

• Moderate-size portlights or windows of safety glass, tempered glass, Lexan, or Plexiglas mounted in strong rigid metal frames.

• Pulpits and lifelines with bolted stanchions, and all fittings through-bolted whenever possible.

• Forward hatch large enough to permit exit. All hatches should have dogs.

• Skidproof decks and ample through-bolted grabrails above and below decks.

• A strong rudder of ample size at an after location, as far as possible from the boat's vertical turning axis.

• Proper electrical grounding approved by a qualified marine electrician for electrolysis and lightning protection.

The prospective buyer of a used boat should have her surveyed thoroughly by a professional marine surveyor before purchase is made. Regardless of its construction, the hull should be examined carefully for deterioration, strains, corrosion, or any construction weaknesses. All fittings, rigging, piping, electrical wiring, and gas-tank installations should be checked. A survey will assure the buyer that he is getting not only his money's worth but also a basically safe and sound boat. This section has only covered hull safety. Safe rigging practices are discussed in Chapter 5. Safety equipment lists are given in Chapter 4 and the Appendix.

RACING POTENTIAL

The third item on our list of considerations for buying a new boat is racing potential. If the boat will be raced at all, "raceability" is an important consideration, almost without regard to how often she will be raced.

To begin with, if the boat has the potential for doing well in races, this will affect her resale value. Then too, she should be able to keep up reasonably well with the rest of the boats; otherwise, she will merely be trailing the fleet around the course, in which case there is hardly any point in racing. Today's racing skipper cannot afford to handicap himself in any way. He must have not only ability, but also a fast boat with a reasonable rating, a capable crew, and good sails (and a little luck doesn't hurt). That is the formula for success, and the boat herself is an important part of it.

A great deal can be learned about a boat's potential performance by studying her plans and looking at her out of water, but it is often difficult to judge racing potential by appearance only. Experienced sailors and even designers have been fooled trying to do this. One way to improve the chances of getting a competitive boat is to look at the records of sister boats being raced in your area. But even this can be deceptive, because a successful boat might have done well at times on account of unusual weather conditions or as the result of an occasional tactical gamble that happened to pay off. On the other hand, a potentially fast boat might have a poor record because she was being sailed badly, or was not properly tuned, had poor sails, or some other reason. Judgments of a design's raceability should be made only after a study of all data and information from all available sources. These might include a study of racing records over a period of time, estimates of the skipper's ability, notations of circumstances affecting performance, performance records of competitors, discussions with owners, a comparative study of handicap ratings, a study of plans and dimensions, and a careful examination of the boat with a trial sail, if possible.

With a new design, however, it is often impossible to study performance records or to take trial sails, so judgments must be based on the designer's reputation and the boat plans. Of course, it is the safest policy to wait until a new design has been proved before buying; but when a new design is introduced, its price is frequently lower than it is a year or so after the boat has been proved. Then too, in IOR racing, many boats are soon outdesigned for maximum competitiveness, although there are now age allowances to improve the chances of the older boats.

The risk of getting a poor racing performer is greatly minimized, even though the design is unproven, if complete data and plans are available. Unfortunately, this is seldom the case. Many designers will not release lines plans, presumably for fear that the plans will be lifted or copied. This is especially true if good racing potential is anticipated. Many advertising brochures for new designs do not even show a midship section of the hull, and a lot of useful information is often missing, such as the centerboard area and aspect ratio, sail-area-to-wetted-surface ratio, prismatic coefficient, metacentric height, location of the longitudinal center of buoyancy, and sometimes even the weight of ballast and estimated handicap rating.

To get a fair appraisal of a boat's racing potential, the prospective buyer should have the following information:

LWL length. This is the most basic determinant of big-boat performance, because it imposes a limit on the speed of a displacement hull. Most handicap ratings are fundamentally based on, or closely related to, either upright LWL or heeled LWL while the boat is underway.

Displacement. This is important because it is directly related to form and wave resistance, stability, and sail area. Advertising literature nearly always gives the displacement in pounds or tons. The displacement-length ratio, discussed briefly in the last chapter, is a useful aid in estimating speed potential. Light boats tend to be fast off the wind in strong breezes.

Sail area. This information, always available, is essential because it is the motivating power. Advertising literature usually gives the square footage of sail area of the working sails, but with the headsail area counted as 100 percent of the *foretriangle* (the area bounded by the foremost mast, jibstay, and foredeck). Sail area is proportional to length, stability, displacement, and wetted surface. The latter is almost never published (although it might be obtained from the designer or the Measurement Handicap System rating certificate); thus it may have to be estimated by looking at the hull or complete plans. A sail-area-to-wetted-surface ratio can be most helpful in determining light-weather performance, as previously stated. A competitive boat usually should have well over twice as much sail area as wetted area, but preferably 2.5 times as much in light-wind areas.

The relationship of sail area and displacement is commonly expressed by the ratio of sail area (in square feet) divided by the cube root of the displacement (in cubic feet) squared (displacement to the two-thirds power). The Cruising Club of America, whose *CCA Rating Rule* influenced American design for about 35 years, considered 15.4 as the ideal sail area-displacement ratio for racing-cruising sloops of all sizes, but this figure may be a bit low for many stiff boats. In simple language, sail area should be as large as possible without overburdening the boat in a strong breeze and without imposing a significant penalty in rating. Careful consideration should be given to the prevailing winds in the racing locality, whether they are predominantly heavy or light.

Wetted surface. This factor is vital to performance in light and even moderate winds. Many prospective buyers make the mistake of judging wetted area by looking only at a profile plan. This tells very little unless the midship section can be seen at the same time. As said in the last chapter, triangular sections or those full at the garboards may have relatively long keels without creating excess wetted surface, but champagne-glass sections with low angles of deadrise must have short, almost fin-type keels in the interest of keeping wetted area low. In the absence of sectional plans or the designer's calculation of wetted surface, this area can only be estimated by looking at the hull out of water or checking the MHS rating of a sister hull.

Beam and ballast. These are the greatest indications of sail-carrying ability in good breezes. Beam is relatively more important at low angles of heel and ballast at high angles of heel. Waterline beam varies from less than 25 percent of the LWL for a large keel racing-cruiser to more than 40 percent of the LWL for a small centerboarder. Small boats need relatively more beam than large boats, and centerboarders need more beam than keel boats. The beam given in sales literature is maximum beam at the rail. Waterline beam usually must be estimated after measuring or observing a plan view or the actual boat, noting flare and tumblehome. Although ample beam is very important for sail carrying, excessive beam increases form resistance and wetted surface, and it can be harmful when beating in a light wind against choppy seas. Ballast-displacement ratios vary between approximately 30 and almost 50 percent. Ballast and beam not only are relative to a boat's length and weight but especially to her sail area.

Draft. This dimension, together with the lateral plane area, has a great effect on windward performance. Sufficient keel depth with an appropriate lateral plane coefficient, as discussed in the last chapter, is needed to prevent excessive leeway. High-aspect-ratio keels or centerboards of deep draft are most efficient, and streamlining them increases lift and decreases drag. Centerboard depth and description are not always published in promotional literature, but the information can be acquired from the dealer or builder. Centerboards should be fairly light (to avoid rating penalties and lifting difficulties), strong, short fore and aft, and deep.

LOA. This basic dimension sometimes determines what class a boat can race in, and when LWL is known, it gives the length of overhangs. These factors have an effect on the boat's rating, her seaworthiness (as discussed previously), and on her sailing length or heeled LWL. Rating rules of today tend to encourage short overhangs, which are acceptable for light-displacement boats that don't need a great deal of reserve buoyancy in their ends. However, there is not enough reserve in the quarters of some modern boats with chopped-off sterns and greatly raking *reversed transoms* (those sloping downward from forward to aft as shown in Figure 3-6). At present, there seems to be a penchant for extreme reverse transoms on IOR boats at least, but their only value to performance is that they keep the stern light to inhibit hobbyhorsing. Concave counters (often seen on some older Sparkman & Stephens and Morgan designs) reduce wetted area when the boat is upright in light airs and lengthen the waterline when she is heeled.

Shape of the hull. This can only be judged by a study of lines plans and photographs, and/or an examination of the boat out of water. On a nonplaning boat, the run can be moderately steep, but it should be easy and sweeping, without an abrupt upward turning of the buttocks. The entrance at the bow should not be excessively full, or windward performance in a head sea will suffer. Flattish, hard bilges tend to provide ample waterline beam and good form stability, while slack, rounded bilges with high angles of deadrise may give less initial stability but less wetted surface. The form of the bilges should be compared to the keel length for evaluation of wetted surface and compared to beam and ballast for evaluation of stability. Integral keels with lead ballast are usually easier to maintain and keep smooth than iron fins or integral keels with external iron ballast.

In general, a round-bottomed hull should have smooth, flowing lines with a minimum of sharp angles or hard edges. Maximum beam and depth of fairbody should not be far abaft or forward of amidships, and hull lines at the bow and stern should not be extremely dissimilar for good balance. As said in the last chapter, a somewhat wedge-shaped hull with the center of buoyancy slightly abaft amidships is usually more suitable for most of today's hulls, especially the small ones, to offset crew weight in the cockpit and to inhibit hobbyhorsing. There should be extra beam above the waterline for reserve stability and good flare at the bows for reserve buoyancy and dryness.

Propeller installation. Propeller drag should be evaluated. It is important to know the prop's lateral location (on or off center), its depth below the surface, its diameter and blade width, the aperture size and location, and whether or not a feathering or folding type can be used. These factors, discussed in the last chapter, affect the rating and speed under sail.

Rating. In judging a boat's racing potential, it is essential to have an approximation of her rating for the handicap rule under which she will sail. It is not enough to feel reasonably sure that the boat will be a good performer. Even though she might do well with her competitors boat for boat, she might have a considerably higher rating that would make her noncompetitive after the figuring of time allowances. When there is a difference of one foot in rating between very small boats of similar speed, the higher-rated boat will have to finish as much as five minutes or more ahead of her lower-rated competitor over a race course of about 20 miles.

The rating of an untried boat can be compared with that of a competitor-to-be whose performance is known. If the new, untried design compares favorably in sail area, LWL, and other vital measures of speed with a successful competitor of similar rating, the chances are that the new boat will be successful also.

If possible, acquire several ratings of sister boats, because there are often substantial variations. Differences in sail sizes, ballast, and propellers can make a foot or more difference in the ratings of otherwise identical boats. Advertising literature for most boats gives low ratings based on the boats' having solid propellers and headsails that are not penalized for overlap.

The prospective buyer should be acquainted with all the handicap rules used in his area, for he might want to race under several rules if the boat qualifies. He should also decide in which class of the cruising division (the division for racing-cruisers) he would prefer to race. Classes are composed of boats within the same rating range (having roughly similar ratings). If a boat's rating happens to be near the dividing line between classes, it might be possible to move up or down into the next class by making a slight change in the boat's rating. Thus, it is important to find out whether a new boat will rate near the top, middle, or bottom of her class. Preference for a class should be based on such factors as the class assignment of sister boats, of boats similar in size and type, and the quality of competition in general. More is

said about this and other aspects of rating in the discussion of handicap rating and measurement in Chapter 7.

VERSATILITY AND ACCOMMODATIONS

This is the fourth item on the list of considerations in selecting a boat. Versatility and accommodations might be listed ahead of racing potential, if racing were not the primary consideration.

Versatility means that the boat can be used successfully for a number of purposes — racing, daysailing, and cruising. Such combinations are quite possible and are not unusual in boats other than the so-called Grand Prix racers, but often some compromises are necessary. The boat's primary purpose is often accentuated at a slight expense to the secondary purposes. An example can be seen in many small boats whose design emphasizes daysailing as opposed to cruising qualities. The daysailer will have the longer, roomier cockpit, while the cruiser will have part of the cockpit space allocated to the cabin.

All racing-cruisers must have at least minimal cruising accommodations. For boats under 30 feet LOA racing under the MORC rules, the minimum accommodations requirements are simply "two bunks permanently installed, 6 feet minimum" and a "stove capable of being safely operated in a seaway" (for offshore and night races).

Figure 3-3 shows three popular accommodations arrangements for small to medium-size boats, perhaps 30 to 38 feet LOA. Most other arrangements are variations of these three. There are many reasons for having the all-important galley in an after location. When aft, it is in a position near the boat's maximum beam for room, it is near the companionway hatch for best ventilation, it is near the transverse turning axis for least motion, and it is near the cockpit for the greatest convenience and accessibility. Also, one of the galley's countertops can often be made to double as a chart table, which must be located near the cockpit, in a position of minimal motion, and where there is good light and good headroom.

The head is usually located in the forward central position shown in the drawings, because this affords maximum privacy, being away from the cockpit and forward of the main saloon (main cabin). On small boats the head door is often designed to close two ways — to close off the head or to separate the head and forward cabin area from the main saloon as shown in arrangement A. Sometimes there is an additional door between the head and the forward cabin, as in B. The

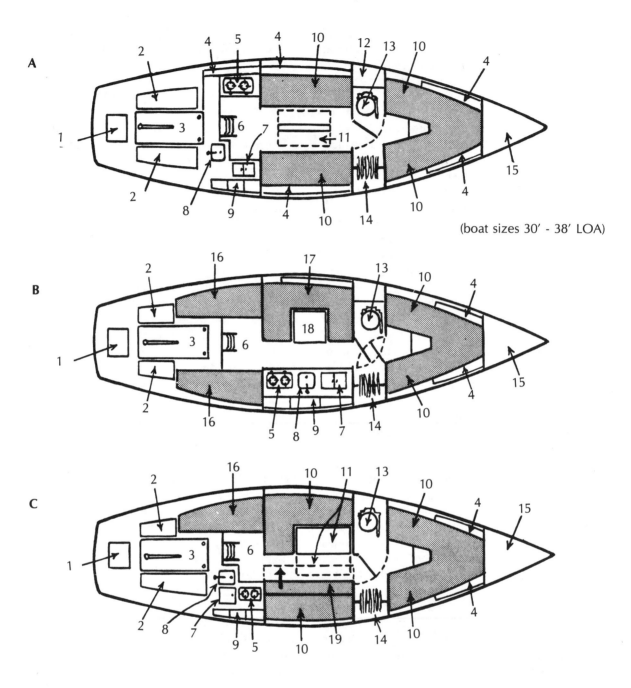

(boat sizes 30' - 38' LOA)

1—lazarette (stowage). **2**—cockpit seat lockers. **3**—cockpit. **4**—shelves. **5**—stove. **6**—companion ladder. **7**—icebox. **8**—sink. **9**—cupboard. **10**—single berth. **11**—dropleaf table. **12**—locker. **13**—WC. **14**—hanging clothes locker. **15**—forepeak (stowage). **16**—quarter berth. **17**—dinette. **18**—table (lowers to make double berth). **19**—transom extension berth (slides out).

Figure 3-3. ACCOMMODATIONS ARRANGEMENTS

advantage of these double-duty door arrangements is that the entire width of the boat may be used for the head area, yet privacy is maintained. Large boats can have an enclosed head, as illustrated in C. This head is large enough to hold a person when the door to the compartment is closed; thus, no double-swinging-door arrangement is necessary. On very small boats the head is usually between the two forward bunks, and it is often hidden with a seat cushion. A curtain or door between the forward and main cabins provides privacy.

Plan A is the traditional and perhaps the most commonly seen arrangement for berths, but plan B has grown in popularity, and for good reason. It provides more bunk space (even though there might be too much emphasis on how many a boat can sleep), and the quarter berths use space that is partly wasted on the conventional arrangement shown in A. The usual quarter berth often makes an excellent bunk for overnight sailing or racing, because it is in a position of minimum motion, and its sides prevent the occupant from being rolled out at substantial angles of heel. For harbor sleeping, quarter berths in very small boats can be hot and cramped when these bunks are in far aft locations under the cockpit seats. It is sometimes possible to install ventilation holes with removable doors that will permit circulation of air when the cockpit seat-locker lids are raised (see Figure 3-5). The holes are at the after ends of the quarter berths. The doors must be watertight and fitted with dogs for safety when at sea or in rough weather.

Another feature considered desirable by many is the dinette (sometimes called settee) arrangement shown in plan B. The table lowers to form a double berth. If there are only four people living aboard (an ample number in a small boat for any period of time), the quarter berths can be used for sleeping, and the table can be left in the raised position to make a comfortable sitting area around a semipermanent table. With the arrangement in A, there is usually a folding table that fits between the bunks for eating purposes, but on small boats this table usually must be removed after meals because it blocks the passageway. With the dinette arrangement, however, the table is off center and, for the most part, out of the way. This is a good arrangement when there are children aboard who need a convenient flat surface on which to put food and drinks, draw, or play games.

Arrangement C is a compromise between A and B. There is only one quarter berth, and the galley is L-shaped. This galley and the one shown in A have an advantage over B in that cooking is easier underway in rough waters, and the sink may be located near the boat's centerline so that there is gravity drainage when the boat is heeled on either tack. The sink arrangement in B might need its seacock or valve closed when the boat is heeled on the port tack. The most satisfactory sink is larger than the size of a large dinner plate. It is preferable that iceboxes open from the top in order to minimize the possibility of spillage and to retain cold air, because the cold air sinks to the bottom of an icebox.

Galley stoves should be gimbaled so that they swing in the transverse direction. Pressurized alcohol types are quite popular, and they are very safe if used properly. Care must be taken not to spill when priming or filling the stove, and a fuel cut-off valve away from the burners should be accessible in case they happen to flare up. A fire extinguisher should always be located in the galley area. For very small boats, the one-burner, bulkhead-mounted, gimbaled stove that burns a solid canned fuel, such as Sterno, is a very satisfactory arrangement for cooking underway in rough weather.

All drawers, locker doors, and even sliding berths should have some simple means of locking or securing in the closed position to avoid their opening at extreme angles of heel. Also, shelves and the dining table should have *fiddles*, or railings, around them to prevent their contents from sliding off. It is important to have sufficient lockers to stow all clothing, stores, and gear. Lack of stowage space is a common fault on many modern small cruisers.

Many stock racing-cruisers have optional accommodations arrangements, usually somewhat similar to those shown in Figure 3-3. In deciding how many bunks will be needed, an estimate should be made of the amount of time the boat will be used for such activities as distance racing, overnighting, or family living. Distance racing requires more bunks than some people might think, because even though half the crew is on watch at night, the total number of crew is usually large, and bunks are occupied with sails or gear. Also, some bunks on the windward side are difficult to use even with *bunkboards* (removable sides), and a dinette area is often used by the navigator. Quarter berths take away from stowage room under the cockpit seats, but they make good stowage areas themselves for sails and other soft gear. For family living, quarter berths are convenient for separating brothers and sisters. The girl can use the forward cabin, while the boy uses a quarter berth. The prospective boat buyer should check the dimensions of the dinette and berths, especially when he or members of his family are very stout or tall.

On medium- to large-size boats, variations of plan A are often used with *pilot berths* and *transom berth extensions*. The usual pilot berth is an elevated or raised

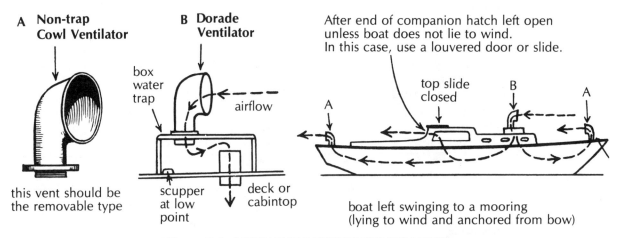

A Non-trap Cowl Ventilator

B Dorade Ventilator

box water trap

airflow

this vent should be the removable type

scupper at low point

deck or cabintop

After end of companion hatch left open unless boat does not lie to wind. In this case, use a louvered door or slide.

top slide closed

A   B   A

boat left swinging to a mooring (lying to wind and anchored from bow)

Figure 3-4. ACCOMMODATIONS VENTILATION

berth near the side of the hull, while the transom is a settee or narrow seat beneath and inboard of the pilot berth, which may be extended or slid out toward the boat's centerline to make a wide bunk (see plan C).

All cabins should be provided with ample ventilation. In most cases there should be two side-by-side *Dorade vents* (named after the yacht *Dorade*), as shown in Figure 3-4; a stern cowl vent (aside from the engine-room vents shown in Figure 3-1); and a cowl vent forward, which can double as a hawsepipe for the anchor line. The cowl vents should be removable and their deckholes provided with screw plate covers. Ventilators should face as shown in Figure 3-4.

Figure 3-5 shows some desirable cockpit features for comfort and convenience. The doghouse or cabintop should not be too high, because it will block the helmsman's view when he is seated. It also increases visibility to have high cockpit seats, and, of course, these provide more stowage space under the seats. As a rule of thumb, the cockpit should be large enough to seat comfortably at least as many people as there are berths below. Cockpits should not be so narrow that knees knock when people sit opposite each other, but on the other hand, they should not be so wide that the crew cannot brace their feet against the opposite seats when the boat is heeling. Leaking seat-locker lids are a constant source of annoyance on some boats. There should be deep, wide gutters under the edges of the lids to carry off rainwater or spray that finds its way through the cracks around the lids. These gutters usually drain into a self-bailing cockpit. Drainage should also be provided to prevent water from collecting between the seat and the coaming when the boat is heeled. This can be accomplished with a scupper and pipe that lead to the bottom of the cockpit as shown in Figure 3-5. Cockpit

scuppers should be large, fairly far inboard, and forward to prevent cockpit flooding from heeling and the quarter wave. They should be covered with a coarse screen to prevent clogging of the scupper pipes or hoses. Outboard cockpit scuppers, subject to flooding, should be provided with plugs. When flooding is a problem, the scupper pipes can be crossed so that the starboard scupper drains on the boat's port side and the port scupper drains to starboard.

Although the engine is usually serviced from below, in the cabin, by removal of the companionway ladder, often there should be some access opening in the bottom of the cockpit to inspect or service the propeller shaft and stuffing box. Flush hatch covers often leak, so it is preferable to have a large, threaded screw plate cover in the cockpit's bottom. Sometimes access to those vital parts can be obtained through a trap door inside a cockpit seat locker or side of a quarter berth.

It is common practice with some designers to rake forward the after end of the cabinhouse as shown in Figure 3-5, but this rake can be very annoying when it is raining, because water can enter the cabin as illustrated, unless vertical slides are put into the companionway hatch. The after end of the cabinhouse should be almost vertical. Cabinhouse sides may rake inboard slightly if there are opening ports in the sides, but if the rake is pronounced, water will lie in the lower lip of the porthole and will spill into the cabin when the port is open. Some ports are now made with sloping lips or drains. Cockpit coamings should be raked outboard slightly for backrest comfort but not to the extent of making cleats, mounted outboard on the coamings, awkward to reach.

A tiller should be hinged to the top of the rudderstock so that it may be lifted up to a height convenient for the helmsman and also in order that it may be folded

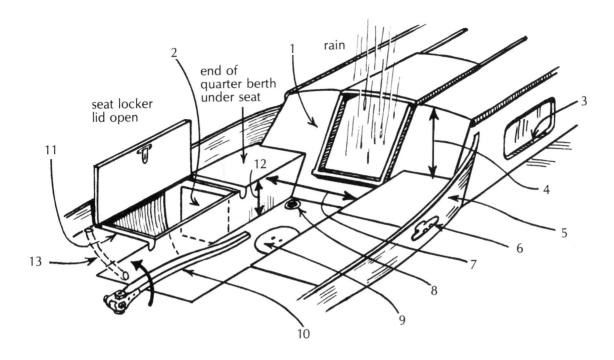

1—minimum rake of cabin trunk's after end. 2—trap door for quarter berth ventilation. 3—lip of opening port horizontal to avoid catching water. 4—minimum seat to cabintop height for visibility. 5—coaming high for backrest and wash protection. 6—coaming slanted outward but not at expense of cleat accessibility. 7—cockpit correct width for seating comfort and leg bracing. 8—scuppers forward to avoid quarter wave. 9—watertight access to prop and stuffing box. 10—tiller not excessively long and hinged to lift completely up. 11—deep, wide gutters under seat locker lids. 12—cockpit depth sufficient for safety but allowing accessibility to engine beneath. 13—scuppers at base of coaming to allow drainage to bottom of cockpit when boat is heeled.

Figure 3-5. COCKPIT COMFORT AND CONVENIENCE DETAILS

back out of the way when at anchor. A tiller should be no longer than is necessary for adequate steering leverage, because when unnecessarily long, it becomes a real obstruction to the crew in the cockpit. Furthermore, it is easy to *overhelm* (use excessive helm action) with too much tiller leverage.

AESTHETICS

Having been trained in the field of visual arts, I hate to put aesthetics in last place on the list of considerations for boat selection, but for most new boat buyers the other considerations we have discussed must come first. Price is a matter of necessity and safety a matter of survival. Most sailors prefer a comfortable, practical boat even if she is somewhat homely, and there are few racing skippers who will tolerate a dog (poor performer), no matter how beautiful she is. Fortunately, though,

beauty is not incompatible with the other considerations, and appearance has a definite place on our list, even if it is last.

Sailing yachts have often been thought of as being among man's most beautiful creations. The graceful flowing lines of a sleek racing hull have been compared to works of sculpture, and even the shapes of seagoing sailing cruisers have traditionally had a functional kind of beauty. In recent years, however, there seems to have been a slight shift of emphasis away from the appearance of many racing-cruisers. This is partly due to the advent of materials such as fiberglass — which tends to give boats a cold, ascetic, nonluxurious look — and it is partly due to a new concept of ruthless practicality and functionalism prevalent especially in the area of small-boat design. I am not against this concept. In fact, I'm very much in favor of comfortable, low-maintenance boats, but there are some unnecessarily ugly boats being produced today.

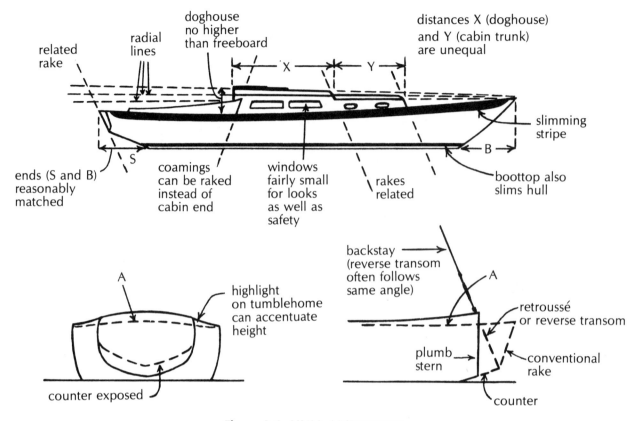

Figure 3-6. HULL AESTHETICS

Designers of these boats argue that small-boat designs should not be miniature replicas of handsome large boats, but that they should be conceived as separate and original entities. This might be considered the essence of the new concept: custom and tradition are put aside, and the boat is designed in strict conformity to the theory that form follows function. There is an unarguable logic to this reasoning, but it is sometimes carried too far.

It is true that it is difficult to scale down a big boat to a small size without sacrificing comfort or certain aspects of performance. But it is perfectly possible for small boats to have good proportions, harmonious lines, and visual unity with little, if any, sacrifice of room or speed. An example of a classic small boat that is not a scaled-down big boat but that has the pleasing and harmonious proportions of a big boat is the Shaw 24 class designed by William H. Shaw. The successful yawl *Trina* is one of this class.

With many of the not-so-good-looking classes, appearance is often hurt by hogged or powderhorn sheerlines, high doghouses, overly large transoms, and needlessly chopped-off overhangs. Moderation seems

most suitable for the sheer, especially if it is reversed. This kind of sheer can be deceptive. On the plans it can look quite graceful, but when the same sheerline appears on the boat, it can make the boat look extremely hogged. One designer noted that a reverse sheer of conservative appearance on the plans could make the boat herself look like a "beached whale." This may be due partly to highlights on the tumblehome. Extreme concave sheers can be ugly, too, especially on a small boat. These can make her look like a toy or rocker, and the turning up of the stern can add to the size of the transom. A compromise for small boats is the nearly straight sheer, with bow higher than the stern, whether the sheer is reversed or conventional.

There cannot be any hard-and-fast rules in the aesthetics of boat design because beauty is so much a matter of personal taste. However, I think that almost everyone agrees that the "barn door" transoms on some of today's racing-cruisers are ugly. Many of the owners will even agree with this. It is questionable whether these sterns are really necessary. They usually are not, and to support this position, there are a number of all-around, successful, small racing-cruisers that have small, hand-

The Esprit 37, designed by Robert Perry, is a fine example of a seaworthy racing-cruiser. (Courtesy Robert Perry)

some sterns. One argument for an extremely wide stern is that it permits extra-large overlapping jibs, because lead points can be located far aft and yet be a maximum distance out from the boat's centerline, although the measurement rules under which most boats race impose such penalties for oversize headsails that they are seldom worth extreme overlaps. Perhaps the most unattractive feature of the "barn door" transom is its height above the water at the boat's centerline. Many could be improved by trimming them down and flattening the sheerline aft, as indicated by the dotted line A in Figure 3-6. If the transom is not too high, a generous width for after sheet leads or some other purpose will not be too objectionable. Also, a stern that is not overly cocked up may give the boat a more streamlined appearance.

It often improves appearance, especially with big boats, when the bottom of the transom is raised above the waterline, exposing the counter. Raking the transom will decrease its top-to-bottom height when it is viewed from astern. With a reverse transom, sometimes called a *retroussé stern* (see Figure 3-6), the sailing length can be increased without adding a great deal to stern weight and without increasing the LWL or length on deck, as shown in the illustration. This type of stern is currently the rage on most IOR boats, and it seems to be admired by many of the younger sailors, who like the racy "fastback" look. When carried to the extreme, however, the ultra-fastback can give a boat a flashy, chopped-off, unbalanced look, one more suitable for a speedboat or sports car. It is perfectly possible for high-performance boats with modern underbodies to have shapely boatlike hulls above the water. A recent example of this is the Paul Kotzebue–designed, canoe-sterned *Tiffany Jayne*. Other attractive classes that are heavier and more seagoing, but sacrifice little in performance, are the C&C Landfall 38 and the Robert Perry-designed Esprit 37.

The cabinhouse frequently can be an eyesore in small

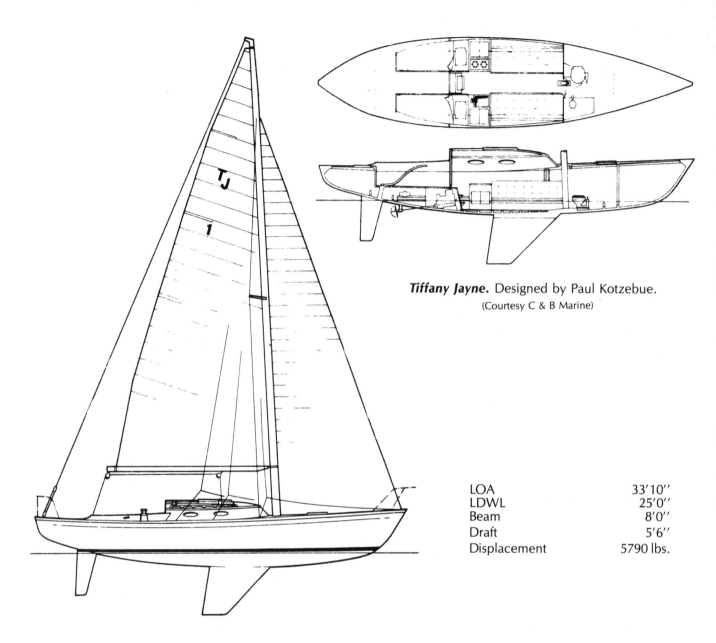

Tiffany Jayne. Designed by Paul Kotzebue.
(Courtesy C & B Marine)

LOA	33'10''
LDWL	25'0''
Beam	8'0''
Draft	5'6''
Displacement	5790 lbs.

racing-cruisers. Sometimes there seems to be a determined attempt, beyond all reason, to get headroom in the very smallest of boats, and this results in doghouses of heights entirely out of proportion to the freeboards. Actually, all that is needed in boats under about 26 feet LOA is sitting headroom. If it is considered essential to have standing headroom in the galley area, then an extra-large companionway hatch with a sliding cover or some kind of foldup tent arrangement can be provided. Thus, boats up to about 26 feet LOA can have well-proportioned and attractive-looking cabinhouses. These can be seen on certain classic small yachts, the Sparkman & Stephens *Dolphin* being a good example.

For a doghouse-type cabin, the Carl Alberg–designed *Electra* is generally agreed to have good looks. For boats slightly larger, full headroom presents a problem, but this usually can be worked out satisfactorily with little sacrifice to looks. The proportionate amount of freeboard can be increased slightly, the cabin sole can be put deep in the bilge if the garboards are full, and a tasteful and harmonious doghouse can be used. It helps appearance if the doghouse slide and cabintops follow radial lines from the stemhead, as shown in Figure 3-6.

Most designers are artistic, but often they are pressured to compromise a boat's appearance not only for accommodations requirements, but also for an optimal handicap rating. The IOR, for instance, has encouraged a somewhat short-ended, distorted, and bloated appearance in many modern boats. While wallsided topsides with no curvature are unattractive, too much curvature with pronounced tumblehome will make the boat look like the proverbial beached whale.

There are many fine points and subtle details that can enhance or detract from the appearance of a design, such as the size and shape of the doghouse windows; *slimming,* or use of a wide band of contrasting color painted below the rail to make the freeboard appear low (see Figure 3-6); the relation of raked cabin ends; size and style of portholes; the *crown,* or camber, given to the cabintop; harmonious rake of lifeline stanchions; the balance of overhangs; and more. Many of these things are discussed in the book *Sailing Yacht Design,* by Robert Henry and Richard Miller.

There are some who argue that beauty is a result of function, and taste a result of exposure — that over a period of time we become so accustomed to certain practical features of design that we eventually find them pleasing to the eye. To some extent this is true. We have gradually grown accustomed to high freeboards, moderate reverse sheers, and the like, but there is much more

to aesthetic evaluation than "handsome is as handsome does." If this weren't so, a garbage scow would be considered a thing of beauty. Down through the ages, handsome vessels of such contrasting types as the Viking longboats, clipper ships, and Gloucester fishermen have had the common denominator of harmonious lines, pleasing proportions, and balanced unity, even though these characteristics were not primarily for beautification. In all probability, these vessels will forever be considered handsome. Let us hope the designers of the future will attempt to make each and every boat a joy to behold. If not, some of us may be forced to buy a fast, practical, but ugly boat. This would be unfortunate, for every sailor should have the opportunity to feel satisfaction and pride in the looks of his boat.

As a last thought on choosing a racing-cruiser, it should be said that the perfect boat doesn't exist. It is one of those elusive things we seek but can never quite find. The new boat may never satisfy all of the considerations mentioned in this chapter, but at least the attempt should be made to satisfy as many as possible. Obviously, the most important considerations should come first, depending on a realistic appraisal of how the boat will be used.

4/ Hull Tuning and Equipping

Tuning is defined as improving, adjusting, and refining the boat and/or her rig to attain the best performance. Tuning the hull includes such considerations as streamlining, smoothing, and fairing underwater surfaces; stowage, ballasting, and distribution of gear, tanks, and other weights in the hull; and planning, equipping, and arranging the deck areas, especially the cockpit, for the greatest racing efficiency.

UNDERWATER SURFACES

Antifouling Paints

The greatest problem with the hull tuning is perhaps that of retaining the smoothest possible underwater surfaces. It is not difficult to get a smooth bottom to begin with. This is often simply a matter of using sandpaper liberally, but the real problem lies in keeping the bottom clean and smooth when haulouts are difficult, expen-

sive, or limited by local racing rules. As all experienced sailors know, in most boating areas bottoms foul quickly with marine growth and barnacles. A slight amount of slime may not hinder speed and a very light coating of certain algae may actually help, but coatings of moss, grasses, and barnacles are disastrous. The most harmful fouling occurs in warm salt or brackish water, but mild fouling takes place even in many freshwater areas.

Fortunately, there are some effective antifouling paints that are a great help, even if they are not a complete solution to the problem. These bottom paints come in two general forms: hard racing enamels and soft *defoliating* types. The former kind gives a hard and smooth racing bottom immediately after the boat is painted, but most of these paints leach their toxins slowly and foul up relatively fast. On the other hand, the defoliating paints create a relatively rough surface immediately after application, but often they are more effective and last longer as antifoulants. These paints slough off and leach out the antifouling poisons over a long period of time. It may be possible to smooth up a defoliating paint slightly with very fine, wet sandpaper, but this reduces the life of the paint. In addition, some of these paints should be immersed before the paint has dried thoroughly. Often this type of paint will become smoother several days or a week after the newly painted boat has been launched.

Hard, smooth bottom paints are being improved all the time, and it is worth using these when the boat will be hauled with reasonable frequency or in areas where marine growth is not a major problem. There are even new slow-leaching types, such as Micron 22, which the manufacturers claim will last for a full season or considerably longer, but these organometallic polymer paints are very expensive and difficult to apply. TBTO (tributyl tin oxide) paints, rather than those containing cuprous oxide, should be used on metal hulls, because copper in conjunction with aluminum or steel can set up serious galvanic corrosion in salt water. On wood or fiberglass hulls, however, there is little to equal the effectiveness of a paint containing more than 50 percent (by weight) cuprous oxide. Before choosing a light blue or green bottom paint, check the copper content on the can's label. It may well be that the brown or dark red color has the greatest amount of toxin.

When haulouts are limited, the next best thing (but a poor substitute) is a bottom scrubbing while the boat is afloat. In some cases, small boats and/or centerboarders are grounded gently, after which the crew jumps overboard and stands in the water. Then, with their feet braced against the ground for leverage, the crewmembers scrub off the boat's bottom with stiff brushes or pieces of burlap bag. In some areas it might be possible to *careen* the boat, or roll her over on her beam ends, by pulling on the halyards, but this puts a lot of unnatural strain on the moderately light mast and rigging of most racing-cruisers, and the boat's bottom may get scratched or scarred at the turn of the bilge if she is grounded. Of course, these cleaning methods are usually most feasible in areas of considerable tide.

When there is no suitable place for careening or grounding, the best means of scrubbing the bottom is with a special long-handled bilge brush such as the one illustrated in Figure 4-1. This can be used from a low floating dock or a dinghy. The brush is equipped with a float that forces the bristles against the boat's bottom. The curved handle allows the brush to reach under the turn of the bilge. Soft defoliating paints are usually easier to clean than hard enamels, because the marine growth sloughs off with the soft paint, whereas the growth often sticks tenaciously to the hard paints. With some soft types, care should be taken not to remove too much paint by overscrubbing.

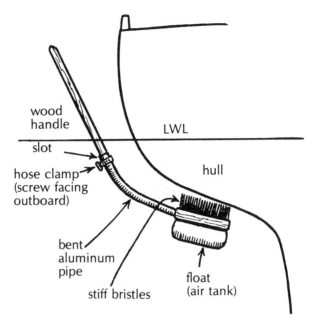

Figure 4-1. BILGE BRUSH

Smoothing, Fairing, and Streamlining

Surface drag is caused not only by the rough surface of the paint itself but also by the irregularities, roughness, and unevenness of the hull surface under the paint. This hull roughness may be due to blisters in fiberglass, scars from ice, marks from resting on the cradle, raised flanges of through-hull fittings, fastenings, and plugs, rudder straps, irregularities in the keel casting, keel corrosion or dents in a lead keel, and squeezed seams on a wooden hull. Molded hulls usually can be kept smoother than conventional wooden hulls because the latter often have problems with seams and fastenings, especially when the wood hulls are stored out of water during the winter. If ice is not a concern, it is best to leave the wooden boat afloat all year, as this prevents the drying out and swelling of the wood that cause problems with expanding and contracting seams. Wooden hulls of strip-planked, edge-fastened, and glued-seam construction are generally easier to keep smooth than conventional plank-on-frame wooden hulls, and when a strip-planked boat can be left afloat, there seldom are serious difficulties with seams. When wood, fiberglass, or aluminum boats are dry-stored for lengthy periods, great care should be taken to see that the hulls are supported adequately. Light metal hulls can get dents, and some fiberglass hulls can be distorted in extreme cases of improper cradling.

Occasionally there are major problems with blisters in fiberglass boats. When there are relatively few large

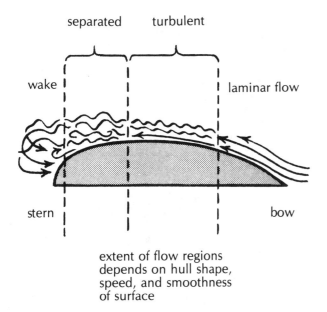

separated   turbulent

wake

laminar flow

stern   bow

extent of flow regions
depends on hull shape,
speed, and smoothness
of surface

Figure 4-2. BEHAVIOR OF THE BOUNDARY LAYER

blisters, they should be treated individually. This consists of breaking them, peeling off the loose material, sanding well, and filling the hole with an epoxy putty. A rash of small blisters in the gelcoat is best treated by sanding heavily the affected area and then coating the surface with clear epoxy. Beware of filling large holes or fairing irregular areas with automobile body compounds. They are easy to work with but will not adhere permanently.

In sanding and smoothing a boat's bottom, particular attention should be given to the forward half of the hull, because the boundary layer (discussed in Chapter 2) is much thinner forward than aft. Figure 4-2 shows the behavioral characteristics of a fluid flowing over a curved surface similar to that of a hull. Forward, the flow is smooth, or *laminar,* but well before it reaches amidships, the boundary layer becomes turbulent, with the outer molecules vibrating back and forth as they move aft. Still farther aft, the flow separates and both the inner- and the outer-boundary-layer molecules begin to bounce off the hull and behave very erratically. Separation can be caused or aggravated by wide yaw angles or an abrupt turning of the hull form. In the wake region, all the way aft, there are low pressures that suck the molecules into back flows or reverse eddies.

There have been attempts to make laminar keels and centerboards where the flow was smooth over the entire surface, but these have not been very successful. However, the laminar-flow region can be extended aft by smoothing, fairing, and proper streamlining. Any

protrusion, bump, or orifice on the forward part of the immersed hull breaks the laminar flow and causes turbulence. In the interest of minimizing frictional drag, there should be a minimum of through-hull fittings, with the smallest possible holes, especially in the forebody. Whenever possible, scupper drains, sinks, icebox drains, and so forth, should use the same outlet. It was reported that one of Richard Carter's most successful One-Ton Cup boats has only one through-hull orifice through which everything drains, even the head. Most yacht owners would not want to go to this extreme, but the example illustrates the importance that a top designer puts on minimizing orifice drag. Centerboarders have an advantage in that some of the drains may empty into the centerboard well.

The flanges of through-hull fittings should be flush with the hull surface. If the flanges protrude, the fittings can be replaced with flush-lip types, or the lips of the present fittings can be ground down to some extent or faired with a filler such as an epoxy cement. Some boats have been fitted with valve-type flaps to cover the holes.

Rough surfaces on the keel should also be filled and faired with cement. If these surfaces are continually peeling, blistering, or rusting, the keel can be covered with fiberglass cloth using an epoxy resin. If blistering recurs in the same localized areas, check to see whether the blisters are caused by weeping plugs. Sometimes there are plugs in the keel for access to keelbolts or for some other reason, and water often will get behind the plugs and weep out, blistering the paint surface. If such is the trouble, the plugs should be removed and the holes dried thoroughly and filled with a permanently waterproof filler.

An ideal streamlined shape for a centerboard, keel, or rudder was described briefly in Chapter 2. Authorities do not entirely agree. Some favor a sharper leading edge than others. A slightly rounded leading edge tends to delay flow separation, which ordinarily does not occur at the usual sailing angles of yaw. It does occur at certain times, for instance, when some rudders are greatly yawed to correct for excessive helm or when a boat loses speed just after tacking. Experts usually agree that the extreme forward end of the keel should be fine or parabolic, as shown in Figure 4-3, whether or not the actual edge is fairly sharp or rounded.

As for trailing edges, there seem to be two schools of thought: that these edges should be very sharp to reduce turbulence, or that they should be fine but cut off square to lessen wetted surface. Sharp-edge advocates sometimes grind down the after edges of their rudders or keels, but when this is not possible, those edges have been fined by extending them slightly farther aft with strips of fiberglass cloth soaked in epoxy resin. Those who advocate squaring off or blunting the trailing edge (see Figure 4-3) to reduce wetted area reason that this has little effect on form resistance, because the edge lies in the area of turbulent wake. This is the view held by the Polish scientist-sailor C.A. Marchaj. A blunted edge should be more beneficial in light airs than in heavy breezes. Most experts agree that the trailing edge should never be rounded, as this would do little to reduce either turbulence or wetted surface. Those sailors who insist on sharp edges should bear in mind that it almost never pays to fine an edge to the point where it becomes fragile and subject to nicking or breaking.

It is generally agreed that ideal centerboard or keel thickness is about one-fifteenth to one-twelfth of its fore-and-aft length, with the maximum thickness being between 30 and 40 percent of the length abaft the leading edge. However, a keel of this shape is not always possible or practical because of the usual placement of ballast at the forward end. A very thick centerboard will require a very wide slot, which could cause excessive drag. When maximum thickness is in after locations, from 35 to 50 percent abaft the leading edge, there may be a slight extension of laminar flow, but with the more forward locations of maximum thickness, 25 to 30 percent abaft the leading edge, tests have indicated that the keel has greater lift at low yaw angles. Centerboard slots should be only as wide as necessary for proper board clearance.

When the rudder is attached to the keel, it should be considered a part of the keel as far as streamlining is concerned. The keel's maximum thickness should not be compared with the length of the keel proper but with that of the keel plus rudder. The rudder's maximum thickness should be at its leading edge and this should be only slightly less than the keel's after edge. The rudder and keel should fit together snugly and be faired as smoothly as possible (see Figure 4-3). A spade rudder, on the other hand, should have an independent stream-lined form, as indicated by the dotted lines showing the cross-sectional shape in Figure 4-3. In the same illustration, an antifouling fin is shown just forward of the rudder. The addition of this fin is advisable in areas where there is even occasional floating seaweed that can lodge between the top of the rudder and the hull. The small fin can be built of wood, metal, or fiberglass.

There is some disagreement among designers regarding propellers in apertures, but all seem to agree that to minimize drag under sail, the propeller and aperture should be as small as possible. Most agree that excessively large apertures in rudders are particularly bad, because in addition to the aperture drag, there is the

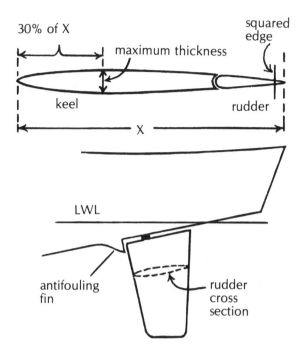

Figure 4-3. STREAMLINING

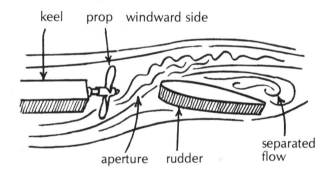

Figure 4-4. ESCAPE FLOW

escape flow through the aperture that detracts from the rudder's effectiveness and makes it necessary to hold the rudder at an extra-wide angle of yaw. This, of course, encourages flow separation (see Figure 4-4). A small keel aperture similar to the one in Figure 2-16(B), located a slight distance ahead of the rudder, has advantages. It allows a two-bladed propeller (turned so that its blades are vertical) to hide behind thicker deadwood, the escape flow is not as damaging to the rudder's effectiveness, and there is no need to cut away the rudder's area. When under power, this propeller might cause some vibration, since both blades will strike the relatively dead water behind the keel simultaneously, but most

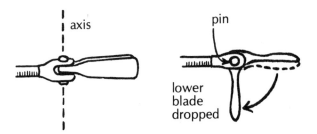

Figure 4-5. FOLDING PROP

racing skippers are willing to tolerate a slight vibration under power in the interest of minimizing drag under sail.

Solid propellers should be as small as possible in diameter and blade width. A general rule of thumb might be a diameter of a half-inch or slightly more to every foot of LWL and a blade width of one-quarter the diameter. High propeller pitch minimizes drag but may cause the prop to be rated as a feathering type. As said in Chapter 2, folding props cause by far the least drag, but they cost dearly in rating. Many skippers, however, think that the reduction of drag is well worth the price. With the folding prop, care must be taken to see that the axis of the blade hinges is vertical. Otherwise, the bottom blade might fall open, as shown in Figure 4-5. Even if the axis has a slight slant away from the vertical the blade might fall open at a severe angle of heel. Some skippers have even gone to the trouble of wiring their prop blades closed immediately prior to starting a distance race to make sure the blade will not open.

To position a folding prop so that its hinge axis is vertical, or a solid prop so that its blades are vertical and hidden behind the keel deadwood, the shaft should be marked so that the prop's position can be noted from inside the boat. Once the prop is in the correct position, it should be locked with the gear shift or a special shaft lock.

Propellers attract barnacles and it is difficult to keep them covered with antifouling paint. One product that is helpful in keeping the prop clean is a grease called Sea Film.

As a final thought on reducing the friction of underwater surfaces, it should be remembered that the topsides are often submerged, so these should be kept faired and smooth also. Usually, this is no particular problem, because they may be painted with high-gloss enamel paints. The topsides of new fiberglass boats need no attention, except occasional cleaning or polishing, but old fiberglass hulls with chalky or scuffed-up gelcoats should be painted. Many of the new two-part polyurethane paints, such as Awlgrip and Imron, will last for many seasons. Smearing the topsides with a liquid detergent may help reduce their friction, because the detergent increases wetting power and somewhat affects the boundary layer. However, only a small percentage of the topsides is submerged in light weather when wetted surface is the primary source of drag. And, of course, detergents soon wash away.

Recent research has revealed that the presence of certain natural or synthetic polymers in the boundary layer can have a damping effect on the molecular oscillations within the layer's turbulent region, thereby extending the laminar flow. It has been suggested that these polymers could be introduced into the boundary layer with slow-leaching paints or small holes at the stem or leading edge of the keel. The USYRU Racing Rules (Rule 65) prohibit releasing substances that reduce skin friction, such as polymers, from containers, but these rules do not prevent leaching them from hull paint. The Cruising Club of America Rule, however, prohibited any use of polymers or similar materials that change water into a non-Newtonian fluid, and this would be a wise prohibition for all the other rules.

In a few regions of the United States, antifouling protection is being provided by *boat baths,* portable boat receptacles into which toxic chemicals are poured to discourage bottom-fouling growth. However, I hope that this practice will not become widespread and that it will be outlawed by many cruising-boat racing associations because of complications, inconveniences, expense, and difficulties involved in the use of these devices, especially when boats use anchor moorings. Boat baths may have their place for certain small keel racers left moored in slips, when fouling is a very serious problem, but let's not make life any more complicated by using chemical baths for large racing-cruisers left at anchor.

STOWAGE AND BALLASTING

As was said in Chapter 2, on most boats pitching is minimized when major weights are concentrated amidships as much as possible. This applies to keel ballast, tanks, engine, and any ballast in the bilge not used for trimming the hull. The same holds true to a lesser extent for loose gear and equipment. If a boat has a tendency to hobbyhorse when beating into head seas, her ends should be kept light and free of gear. This is especially true with long overhanging ends and modern IOR-type boats with tall masts and deep, heavy keels. Heavy coils of line, chain, anchors, batteries, and rubber liferafts should be kept out of counter lazarettes or forepeaks, and of course crew weight should be kept amidships. If hobbyhorsing is a serious problem, consideration should be given to moving tanks, batteries, exhaust blowers, or engine mufflers when they are located far aft. Extreme forward and after spaces can be used to stow light gear such as flags, light sails, light lines, aluminum swimming ladders, plastic pumps, plastic buckets, and so forth.

A small amount of inside ballast is often used for correcting the hull's fore-and-aft trim. It is important that the hull be trimmed so that it sits on or near its designed waterline, so that it is not excessively down by the bow or stern. On many small and even medium-size boats, however, it may be preferable to trim the hull very slightly down by the bow (provided this is allowed under the measurement rule) to offset crew weight in the cockpit. Occasionally, it can be helpful to trim some boats slightly down by the stern when they are reaching or running, in order to lengthen the waterlines of boats having long overhanging counters or to increase stability when the maximum beam is located somewhat abaft amidships. A further benefit of temporarily trimming down by the stern is to prevent a fine bow from burying when running before steep following seas. Any change in trim while racing, however, must be done with crew weight, because after a boat is measured, her ballast and heavy gear cannot be shifted. The effect of trim on helm balance is discussed in Chapter 5.

The stowage of inside ballast should be influenced by considerations other than hull trim. The ballast should be as low as possible for the sake of stability, and it should be placed so that it cannot shift position during the most severe knockdown. *Boats have been lost because of shifting inside ballast.* If inside ballast is used for trimming purposes, of course, it cannot be placed amidships. In most cases, however, it is probably better not to place the ballast in the ends but to put it closer to amidships, and use more ballast as necessary.

Aside from ballast, all weights should be placed with consideration not only for how they affect pitching, but also for stability. Of course, the lower the weights, the more effective they are in making the boat stiff. Some sailors believe that the more they load their boat with gear and supplies, the stiffer the boat becomes, but this theory is often erroneous, because most modern racing-cruisers have their centers of gravity above their centers of buoyancy. Walter J. Bloemhard, who wrote a series of articles on sailing-yacht design for *Motor Boating* magazine, tells us that if gear cannot be stowed well below the vertical center of gravity, initial stability might be increased by taking gear off the boat. The

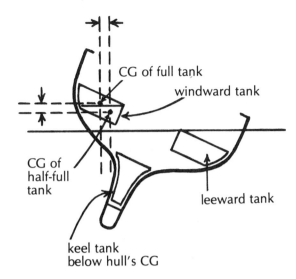

Figure 4-6. TANKS AND STABILITY

center of gravity of most racing-cruisers is not very far from the LWL, so for the sake of stability, all heavy stores should be stowed as far as possible below the waterline. This means that canned goods, tools, spare parts, and heavy cooking utensils should be stored in the lower drawers or lockers, under the lowest bunks, or even in the bilge when there is no problem with bilge water.

Batteries and tanks also should be placed as low as possible. Some integral-keel boats have water tanks deep down in the hollow of the keel and these can be very helpful to stability. Occasionally one hears arguments that side tanks, as illustrated in Figure 4-6, contribute to stiffness more than a keel tank (similar to the one illustrated) whose volume is equal to that of both side tanks. However, the boat's CG remains on the centerline when the boat heels. Although the windward tank is helpful to stability, the leeward tank is detracting from stability. A keel tank, on the other hand, lowers the hull's CG very slightly and there is no offsetting force. Tanks that are shallow and flat, of the same type as the side tanks in Figure 4-6, have a disadvantage in that heeling causes the CG to shift quite far to leeward when such a tank is only partially filled, as illustrated in the diagram. To avoid this, such tanks may be kept full or empty. However, a USYRU rule (Rule 22) forbids the filling of tanks after 9 p.m. on the day before a race. Unfortunately, violations of this rule are frequent, probably because some boat owners are not aware of the rule's existence. Also, under some measurement rules, certain tanks that are empty at the time of measurement must be kept empty while racing.

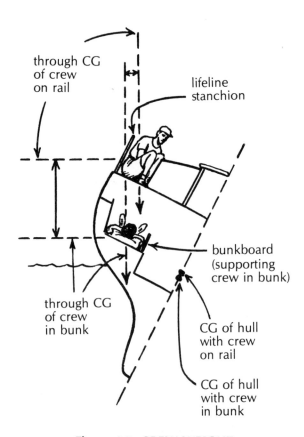

through CG
of crew
on rail

lifeline
stanchion

bunkboard
(supporting
crew in bunk)

through CG
of crew
in bunk

CG of hull
with crew
on rail

CG of hull
with crew
in bunk

Figure 4-7. CREW WEIGHT

It is obvious that crew weight should be kept on the windward side for the sake of stability. Occasionally, one hears of some "gung-ho" ocean-racing skipper rousing out the off-watch crew to man the windward rail when it breezes up in the middle of the night. However, a crewmember might add just as much or even more to stability on a windward bunk down below, where he is warm and dry and is getting needed rest. Figure 4-7 shows that the lower crew's weight is farther outboard, and because it is also lower, it slightly lowers the hull's CG. Most offshore or night racing regulations and the latest USYRU rules state that the crew must keep their torsos inside the lifelines, so this prohibits any hiking out. Another advantage in keeping the crew below is the reduction of windage.

During the sailing season, most racing-cruisers tend to grow heavy from accumulated gear and supplies. It is a good idea to periodically give the boat a thorough cleaning and lightening, provided she is kept close to her measured condition of trim and weight. It is my personal opinion that overloading is harmful to the speed of most boats. This is especially so with light-displacement boats.

COCKPIT AND DECK LAYOUT

The Helm

In the last chapter we discussed the cockpit from the standpoint of comfort, but now we shall discuss it from the standpoint of racing efficiency.

A first consideration might be the type and location of the helm. It is always desirable to have a tiller for a small- to medium-size boat that will be raced. If the boat has a heavy rudder, poor helm balance, or a helm that requires great physical strength to handle, then she needs a wheel for its greater mechanical advantage. However, when the boat is well balanced and does not have a heavy helm, a tiller will give quicker response and usually a more sensitive feel. Tillers are especially useful when a boat is running before following seas with the spinnaker set, when there is a tendency to yaw. Under these conditions, helm control usually requires a lot of tiring spoking or spinning of the wheel.

If a wheel is used, it should be of a gear ratio that requires a minimum turning for response. Captain J.H. Illingworth has suggested a general rule of three-quarters of a turn from amidships to hard over for the wheel of a small yacht. Of course, this depends on the boat's balance, size and weight of rudder, and so forth, but it serves as a rough guide. Most sailors who have raced modern yachts in difficult downwind conditions prefer that the spokes be covered by an outside steering rim (see Figure 4-8). Exposed spokes may be romantic-looking, but they tend to catch on everything and they often bark the helmsman's wrist or knuckles.

Opinions differ as to the best location for the helm. At one time, there was a rage for a forward location, placing the helmsman right up against the after end of the cabinhouse. Arguments for this arrangement are that the helmsman's vision is less hampered by the crew working the jibsheet winches in front of him; that the helmsman is closer to the companionway for communication with the navigator; that a measure of protection from spray or weather is afforded by the cabinhouse; that the helmsman gets a better view of the headsail; and that there is more room to extend the tiller for better steering leverage. However, there are many arguments in favor of the helmsman being located farther aft. Some of these are that crew may be placed ahead of the helmsman to keep their weight out of the stern; that the skipper who is usually at the helm can see what his crew is doing; that if the doghouse is high, the helmsman can see over it better when farther aft; that when seated aft, he can see better to leeward of the jib; and in this location he does not have to crane his neck backward to see the masthead wind indicator. Many of these advantages and disadvantages are shown in Figure 4-9.

Of course, the helm position sometimes will depend on the location of the rudderstock, because the tiller usually is fastened to the head of the rudderstock. However, if the stock happens to put the tiller in a particularly awkward location, a wheel can be substituted, or a steering shaft with linkage to the rudderstock can be used, as in E.G. Van de Stadt's Excalibur class. This is illustrated in Figure 4-8. On some boats with rudderstocks in the middle of the cockpit, the tiller can be folded back so that the helmsman sits abaft the stock. In this case, steering control is reversed, with the bow turning in the direction the tiller is pushed. Steering in this manner requires a very strong tiller-to-rudderstock connection.

In general, I tend to favor the after location for the helmsman in small to medium-size boats, primarily because it tends to keep crew weight always closer to the boat's CG. Also, with the helmsman located forward, the jibsheet winches usually must be located behind him, and when he sits to windward, this means that after every tack or even change in jibsheet trim, some of the crew must climb around the helmsman to return to their usual heavy-weather station, amidships on the weather rail. Of course, the crew sometimes interferes with the helmsman's view when he is in an after location, but he can sit to windward, where his view is unobstructed for the brief time that the jib is being trimmed just after tacking. Thereafter, the helmsman can sit to leeward if he so desires, and there is no need for more than one jib-trimming crewmember to be in his way. In good breezes, the helmsman should usually be sitting to windward, because there he can watch approaching waves and puffs for the most effective steering, and his weight there helps stability. Another advantage in being to windward is that the helmsman guards against fatigue by *pulling* against the tiller's customary weather helm rather than having to *push* against the weather helm, a much more tiring activity over a period of time. On the windward side, the helmsman probably will have his vision blocked less by the crew on the weather rail when he is sitting aft than when he is forward. It is especially important to keep the crew forward on most small boats with overhanging sterns and cockpits extended almost to the transom. Some of these points are illustrated in Figure 4-9.

Some tillers that attach to nearly vertical rudderstocks on the floor of the cockpit can be most annoying. When these tillers are held low for efficient leverage, they often strike the cockpit seats or, worse, the legs of crewmembers seated in the cockpit, when the helm is

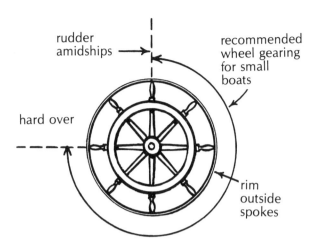

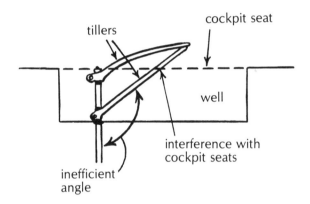

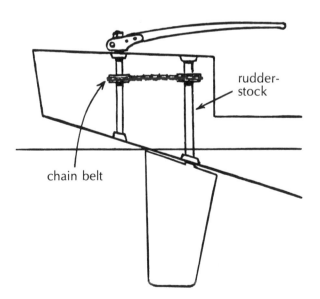

Figure 4-8. STEERING DETAILS

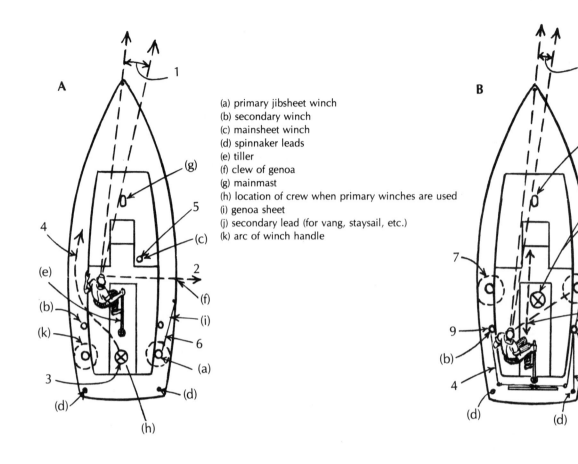

(a) primary jibsheet winch
(b) secondary winch
(c) mainsheet winch
(d) spinnaker leads
(e) tiller
(f) clew of genoa
(g) mainmast
(h) location of crew when primary winches are used
(i) genoa sheet
(j) secondary lead (for vang, staysail, etc.)
(k) arc of winch handle

Advantages

1—Wider view of jib luff for helmsman.
3—Crew working winches don't obstruct helsman's view.
6—There may be no need for a turning block (see text), and primary winches can be used for spinnaker.

Disadvantages

2—Genoa blocks helmsman's view to leeward.
3—Crew weight too far aft in small boats when winches are used.
4—Crew must climb around helmsman to man weather rail.
5—Extra winch is needed for mainsheet.
6—Spinnaker and genoa sheets must be transferred or crossed.

Advantages

3—Crew weight farther amidships.
2—Helmsman has better view to leeward, and he can more easily see masthead fly.
4—Secondary winches can be used for mainsheet.
8—Secondary winches (of ample size) can be used conveniently for spinnaker.
7—Widest part of deck for winch handle clearance on boat with narrow stern.

Disadvantages

1—Poor jib luff view when helmsman sits to weather.
9—Secondary winches in helmsman's way.
10—Helmsman separated from navigator.
11—Lines from secondary leads may have to cross primary winches.

Figure 4-9. COCKPIT LAYOUTS

put hard over. This problem is avoided when the rudderstock is abaft the after end of the cockpit's well and when the head of the stock is raised nearly to the level of the cockpit seats. When the rudderstock is so far forward that it must come through the cockpit floor, then a linked-shaft arrangement similar to Excalibur's could be used, or the head of the rudderstock could be raised off the cockpit floor, as shown in Figure 4-8. This has been done on the popular Sparkman & Stephens-designed Tartan 34. Such an arrangement minimizes tiller interference and allows the helmsman to stand up yet keep an efficient tiller-to-rudderstock angle, as illustrated.

Sheets and Winches

Once the helm's position is determined, the next consideration is the location, size, and number of sheet winches. A small sheet winch is illustrated in Figure 4-10. The drawing shows the usual top-action winch with handle on top, but the dashed line also shows a less-common bottom-action handle.

Medium-size boats, perhaps 30 to 40 feet LOA, usually have four headsail winches, two on each side of the cockpit. However, if economy is a major consideration, smaller boats can get along with only one per side. When there are four winches, the large primary ones are used for genoa sheets and the smaller secondaries for the spinnaker guy and sheet.

Winches are numbered according to size, but there is no uniform numbering system for all different makes. The only consistent feature is that the larger the number, the larger the size. For example, number 8 Enkes, number 10 Barients, or number 16 Barlows, which might be used on the smallest boat with a 200-square-foot genoa, are considerably smaller than number 20 Enkes, number 24 Barients, or number 25 Barlows, which are recommended sizes for a 30- to 35-foot boat with a 350-square-foot jib. Of course, there are no set rules for winch size. It all depends on your pocketbook, your age, the strength of your crew, and other factors. But most stock boats seem to have standard winches that are roughly one size too small. The owner of a new boat with undersize winches might do well to buy new, larger winches for primary use and then use the originals as secondaries. For boats around 35 feet or longer, two-speed winches are a good choice, because they afford speed and then power by cranking in the reverse direction.

The power of a winch is determined by the length of its handle, the radius of its drum, and, when it is geared,

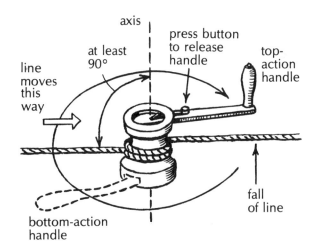

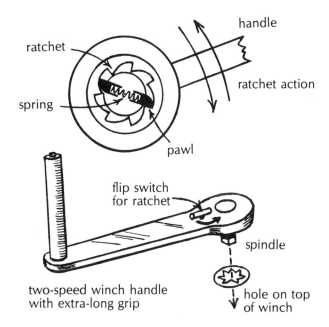

Figure 4-10. WINCHES
(From *Sailboat Maintenance* by Eric Jorgensen)

by its gear ratio. The *power ratio* of a direct-drive, nongeared winch is obtained by dividing the handle length by the drum radius. To figure the power of a geared winch, multiply the ratio of the handle length to the drum radius by the gear ratio, which is a comparison of the drive gear's rotation with that of the drum. A 3:1 gear ratio would mean that the gear turns three times to one turn of the drum. A winch with this gear ratio having a handle of 10 inches and a drum with a radius of 2 inches would have a power ratio of 15:1.

The advantage of a two-speed winch is that when the handle is turned in one direction to give high speed, the jib can be brought in very fast. When power is really

BARIENT No. 22 — SHEET WINCH

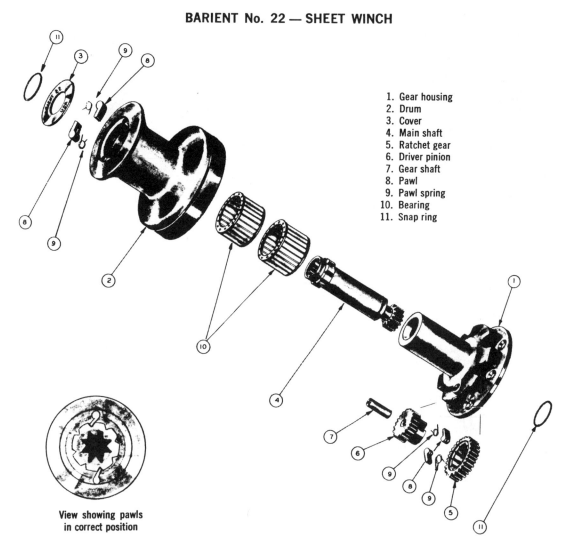

1. Gear housing
2. Drum
3. Cover
4. Main shaft
5. Ratchet gear
6. Driver pinion
7. Gear shaft
8. Pawl
9. Pawl spring
10. Bearing
11. Snap ring

View showing pawls
in correct position

(From *Sailboat Maintenance* by Eric Jorgensen)

needed, usually when the jib's clew is a few feet from the point of proper trim, then the handle's direction or rotation can be reversed to operate the slow but powerful low gear. Normal American-made one-speed winches turn clockwise to turn the drum, but when the handle is turned counterclockwise, the drum is locked in place by ratchet pawls (see Figure 4-10). This ratcheting feature allows the winch-cranker to make short, back-and-forth turning motions with the handle instead of turning the handle entirely around in a circle. This enables the winch-cranker to use his weight in the most effective manner for the greatest power during the last few inches of trim. Of course, two-speed winches do not

have this kind of ratcheting, because when the handle's direction of rotation is reversed, the winch operates on high gear. However, it is possible to obtain a special ratcheting handle for two-speed winches. This is recommended highly. This handle usually has a flip switch on top to change from ratcheting to nonratcheting (see Figure 4-10).

The illustration of the ratcheting handle in Figure 4-10 shows an extra-long hand grip. It is a good idea to have this on one of the handles so that a cranker can use both hands or two men can grip the handle for extra power in strong winds. Some handles are made with an extended hand grip that is twice as long as the single standard hand grip, but this is too long for many small boats. Such extra-long hand grips are clumsy, and they can catch on the lifelines, interfering with complete rotation. It is better to have an extended handle made slightly over 1½ times the length of a single grip.

All winches should be *freewheeling,* that is, when slack is taken in by pulling on the fall of the line, the winch drum should be able to turn without spinning the handle when it is not held. Nonfreewheeling winches can be annoying and even dangerous, because if someone pulls on the fall of the sheet while the handle is inserted, it can spin around and knock a crewmember (often the one who does the pulling) on the arm or head.

Figure 4-10 shows a square spindle at the bottom of the winch handle that fits into a hole on the top of the winch. This is the best arrangement, rather than the spindle on the top of the winch and the hole in the handle, because sheets can foul on a winch-top spindle. Also, every so often someone will accidentally sit on it, which can be a painful experience. The star-shaped spindle hole shown in the illustration is usually better than a square hole, because it is easier to insert the spindle into a star hole while the winch is turning.

A bottom-action winch with its handle inserted at the bottom of the drum, as shown in Figure 4-10, has one slight advantage in that loops of the sheet can be put around the drum without removing the handle, but this advantage is more than offset by the fact that the handle cannot be turned in a 360-degree circle without the winch-cranker's hand bumping into the sheet. Halyard winches are discussed in Chapter 5, and the operation of winches is discussed in Chapter 9.

A fairly recent development is the self-tailing winch with line guide and grips or cleating grooves on top of the drum (see accompanying photograph). There are also self-tailing adapters, such as the simple Elvstrom Winchers, which are specially shaped rubber rings that fit over certain sizes of existing winches. The advantage of self-tailers is of course that there is no need to pull on the tail of the line, and one person can easily handle the whole winching operation. Obviously, self-tailers are most valuable when sailing shorthanded.

The location of sheet winches should be very carefully thought out. Some factors that will influence their location are the tiller location, the number of winches used, the mainsheet arrangement, width of the side deck, location of lifeline stanchions, the height of the cockpit coaming, beam at the stern, buoyancy aft, and the amount of jib overlap. Some sailors like to put their primary winches abaft the secondary winches, as shown in arrangement A, Figure 4-9, while others like to put the primary winches forward of the secondaries, as

The rubber ring around the top of this sheet winch is a Watski Wincher, which gives an ordinary winch self-tailing and cleating capabilities. The winch is a Barient 28, about the largest size on which a Wincher will fit. (Rip Henderson photo)

shown in B. I tend to favor the latter arrangement whenever possible, but this depends on many of the factors just listed.

Tiller location is a key factor because the winches must be placed so that the winch-working crew is not in the helmsman's way. This usually means that if the helmsman is forward, the primary winches should be aft, and if the helmsman is aft, the large winches should be forward. As said before, if a small boat's cockpit extends far aft or if the boat lacks buoyancy aft, the crew weight should be kept forward of the helmsman if possible. Width of the side deck and position of lifeline stanchions are important because the handle must be able to make a 360-degree rotation without skinning the winch-cranker's knuckles. The beam aft largely controls the location of the spinnaker sheet leads. If the beam is wide, those leads usually will be all the way aft at the corner of the transom, but if the stern is narrow, the leads will be farther forward on each quarter. The secondary winches should be where the spinnaker sheets can be led to them effectively and fairly, without chafe.

The same is true for the genoa leads and the primary winches. There should be a carefully thought out relationship between the winch and the lead point. This will depend largely on the genoa's overlap; whether or not

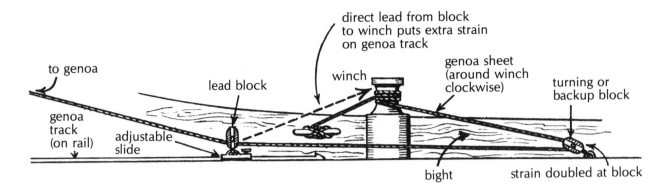

Figure 4-11. TURNING BLOCK

there is a *turning,* or backup, block as shown in Figure 4-11; and the height of the cockpit coaming. Also, it will depend on whether or not the genoa leads to the rail or to an inboard deck track. If the primary winches are aft, as in Figure 4-9(A), and the cockpit coaming is low, turning blocks may not be necessary. In that case, the sheet's angle from the lead block to the winch will be nearly fore and aft to minimize the pull on the genoa's lead track, and the sheet will be nearly parallel to the deck since the winch is low. However, in many cases, even when the primary winches are aft, it is a good idea to use turning blocks to eliminate side pull and the extra upward strain illustrated in Figure 4-11. Some outboard genoa tracks cannot be through-bolted, for they are mounted on the rail or very near the boat's side; and when a track is secured only by screws, it can be lifted or pulled loose.

Turning blocks should be extra-strong (usually the foot-block type) and through-bolted, because the jib-sheet's pull is the same leading to the block as it is going away from it, and this doubles the strain on the block. In other words, if there is a 500-pound pull on the sheet before it turns through the block, there is also a 500-pound pull on the line after it turns and doubles back to the winch, and this puts 1,000 pounds of strain on the block. For this reason, in the interest of safety, no one should ever stand or rest his arm within the *bight,* or angle, of the line running toward and away from a turning block.

Another point to consider when leading a sheet to a winch is the angle of the sheet to the turning axis of the winch. Sheets generally cannot be led down to a winch, unless it is canted slightly, without the sheet turns *overriding* (one turn riding up over another and jamming). Usually, a sheet should be led slightly up to a winch or at right angles to the drum's axis, as shown in Figure

4-10. Some winches are mounted at a very slight outboard cant to improve the lead angle.

Some consideration should also be given to the crossing of sheets, as in the infrequent case where a large jib and a spinnaker are being carried simultaneously. Crossed sheets are not always bad, but chafe and entanglement are apt to occur.

The mainsheet arrangement has a bearing on the location of the headsail sheet winches because it may be possible to utilize the secondary winches for the mainsheet. Figure 4-12 shows three common mainsheet arrangements, and A illustrates how the secondary winches, which ordinarily would be used for the spinnaker, could double for use with the mainsheet when beating to windward. Most mainsheets consist of a tackle with a self-contained cam cleat. The tackle should have enough purchase to make a mainsheet winch unnecessary, except when the mainsail is strapped in while beating in a fresh breeze. Such an arrangement is seen in Figure 4-12(D), and the tackle illustrated produces a 4:1 purchase, or a 400 percent tension, as represented by the four heavy arrows between the blocks. The force for any tackle system is determined by the number of lines of the tackle that are carried by movable blocks. The cam cleat is shown at the bottom left-hand side of the mainsheet tackle. It is not desirable to have tackles with too many parts, as this results in an excessively long sheet and makes it difficult to push the boom out in light airs.

An important rule for the mainsheet's location is that it be within easy reach of the helmsman. This is necessary because there are times when the helmsman might have to slack his mainsheet instantly when there is no crewmember near the cleat. Also, there are times when the owner might want to sail shorthanded or even alone. It is possible to singlehand a large boat, as many

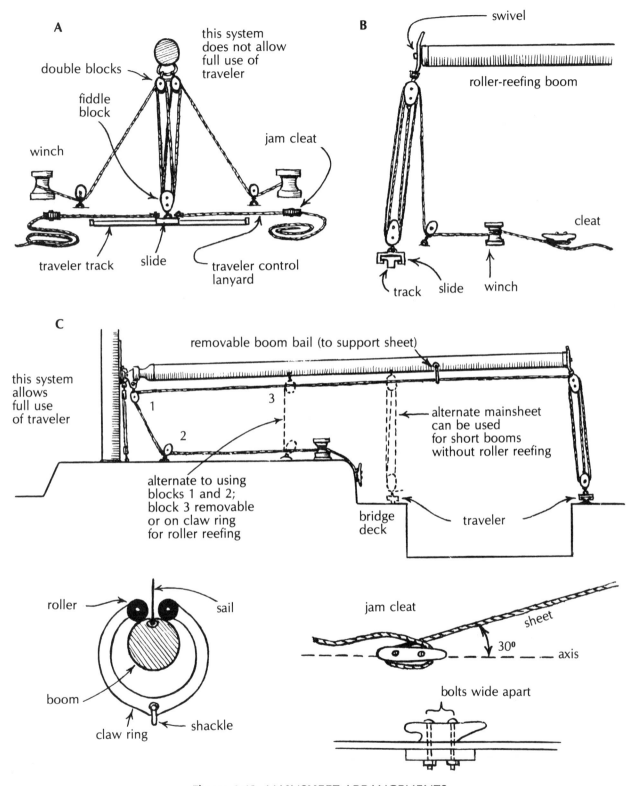

A

this system
does not allow
full use of
traveler

double blocks

fiddle
block

jam cleat

winch

traveler track   slide   traveler control
lanyard

B

swivel

roller-reefing boom

cleat

track   slide   winch

C

removable boom bail (to support sheet)

this system
allows
full use
of traveler

1

2   3

alternate mainsheet
can be used
for short booms
without roller reefing

alternate to using
blocks 1 and 2;
block 3 removable
or on claw ring
for roller reefing

bridge
deck

traveler

roller   sail

boom

claw ring   shackle

jam cleat   sheet

30°   axis

bolts wide apart

Figure 4-12. MAINSHEET ARRANGEMENTS

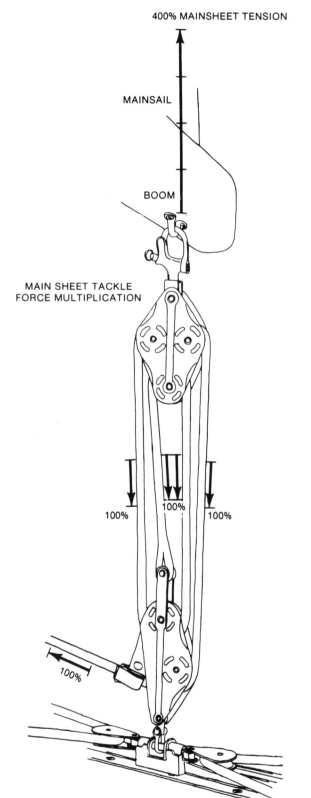

Figure 4-13. NICRO/FICO MAINSHEET ARRANGEMENT

(Courtesy Nicro Corp.)

contestants in the OSTARs (Observer's Singlehanded Transatlantic Races) and other lone voyagers have demonstrated. With a helm that is located near the after end of the cockpit, sheeting arrangement A or B in Figure 4-12, or B with a cleat on its tackle, might be suitable, but with a forward helm position, arrangement C, with the mainsheet winch and cleat on the cabin-house would be appropriate.

To some extent, the type of mainsheet arrangement will depend on whether or not the boat has roller reef-ing. Since a roller-reefing boom must be turned to roll up the sail, the sheet usually must be attached to the ex-treme after end of the boom by a swivel or revolving ring, as shown in Figure 4-12. Occasionally a *claw ring,* also illustrated in Figure 4-12, is used, but the ring can slip in a fore-and-aft direction and chafe the rolled-up sail. Most boats now use the so-called jiffy-reefing system, which is described in Chapter 9 (see Figure 9-4). With this method, of course, fittings can be attached anywhere along the boom.

When roller reefing is not used and there is no need to rotate the boom, the mainsheet can be secured to the boom some distance forward of its after end, as shown by the dotted lines in Figure 4-12(C). If the boom is a long one, however, and the sheet is secured near the boom's middle, individual tackle blocks should be somewhat spread out along the boom to distribute the load, thereby minimizing any risk of breaking the boom. This arrangement has advantages, because it pulls the boom down in its middle, thereby counter-acting the sail's upward pull, which tends to make an in-sufficiently rigid boom bow upward. If a boom's middle bends up, this can be harmful to the sail's shape, especially in a strong wind. When it blows, we often want to bend the boom down, not up. For this reason, and the fact that jiffy reefing is faster, easier, and af-fords outhaul tension, most modern sailors have con-verted from roller reefing to the jiffy method.

Whenever possible, mainsheets should be fitted with travelers. These are often through-bolted, transverse tracks with slides similar to those used for genoa leads (see Figures 4-12 and 6-16), but it is preferable that the slides move on rollers or races with ball bearings. A traveler slide with attached blocks to increase the pur-chase on the control lines is shown at the base of the mainsheet in Figure 4-13. If the boom is short, the traveler might run across the bridge deck, but if the boom is longer and the boat has roller reefing, it might be necessary to run the traveler across the middle of the cockpit. Most racing skippers feel that a traveler is an essential piece of equipment, but a makeshift substitute is a vang at the boom's after end, secured near the rail.

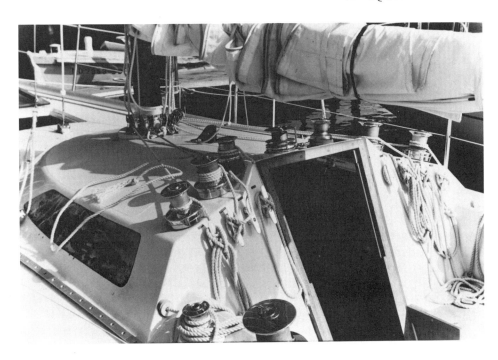

Most of the mast winches on a Chance Offshore One are located on the after end of the cabintop. This arrangement helps keep crew weight off the foredeck of a racing-cruiser. (Sally Henderson photo)

However, this means that an extra adjustment will have to be made every time the sail's trim is changed. Vangs, travelers, and some fine points of trimming are discussed in Chapter 6.

Careful thought should also be given to the type and location of cleats. Of course, this will depend on the layout of the various lines. On small racing-cruisers, it is customary to lead the halyards, the spinnaker-pole lift, and sometimes even reefing lines from blocks at the base of the mainmast through fairleads and across the top of the cabin trunk to the cockpit. This arrangement keeps crew weight aft, where it will not be detrimental to boat speed, and also allows the helmsman at the forward end of the cockpit to lend a hand. This layout normally requires winches and cleats at the after end of the cabin trunk on either side of the companionway. In some cases, one winch can be used to serve a number of lines. This is made possible by using *line stoppers,* which are illustrated in the accompanying photograph. A line led through a stopper ahead of a winch may be locked by pulling the stopper handle. This allows it to be removed from the winch so the winch can be used for another line.

Larger boats may not have many lines led to the after end of the cabintop. This is partly because these craft are not so sensitive to crew weight forward. Also, many operations, such as reefing and lowering the jib or setting the spinnaker, may be easier from the foredeck. Another consideration is that oceangoing yachts may need a dodger coaming to keep water from washing under the dodger in heavy weather offshore. Holes

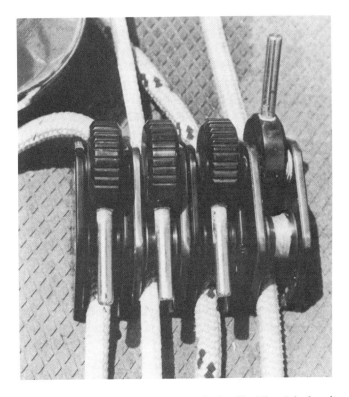

These devices are line stoppers or lock-offs. The right-hand stopper is locking the line, while the others allow the lines to run free. (Courtesy Yachtspars)

through the coaming for lines can let a surprising amount of water through. It is also true that lines led from the base of the mast through blocks and fairleads increase friction and therefore require greater power applied to the lines. Large boats with such a layout and keel-stepped masts normally require a tie rod connecting the partners area to the keel.

The size of a cleat should be proportional to the size of the line it accommodates. This is especially true with jam cleats. As a rough guide for selecting the proper sheet size, a 200- to 300-square-foot genoa might take a sheet ⅜ inch in diameter, a 300- to 400-square-foot genoa might take a ½-inch sheet, and a 400- to 700-square-foot jib might require a ⅝-inch sheet. Prestretched Dacron is the best sheet material because it is very strong and has minimal stretch. In addition to strength requirements, sheets should be sufficiently thick to allow easy hand gripping. Jam cleats with a wide space at one end and a narrow space at the other (see Figure 4-12) are very practical, but they must be mounted facing the proper way, so that the sheet goes around the wide end first and then wraps around to jam in the narrow end.

Cleats mounted on the outside of the cockpit coaming are out of the way, but they are sometimes hard to reach, especially if the cockpit coaming rakes outboard, away from the vertical. If possible, the primary winch cleat should be mounted horizontally on a block or pedestal near the winch. A cleat usually should not be placed in line with its sheet, but the cleat's axis (from one end to the other) should be slanted slightly away from the direction of the sheet, as shown in Figure 4-12. Cleats on the boat's port side do not have to be placed in the same corresponding position as cleats on the starboard side, because most American yachts are equipped with clockwise-turning winches on both sides. This means that a sheet will lead off the outboard side of the winch on the starboard side and the inboard side of the winch on the port side. All cleats must be through-bolted.

Sheet stowage presents a problem on many small boats. If possible, sheets and other frequently used gear should not be kept in the seat locker on which the helmsman usually sits. Sheets might be kept in temporary handy locations — for instance, on hooks just inside the companionway or on hooks accessible from the forward hatch. On medium- to large-size boats, waterproof deckboxes, placed out of the helmsman's way in the cockpit or perhaps just forward of the doghouse, are very convenient for stowing constantly used gear.

There should be consistency in the stowing of gear.

Items should always be stowed in the same location so that they can be found quickly. It is a good idea to mark sheets with colored tape or use different-colored lines for identification purposes. A simple means of differentiation is to have some sheets of braided or woven line and others of laid or twisted line. Some braided lines have a slight disadvantage in that they can slip on smooth winch drums a little more easily than laid lines, but braided lines are less apt to kink.

A winch handle should be stowed in a convenient location near the winch it operates. Some boats are provided with handle compartments in the winch bases, but if there are no such compartments, special winch-handle holders can be obtained from a good chandlery. Some holders made of rubberlike PVC are usually very satisfactory, but an extra-large holder is required for a geared winch handle that has a spindle, because this can catch in the holder and make it difficult to remove the handle. A simple solution for stowing winch handles is to fasten a holding strap across a corner of the cockpit or where the after end of the cabin joins the cockpit coamings.

All fittings should be kept properly lubricated, but this should not be overdone. Too much oil or grease can drip on teak decks, coamings, or rails and can stain the sails. In some cases, such as with slides on tracks, wax or cake paraffin may be used effectively without any risk of staining.

Keep the Decks Clear

When tuning for racing, unessential, lightweight deck gear that could be fouled by sheets and other lines or sails should be stowed out of the way. This is especially true on the foredeck. Most measurement rules specify that heavy deck gear such as anchors must be kept in the same location as when the boat was measured. (Of course, this only applies while the boat is racing.) It is a good idea to be measured with anchors off the foredeck, perhaps mounted on the cabintop or where there is little or no chance that they will be fouled. If there is a ventilator on the foredeck, it should be removed and replaced with a cap during a race. Even the engine-room vents may be removed temporarily, for the Coast Guard has ruled that: "Sailboats used for pleasure purposes need not be ventilated when under sail alone, and may block off cowls and ducts leading to the engine and fuel compartments when under sail alone." In rough weather, racing offshore, sealing ventilators is a safety precaution for the watertight integrity of the hull, but the engine room should be provided with some ventilation from below, in the cabin. Also, the engine compartment should be well ventilated and thoroughly sniffed for gas fumes before the engine is started.

A common problem with a small boat's cockpit layout is an awkward compass location. On large boats with steering wheels, the compass can be mounted in a binnacle on top of the steering pedestal, or in a separate binnacle on its own pedestal immediately forward of the wheel. On small boats, however, compasses must usually be mounted on the bridge-deck bulkhead or on the after end of the cabin trunk. One difficulty with hanging the compass on the outside of a bulkhead is that sooner or later it will be fouled, stepped on, bumped into, or hit with a winch handle. It is better to cut a small port or window through the cabin or bridge-deck bulkhead and mount the compass where it is protected on the inside of the bulkhead, just below the window. Some boats have twin compasses, one mounted on each side of the cockpit for easy reading from either side of the boat. The trouble with this arrangement is that, aside from the double cost, the two compasses seldom agree exactly, and adjustments and deviation cards may have to be made for each. Careful thought must be given to mounting the compass where it is as far as possible from magnetic influences such as ferrous metals and electrical equipment, because these can cause serious compass errors. Deviation can be caused by the engine, instrument panel, engine controls, fire extinguishers, some steel winch handles, radios, fathometers, voltage regulators, and so forth. Even beer cans near the compass can affect it.

SAFETY EQUIPMENT

So far we have not talked about equipment that is intended entirely or primarily for safety. To begin with, all boats must have the equipment required by federal law, such as approved life preservers for every crewmember; backfire flame arrestors for carburetors; bells, visual distress signals, whistles, fire extinguishers, marine sanitation devices, lights, and ventilators for engine rooms. Exact requirements should be obtained from your local Coast Guard, especially the rather complicated rules for engine ventilation. Basic ventilation and other regulations are set forth in the Coast Guard pamphlet, entitled *Federal Requirements for Recreational Boats*. There are many variations in the engine arrangements of sailing auxiliaries, and there may be several alternatives in meeting the Coast Guard requirements.

In addition to the above equipment and any extra items required by state laws for the waters sailed, local yacht-racing organizations have minimum safety equipment requirements. Typical safety lists for small racing-cruisers are the MORC requirements, which have a provision for minimum requirements, Category B, for use during day races in relatively protected waters, and Category A, additional equipment for offshore and night races. Structural features for these categories have already been mentioned, but portable and semiportable equipment has not been discussed. In Category B, these items include: one manual bilge pump; one anchor and cable; flashlights (one of which is suitable for signaling), water-resistant, with space batteries and bulbs; first-aid kit and manual; compass, marine type, properly installed and adjusted; heavy-weather jib and reefing equipment for mainsail; tools and spare parts including a hacksaw; radio receiver capable of receiving weather bulletins; softwood plugs, tapered and of various sizes; whistles, referee type, attached to life jackets; lifering, U.S.C.G.-approved, or horseshoe, equipped with a whistle (referee type), dye marker, automatic water light, drogue (must be within easy reach of the helmsman); and safety belts, harness type, one for each crewmember. Additional Category A requirements include: a stove capable of being operated safely in a seaway; the bilge pump provided in Category B must be operable with all cockpit seats, hatches, and companionway closed; one additional anchor with cable; radar reflector; spare compass; charts, light list, and piloting equipment; emergency steering equipment; and distress signals, to be stowed in a waterproof container (four red parachute flares and launching device, four orange smoke flares, and four white flares). Dinghy or raft and lifeline requirements for MORC boats have already been given in Chapter 3.

For larger boats (and even small boats), many yacht-racing organizations are using the ORC (Offshore Racing Council) requirements obtainable from the USYRU. These regulations actually apply to International Offshore Rule racing, but they form a good basis for equipping any offshore boat. Equipment can vary according to the category of offshore event, and this is explained in Part 5 of the regulations.

The ORC regulations appear in the Appendix.

Some of the ORC ocean-racing equipment requires a few words of comment. The man-overboard pole or *Dan-buoy* attached to a lifering is important at sea where the waves have deep troughs that can hide an ordinary lifebuoy. There is an excellent pole on the market that is fitted at its upper end with a very bright strobe light. A less effective but simpler alternative to this pole

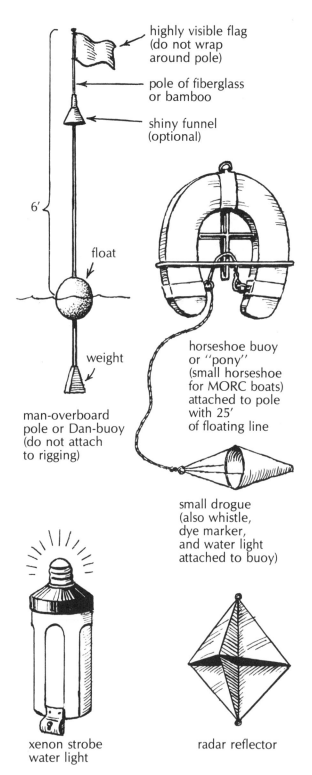

highly visible flag
(do not wrap
around pole)

pole of fiberglass
or bamboo

shiny funnel
(optional)

6'

float

weight

man-overboard
pole or Dan-buoy
(do not attach
to rigging)

horseshoe buoy
or "pony"
(small horseshoe
for MORC boats)
attached to pole
with 25'
of floating line

small drogue
(also whistle,
dye marker,
and water light
attached to buoy)

xenon strobe
water light

radar reflector

Figure 4-14. OFFSHORE SAFETY EQUIPMENT

light is a small, shiny metal cooking funnel placed over the upper end of the pole (see Figure 4-14). This can make a pole visible by flashing in the sun or reflecting a searchlight at night (of course, this reflector is no substitute for the required water light attached to the horseshoe ring). The Dan-buoy and ring should not be lashed to the rigging, because they take time to unlash and could be inaccessible in the event of a dismasting. They should rest in holders that allow instant removal. They may be secured to the lifelines or stern pulpit. The required drogue is a miniature sea anchor to lessen drift.

Safety belts are among the most valuable items of equipment for the ocean-racing crew. The harness type required has a chest belt with shoulder straps. A short, stout lanyard is attached to the belt with a safety snaphook, and at the end of the lanyard is another large, strong snaphook suitable for snapping onto strong points or some part of the rigging.

Bilge pumps should have a filter or heavy screen at their intakes to guard against clogging. The filters should be accessible for easy cleaning if the pump is mounted permanently. Bilges must be kept clean, and all paper labels should be removed from canned goods stowed in the bilge to prevent pump clogging. One bilge pump should be near or accessible from the cockpit, but it should not be mounted inside the cockpit seat locker or lazarette. It is always wise to carry spare parts for the pump. A pump's outlet should be above the waterline, and the discharge line should be looped and vented to prevent water from siphoning back into the bilge. It is a good idea to have an additional portable pump so it can be put in the deepest part of the bilge at any angle of heel and so it can be moved to a new location if the usual pumping area becomes inaccessible.

A radar reflector is normally a geometric shape made of folding, lightweight metal hung in the rigging to warn radar-equipped ships or boats of your presence (see Figure 4-14). This should be used at night or in foggy weather, especially near shipping lanes.

Some ocean-racing sponsors do not require seacocks on deck scuppers with outlets close to the waterline. However, it is the safest policy to have a seacock on every outlet, because the discharge lines could rupture while the boat is heeled with the outlet deeply submerged. A valve should be used on the engine exhaust to prevent water from entering in a following sea.

Suitable tools and spare parts for long-distance ocean races should include such tools as pliers, screwdrivers, assorted wrenches, hatchet, hammer, hacksaw, wood saw, chisel, spike, drill, brace and bits, files, and a crowbar. Spares should include sails, line, an extra spreader, tiller, the longest stay, a coil of flexible wire, batteries, bulbs of every size, fuses, hoses, turnbuckles of every size, shackles, blocks, tangs, wire clamps, winch handles, stops, sail slides, hanks, and battens. Also, there should be sewing and repair kits for sails, fiberglass, the head, liferafts, etc., and there should be an assortment of caulking materials, underwater epoxy, tape, glue, binding wire, small sheets of soft metal, nails, screws, pins, bolts, and soft wooden plugs tapered so that they can be driven into any through-hull orifice.

In addition to equipment required in the ORC lists, there is other safety-related gear that many offshore sailors deem essential or desirable. This equipment includes such items as a suitable bosun's chair for going aloft at sea; a face mask for underwater inspections; a Xenon strobe masthead light that flashes so brightly it can be seen in fog or daylight; deviation cards for all compasses; a barometer; *weather cloths* secured to the lifelines to give protection to the cockpit; safety nets secured to the lines forward for the protection of the foredeck crew and to prevent headsails from washing overboard; a *collision mat* (a piece of canvas with lashings that can be hauled under a boat to help stop a leak or cover a hole); a sea anchor or some kind of drogue (even a small auto tire) to lessen drift or slow a boat in extremely heavy weather; a storm mizzen or suitable riding sail set on the permanent backstay of a sloop; strong covers for large doghouse windows over approximately eight inches in height, even if they have an area less than two square feet; adequate engine fuel in case of a dismasting; an easily removable fuel-line filter that can be cleared readily in rough weather; and at least one EPIRB (Emergency Position Indicating Radio Beacon) approved by the FCC.

Another useful item is a hand clamping tool (such as Nicopress) to install compression sleeve fittings on wire cables to make rigging repairs. Optional masthead running lights allowed under the International Rules of the Road are a very sound idea when normal lights are obscured by racing sails. Another suggestion is the use of *jack wires,* which often are installed on British offshore racers but seldom on American yachts. A jack wire running along the rail or cabin trunk accepts a safety belt lanyard's snaphook and allows it to slide fore and aft so that a crewmember can travel between the cockpit and the foredeck in safety at night or in extremely rough weather.

All of this may sound like a lot of gear, and such a list may seem to conflict with advice given earlier about not overloading the racing boat. However, there is not as much equipment as there appears to be. Robert Manry had much of this gear (and more) in his 13½-foot *Tinkerbelle* when he sailed her across the Atlantic, and she was not seriously overloaded. As said before, only light-displacement boats will have their speed greatly affected by overloading. Of course, all the equipment listed is not needed for short day races, but for long races at night and in unprotected waters, safety must be the primary consideration.

Personal gear is not a part of hull safety, but it is appropriate to say here that for safety, each crewmember should wear nonskid deck shoes and carry a knife. Foul-weather gear should be orange or yellow for best visibility, and the jacket should open in the front with snaps or Velcro, because this is the easiest type to put on or take off.

Hull safety was discussed in the last chapter; rigging safety is discussed in the next.

5/ Selecting and Tuning the Rig

CHOICE OF RIG

The most common rigs for modern racing-cruisers are sloops, cutters, and yawls, with sloops being the most popular. There is often confusion as to what distinguishes a sloop from a cutter. Of course, both are single-masted, but the cutter has her mast farther aft, and she usually is *doublehead-rigged* (with two headsails, a forestaysail, and a jib). One practical definition requires that a cutter have her mast located at least two-fifths of her LWL length abaft the forward LWL ending. By this definition, most single-masted boats racing today are sloops, although some are cutters, and many come very close to being cutters.

There are a few schooners that are raced successfully, the veteran *Nina* and the smaller *Ingenue* being two good examples. It is doubtful, however, that this rig will ever regain great popularity, because it requires a relatively large number of tricky-to-handle sails and a large crew to handle them. Furthermore, single-masted boats are usually more efficient for windward sailing,

and they are easy to shorten down with modern reefing systems. Conventional schooners have always been able to "pick up their skirts" on a beam reach, but for the varied points of sailing over a modern closed course, the schooner usually needs a taller-than-normal foremast to support large jibs and spinnakers. Most schooners are not especially close-winded, but the *Nina,* with her modern staysail rig, is an exception to this rule.

The ketch rig is excellent for cruising, but it is not the most efficient rig for closed-course racing. The large mizzen divides the sail area for ease of handling, easy reduction of sail, and helpfulness in balancing the helm for self-steering. However, the rig allots too much sail area to the mizzen for optimum efficiency to windward, the foretriangle is smaller and less powerful than it could be, and the center of effort of the total sail area is lower than it should be for fast light-air sailing. Furthermore, there is a large gap between the mizzen and a marconi main that is difficult to fill efficiently with sail. One of the few successful small racing ketches of recent times, *Chanteyman,* owned by sailmaker Edgar Raymond, carries an unusual sail called a *mule* to fill this gap, but the sail has a very limited range of maximum effectiveness in terms of the points of sailing on which it will set without interfering with other sails.

After considering efficiency, rating, and all other factors, the most satisfactory rigs for racing are sloops and yawls.

The above remarks apply only to small and moderate-size boats. Large ketches sacrifice little in speed, because their size normally requires dividing the sail area anyway for ease of handling, and on a large boat it is possible to provide sufficient space between masts to minimize harmful wind interference. A prime example is the 79-foot ketch *Ondine,* which set the Bermuda Race elapsed-time record in 1974 (not broken until 1982). She carries an enormous mizzen with great space between the mizzenmast and the end of the main boom.

A recent development is the "rediscovery" of the cat ketch rig, which consists of two masts carrying sails of nearly equal size, with the forward mast stepped far forward, catboat-fashion. There is no jib set ahead of the forward mast, but the after mast can carry a staysail, which must be lowered when coming about. The first modern cat ketch to gain wide recognition was *Cascade,* which made a shambles of her class in IOR racing in 1973. She did well primarily because of her handicap rating and became much less competitive after the closing of a loophole giving too much credit to her rig. Other well-known cat ketches are the Freedom boats promoted by Garry Hoyt. These are interesting and in some respects handy rigs, but, having sailed on and against Freedom 40s, I think their speed, especially to windward, is overrated.

Yawls vs. Sloops

The modern yawl rig is altogether different from the marconi yawl rig of the 1920s and 1930s. The early boats had larger mizzens that divided the rig for ease of shortening sail in heavy weather. The typical contemporary racing yawl, however, is more like a sloop with a small balancing sail at the stern. The mizzen adds very little drive, and the mizzen staysail is greatly overrated (usually by sloop owners) when set from most of today's short, atrophied mizzenmasts. The mizzen staysail has a very narrow point-of-sailing range when it can be carried effectively, and the extreme slant of its luff away from the vertical often makes the sail quite inefficient for its area. This sail, together with the mizzen, is inefficient also in that it can require an extra crewmember to handle the sail combination.

The modern yawl rig has an advantage over the older

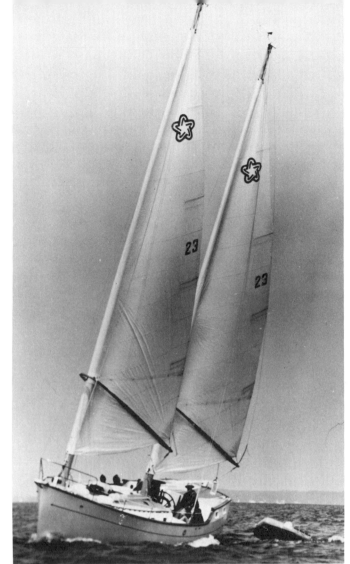

A Freedom 40 with a cat ketch rig. Since there are no shrouds, the sheets may be slacked to carry the booms broad off for better utilization of lift when sailing far off the wind. (Sally Henderson photo)

rig, however, because it is generally more weatherly or close-winded. As a rule, cutters and especially sloops are considered more close-winded than yawls, partly because when sailing to windward, a mizzen is severely back-winded and thus is as much a hindrance as an asset. To some extent this is true, but a mizzen can be a help as a balancing sail, especially when working to windward in light airs. Some sloops tend to be too perfectly balanced or slack-headed with no helm feel because of insufficient weather helm in light airs, but a mizzen sheeted flat can give the rudder a little bite on the water. This not only gives the helm a feel but also helps keel lift and the prevention of leeway when the rudder is hung on the keel.

In my sailing area, the Chesapeake Bay, there were a number of yawl-rigged sister boats competing against each other. Two of these boats tried racing a year or two without mizzens. No part of the rig was changed, except that the mizzens were removed. This had the effect of lowering their rating slightly, but it moved the sails' total center of effort farther forward, and of course, they lost the sail area of the mizzen and mizzen staysail. After racing a yawl-rigged sister against these boats converted to sloops, I concluded that there usually was not much difference downwind, but upwind the yawl was slightly superior in light to moderate winds. This seems to support my contention that the mizzen and mizzen staysail are overrated downwind and that the mizzen is underrated upwind. Of course, in this particular example, the two converted boats might have been much more effective to windward and downwind as well if they had added to their mainsails the sail area lost in the removal of the mizzens — but then, of course, their rating would have been higher.

For cruising, the yawl has several advantages over the sloop, especially for shorthanded sailing. In heavy weather or in a sudden squall, the mainsail can be lowered and good balance is retained under jib and mizzen alone. Also, the mizzen alone is often useful for holding the boat's bow to the wind, as, for example, when the boat is anchored lying to a current and rolling to a beam swell. A disadvantage to the mizzen is that it adds to cost and upkeep. There are extra spars, rigging, and sails to buy, maintain, and replace.

To sum up the pros and cons of yawls versus sloops, it seems that in most cases yawls are better suited for cruising, especially when economy is not the prime consideration, but sloops generally are better for racing, except in the larger boat sizes. Very few yawls are seen today in IOR racing, but the rig is popular in PHRF and MHS racing.

Size of Rig

The amount of sail area in the rig depends on a number of factors, but primarily on stability of the hull, displacement, wetted area, and the lateral plane. The relationship of sail area to displacement and wetted surface has been mentioned in Chapters 2 and 3. As previously said, the old CCA ideal sail area–displacement ratio was 15.4 for sloops, but many racing cruisers have ratios higher than this. The lighter a boat, the less sail area she will need. The sail area–wetted surface ratio (SA/WS) should be well over 2 and preferably 2.5 for good light-weather performance.

Since the wind on the sails exerts a considerable side force against the hull, sail area should also be related to the lateral plane. As a general guide for a modern racing-cruiser, the sail area might be at least seven times the area of the lateral plane. The draft times the LWL times the lateral plane coefficient (described in Chapter 2) gives an estimate of the lateral plane area. Thus, a normal, moderately heavy, keel ocean-racer, with a lateral plane coefficient of .60, drawing 5 feet, and with a waterline length of 25 feet, would have a lateral plane area of 75 square feet, so her sail area should be 525 square feet or slightly more. This rough guide can be used to determine the sail area when the lateral plane is known, or to determine the lateral plane when sail area is known.

The side force exerted on the sails (and resisted by the keel) causes heeling, and, of course, this is directly related to the size and shape of the sail area. A high-aspect-ratio rig has a relatively high center of effort and therefore exerts a greater heeling force than a low-aspect rig. In this respect, it might seem that a yawl with its divided rig has a slight advantage over a sloop, but the distribution of sail area in the yawl is still relatively inefficient.

One way of evaluating sail area with respect to stability is the Dellenbaugh coefficient method described in *Skene's Elements of Yacht Design* (revised by Francis S. Kinney). This gives a comparison with other boats for the angle of heel when the wind exerts a force of one pound per square foot on the sails (when the wind blows at about 16 m.p.h.). The formula is

$$\text{Angle of heel} = \frac{57.3 \times \text{sail area} \times \text{heeling arm} \times 1(\text{lb. per sq. ft.})}{GM \times \text{lb. displacement}}$$

The heeling arm is the length from the sails' center of effort to the center of the lateral plane, as shown in Figure 5-1. GM, the metacentric height (see Figure 2-25), can be obtained from an inclining test used when a boat is measured under certain handicap rating rules (see Chapter 7). An inclining test, which is also useful for determining proper mast and rigging size, is illustrated in Figure 7-4. The GM is the boat's righting moment for one degree of heel times 57.3 divided by her displacement in pounds. RM1° is the weight in pounds added to the inclining boom (see Figure 7-2) sufficient to heel the boat one degree multiplied by the distance in feet that the weight is from the boat's centerline. The Dellenbaugh angles usually vary between 10 and 22 degrees. Centerboard boats are generally about 10 percent stiffer than keel boats, and large boats are generally stiffer than small ones. A moderately stiff keel sloop of 22 feet LWL might have an angle of about 21 degrees, a 25-footer might have 19 degrees, and a 30-footer might have 17 degrees.

In conclusion, sail area should be low in the interests of heavy-weather performance and a favorable handicap rating, but the area should be high enough for good light-weather performance. A light-displacement boat with low wetted surface and a fairly high rating, racing in areas where fresh winds are the norm, should have a small to moderate sail area; but stiff, heavy boats with low ratings and considerable wetted surface, racing in calm regions, should have plenty of sail area.

MASTS AND STANDING RIGGING

The most practical standing rigging (the stays and shrouds) for today's racing-cruisers is composed of 1 x 19 construction stainless steel wire (one strand made of 19 wires). Unless the more expensive solid-rod rigging is used, prestretched 1 x 19 wire permits the least amount of stretch, an extremely important factor, especially where a racing boat is concerned. This wire is very stiff and cannot be spliced readily, but it is customary to use swaged eyes or jaws at the wire endings that secure to *tangs* (mast straps for shrouds or stays) or turnbuckles (see Figure 5-2). Swaged terminal fittings give up to 100 percent of the wire rope strength, whereas splicing gives only up to 80 percent strength. The greatest weakness with swaged terminals is that salt water works its way into the top of the fitting, and, in time, corrosion or expansion from ice in freezing weather can cause tiny hairline cracks in the terminal where it joins the wire. One effective solution to this problem is to oil or coat the terminal tops with Rustoleum 769 Damp Proof Red Primer; or use removable terminals with swage inserts (such as Norseman brand).

On the so-called Grand Prix IOR racers it is common practice to use rod rigging, especially for shrouds, since it stretches even less than 1 x 19 wire and is stronger, so it can be used in smaller sizes for less windage. Modern stainless steel rod is much more reliable than it used to be, and the problem of breakage at terminal fittings has largely been solved with the cold-formed, flared head (sometimes called a mushroom head). Nevertheless, there still are two problems with rod — its very high cost and its completely unyielding nature. Roderick Stephens, the rigging expert at Sparkman & Stephens, has written: "The very slight ability of the wire to give in the face of excessive peak loading clearly adds to the overall safety and security of the rig." Failure of rod to give may put unnecessary strain on the hull as well as the rig. When racing is the prime objective, rod may be the best choice (when cost is not an overriding consideration), but when a lot of cruising is planned, especially in out-of-the-way areas, wire is more sensible.

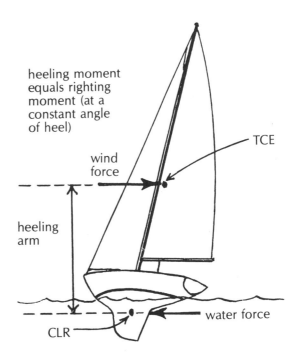

Figure 5-1. HEELING ARM

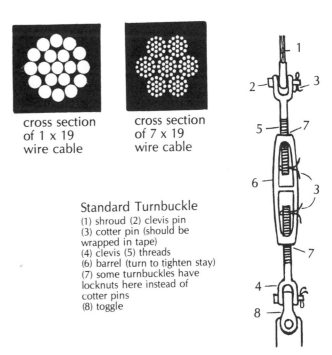

cross section of 1 x 19 wire cable

cross section of 7 x 19 wire cable

Standard Turnbuckle
(1) shroud (2) clevis pin
(3) cotter pin (should be wrapped in tape)
(4) clevis (5) threads
(6) barrel (turn to tighten stay)
(7) some turnbuckles have locknuts here instead of cotter pins
(8) toggle

Figure 5-2. STANDING RIGGING DETAILS

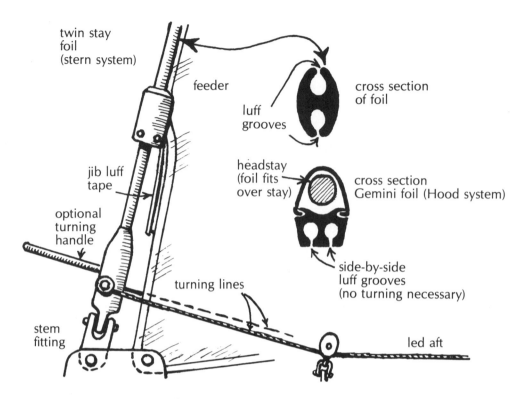

twin stay
foil
(stern system)

feeder

luff
grooves

cross section
of foil

jib luff
tape

headstay
(foil fits
over stay)

cross section
Gemini foil (Hood system)

optional
turning
handle

turning lines

side-by-side
luff grooves
(no turning necessary)

stem
fitting

led aft

Figure 5-3. LUFF FOILS

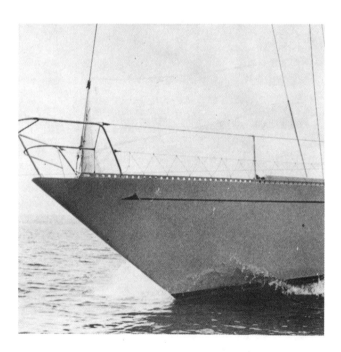

The bow of a racing-cruiser showing a grooved luff foil supporting her jib. The network of lines on the lifelines helps prevent the hankless jib from washing overboard. (From Sail and Power, *Third Edition)*

As for jibstays, most modern racing boats are now using aluminum (or plastic) slotted foils similar to the ones shown in Figure 5-3. The slots, which run nearly the full length of the stay, accept the jib's luff rope. The greatest advantage of these devices is that when there are pairs of luff grooves and two jib halyards, sails may be changed without lowering one jib before the other is hoisted. A disadvantage is that when the jib is lowered, it is hard to control, because it is not attached to the stay with hanks. Here again, it may be preferable to use slotted foils when the accent is on serious racing, but 1 x 19 wire when racing is less frequent and more casual.

The size of the standing rigging depends not only on the boat size and the amount of sail area but also on stability. Stronger rigging is needed on a stiff boat than on one that is tender. A very rough rule of thumb is that for a moderate, medium-size cruiser of good form stability but with a modest ballast-displacement ratio, the breaking strength of the upper shroud should be equal to twice the weight of the keel ballast. In some cases this might be a little heavier than necessary, but it allows an ample margin of safety for offshore sailing. Breaking strengths of a few of the common sizes of 1 x 19 wire used on racing-cruisers are 2,100 pounds for ⅛-inch diameter, 4,700 pounds for ³⁄₁₆-inch diameter,

8,200 pounds for ¼-inch diameter, 10,300 pounds for ⁹⁄₃₂-inch diameter, 12,500 pounds for ⁵⁄₁₆-inch diameter, and 17,500 pounds for ⅜-inch diameter. Lower shrouds need not be this heavy when there are two of them at the same location on the mast. Headstays and permanent backstays generally are the same diameter as the upper shrouds, although some owners use slightly heavier jibstays in an attempt to lessen stretch and sag. A few years ago it was customary for some naval architects to specify extra-heavy backstays for offshore racers. Presumably this was done to cope with the jerking strains of alternately collapsing and filling heavy-weather spinnakers in hard-driving downwind conditions. But the practice of disproportionately "beefing up" the backstay has largely been abandoned, perhaps partly because the backstay angle is more advantageous.

All shrouds and stays should be fitted with toggles, as illustrated in Figure 5-2. These serve as a universal joint to prevent fatiguing of the wires and especially the turnbuckles. Some say that the jibstay or headstay should have a toggle at the top as well as the bottom of the stay. There is extra strain on the headstay because it is usually set up tight for windward work, the jib exerts a lateral force as well as a fore-and-aft force, and the spinnaker pole often lies against the stay. Furthermore, with an extra-taut stay there is little mobility in the joint action of the toggle. For this reason, the headstay turnbuckle should be extra-large and strong. Some yachtsmen eliminate the headstay turnbuckle entirely, resorting to the backstay turnbuckle's pull aft on the head of the mast to tighten the headstay. I don't like this practice because the masthead must be moved to change tension on the headstay, and this can alter the tune of the other stays and shrouds as well as give an unwanted mast rake. There is no great danger of parting a headstay turnbuckle if it is strong enough, has toggles, and is inspected continually. Although some sailors have a fear of parting the headstay when beating and having the entire rig fall back into the cockpit, in most cases if the stay breaks, the wire in the luff of the jib will hold the mast temporarily. In such an accident, some helmsmen might instinctively luff into the wind, but the better action would be to bear off immediately so that the wind exerts its force forward. Then, of course, the mainsail should be lowered, and the jib left hoisted until masthead halyards or other preventers can be made fast to the stemhead to hold the mast forward.

Many racers now carry hydraulic backstay adjusters (see accompanying photograph), which increase tension on the stay with a hydraulic pump. This is a quick and effective method of tightening the backstay and thus the headstay, but hydraulic adjusters are expensive, and

A hydraulic backstay adjuster. Note the wise precaution of having a turnbuckle above the cylinder in case the adjuster should suffer from a fluid leak or other operational failure. (Sally Henderson photo)

sailors unused to these devices should be warned that damage can be done easily by overtensioning the stays. Also, it is wise practice to have a turnbuckle on the backstay in addition to the hydraulic adjuster, because the latter can leak fluid or otherwise fail, and then the turnbuckle can serve as a backup.

The safest fittings are forged, extruded, or machined from bar stock. Cast fittings are apt to have hidden flaws. A fitting of top-quality stainless steel is harder and generally has greater tensile strength than a good bronze fitting of equivalent size. However, the stainless steel fitting is usually more expensive and perhaps more subject to fatigue or crystallization from constant bending pressures. Also, stainless turnbuckles have been known to bind and peel their threads. It is important to be sure that there is ample shank length screwed into the turnbuckle barrel, because there is great strain on the threads. Some turnbuckles have lock nuts, but these can back off, and, when they are set up extra-tight to prevent this, they put extra strain on the threads. Recommended sizes for forged bronze turnbuckles are: for ⅛- to ⁵⁄₃₂-inch stainless steel 1 x 19 wire, ⁵⁄₁₆-inch turn-

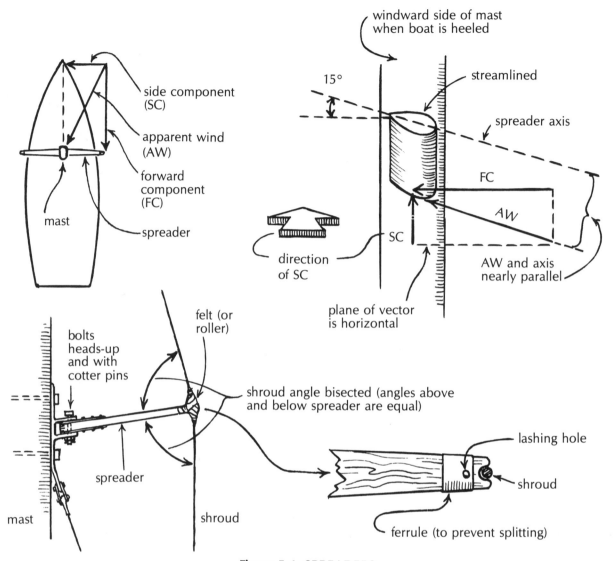

Figure 5-4. SPREADERS

buckle; ¼- or ⁹⁄₃₂-inch wire, ½-inch turnbuckle; and ⁵⁄₁₆- or ⅜-inch wire, ⅝-inch turnbuckle. The most thorough way to check for flaws or hidden cracks in a fitting is to have it X-rayed, but a simpler method of looking for hairline cracks is to paint the fitting with Spotcheck, made by the Magnaflux Corporation, or with a mixture of Mercurochrome and liquid detergent. After application, the solution is wiped off and the fitting is carefully examined with a magnifying glass. Any cracks should be clearly visible.

The great majority of racing boats now use aluminum masts, because they are light, strong, stiff, easy to maintain, and not unreasonably expensive. However, wood masts have not been entirely outmoded. In fact, I have a friend who makes a good living from building spars of

Sitka spruce (and a few of fir). In defense of wood masts, they are quiet (halyards make an awful racket on aluminum masts), they may be tapered easily their entire length to lower the center of gravity, and they are handsome when varnished. Some of the older classic boats do not look right without wood spars. On the other hand, aluminum masts are the best choice when the major considerations are the most competitive racing and low maintenance. Varnished wood booms go a long way to dress up fiberglass boats, and they are heavy enough to inhibit riding up without constant use of boom vangs. Aluminum booms, however, have plenty of room inside for running internal outhauls and reefing lines, and their light weight is beneficial in light airs.

Spruce spreaders can be properly tapered and stream-

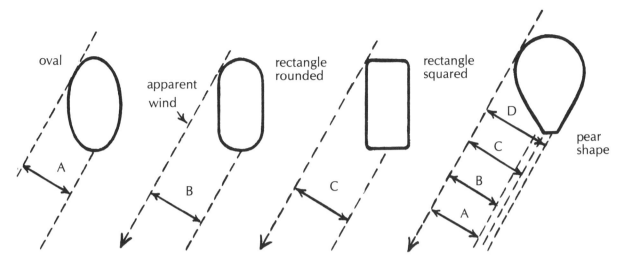

Figure 5-5. MAST SECTIONS

lined to reduce weight, windage, and interference with the airflow around the sails. It is a good idea to paint varnished spreaders with white or aluminum paint on their tops so that the sun will be reflected and thus discourage deterioration.

A streamlined spreader's leading edge should be angled down perhaps 7 to 15 degrees, as shown in Figure 5-4, to reduce windage when the boat is heeled. If this is not done, the spreader exposes its wide underside to the wind even at normal heeling angles. This is explained in the diagram. Of course, it is very important that the spreader's length be angled upward so that it bisects the shroud angle as illustrated. This is done to prevent any unnecessary bending moment or any tendency for the spreader tip to slip on the wire. Naturally, the tip should be lashed or otherwise fastened securely to the shroud to prevent slippage. More than a few masts have been lost because a spreader slipped. A wooden spreader tip should be fitted with a metal band or ferrule to prevent the shroud from splitting the wood (see Figure 5-4), and tips should be fitted with a roller or wrapped in felt to prevent chafe on genoa jibs.

One of the main problems with any mast is windage and the fact that it interferes with the airflow around the sail it supports. To minimize this interference, a mast's diameter should be as small as possible without sacrificing rigidity. Actually, some compromise is nearly always involved between rigidity and diameter. Fore-and-aft stiffness is especially important because lateral mast bend is usually easier to control with the shrouds and spreaders than is fore-and-aft bending.

In choosing the sectional shape for a mast, it should be kept in mind that, when close-hauled, the apparent wind blows against the mast at an angle of 25 to 30 degrees from the fore-and-aft centerline. Thus a streamlined section for a fore-and-aft flow is often a poor shape aerodynamically for nonrotating masts when underway. Another consideration, sometimes overlooked, is that it is of greatest importance to minimize mast interference on the leeward side of the sail, because most of the sail's pull comes from this side. Square or square-ended rectangular mast sections are bad from the standpoint of interference; round sections cause minimal interference but often lack fore-and-aft strength; and pear-shaped sections cause interference on the mainsail's important leeward side. Oval sections are a good compromise, because they have fore-and-aft strength yet cause minimal interference to leeward. Testing has shown that a rectangular section with round ends is quite successful (see Figure 5-5). A recent development is the so-called Beta section, which is a full-shaped oval with a flat after side. Its designers claim that the flat side aft gives strength to the mast, while the rounded shape forward with fullness aft prolongs the attachment of airflow.

On many small to medium-size racing-cruisers, the mast is stepped on top of the cabinhouse. There are pros and cons for this practice. Some of the advantages are that the mast does not take up space or block passageways below decks; since the mast does not pass through the cabintop or deck, there is no problem with leaks around the *mast collar* (the canvas strip that fits around the mast at the mast partners to keep water from running down to the mast step); the mast is shorter, which saves weight and size for convenience in winter storage; a *tabernacle* (pivot at the heel of the mast) may be used to lower the mast for low bridges or to raise the mast without a crane; and there is often less strain on the

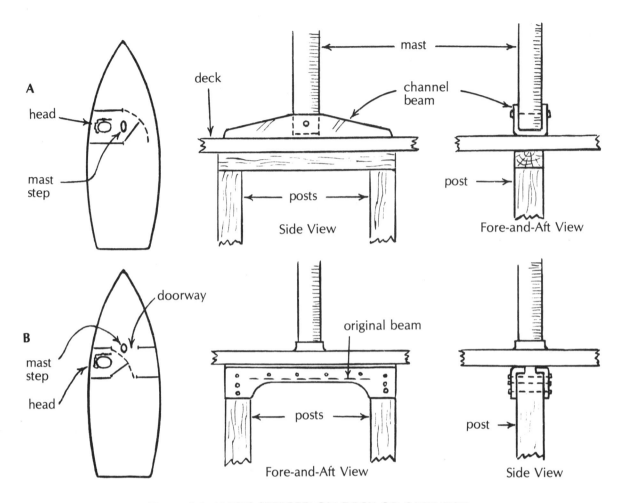

Figure 5-6. MASTS STEPPED ON DECK OR CABINTOP

boat's garboards than there is with the mast that penetrates the deck to a mast step on the floors.

One disadvantage of stepping the mast on the cabintop or deck is the difficulty in keeping the mast from developing compression bends, because it behaves like a column with two pin ends, as an engineer might say, as opposed to a mast passing through the deck, which behaves like a column with a pin end at the top, but a fixed lower end. Another drawback to deck or cabintop stepping is the structural difficulty of supporting the tremendous downward thrust of the mast when stays are set up and the sails are strapped in while beating to windward. In some cases it is possible to transmit the load to the keel with a permanent pipe under the mast step. However, there must be adequate floors at the point under the mast to prevent straining the garboards. Without strength in this region, especially when pounding in a seaway, wood boats can begin to leak and fiberglass boats can develop cracks.

In most cases, a pipe under the mast is not practical

because the step is usually over a bulkhead doorway into either the head or the forward cabin, as shown in Figure 5-6. In case A, the head is enclosed, and its bulkheads extend out to the boat's centerline. There are heavy posts that can support the mast load on either side of the head doorway, but the mast step lies over the middle of the doorway, and the load must be supported by a fore-and-aft horizontal beam across the top of the posts. With arrangement B, often used on smaller boats, the load is supported in the same manner, but the beam runs athwartships instead of fore and aft. These beams are not always adequate, and they sag in time. One solution to the problem is the addition of metal beams, as shown in Figure 5-6. In case A, a channel beam has been added to span the posts above the deck. In case B, the transverse beam might hurt appearance above deck, so an inverted channel beam with concavely curved undersides for headroom (or two right-angle beams fitted together for easier installation) has been put under the deck.

As stated in Chapter 3, it is more convenient and safer to leave an anodized aluminum mast stepped the year round when the boat is left afloat, because the anodizing may become scratched with repeated spar removal and storage. However, the rigging should be slacked to allow for contraction in cold weather, and the wire ends of the halyards should be hauled aloft on *gantlines* (old or light pieces of line used for this purpose) so that the rope ends of the halyards may be protected under the winter cover. The wire halyards and gantlines must be carefully tied away from the mast. Of course, in the spring when the boat is commissioned, the owner or a reliable crewmember should be hauled aloft to oil blocks and sheaves, seize and wrap the spreader tips, and carefully inspect all tangs and masthead fittings. Even if masts are left standing most winters, however, they should be removed every few years for the most thorough inspection and maintenance.

It is better for varnished spars to be removed from the boat during the winter for protection from the weather. They should be stored off the ground and *should be properly supported so that they lie straight.* A good spar can be permanently bent by being stored improperly.

RUNNING RIGGING

Running rigging comprises the movable lines and wires used to hoist, trim, and adjust the sails. (Sheets were discussed in connection with sheet winches in the last chapter, so here the discussion is limited to halyards.)

On racing boats, wire is used for halyards for jibs, mainsails, and mizzens to minimize windage and stretch. Flexible wire rope of 7 x 19 construction (seven strands, each made from 19 wires) is the best wire for halyards. To minimize fatigue, sheaves of large diameter are recommended. This is one reason that sheaves installed in the masthead, as shown in Figure 5-7, are preferable to small blocks hung at the *truck* (mast top). When halyards are external, mast sheaves should project slightly beyond the after side of the mast, as shown, so that the halyard can be led fairly to the head of the mainsail for proper sail setting and the reduction of chafe. The main halyard should be on the starboard side of the mast and the jib halyard to port. This is done partly for safety, because most crew expect this arrangement. It is also done for efficiency, because the main halyard leads down the forward side of the mast, and its winch, located near the base of the mast, usually turns clockwise, so the halyard must lead to its forward side.

The architectural drawing of a masthead on page 86 is for a U.S. Naval Academy 44-foot Luders yawl. It includes a sheave box that houses three sheaves, one for

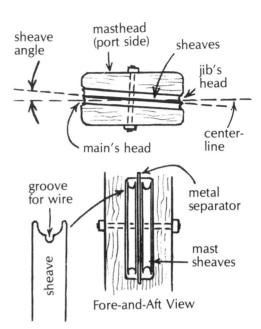

Figure 5-7. MASTHEAD DETAILS

the main halyard and two for jib halyards. The projections at the top of the mast are cranes for two spinnaker halyards. If two spinnakers are set simultaneously (during a change), another U-bolt would be added to the port crane. The large, flat, horizontal plate on top of the mast will accommodate such things as a masthead light, wind indicator, and antennas. Note the toggle at the top of the headstay.

When there are two side-by-side mast sheaves, it is wise to have them installed on a slight slant away from the boat's centerline (see Figure 5-7), so that the main halyard's after part is near the centerline. This will help fairleading, to prevent chafe on the lips of the sheaves, and it will help prevent one halyard from jumping over the top of the other and jamming. It is best to have a thin metal separator between the sheaves, as illustrated, to ensure that each halyard remains where it belongs. Be sure that there is the very minimum of space between the sides of the sheaves and the mast or separator, because if the halyard jumps the sheave, it can jam with the sail hoisted. Such a jam cannot be cleared without going aloft or even unstepping the mast in extreme cases.

The same thing holds true with blocks. Be sure that all blocks used for wire are intended for that wire and that a block is fitted with a swivel when the lead direction of its wire rope is expected to change. Be wary of using wire on sheaves without a deep groove for the wire and of using wire in sheaves made of Tufnol or other laminated cloth and plastic types that can be chewed or even split open by the wire. The minimum recom-

Luders fiberglass yawl, mainmasthead detail
(*From* Sail and Power, *Third Edition*)

mended sheave or winch drum size for a 7 x 19 wire halyard is 20-to-1 (sheave or drum diameter 20 times diameter of wire). Be sure that all nonmetal blocks have metal straps connecting the sheave pins to the eyes by which the blocks are hung.

Halyard winches on small to medium-size boats are similar to the top-action, ratcheting sheet winches discussed in the last chapter, but larger boats often use reel winches. This type is similar to a fishing line reel in that it winds the entire halyard on its drum. Reel halyard winches offer the advantage of always allowing the sail to be supported by wire, even when reefing, and, of course, there is no need to coil the halyard's end. But some of these winches can be extremely dangerous if they are not handled with care. The primary danger comes from the older makes of winches that have on/off brakes and require lowering sail with the crank handle inserted. When this is done, there is some risk that the handle may slip out of the winch operator's hand and spin around, striking the operator or someone else on the head. Newer types of reel winches, such as those made by Barient, are much safer, however,

because they have screw-toggle brakes that release slowly so that the sail is lowered without inserting the crank handle. Also, these winches allow hoisting with the brake on, in case the handle should slip out of the operator's hand while he is hoisting. Some sailors even say that reel winches should never be used, but I think they can be valuable if they are the safest kind and are used properly. The best policy is to remove the handle before lowering sail and to release the brake gradually, so that the sail will not suddenly tumble down and cause a backlash in the wire.

When standard ratchet winches are used, the halyards are wire but with rope tails, the rope part being spliced to the wire. When the sail is fully hoisted, the wire part is around the winch drum, but the rope tail is made fast to a cleat. The splice should lie between the drum and the cleat. A worn-out rope tail is sometimes difficult to replace when it cannot be rove through the mast sheave designed to accommodate the wire only. Thus it is a good idea to use sheaves with double grooves, as shown in Figure 5-7. The small groove at the bottom of the large groove accommodates the wire.

Well-organized halyards at the base of a mast. The pipe rail, or "sissy-bar," forward of the mast provides crew security. (Sally Henderson photo)

There are two ways to join the wire and rope: by eye-splicing the rope to an eye that is spliced, swaged, or formed with compression sleeves in the end of the wire, or by a wire-to-rope splice. The latter method is probably the most satisfactory when the splice is made properly, but make sure it is well done, because the splice can pull apart or wire snags can work their way through the rope strands, much to the discomfort of the crew. Most reputable riggers and yacht handlers, however, do a neat and strong job of this rather difficult splice. Avoid leaving wire-to-rope splices bent around winches, especially if their drums are of small diameter, because continual bending of the splice can weaken it. Never bend such a splice around a cleat.

When halyards are external (on the outside of the mast), there is usually no serious objection to joining the wire and rope with two eyesplices, except that the eyes are liable to chafe the mast unless the halyards are tied off. With this linkage, also, the splices should lie between the drum and the cleat when the sail is fully hoisted. All halyards should be tied away from the mast when at anchor to prevent their rapping against the spar in a breeze and causing chafe. This is also important with aluminum masts because of the problem with noise.

The rope parts of halyards should be of Dacron because it is strong and easy to handle and resists rot and stretch. Be sure that the ends of internal halyards are knotted so that they cannot escape back into their mast exits. It is also a good idea to run the knotted ends of external halyards through cleat bases to prevent them from escaping aloft.

HELM BALANCE AND THE RIG

Good helm balance is essential to top sailing performance, yet achieving it is one of the most perplexing problems for the yacht designer, since there is no entirely scientific way of balancing all boats properly for varying speeds and weather conditions. Once the hull is designed, it becomes a question of where to place the rig so that the center of effort of the sails (the geometric center of the sails' lateral plane) relates properly to the center of lateral resistance (the geometric center of the hull's underwater lateral plane). The wind's side force, theoretically concentrated at the sails' center of effort (CE), exerts its pressure laterally in one direction, while the water's side force, concentrated at the center of lateral resistance (CLR), exerts its pressure on the other side of the boat in the opposite direction. This is the simple, basic (not entirely correct but convenient) assumption we start with — that the CE and the CLR are two opposing forces on opposite sides of the boat. It would seem that if the two forces were directly opposed, working in the same vertical transverse plane, the hull would be in balance; however, this is not true — for several reasons.

In the first place, neither the sails nor the hull's underbody are flat planes. They are, of course, curved surfaces. The hull's true center of lateral pressure is normally forward of the CLR, especially when the boat is sailing close-hauled. Then, too, there is the thrust, or forward component, of the wind's force on the sail, which acts to leeward of the boat's turning axis and so also tends to turn her into the wind or give her weather

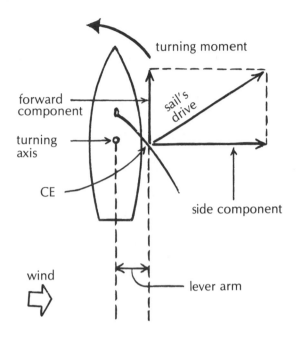

Figure 5-8. WEATHER HELM WHEN REACHING

helm. When the sheets are started and the main boom is broad off on a beam reach, the thrust is especially far to leeward, which increases the turning moment. This helps explain why so many boats have severe weather helms when reaching (see Figure 5-8).

It is convenient to consider balance as a problem of hydrostatics, but hull movement is very much involved, and the CLR shifts its position when the boat is underway. This center will often wander considerably, but its exact position will depend on hull shape, yaw angle, speed, and angle of heel. (Hull shape in respect to balance was discussed in Chapter 2.) The fish form tends to develop lee helm, whereas the wedge form develops weather helm when heeled. This phenomenon may be explained by the fact that the fish form trims down by the stern, moving the CLR aft when heeled, while the wedge form does the opposite. Also, there is greater curvature forward on the leeward side of the fish-shaped hull, which lowers the pressure (according to Bernoulli's principle) forward of the CLR, but on the wedge form this pressure is abaft the CLR. This is shown in Figure 5-9. Notice that the greater friction on the leeward side also has a slight influence on balance. Of course, the yaw angle has considerable influence. Hull A should have its keel well aft to improve balance, while B should have its keel extended well forward.

If the helm is extremely unbalanced because of the hull's shape, it may not be possible to correct the prob-

lem simply by changing the position of the CE of the sailplan. In many such cases, the keel must be extended or shortened, or sometimes a fin or skeg may be added. Balance is often easy to control with tandem centerboards, but these are seldom used on racing boats because of rating, increased drag, extra maintenance, or some other reason. The British ocean-racer *Outlaw* had a retractable daggerboard aft, which moved her CLR aft and gave her greater directional control downwind without the need for a spade rudder. A few American yachts have lifting rudders (see Figure 2-23), which may be used to alter the position of the CLR, and the Halsey Herreshoff–designed *Alerion* originally had a retractable skeg, although it was later changed to a fixed skeg. Two boats that I am familiar with had small fins added forward of the keel (one was movable like a bow rudder) in an attempt to correct for slight lee helms, although in these cases, balance probably could have been improved with rig changes. Bow rudders, of course, are very vulnerable to damage.

Lee helms (counteracting the tendency of the boat to fall away from the wind) are usually more harmful than weather helms (counteracting the tendency to round up into the wind). The reason for this is that, with lee helm, a rudder does not supply any lift, and a rudder attached to the keel no longer contributes to the keel's hydrodynamic lift (explained in Chapter 2 and Figure 2-27), and, as a result, leeway and forward resistance increase. Furthermore, it is difficult to feel a boat and work her to windward when she has a lee helm. A boat that turns to leeward when she heels over in a breeze not only will suffer in performance, but she can be positively dangerous, because she will not round up into the wind during a knockdown. Fortunately, there are few boats with extreme lee helms. Most of today's hulls are not of the extreme cod's-head-and-mackerel-tail form, but are modifications of symmetrical or moderate wedge forms. These forms are usually fairly well balanced and have some weather helm when heeled.

A mild weather helm is usually desirable on all boats, but especially on those with keel-attached rudders, in order to attain hydrodynamic lift from the keel-rudder combination when beating to windward. Optimum rudder angles vary from about three to five degrees for most racing-cruisers. In other words, at a moderate angle of heel when beating, a tight tiller (with no play between it and the rudderstock) should be held about three to five degrees to windward of the boat's centerline to hold the boat on a straight course.

The next consideration after hull form in the attainment of proper balance is obviously the location of the CE of the sailplan. Figure 5-10 shows how the CE of a

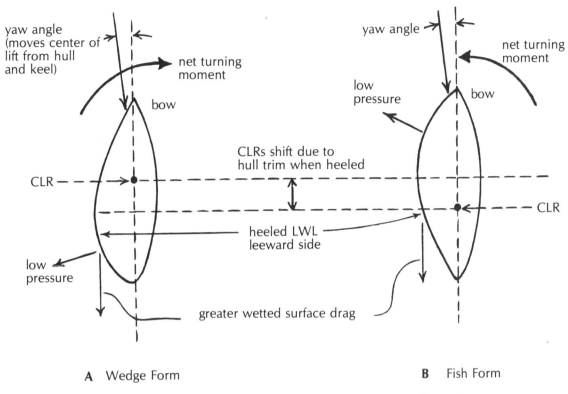

A Wedge Form **B** Fish Form

Figure 5-9. WATER FORCES PRODUCING UNBALANCED HELM

triangular sail is found. Each side is bisected by a straight line drawn from the side's opposite angle, and these lines intersect at the triangle's geometric center, the sail's CE. If the boat is sloop-rigged, the CEs of the jib and mainsail are found, and their combined or total center of effort (TCE) must be located. This can be done by drawing a line between the two CEs and locating the TCE on this connecting line at a position that is in accord with the comparative areas of the sails. A simple method of finding the position of the TCE is illustrated in Figure 5-10. As shown, if the main's area is double the jib's, the TCE on the connecting line would be twice as far from the jib's CE as from the main's CE. To locate the TCE when a genoa jib is carried, take the area of the foretriangle, multiply this by the distance in feet between the center of the main and the center of the foretriangle, and divide by the total area of main and foretriangle. The result gives the distance in feet of the TCE from the main's CE.

The CLR can be found by balancing the underwater profile on a ruler or hanging it from a pin, as illustrated in Figure 5-10. Once these two centers are located, it is a question of where the TCE should be located relative to the CLR. Some yacht designers will tell you that the TCE's designed position is the result of an educated

guess based on knowledge of some fundamentals and the observation of various boats. One thing is nearly always certain — that the TCE should be forward of or *lead* the CLR. The lead may vary from 2 to 20 percent of the waterline length, but, in general, a fairly flat-bilged, beamy, fin-keel or centerboard racing-cruiser might have a lead in the neighborhood of 15 percent of the LWL, whereas a narrow, but heavily ballasted, fairly symmetrical hull with a fine entrance and longer keel might have a lead of only about 8 percent.

Since the exact optimum lead of the TCE is very difficult, if not impossible, to pinpoint, many boats suffer from minor balance faults that must be corrected through tuning. The TCE and CLR may be moved slightly to alter the lead by: (1) changing the mast rake, (2) raising or lowering a pivoting centerboard, (3) altering sheet trim, (4) altering the mainsail's leech tension, (5) changing the fore-and-aft trim of the hull, (6) lowering the mizzen on a yawl, (7) setting higher or lower jibs, (8) increasing or decreasing the ballast, (9) changing the rig or the position of the mast step, or (10) changing the lateral plane profile. Of course, the first methods should be tried first because they are easier. The latter methods should only be tried in cases of extreme imbalance.

Raking the mast aft will move the CE aft and

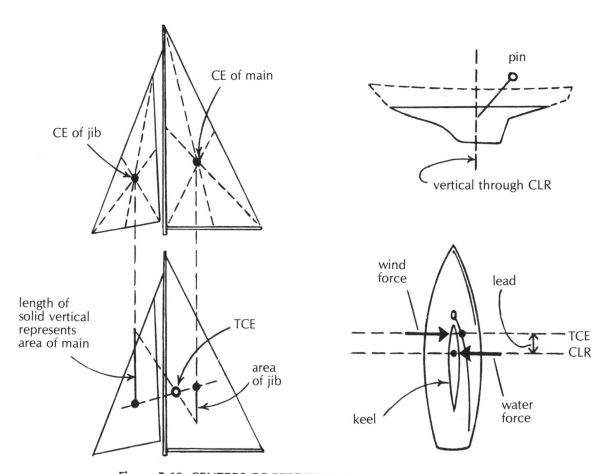

Figure 5-10. CENTERS OF EFFORT AND LATERAL RESISTANCE

therefore increase weather helm, whereas a forward rake will have the opposite effect. Raising the centerboard slightly will move the CLR aft, thereby decreasing weather helm. However, most boats should be tuned so that they balance well with the board fully lowered for maximum draft. In a strong breeze, it helps to ease the mainsheet to relieve a weather helm. This not only moves the CE forward but also helps reduce heeling, which often causes weather helm due to the asymmetrical shape of the hull when heeled. Leech tension can be adjusted with the boom vang or with a special adjustable *leech line* sewn into the leech tabling (edging), or tension can be altered by a sailmaker. However, any permanent alteration should be made with caution, because it can harm the efficiency of the sail's shape. More is said on this subject in the next chapter. A tight mainsail leech will increase weather helm, and a loose leech will ease weather helm.

Trimming the hull slightly down by the bow will move the CLR forward, thereby increasing weather helm, whereas trimming the hull down by the stern will have the opposite effect. At the same time, however, mast

rake will be changed by the hull trim, so the change of CE due to the altered rake will partially counteract the relocation of the CLR due to the altered hull trim. Moving the crew slightly aft on a moderately wedge-shaped hull may relieve weather helm not only by moving the CLR aft but also by improving stability through extra bearing and weight leverage at the hull's beamiest part. Of course, the addition of ballast will also relieve weather helm caused by excessive heeling.

Setting small or large sails forward or aft obviously moves the TCE, with a larger area forward tending to produce lee helm or reduce weather helm, while the larger area aft has the opposite effect. With this method or any method of changing balance, the improvement in balance should not be made at the expense of overall performance. Setting a small jib in light weather, for example, may produce a better feel to the helm, but the boat will lose power and speed.

If it becomes necessary to change the rig or the underwater lateral plane for an extreme case of poor balance (and this is seldom the case with a boat designed by a reputable naval architect), the simplest, least expensive method should probably be tried first. It may be simpler to reshape the rudder or add a skeg or balancing fin than to relocate the mainmast, for this might entail moving chainplates, changing major structural supports under the mast, and buying new sails. Of course, changing the sailplan may greatly change the boat's rating, too.

TUNING THE STANDING RIGGING

Most modern racing-cruisers have either of two basic rigging plans, the masthead or the fractional rig, illustrated in Figure 5-11. Small or large boats may be rigged using either plan, but usually no matter which plan is used, the larger the boat, the more rigging she needs to hold and control the mast. Boats above the medium size often need *intermediate shrouds* (between the upper and lower shrouds, as illustrated), with an extra pair of spreaders. One thing seems certain, however: the rig should be the simplest version that will do the job for which it is intended. Extra rigging causes windage and adds unnecessary weight aloft. Windage reduces speed far more than many people realize. A 2½-pound weight at 40 feet above the water is equivalent to subtracting 100 pounds of keel ballast.

Many of today's small to medium-size racing-cruisers use the masthead rig shown in Figure 5-11(A), although there has been a revival of the fractional rig in IOR racing recently. The masthead plan is a simple, effective arrangement, with the headstay being directly opposed by the permanent backstay. Some of the modern fiberglass boats have only single lower shrouds, thus allowing the main boom to go farther forward when running. However, I prefer the lower shroud's chainplate to be somewhat abaft the upper shroud's for better control of mast bend without the need for running backstays. The upper shroud's chainplates should be exactly abeam of the mast's lateral centerline on a racing-cruiser with a nonflexible rig and spreaders that are not swept back or hinged. Otherwise, the downward pull of the upper shrouds will tend to bend the spreaders and perhaps even the mast. When the lower shrouds are directly abeam of the mast, most boats need a *baby stay,* or short forestay, leading to the foredeck to control mast bend. This stay is usually attached to a slide on a track for the adjustment of tension and for removal when the spinnaker pole is dipped (see Chapter 9).

Aside from letting the main boom go forward when running, another advantage in locating the lower shrouds directly abeam of the mast is that this arrangement often allows all the shroud chainplates to be fastened to the same transverse bulkhead in way of the mast (see Figure 5-11). This not only provides a convenient and effective means of construction but also allows the chainplates to be moved easily inboard of the rail for close trimming of the genoa when beating to windward.

This close trim also requires short spreaders, but they should be long enough to give the shrouds an effective angle with the mast, to prevent too much compression on the mast. Shroud angles should be at least 10 degrees but preferably larger. With modern aluminum masts of proper section, it is possible to keep the spreaders short and still keep a reasonable shroud angle by attaching the shrouds to the mast a short distance below the masthead. Another way to keep the spreaders short, of course, is to have more than one pair, but this creates additional windage and weight aloft.

Fractional rigs with small foretriangles and large mainsails have been given a break under recent handicap rating rules, but they have several drawbacks for racing in light-air regions. Large, powerful jibs and spinnakers cannot be carried with this rig, and it is difficult to control mast bend without runners (running backstays), which add to handling complications. Nevertheless, a fractional rig has some advantages in that the mast can be bent significantly to control the shape of the mainsail, and shortening down is easier in a blow, because there is not as much need to change headsails. Often the jib can be left up and the main reduced with a jiffy-reefing system (see Chapter 9).

Even masthead-rigged boats require runners, of course, when they are doublehead-rigged, because the runners are needed to oppose the pull of the forestaysail. In light airs, however, doublehead-rigged boats will make better speed with large masthead genoas or reaching jibs, and the forestaysail stay will interfere with the large jib when tacking. It is customary, therefore, to fit forestaysail stays with quick-release fittings (see accompanying photo) so that they can be disconnected and brought aft to the mast to leave the foretriangle open. Neither the forestaysail stay nor runners are needed for mast support in light airs.

Adjustment of the standing rigging for proper tune is a controversial subject, because not all boats respond well to the same kind of treatment. Some sailors advocate loose rigging and others insist on tight rigging. Generally, small boats with bendy or semiflexible rigs (having masts that can bend aft to alter sail draft) sail better with their shrouds fairly loose, unless taut shrouds are needed to tighten the jibstay; many larger racing-cruisers, especially those with masthead rigs, perform best with their rigs set up quite taut.

To begin with, let us consider the adjustment of the shrouds as we view the mast from the bow or stern. A basic uncontroversial premise is that the mast should be

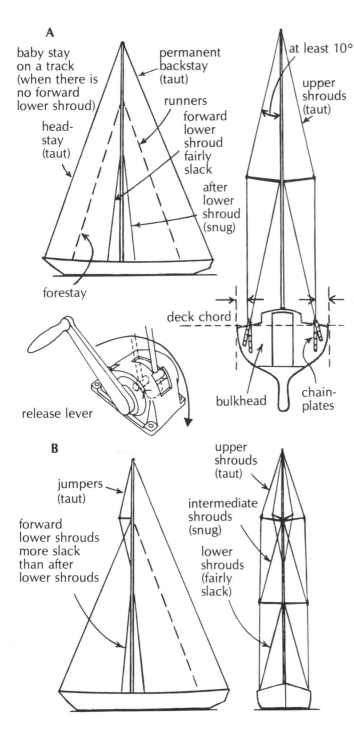

A

baby stay
on a track
(when there is
no forward
lower shroud)

head-
stay
(taut)

permanent
backstay
(taut)

runners

forward
lower
shroud
fairly
slack

after
lower
shroud
(snug)

forestay

release lever

at least 10°

upper
shrouds
(taut)

deck chord

bulkhead   chain-
plates

B

jumpers
(taut)

forward
lower shrouds
more slack
than after
lower shrouds

upper
shrouds
(taut)

intermediate
shrouds
(snug)

lower
shrouds
(fairly
slack)

Figure 5-11. TUNING THE RIG
(Release lever courtesy Schaefer Marine)

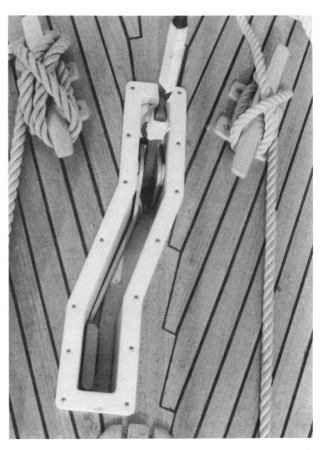

A quick-release lever in a deck well to prevent fouling from lines or sails. (Sally Henderson photo)

vertical when the boat is not heeled, as shown by the horizontal dotted line in Figure 5-11. Of course, when the boat heels, the force from mast and sail weight and wind pressure pulls against the windward shrouds, stretching them taut and causing the leeward shrouds to go slack. This is perfectly normal; however, the shroud adjustment should be tight enough to prevent excessive leaning of the mast to leeward when the boat is heeled. The 90-degree angle of the mast with the deck plane cannot be preserved, but the angle should not be allowed to change a great deal for the sake of minimizing loss of sail efficiency due to heeling. Beyond small angles of heel, a sail begins to lose projected area, and the sail's drive, the resultant of the wind's side force and the forward thrust, begins to be directed downward instead of straight ahead.

From this same fore-and-aft view, the mast should be kept approximately straight. This means that the upper shrouds should be kept more taut than the lowers, because the uppers are longer, pass over spreaders, and consequently have more stretch. If there are intermediates, they should be slightly more slack than the uppers but more taut than the lowers. This is a basic rule. There are some small-boat sailors, however, who think it advantageous to let the head of the mast bend slightly to leeward in a fresh breeze in order to minimize heeling and open up the jib slot. On a racing-cruiser the mast should be approximately straight when viewed from the bow or stern, but if it becomes necessary to tighten the after lower shrouds to control fore-and-aft mast bend (when viewed from the side), a very small amount of lateral bend to leeward is tolerable if this has no adverse effect on the shape of the mainsail. However, the mast rarely should be allowed to bend so that its top hooks to windward, and S-curves in the mast are usually harmful.

Viewing the mast from the side, we are concerned with rake and fore-and-aft mast bend. Both of these are controversial subjects. There has been talk about raking the mast according to the so-called *lift-line theory.* According to some sailors' interpretations, this calls for a considerable amount of rake aft. The *lift line,* a line drawn through the centers of lift (where the lift is concentrated) at all heights up the sail, and the *aerodynamic axis,* a line drawn through the centers of pressure (where the pressure is concentrated) at all heights up the sail, are essentially at the same location on the sail, although the forces act in different directions. The lift line drawn through these centers of lift and pressure will lie about 25 to 40 percent of the sail's width (from luff to leech) abaft the luff when sailing close-hauled (see Figure 5-12), depending on the exact boom angle and the draft or *camber* (curvature) of the sail. As can be seen in the illustration, the mainsail's lift line rakes forward considerably. Proponents of the lift-line theory advocate considerable rake aft when beating, especially for *una-rigs* (catboats with single sails), in order that the line be vertical, because maximum drive, which acts almost horizontally, will be most efficient at right angles to the lift line.

This theory may hold true for una-rigs, but for boats with jibs, the lift line rakes aft on the headsail. Also boats with low booms and bendy rigs usually have their masts bowed aft when beating. Therefore, except with some una-rigs and possibly a sloop with a fairly high boom and very small jib, rake aft should not be any more than moderate.

There is also another factor to consider with this theory. When a boat heels moderately, as she usually does when beating, a forward-raking lift line almost meets the apparent wind at right angles. This is shown in Figure 5-12. Thus a racing-cruiser that is not sailed upright need not carry a lot of rake aft to satisfy the lift-line theory.

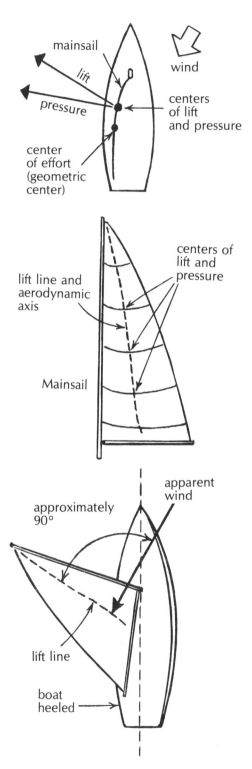

Figure 5-12. LIFT LINE

Mast rake affects the tune of a boat in many ways, but perhaps the most significant effect is on balance. As has been mentioned, a rake aft will increase weather helm, so raking the mast for optimum balance should be the first consideration. An important benefit of some after rake is that it helps tighten the jibstay or headstay for effective windward work. However, a pronounced rake aft is detrimental to downwind performance for three main reasons: gravity adversely affects the mainsail, the wind doesn't meet the vertical plane of the sail at right angles, and the center of effort is farther aft than it would be if the mast were plumb or raked forward. For steering control downwind, it is advantageous to have the CE forward. Also, with rake, area is lost in the foretriangle, an important consideration for racing-cruisers, and the mainsail loses area if it becomes necessary to raise the end of the boom for clearance.

A few relatively minor benefits of rake aft are that the masthead is slightly farther amidships to lessen hobbyhorsing; there may be slightly less windage because the rigging is inclined farther from the vertical; gravity lets the mainsail hang more effectively when sailing on the wind (but less effectively off the wind, unless the backstay can be eased to let the mast go forward a small amount); the CE is lowered somewhat, which is beneficial in heavy winds (but not in light winds); the foot and clew of a sail will be lower, a benefit at times (but, of course, this should be accomplished by the original cut of the sail based on estimated rake); and mast rake will raise the outboard end of a boom when it is broad off to lessen the possibility of tripping in a seaway.

The major considerations should be the effect of rake on balance and sail area, and on the tautness of the headstay. Most racing-cruisers are designed to carry a slight rake aft, and, of course, the designed rake should be tried first. If this doesn't work, the mast should be moderately inclined farther aft or forward. Seldom should a mast be raked more than slightly forward of the vertical. The average, well-balanced racing-cruiser with a mainsail luff of 35 feet may carry a rake aft of about one foot (measured at the base of the mast from a plumb line attached to the hoisted halyard to the after side of the mast).

Another controversial subject is mast bend. It has long been common practice in dinghies and small racing boats to bow the mast so that its head bends aft and its middle part bows forward. Now this is being done on large racing-cruisers. The primary purpose of a bendy or flexible rig is to increase the versatility of the mainsail. A full main with a lot of draft or camber can be used on straight spars in light airs, and when it blows, the spars can be bent to flatten the sail. The mast bowing forward at its middle will take up slack in the sailcloth between the luff and the leech, while the masthead bending aft will ease tension on the leech. It is also possible to increase sail area with a bowed mast.

Despite the benefits of bending masts, the practice has drawbacks for large racing-cruisers with masthead rigs. First of all, spars must be designed to be bent, and sails must be specially cut to fit the bent spars. Otherwise, the spar can be strained or broken and the sails badly distorted. Second, bending the mast on a boat that is masthead-rigged (the most common rig for small to medium-size racing-cruisers) can lead to detrimental complications. Some of the effects of bending a masthead rig are that the masthead will be lowered, thereby slacking off the rigging; area is lost in the foretriangle, a region of special importance in the masthead plan; and the headstay and other rigging cannot be kept as taut because a column bent in compression is not as stiff as a straight one. Furthermore, many experienced sailors feel that bending a long mast when offshore in heavy winds puts serious, if not dangerous, stresses on the rig. A safe and conservative mast bend for a masthead-rigged offshore boat is achieved by moving the mid-luff forward a distance equal to half the fore-and-aft sectional dimension of the mast. This can be done by tightening the backstay and the baby stay.

With many fractional rigs, especially those with small foretriangles, bending can be much greater. These rigs allow easier, more controlled bending without the need to bow the mast through almost pure compression, which would detract considerably from mast strength. Although obviously there is compression loading on a bowed mast that is three-quarter-rigged, most of the bend is induced when the permanent backstay pulls the top of the mast aft while the jibstay pulls the lower part of the mast forward. A major consideration when bowing a mast is to see that the jibstay remains tight. If the bend is achieved at the expense of a slack jibstay, there will be little or no benefit, even when the main is large and the jib small. Experiments should be made to see how the mast can be bent most effectively without slacking the jib's luff. In some cases, this can be done by tightening the upper shrouds when they are attached to the mast near the jibstay and having their chainplates set well abaft the mast. Hinging spreaders allow the mast to bow without putting any bending strain on the spreaders. However, there should be closely spaced stops to limit the fore-and-aft swing of the spreaders, because they could swing too far and cause the mast to collapse. Hinged spreaders should not be used for rugged offshore sailing, because they move too much in a seaway.

The jibstay or headstay should be kept taut for the

most effective sailing to windward, but this has become almost a fetish with many racing skippers. Complete elimination of headstay sag is impossible, even with rod rigging. If there were no sag, the stay loading would approach infinity when beating in a strong breeze. Sailmakers realize this and allow for some sag when cutting a jib; thus a slight sag will not be harmful to the set of the sail. An extremely tight headstay can put harmful compression bends in the mast, strain the hull and stem, introduce extra stress at the mast step, and pull the rig forward (or aft when the backstay is set up). A common mistake is made by those who carry the jibstay too tight in light airs when the luff should have a bit of sag for optimum camber.

The backstay needs frequent adjusting either for altering tension on the jibstay or for bending the mast or both. The most desirable backstay adjusters for large boats are probably the hydraulic types mentioned earlier, but a wheel adjuster or a turnbuckle with folding, locking handles is less expensive and perfectly satisfactory. Even an ordinary turnbuckle will do. Its main drawback is the need to remove cotter pins for every adjustment, but that operation can be simplified by using metal, shower-curtain rings as cotters. They have to be replaced often, but they are inexpensive. I have used them without problems for years.

Another backstay-adjusting system used on small racing-cruisers is two permanent backstays or one split into two legs leading to each quarter. Then a tackle or sliding donkey is rigged between the stays so that they can be pulled together somewhat, thereby increasing the pull aft on the head of the mast. This system has some drawbacks, however, in that precise adjustment is difficult, and the stays are pulled out of alignment with their chainplates. Whatever method you use, be sure to slack off the backstay after racing — this gives the hull a chance to relax and thus inhibits permanent distortion.

When adjusting the rigging, sight up the mast track at the after side of the mast to make sure that the mast is not being bent adversely. The track should be viewed from the side and from aft. After the rigging is adjusted, the mast should be examined while underway. Sight up the track while the boat is heeled when beating, to see if it remains reasonably straight. Also, watch the mast movement when the boat pounds into head seas. The mast should not be absolutely rigid, but excessive mast movement should not be allowed. When the shrouds are too loose, mast movement may strain the hull or rig and shake some wind from the sails. If, on the other hand, the rig is too tight, the mast cannot give to the boat's motion, and the wind may be bounced or jolted from the sails. It is not wise to make rigging adjustments while underway, because, when sailing, strains on the rigging are distributed unevenly, and it is difficult to estimate the amount of adjustment needed and to duplicate exactly the shroud adjustment on both sides of the boat.

The standing rigging will need periodic inspection and adjustment because the wire may stretch a little over a long, active season. Be sure to keep cotter pins well taped so they can't snag sails, and keep all toggles and turnbuckles well lubricated. If turnbuckle threads corrode, they can gall and peel, thus seriously weakening the fitting.

6/   Sail Selection, Shaping, and Trimming

Today the standard basic cloth for racing sails is nearly always made from one of two synthetic materials — nylon or polyester (most often Dacron in the United States and Terylene in England). Recently, Mylar, a polyester film made by the DuPont Company, and Kevlar, a DuPont high-tensile-strength fiber developed from long-chain polymers, have been used on the Grand Prix racers, but these relatively new materials are not substitutes for basic sailcloth. In fact, Kevlar has been banned for IOR racing beginning January 1, 1984. The new materials are most often used in a reinforcement or laminated form bonded to (or, in the case of Kevlar, interwoven with) Dacron to improve its strength and especially resistance to stretch. Nylon and Dacron are both highly resistant to rot, mildew, and water absorption. Unlike the old cotton sails, modern synthetics need little if any breaking-in. The major difference between Dacron and nylon, however, is that the former is *stable,* or resistant to stretch, while the latter is elastic, stretching out of shape in a strong wind, but recovering its original shape. With mainsails, genoa jibs, working jibs, forestaysails, mizzens, and other sails carried to windward in fresh breezes, stability of the sailcloth is extremely important. But with certain sails carried downwind or upwind in very light airs, such as spinnakers, spinnaker staysails, and drifters or *ghosters* (lightweight reaching jibs), some stretch can be tolerated, and nylon of great strength is made in very light weights.

Although Dacron cloth is very resistant to stretch compared with other materials, every woven cloth is subject to *bias elongation*. This occurs when the cloth is pulled diagonally to the direction of the weave. We can demonstrate this with an ordinary pocket handkerchief. If we hold a square handkerchief with both hands, each grasping the middle of two opposite sides, and pull our hands apart in an attempt to stretch the handkerchief, there will be very little noticeable stretch in the cloth. This is because the pull is in the direction of the weave, which runs parallel and at right angles to the edges. However, if we hold the handkerchief at two diagonally opposed corners and pull our hands apart, there will be very noticeable elongation of the cloth (see Figure 6-1).

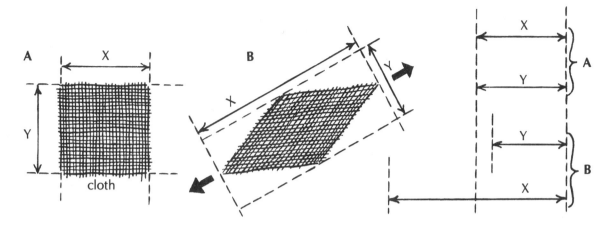

Figure 6-1. BIAS ELONGATION

Only a small part of this elongation is due to fiber stretch. Most of it is caused by slippage or realignment of the fibers when the cloth is pulled at a 45-degree angle to the direction of the weave. Essentially the same kind of elongation can take place even with nonstretch Dacron cloth. Diagonal tension will distort the square configuration of the weave, causing the cloth to become longer in one direction and shorter in the other. Dacron can yield to bias tension more easily than some other fabrics because it is smooth, hard, and slippery.

Excessive bias elongation is harmful to a sail, because as the wind increases, the sail will lose its proper, designed shape. In a fresh breeze, the draft or curvature tends to move from the sail's forward area to its after area. This not only causes loss in drive but also increases weather helm and adds to the heeling moment.

Minimizing this bias elongation is one of the sailmaker's biggest problems. There are several methods of combating this problem: (1) increasing the weight of the cloth, (2) arranging the cloth panels of the sail so that bias tensions occur in the least harmful locations, (3) cutting the sail to allow for a predicted change in shape, (4) weaving the cloth as tight as possible, (5) using resin filler between woven fibers to lock the threads in place, (6) using a resin coating on one side of the cloth, and (7) laminating or bonding the cloth to Mylar film, which will not elongate on the bias. The first five methods usually are used on all standard, unlaminated racing sails in varying degrees, but some sailmakers and skippers favor an extra-tight weave with little resin, and others prefer heavily filled or coated resinated cloth.

There is some disagreement among sailmakers about the use of resins. Some claim they break down in time and permit stretch, while others say they remain effective even after years of hard use. Heavy resination,

especially with coatings such as Yarn Temper, gives sails a hard, stiff, slippery, parchmentlike finish, whereas sails filled with more pliable resins are relatively soft and easy to furl and handle. The latter system may be the best compromise for the cruising sailor, who only races his boat occasionally. A certain amount of stretch resistance is sacrificed with these sails, but when they are cut properly, their shape can be adjusted by spar bending and tensioning of the edges, especially the luff. The less stable sails can be kept well shaped, but they require more frequent adjustment. One advantage, not always appreciated, is that when these sails are not too light, they normally have good recoverability after being stretched out of shape, whereas a heavily resinated sail may lose some of its optimum shape permanently if it is stretched badly in a blow and the resin breaks down. Thus, another consideration is whether or not you have a grooved jib-luff system that permits quick, easy sail changes. If you might be forced to lug a sail in winds that are too heavy for it because of difficulties in changing, then a sail with good recovery might be the best choice to minimize risk of damage.

Mylar sails have not yet reached their peak of development, but even the present sails offer advantages for the all-out racer. Aside from very high resistance to stretch, Mylar sails are of significantly lighter weight. On the negative side, the Mylar film can peel away from the Dacron cloth if the sail is carried in a wind much stronger than it was intended for, and the film can tear easily if it is punctured. Also, the shape of a Mylar sail is so stable that it cannot be altered much by adjustments. This means that although a lightweight Mylar sail will hold its shape in various strengths of moderate wind, the shape cannot be changed for minor improvements in fluctuating wind strengths and on various points of sailing; it can't be optimized with adjustments for every condition. If you get a well-shaped Mylar sail, it will stay well shaped with proper care, but if you get a not-so-good sail, there is little you can do to improve it.

At present, moderately resinated Dacron sails are the best choice for the average dual-purpose boat that competes mostly in club races and occasional long-distance events. Such sails are relatively expensive and durable, allow easy handling and flexibility in adjustments, and don't need pampering. Dacron weight is figured in ounces per yard for the American standard width of 28½ inches, and weights vary between 2 and 12 ounces. A rule of thumb for selecting the proper weight of cloth for the mainsail consists of adding the LOA in feet to the main's luff length in feet and dividing by 10 to obtain the weight in ounces per yard. This gives a rough idea of mainsail weight. It may be slightly heavier or lighter, depending on the expected average strength of sailing wind in areas where the wind is fairly steady or consistent, and also depending on the weave and finish of the cloth. The heavier weight is best in most cases, unless the vast majority of races will be sailed in light airs, because weight gives the sail a little more body to hold its shape, especially when it is exposed to backwind from a large genoa. Furthermore, racing-cruisers usually are restricted to one mainsail, which must be carried over a wide range of wind velocities. A special light- or heavy-weather main may not be used.

Although it is much smaller than the mainsail, the mizzen should be almost as heavy if not the same weight as the mainsail, because it is needed for balancing sails in the heaviest weather. For this reason, the mizzen rigging should be amply strong despite the added windage.

The weight of genoas depends on how many are carried. If there is a choice among three or four genoas, then the largest can be quite light, but if only one genoa is carried, it should be a versatile sail capable of performing well over a wide range of conditions. Such a sail might be about 75 percent of the mainsail's weight or slightly lighter. With the working jib, weight also depends on how many are carried. If there is a small storm jib, this should be the same, or nearly the same, weight as the mainsail, and a large working jib could be perhaps 20 percent lighter than the main. But if only one medium-size working jib is carried, it should be the same weight or only slightly lighter than the main. A storm trysail should be about the same weight as the mainsail, but slightly heavier in a very large boat (over about 50 feet LOA).

Thus far we have only talked about Dacron sail weights. Recommended weights for nylon sails are discussed in the next section.

SAILS NEEDED

The selection of sails depends primarily on two factors: cost and intended use. If a great deal of distance racing will be done offshore, then many sails will be needed, but for club racing round the buoys in protected waters, a large sail inventory is not necessary. It can be an advantage to have a limited number of versatile sails rather than a large variety of sails on short races, because there is less chance of carrying the wrong sail and of wasting time changing to the correct sail when conditions of wind or sea change in the middle of the race, as so often happens. Of course, changing time is greatly decreased with double-grooved luff foils, but boat speed still suffers from the weight of crew on the bow, and it takes time to adjust new sheets and get the boat moving at her best. The most basic sails for light and heavy air are shown in Figure 6-2.

The minimum sail inventory needed to begin racing a small to medium-size sloop is: (1) a large, general-purpose mainsail, (2) a number 1 (largest size), general-purpose genoa jib, (3) a large, nonoverlapping working jib or a number 2 (next smaller size) genoa or a number 3 (still smaller) genoa, and (4) a large, general-purpose parachute spinnaker. Unless you race in a nonspinnaker or working canvas division, which has a restriction on racing sails, you cannot race successfully with fewer sails than those listed, but many sailors start off with this combination and gradually add other sails in following years. Obviously, it is much better if you can afford both a small genoa and a working jib. The latter will be handy for cruising shorthanded and will be needed for racing or cruising in a blow, while the small genoa often will be just the right sail for racing or daysailing with a full crew in moderately heavy weather. The most competitive racing boats also carry light-air, number 1 genoas made of lightweight cloth, in addition to a heavier, all-purpose number 1. If the boat is yawl-rigged, of course, a mizzen and mizzen staysail should be carried, and obviously, if she is doublehead-rigged, she will have a forestaysail.

When only one spinnaker is carried, it should be very versatile, one that can be used effectively on most downwind points of sailing in various wind conditions. For the majority of U.S. sailing areas, such a spinnaker should be a ¾-ounce nylon radial-head 'chute (with radiating seams at the head) or tri-radial 'chute (with radiating seams at all three corners). Some experienced skippers and sailmakers feel that a ¾-ounce spinnaker is so important that when a second 'chute is carried, it should be a duplicate in case of damage to the first. In light-air regions, the most competitive boats carry

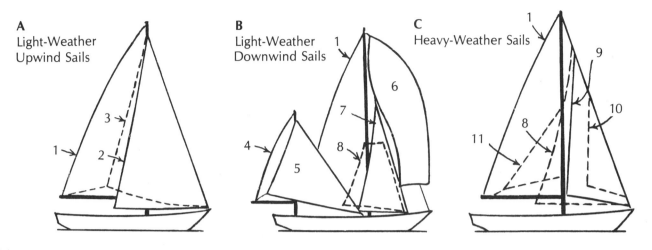

A
Light-Weather
Upwind Sails

B
Light-Weather
Downwind Sails

C
Heavy-Weather Sails

1—mainsail. **2**—no. 1 genoa. **3**—drifter or reacher (sheeted to main boom or deck). **4**—mizzen. **5**—mizzen staysail. **6**—spinnaker. **7**—spinnaker staysail. **8**—no. 2 genoa. **9**— working jib. **10**—storm jib or spitfire. **11**—storm trysail (sheeted to main boom or deck).

Figure 6-2. BASIC SAILS

Two sister boats racing under spinnakers. The boat on the left is carrying a tri-radial, while the other carries a star-cut spinnaker. (Courtesy Murphy and Nye)

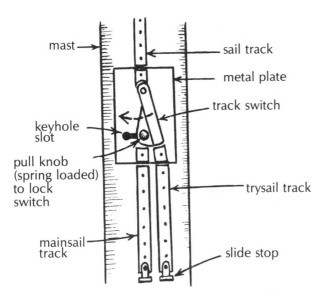

mast

sail track

metal plate

track switch

keyhole slot

pull knob (spring loaded) to lock switch

trysail track

mainsail track

slide stop

Figure 6-3. TRACK SWITCH

½-ounce spinnakers, generally radial heads, which are the lightest possible weight. But in a heavy-air region, such as San Francisco Bay, an all-purpose 'chute for a moderate-size boat might be made from 1.2- or 1.5-ounce nylon. A few years ago, star-cut spinnakers (tri-radials with radial seams extended as far as possible toward the sail's center) were in vogue for close spinnaker reaches. Now these sails are considered marginal for close reaching, but since they are made of heavy nylon (normally 1.5- or 2.5-ounce cloth) and have narrow shoulders, they are good sails for running or broad reaching in strong winds.

For offshore distance racing or any sailing away from sheltered waters, a few more sails are necessary, particularly a storm jib or a small, heavy working jib and a storm trysail. Some storm trysails are rigged with a double full-length track or short track and *switch,* as illustrated in Figure 6-3, so that this sail can be set in the quickest, most convenient way. The trysail may trim to the side deck (to a through-bolted fitting, often the base of a stanchion) or its clew can be secured to the main boom. In the latter case, the trysail can be used as a substitute for a triple-reefed (reefed to a third row of reef points or a very deeply reefed) mainsail. Used in this manner, the trysail becomes more than a mere storm sail; in combination with a small genoa, it can drive the boat to windward effectively when racing in heavy weather. It is wise to give the main boom some support with the topping lift when the trysail is carried in this way. Also, the sail track on the mainmast should be bolted to the mast opposite the head of the trysail.

It is advisable to have a high-cut number 3 genoa or moderately long luff *lapper* (slightly overlapping jib) for racing at sea or in heavy weather. A headsail of this type should be raised a foot (or slightly less) off the deck with a *tack pendant* (a short wire strap) so that seas and/or the bow wave will not break against its foot. Any headsail that is short on the luff (a working jib, small genoa, or storm jib) should be fitted with a *head pendant* that extends the length of the jib halyard so that when the halyard is part wire and part rope, only the wire goes around the winch. The head pendant should make up for the lower position of the head of a smaller jib so that the load of the sail will not be supported by a wire-to-rope splice.

After those already mentioned, the next most important sails are a spinnaker staysail; a reaching jib, or *reacher,* for long-distance racing; and a very lightweight, high-cut jib called a *drifter* for light-weather regions. Another sail considered important by some racing sailors, especially those who have boats with short main booms, is the so-called *blooper.* This is a baggy, jiblike sail with a hollow luff that is carried opposite (to leeward of) the spinnaker. It is normally carried on a short tack pendant, with the halyard well slacked, so that it flies out far to leeward of the spinnaker and is minimally blanketed by the mainsail. Not all sailors think the blooper is worthwhile, and it is prohibited on boats racing under the Measurement Handicap System (see Chapter 7). Nevertheless, it augments the sail area opposite the spinnaker and improves downwind balance on boats with short booms.

The reaching jib is valuable for long reaching courses when the apparent wind is well forward of the beam, because it is high cut and thus inhibits excessive twist. A low-cut genoa carried on the same point of sailing would twist so much that its clew would be backwinding the main, while its head would be luffing. The high clew also enables the reacher to be trimmed to the end of the main boom, which may be an advantage when the boom is fairly long and is quite far off. For the best handicap rating, the boom may need a painted band (normally red), which marks the limit on the boom beyond which no lead for headsail sheets shall be attached. Without a band, the boom length would be measured to the boom end. Consult your rating rule for details.

The drifter also has a high clew, and sometimes it is possible to combine this sail with a reaching jib and have what is called a *drifter-reacher.* I have such a sail made of 2-ounce Dacron, and it is set flying on its own luff wire but has two hanks on the luff to hold the luff straighter when sailing moderately close to the wind. Obviously, it is not a close-winded sail, and it should not be carried to windward when there is any breeze. But in very light conditions, it affords sufficient power for a respectable speed-made-good to windward. This sail has been successful when used as a blooper, racing in the PHRF nonspinnaker division. It is carried opposite a boomed-out genoa and given fairly clean air by slacking its halyard and allowing the sail to flow out to leeward of the mainsail. This is presently legal, and under certain conditions in a fresh breeze, we can keep up with boats flying spinnakers, often with much better steering control.

A true drifter, of course, is a very specialized sail, and it is used where there is only a breath of air. Normally, the sail is made of light nylon, and it is fairly small, with a high clew so that it will be filled out by the lightest zephyr.

Spinnaker staysails, or cheaters, have changed over the years. Originally, they were intended to fill in the space under a lifted spinnaker, and they were low on the hoist. But modern staysails are much taller, because it was later realized that, in reaching conditions when the sail is most effective, a long luff supplies much more drive with minimal interference to the spinnaker. Some of these staysails go almost to the masthead, but slightly shorter luffs may extend their range. They are most efficient between a quarter and a beam reach, while a blooper is best when the wind is farther aft, just abaft the quarter.

A few years ago there was some interest in the light-air, doublehead rig, which consists of a lightweight genoa staysail (an overlapping forestaysail with low foot) and a jib topsail or Yankee jib cut like a drifter (see Figure 6-8). This rig is designed to give maximum headsail area for a given handicap rating. On some boats the rig has proven quite effective when beating in light airs and when close reaching in all but very strong winds, but there are times when it is difficult to trim the two headsails so that they will not interfere with each other. Of course, this rig also requires greater crew effort and coordination, especially when tacking. It may be worthwhile, in the interest of economy and versatility, to investigate the possibility of having a drifter that can double as a light-air jib topsail, and a cheater for beam reaching that can double as a genoa staysail for sailing on the wind. In this case, both the staysail and the jib should be made of the lightest Dacron so that they will hold their shape when beating in light to moderate breezes. The jib topsail normally is cut to trim from the spinnaker lead position near the quarter, while the staysail is cut to trim from a position slightly inboard of the genoa track. Usually, the staysail will have a wire luff to prevent sag, and unless the boat has her

shrouds set will inboard of the rail, the staysail probably will be cut so that its leech is under the lower spreader, with the foot passing through the slot between the upper and lower shrouds. More is said about the size of these sails in the discussion of the LP measurement later in the chapter, and more is said about spinnaker staysails in Chapter 9.

A brief mention should be made of a few sails that seldom are used for racing. These are roller-furling headsails and poleless spinnakers usually called *flashers* or *MP* (multipurpose) sails. Roller-furling headsails are furled by winding them up on their stay, which is turned with a furling line wound around a drum below the tack

The Ulmer Flasher, a poleless spinnaker. The sail is asymmetrical, with the clew higher than the tack. (Courtesy Jack Quinn, Ulmer Sails)

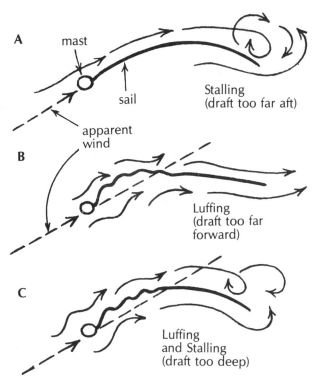

Figure 6-4. LUFFING VERSUS STALLING

of the sail. The system is a handy one, because sail can be set or removed without hoisting and lowering, but it has two major disadvantages for racing: It is hard to prevent excessive luff sag, and the roller drum keeps the tack and foot of the sail high off the deck. Foil-type roller stays help prevent luff sag but the tack still must be high. Partial furling is sometimes practiced to reduce the size of the headsail when sailing in a fresh breeze, but this seldom produces a well-shaped, proper setting sail, and the torsional strains are severe. A jib intended for reduction by standard roller furling should be cut extra flat.

Flashers and similar sails are currently in vogue on cruising boats that seldom race. These sails are asymmetrical spinnakers (with one clew higher than the other) carried without poles. They can provide considerable speed downwind, but they are not as efficient for racing as conventional spinnakers, especially when running. Flashers are usually prohibited in PHRF non-spinnaker racing. When a flasher is carried, its tack is secured at the foot of the jibstay rather than on the end of a pole. This makes its setting and handling easier, while obviating the need for spinnaker gear. Actually, a conventional spinnaker can be used in a similar way (when not racing), except that its clew will be much lower and the sail will be more difficult to trim.

DRAFT AND CUT

Draft, or camber, is the luff-to-leech curvature that gives a sail an efficient airfoil shape. This curvature should correctly bend or change the direction of a maximum amount of air flowing around the sail. On most points of sailing, the flow moves from forward to aft, and it moves faster on the leeward than on the windward side of the sail. Thus, in accordance with Bernoulli's principle, the pressure to leeward is lower, and it exerts a leeward pull acting approximately at right angles to the sail's surface. The efficiency of a sail depends to a very large extent on the amount and character of its draft.

If the draft is such that it bends the wind too abruptly, the flow to leeward will separate and break away, and the sail will *stall,* as shown in Figure 6-4. On the other hand, if the wind is bent only slightly, stalling is avoided, but the sail may lack maximum effectiveness as an airfoil. A deep draft that fails to bend the wind at a close *angle of incidence* (angle of trim or inclination to the wind) will often make the sail luff, as illustrated in Figure 6-4. Both luffing and stalling are caused by the depth and location of draft and the wind's angle of incidence, often called *angle of attack,* as in airplane terminology. Excessive draft near the luff will encourage luffing, but excessive draft near the leech will encourage stalling. A very deep draft near the sail's middle may cause luffing at the luff and stalling at the leech simultaneously. See Figure 6-4(C).

In Chapter 2, we discussed the keel's action as a hydrofoil and mentioned that the yaw angle created lift and drag forces (refer to Figures 2-19 and 2-27). Essentially, the same forces act on the sails but on the opposite side of the boat. These are illustrated in Figure 6-5. When sailing upwind or somewhere higher than a broad reach, the principal force giving drive to the sail is lift, while before the wind, the primary forward drive is caused by drag. In other words, when running we want a sail shape that will give maximum drag, but for sailing higher, and especially to windward, we want a high-lift sail. In the foretriangle we can change sails for optimum shape on various points of sailing, but the mainsail must be an extremely versatile sail able to perform reasonably well both to windward and downwind.

Such a mainsail might have draft curves approximating those in Figure 6-6. These curves are shown at approximately one-third of the luff measurement up from the boom and at another position about two-thirds up. The maximum draft may be slightly less than 10 percent of the chord length at the top position illustrated, but slightly greater at the lower position, and it will lie

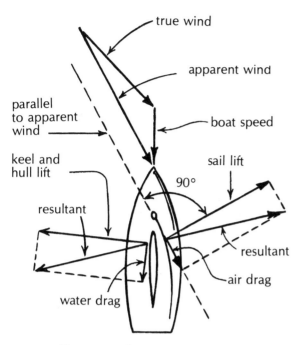

Figure 6-5. SAIL LIFT AND DRAG

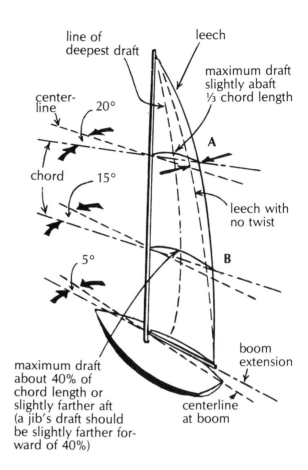

maximum draft
about 40% of
chord length or
slightly farther aft
(a jib's draft should
be slightly farther for-
ward of 40%)

between one-third and one-half the chord length abaft the luff. On the mainsails of many modern racing-cruisers, the deepest draft is closer to half the chord length. Notice that the chords are angled progressively farther away from the boat's centerline, the higher they are located. This is caused by sail twist, or the falling off of the leech. A certain amount of this is important to allow for the fairing of the apparent wind at greater heights above the water. There are conflicting opinions concerning the optimum angle of twist. C.A. Marchaj has written that the twist allowance should be only about seven degrees (this would be added to the boom's angle), but the sailmaker-sailor Lowell North has suggested a greater leech curve of about 6 percent of the leech length (the distance between the arrows shown at A, top chord, Figure 6-6) when close-hauled. This would give a slightly wider angle than the one illustrated for a sail of medium aspect ratio.

Optimum sail twist and draft actually depend on a number of factors. If the boat is large and fast, her sails should not have a great deal of draft. If the average winds are strong but the waters are fairly protected in the sailing locale, draft should be moderate. But for rough seas or light airs, draft should be considerable. For distance racing, or when it is expected that down-wind sailing will predominate, the sails should have ample draft located nearly midway between luff and leech. To emphasize upwind ability, the mainsail should

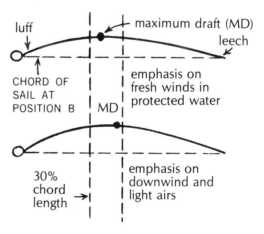

Figure 6-6. DRAFT AND TWIST

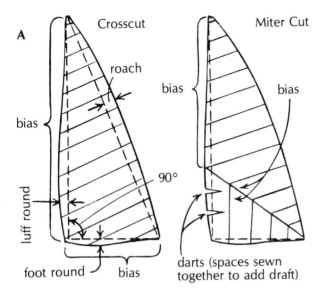

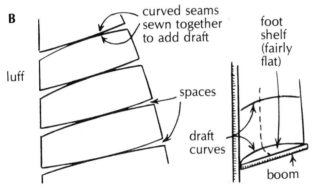

Figure 6-7. COMMON SAIL CUTS

boat backward instead of ahead when the sail is trimmed in for beating. In addition, this draft near the after part of the sail causes extra heeling. The so-called Frisbee shape formerly advocated by North Sails conjures up images of a hooked leech, but the draft curve of such a sail is by no means exactly like a Frisbee. The curve is merely fattened in its middle in an attempt to improve airflow and move the draft away from mast turbulence. The area just forward of the leech is curved more than that of a normal sail, but the leech is not hooked. Apparently the Frisbee shape did not prove very successful, since it is no longer being promoted.

Draft is built into a sail by using one or a combination of two methods: by cutting *rounds* (slight roaches) at the luff and foot, or by tapering and/or slightly overlapping the seams, commonly called *broadseaming*. Both these methods are illustrated in Figure 6-7. With the round method (6-7(A)), the draft forms in the sail abaft the luff when this rounded edge is set on a straight mast, while draft forms above the foot when it is bent to a straight boom. The roach at the leech has nothing to do with adding draft. It simply adds area, which has been unpenalized in most measurement rules. Under the latest form of the IOR, however, reduced mainsail roach will lower a boat's handicap rating.

With the tapered construction (Figure 6-7(B)), the individual *cloths* (cloth panels) are cut wider in their middles than at their ends. When the spaces, shown in the illustration, are sewn together, more material, and therefore draft, is put into the sail's middle. Often the width of the seams also is varied to help shape the draft. For sails carried upwind, the very stable Dacron sailcloth is suitable for the tapered construction. A slightly softer, springy cloth is often used for the round construction, because this lends itself to draft adjustment through altering edge tension.

The principal methods of arranging the cloths are shown in Figure 6-7. The crosscut sail is the most common arrangement for large mainsails, but the miter cut is occasionally seen. With both cuts, bias elongation at the leech is minimized. This is highly desirable, since leech control is vital to sail efficiency. It is an area under great strain, especially when the sail is strapped in when beating. Notice that on the crosscut sail, the luff and foot seams are at angles of less than 90 degrees, which allows some bias stretch along the mast and boom. This permits some draft alteration through the adjustment of the sail's outhaul and downhaul or halyard. With the miter cut, however, the foot and luff below the miter seam are not subject to bias stretch. This may be beneficial in some ways, but it does not allow effective, evenly distributed draft alteration through alteration of

be cut fairly flat when carried behind a large genoa. Twist should be greater at the top of the main on a seven-eighths-rigged boat than on one with a masthead rig. One theory holds that twist is helpful when beating in rough water, and, of course, a lot of twist increases the boat's stability by slacking the leech and creating greater chord angles aloft. Tender boats in fresh breezes might need sails with moderate draft located low and forward. Then, too, the stability of the cloth and the cut of the sail have a very important effect on adjusting the draft for changing conditions. Some variations of draft curves (used on sails made of soft cloth) illustrating these points can be seen in Figure 6-6. The curves are slightly parabolic, flattening near the leech, even when the maximum draft is near the sail's middle. This is necessary because too much curvature in the area just forward of the leech will cause lee-side suction, acting nearly at right angles to the sail's surface, to pull the edge tension. Recently, North and Haarstick sailmakers have rediscovered the vertical cut, which arranges the cloths so that they run parallel to the leech. Formerly, these sails had to be cut very flat, but with advanced computer technology it is claimed that adequate draft can be built more easily into modern sails with vertical seams. The main advantages of such a cut are resistance to horizontal splitting in strong winds and great strength and less stretch along the leech by using heavier cloth in that area, which is subject to tremendous strain. Other sailmakers are improving the leech strength by using more conventional cuts (mainly crosscut panels) but with two- or three-ply construction at the leech. When the leech and other high-stress areas are heavily reinforced, the rest of the sail can be lighter in weight without any harmful loss in overall strength. A minor disadvantage of vertical seams is that they cause more drag than crosscut seams, being aligned against, rather than with, the airflow. Lightweight, vertical-cut sails should be made from fabrics that are fairly heavily resinated.

For maximum area, all mainsails and mizzens should have a tack angle, the angle between the chord of the luff and foot, of exactly 90 degrees, as shown in Figure 6-7. Some sailors insist on a tack angle greater than 90 degrees (giving a droopy boom appearance) in the belief that the obtuse tack angle gives the greatest untaxed area, but this notion is erroneous, as can be proved by simple geometry.

Genoa jibs are usually miter cut, although a few are either crosscut or "spiderweb-cut" (with two or more miter seams), and others have quite unorthodox arrangements of paneling at the foot. Most sailmakers use a very sophisticated, scientific approach, even utilizing computers for sail designs, and this sometimes results in unusual cuts. The computer approach is not just an advertising gimmick; it can be very effective. However, results are only as good as the information fed into the computer, and much of this information is based on assumptions and estimates. The computer does the complicated arithmetic based on the sailmaker's even more complicated judgment. One prominent sailmaker recommends that a jib's maximum draft be located 40 to 45 percent of its chord length abaft its luff for effective windward work. Maximum draft is generally slightly closer to the luff on a jib than on a mainsail. The exact location and amount of draft, however, will depend on the sailcloth and other factors. If a very stable cloth is used, maximum draft can be located slightly farther aft, compared with the draft location on a sail made of less stable cloth. A sail made of stable cloth can also have a little deeper draft than one having greater stretch. Draft

will also depend on whether the jib is intended for light or heavy weather. Number 2 and number 3 genoas are usually cut a little flatter than number 1 genoas. Headsail draft should be designed with consideration for the mainsail. Too much draft, draft located too far aft, or a tight leech on a genoa can hurt the efficiency of the slot between the jib and the main, causing the latter to be backwinded.

Most authorities agree that a genoa should have some *reverse roach* (concave "round" on the leech). Speaking from experience, I noticed great improvement in the performance of a genoa that suffered from a badly curling leech after it was given a greater reverse roach. The loss of area from recutting resulted in little reduction of speed when reaching. The leech area, so often a problem on genoas, was greatly improved to increase speed on the wind.

The area of a genoa is controlled by the LP measurement shown in Figure 6-8. This is a perpendicular from the luff to the clew and is the altitude in the formula used to obtain the area of a triangle: area = ½ base x altitude), the base being the luff dimension. Most big-boat handicap rules charge a small graduated penalty for an overlap greater than 150 or 155 percent of the foretriangle base (see Figure 6-8). Most racing genoas vary between 150 and 180 percent, as shown in the illustration. Any jib greater than 180 percent seldom pays, because there is too much penalty for what little benefit (if any) is gained by the extra overlap. In Figure 6-8, the same LP dimension will allow a variety of jib shapes. They may be low to the deck, as with jib A, or have the foot off the deck and have more overlap, as with jib B. The latter jib has an advantage in that it may have additional unpenalized area by having a comparatively large foot roach (shown by the dotted line). However, there is a practical limit to this foot-roach concept, because the sail cannot be trimmed and set efficiently if the curve is too great. If the sail is cut high enough, a small staysail might be set beneath it to add area. This is the principle of the light-air, doublehead rig discussed earlier. The rig can create an area more than 30 percent larger than a 180 percent genoa, but without penalty for exceeding 150 percent overlap However, two headsails may not always operate with the same efficiency as a single jib, and, as mentioned, there are certain handling difficulties with the doublehead rig.

The low jib, A, does not have as much overlap, but it is close to the deck, which is an advantage in that it helps prevent the escape of air from the sail's high- to its low-pressure side. Some jibs, called *decksweepers,* are so low that they touch the deck, but such a sail has a

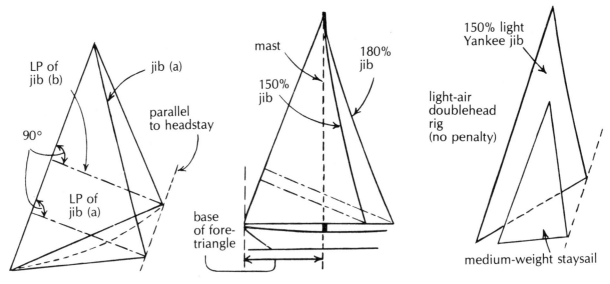

Figure 6-8. JIB AREA

practical disadvantage in that it completely blocks the helmsman's view when he is looking forward to leeward, and the sail is more apt to scoop up the bow wave when reaching. Most decksweepers on modern, broad-beamed boats are trimmed to deck tracks inside the lifelines when beating, but they can cause some difficulties when trimmed to the rail. More is said about this at the end of the chapter.

Some mainsails are made with a so-called *foot shelf,* which is a flat area (nearly horizontal) in the sail just above the boom (see Figure 6-7). This allows a proper, sufficiently deep-draft curve to be located at the foot of the sail. It may also have the effect of helping to prevent the downdraft under the boom. In this case, the foot shelf may act as an end plate, or "fence," similar to that on the keel shown in Figure 2-22.

Determining the proper size for the number 1 genoa, between 150 and 180 percent, can be a difficult decision. This depends on several factors: the size of the fore-triangle base, the average wind velocity in the sailing locale, the character of the race courses (the amount and length of windward and reaching legs), and the ease with which the hull can be driven. But perhaps the most important and easily estimated factors are the shape of the mainsail and the shape of the hull above the waterline. Results of a wind-tunnel test at Southampton University in England (according to C.A. Marchaj) indicated that the headsail leech should come abaft the point of maximum draft on the main for greatest advantage. Thus, the location of the mainsail's draft would have an important bearing on the genoa's overlap.

A commonsense rule for the overlap of genoas that

trim to the rail has been given by Wallace C. Ross, former president of Hard Sails. Under this rule, overlap is determined by the beam, the half-breadth shape of the hull, and the shroud location. Since the genoa passes outboard of the shrouds and in this case trims to the rail, Ross suggests that the lead position be located no farther aft than a point where the rail is intersected by a line drawn from the outboard shroud parallel with the boat's centerline. This is illustrated in Figure 6-9. Of course, the genoa's clew would be some distance forward of the lead position, depending on the height of the clew, but most low-cut genoas would have their clews only slightly forward of the lead block when beating. The illustration shows two correct-size genoas and two incorrect, oversize jibs. In the correct examples, the suction force to leeward of the sail does not pull in a backward direction, but in case C the force near the leech pulls backward. This is due not only to the tremendous overlap, but also to the fact that boat C has such a narrow stern. Boat B, on the other hand, has a wide stern, so she may carry a fairly large overlap without developing negative forces at the leech. Boat D has her shrouds set inboard with the chainplates mounted on a transverse bulkhead or on the cabin sides. This allows the jib to be trimmed in so that the leeward force components are forward; but the jib is trimmed so flat that it closes the slot, blocks the flow between the sails, and severely backwinds the main. This overlap might be tolerated and even prove advantageous, however, if the main were trimmed in much closer with the main boom on the boat's centerline.

A similar principle is involved when the genoa is

trimmed to a deck track inboard of the rail. If the leech hooks too much to windward of a line drawn through the outboard shroud parallel to the centerline, the after end of the genoa may cause too much drag when close-hauled. I saw this principle demonstrated many years ago when a cutter with a narrow stern carried a genoa with more than 200 percent overlap. It made the boat fly on a reach, but when the sail was trimmed in for a beat in any breeze fresher than a light air, the boat slowed dramatically, and the handicap penalty paid for the sail was not worth its light-air reaching benefits.

DRAFT CONTROL

Since the mainsail, especially, must be a very versatile sail, good upwind and downwind in a variety of weather conditions, there should be some means of controlling or adjusting draft. The usual means of draft control for racing boats are: spar bending, edge tensioning, and zippering or foot lacing. Although mast bowing was discussed in the last chapter, there was no mention of boom bending.

There are a number of difficulties in flexing the boom on a racing-cruiser. In the first place, the boom would have to be bent a great deal for this to have any significant effect on flattening the sail; second, if the boom were limber, the boom vang would tend to bend it when reaching, just when a straight boom and maximum draft in the sail are needed. Furthermore, using a limber boom causes difficulties in controlling unwanted sideways bend and could allow an upward bow when the sheet is secured to the boom's end.

Edge tensioning is an ancient but effective means of changing draft that is not always exploited fully by racing-cruiser skippers. Almost any sailcloth except the most ultra-stable will respond to edge tensioning, although sails that are not highly resinated and those with luff and foot rounds respond best. Also, these sails should be crosscut or otherwise have their panels oriented on the bias at the luff and foot (when it is attached to a boom). For best results, these adjustable edges should be sewn to cloth tapes or *boltropes* while under uneven tension (with less tension near the tack). To prevent overstretching the tapes, a loose floating luff wire may be sewn into a luff sleeve, as illustrated in Figure 6-10. This limits the extent of stretch. With boltropes, prestretched Dacron rope is often used to prevent overtightening of the luff. It is a good idea to put a scale on the mast with which a mark on the halyard can be aligned to determine the right adjustment for a given wind condition or point of sailing.

When beating in a breeze, a sail should be flattened

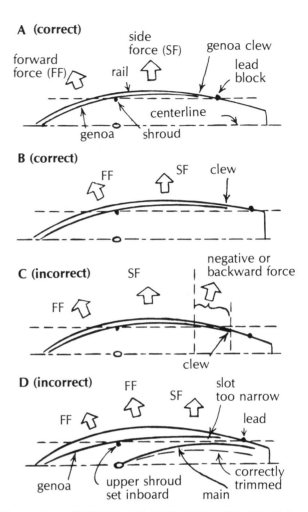

Figure 6-9. OVERLAP OF RAIL-TRIMMED GENOA

and have its draft pulled forward by tightening its luff, and if the sail has a boom, its lower part can be flattened to some extent by tensioning the foot. When running and reaching or beating in light airs or rough water, the luff and foot should be slacked for generous draft. In drifting conditions, however, it may pay to flatten the sails to achieve maximum projected area and to help prevent the sails from slatting in motorboat swells. It is especially important to stretch out the luff on a fresh-wind beat to keep the draft from moving aft and thus cause more heeling than forward thrust.

Edge stretching is usually accomplished by tensioning halyards, downhauls, or outhauls, but racing boats normally have their luff lengths (and foot lengths when boomed) limited by *measurement bands*. These are one-inch-wide painted bands (normally black unless the boat has black spars) circling the spars at the corners of the sail. They mark the limit of sail extension for the sake of optimizing the boat's handicap measurement rating.

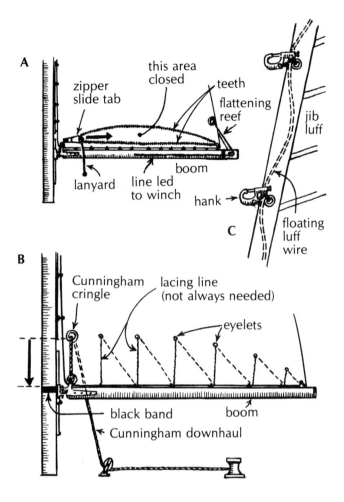

Figure 6-10. DRAFT CONTROL

and the black band so there is room to stretch the foot. The flattening reefing line is led through a cheek block quite far aft so that the cringle is pulled aft as well as down to tighten the foot. From the cheek block, the line runs forward to a winch on the boom, or sometimes the reefing line may be led through the boom and down to a winch on the mast, or through fairleads to a winch on the cabin trunk. Of course, the flattening reef also reduces the area of the sail slightly while folding up any deep draft just above the boom, and all of this will be helpful for sailing in a breeze.

Miter-cut and/or foot-shelf-type mainsails that don't respond well to alteration through edge tensioning sometimes are fitted with a foot zipper or foot lacing, often called a roach reef. Figure 6-10(A) shows a sail zipper in the open, full-draft position. When the zipper is pulled aft, the area between the teeth is closed, and a certain amount of draft is reduced. The same end is achieved with the lacing shown in Figure 6-10(B). Notice that the eyelets through which the lacing runs form an arc from the Cunningham cringle to the clew, so the greatest area above the middle of the boom is reduced the most, thereby flattening the draft curve. Nowadays the flattening reef is more often used than zippers or roach reefs, because it is simpler and quicker.

BASIC SAIL TRIM

The successful racing sailor must develop an instinct for sail trim. The approach to proper trim may be intuitive, but it should be based on, or developed from, an understanding of the basic aerodynamic principles involved. This does not mean that a sailor should try to trim his sails at precise angles derived from scientific theory. The approach should be primarily empirical and experimental, based on trial and error. However, a knowledge of the wind forces and sail reactions should be helpful in establishing basic trim positions from which deviations and fine adjustments can be made.

Figure 6-11 illustrates the basic wind, course, and trim angles when beating to windward in a medium-size racing-cruiser in moderate conditions of wind and sea. These angles are based on the performance of a club racer of conservative design with average windward ability. Many of the modern IOR racers with extremely short keels can sail much closer to the wind, but in doing so they often will make much more leeway. Obviously, a boat's forward speed brings the apparent wind considerably forward of the true wind; and, of course, the apparent wind direction is shown by the *telltales* (ribbons or threads on the shrouds) or the masthead in-

When a sail has been stretched to the banded limit and it needs further stretching for best shape, then a *Cunningham downhaul* or *flattening reef* is rigged, as shown in Figure 6-10. The Cunningham supposedly was named after a contemporary yachtsman, although a Cunningham reefing system was used long ago on square-riggers. As the illustration shows, the modern version requires a cringle a short distance above the tack. A line rove through the cringle is tightened with a winch (or tackle), and this rig enables the luff to be tightened without letting the sail go past the black band. The same principle applies to the flattening reef. A cringle in the leech, perhaps a foot or so above the boom, accepts a line that hauls the cringle down to the boom and thus creates some space between the leech

dicator. The latter, however, might show the wind to be a little more fair (farther aft) because the wind velocity usually is slightly greater at the higher altitude. The apparent wind angle, shown at 30 degrees, is the angle between the boat's heading and the apparent wind. The angle of attack is the angle between a forward extension of the sail's bottom chord (or the boom) and the apparent wind. The boom angle (in this case, 5 degrees) subtracted from the apparent wind angle gives the angle of attack. The angle between the boat's heading close-hauled on the starboard tack and her close-hauled heading on the port tack will be about 86½ degrees, but, due to an assumed 3½-degree angle of leeway or yaw, the angle between the actual courses on the two tacks is about 93½ degrees. Although the main boom is trimmed in to within 5 degrees of the boat's centerline, the genoa's chord is at approximately 12 degrees. As a general rule, when one sail lies behind another, the after sail must be trimmed flatter, especially when there is an overlap. Some modern boats with deck genoa tracks allowing close headsail trim carry their main booms on the boat's centerline to minimize genoa backwind. The airfoil shape of the genoa deflects the wind so that its luff is sailing in a lift (favorable change of wind direction), while the deflection causes the mainsail to sail in a header (unfavorable change of direction).

Figure 6-12 illustrates the basic boom positions for the various points of sailing, considering the mainsail without jib interaction. Exact boom positions will vary with the boat size, wind and sea conditions, sail draft, aspect ratio, and especially with the addition of a headsail. The close-hauled point of sailing shows the main to be trimmed correctly for when a genoa is carried. But with the successive points of sailing, the farther away the boom is from the centerline, the more the jib will turn the airflow against the mainsail's lee side, until the jib is blanketed by the mainsail when the wind is quite far aft. The lift-drag forces illustrated are rough estimates that will vary, of course, with different hull forms and sailplans. Lift acts at right angles to the apparent wind, while drag acts in the same direction as the apparent wind. The optimum angle of attack, in most cases, might lie between 25 and 30 degrees, closer to 25 degrees when close-hauled, but closer to 30 degrees when the wind draws aft. The lift force is utilized principally until the wind is slightly forward of the quarter. When broad reaching or sailing somewhat farther off the wind, some sailors trim the main so that it is almost square to the wind, but this is usually not correct. The sail should be eased considerably more to utilize optimum lift-drag and to align better the direction of the sail's pull with the boat's heading.

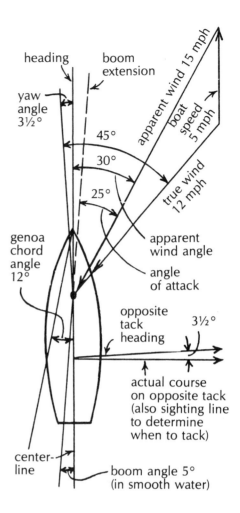

Figure 6-11. WINDWARD TRIM, COURSE AND WIND ANGLES

When the boat bears off beyond the near quarter reaching point of sailing (Figure 6-12(E)), interesting things begin to happen. This point of sailing was discussed in a fascinating article by Eugene M. Reardon in *One Design and Offshore Yachtsman* magazine (March 1967). When the apparent wind is approximately 127 degrees off the bow, there are theoretically two optimum boom angles — one with the boom far off (position number 1 in the diagram), which continues to utilize lift principally at about a 30-degree angle of attack, and the other boom angle much narrower (position number 2), which utilizes the drag force at an angle of attack of about 60 degrees. These positions are based on a lift-drag polar diagram (curve) similar to the one shown in Figure 6-13. The curve is made up of points at the end of an infinite number of lift-drag vector resultants, as illustrated. The dashed lines show examples of lift and drag forces, with their resultants shown as arrows. Numbers indicate angles of attack.

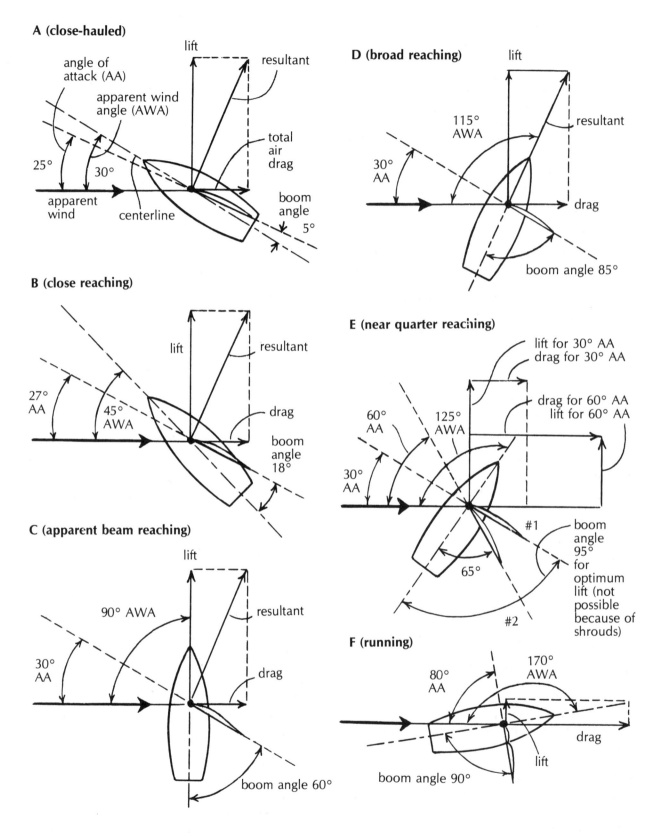

Figure 6-12. BASIC BOOM POSITIONS

The curve illustrated is for a modern, light-displacement boat with one marconi sail, but it shows the character of most sail polars in that lift increases to its optimum point (around 27 degrees in Figure 6-13), then drops sharply when stalling occurs, and then rounds out (although there may be an additional slight hump in the curve) as lift decreases more slowly and the drag increases rapidly. The hollow part of the curve, shown extra-heavy in the diagram, should be avoided, because at these angles of attack (between 30 and 53 degrees for this polar), we are not getting properly directed optimum lift or drag.

As Reardon points out, this study does not allow for the considerable effects of a jib or spinnaker. In applying this information to a racing-cruiser, we would have to eliminate optimum position number 1 (Figure 6-12(E)) because of the interference of shrouds with the boom. This would mean that on this point of sailing, we should shift from using optimum lift to optimum drag, and this could even mean that, as we bear off (at the time of shifting), we *might* slightly *trim in* the main rather than slack it off, as is customary.

To generalize and perhaps oversimplify, we might suggest keeping the main well eased out to the verge of luffing until it is interfered with by the shrouds or especially by headsail backwind. Then, if we need to bear off more, we might trim in slightly (or slack off no more) when shifting to utilize drag. After this point of trim, we slack the mainsheet progressively, the farther we bear away, until the boom touches the shrouds. Some of the new boats, such as the cat ketches mentioned earlier, which do not have shrouds, may have an advantage in being able to carry the boom out so that it is forward of the beam when running. By doing this, they can almost continually utilize lift from their sails rather than drag.

When carrying the spinnaker, we will probably have to shift from using optimum lift to optimum drag much sooner. If the spinnaker is carried on or just below a beam reach, the main must be trimmed in closer than indicated in Figure 6-12(C) to prevent excessive backwind, but the main should be out as far as possible to make the most of lift, because this acts in nearly the same direction as. the boat's heading. At broader angles to the wind, it can help to use optimum drag forces in order to open up the slot between the main and the spinnaker to avoid backwind. An example is shown in Figure 6-14, where the boat is headed 105 degrees from the apparent wind. Obviously, if the boom were slacked off to about 75 degrees, the main would give the greatest forward drive by utilizing optimum lift, but at the same time, the boom might be too close to the clew of the spinnaker. If

(For Above-Water Portion of a Una-Rigged, Light-Displacement Boat)

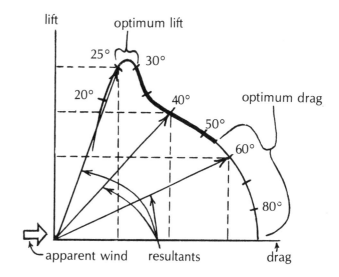

Figure 6-13. CHARACTER OF A LIFT-DRAG POLAR

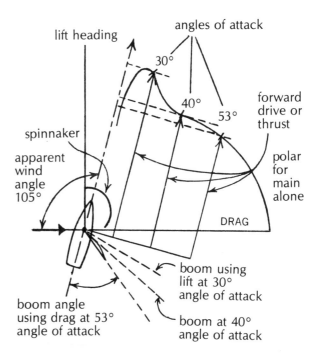

Figure 6-14. SPINNAKER INFLUENCE ON MAINSAIL TRIM

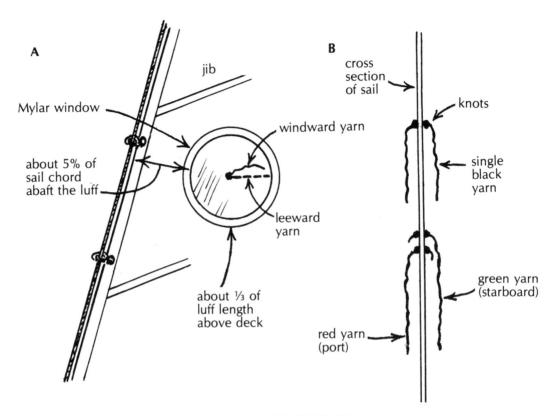

Figure 6-15. LUFF TELLTALES

the angle of attack were increased to 40 degrees, there would be considerable loss of forward drive component, and the slot would not be opened a great deal. However, if the angle of attack is increased to 53 degrees, there is little additional loss in the forward component, and the slot is opened up considerably. Of course, we cannot be sure of the polar's exact shape when the spinnaker is set, but the example illustrates that we probably shift from lift to drag much sooner when the spinnaker is set. Also, the main boom angle may be little if any greater on this point of sailing than when beam reaching. If a racing-cruiser's main, at optimum trim, is badly backed by the spinnaker, a good reaching jib might be more effective than the spinnaker when beam reaching. Spinnaker trim is discussed in Chapter 9.

Considering the points of sailing above a beam reach, when the genoa is carried instead of a spinnaker, we might say that the old rule of keeping the sails eased out until they are on the verge of luffing holds true. If we decrease the angle of attack by slacking sheets, this causes luffing, and if we increase the angle of attack by overtrimming, the sails tend to stall. A great aid in ensuring that the jib will not be stalled from overtrimming is the luff telltale, a piece of dark yarn or ribbon fas-

tened to the jib's luff about 10 inches or so abaft the jibstay. Usually a yarn is threaded through the sail and knotted as shown in Figure 6-15, but a ribbon might have to be sewn or taped on. Telltales on the windward side of the sail show when the sail is luffing by fluttering violently, but telltales on the leeward side indicate stalling when they twirl. Let the sail out or head the boat closer to the wind until the twirling stops. Theoretically, the trim is perfect when the telltales on both sides fly straight aft and move very little, but it may pay to allow the windward telltale to lift or wave slightly when beating to windward.

Sails normally are translucent enough so that leeward telltales can be seen through the cloth, but sometimes they can't be seen when bright sun shines on the windward side of the luff. To solve this problem, sailmakers put small plastic windows in the luff. The best ones are round windows with short yarns in the center, as shown in Figure 6-15(A). This design prevents the yarns from sticking to the stitching when they twirl. If one window is used, it should be located near the middle of the luff, but low enough to allow the helmsman good visibility. Telltales near the top and bottom of the sail indicate twist; this is discussed later.

Mainsail stalling is delayed by the Venturi effect of any overlapping jib, but a genoa, especially, will often throw backward against the main and cause premature luffing. There are some indications that, at times, more of this backwind can be tolerated than realized, particularly when the main is heavy and stable, with some "body." The principal consideration is to keep the proper-width slot between the main and the jib. If the slot is too wide, it will lose its Venturi effect of speeding up the flow to leeward of the main. But if the slot is too narrow, the flow will be constricted and blocked. The slot should be wider in fresh winds than in moderate weather. The jib should be kept on the verge of luffing, and the helmsman should use the jib luff rather than the partially backwinded mainsail luff as a guide to optimum pointing.

An occasionally maladjusted slot is the one between the mizzen and the mizzen staysail. Some sailors trim these sails so that the slot is too constricted. If the mizzen is badly backwinded, the staysail sheet should be eased, but if this results in undue luffing, the mizzen or staysail should be lowered. In general, all light downwind sails should be eased off and allowed to flow and lift as much as possible. More is said of this later in the discussion of spinnakers.

Optimum sail trim must change constantly with every wind shift or change in boat speed or wind velocity. Thus, sheets should be adjusted, or "played," continually. Sheet playing will be less frequent if the helmsman changes course for wind changes, but the sheets will require more tending when the helmsman holds a comparatively steady course. During lulls, the sheets should be eased, but in puffs they should be trimmed back in. When the boat picks up speed, such as after tacking, sheets should be eased out. To reiterate, theory merely gives us a point of departure for proper trim. The real test is how the boat performs when sailing alongside of her competition. A fine instinct for sail trim develops from an awareness of the problems involved, astute observation, experience, and a penchant for experimentation.

VANGS AND TRAVELERS

Boom vangs and travelers control sail twist and to some extent the draft curvature. When a sail is twisted, its head has a broader angle to the boat's centerline than its foot (see Figure 6-6). Sail twist becomes progressively larger as the boom is slacked off, until the sail begins to lie against the spreaders and shrouds. Twist results when the sheet pulls the sail mostly inward, toward the boat's

centerline, rather than downward. This allows the boom to ride up and twist the sail. A boom vang supplies downward pull when reaching and running, while a traveler performs the same function when beating. As said in Chapter 4, a vang led to the leeward side deck when beating has somewhat the same effect as a traveler, but the latter is much more convenient because a side deck vang needs adjustment at every change in sheet trim.

On small boats, boom vangs usually can be secured at the boat's centerline near the base of the mast. Of course this eliminates the need for adjustment when the sheet's trim is changed. On racing-cruisers, however, this on-center vang sometimes cannot be used (unless the main boom is quite high) because of interference with the cabinhouse or too little space between the gooseneck and the cabintop or deck. Thus an off-center vang, sometimes called a *go-fast,* often must be rigged to the side deck. These are illustrated in Figure 6-16. The on-center vang tends to thrust the boom forward against the mast when the sail is trimmed in, but when the sail is slacked off for reaching or running, the thrust is lateral against the gooseneck track. On these off-the-wind points of sailing, there is a tremendous sideways strain at the gooseneck, so if an on-center vang is used, the gooseneck should be extra-strong and its slide track should be bolted to the mast. Some of the larger new boats are fitted with hydraulic vangs, and these have a lot of power. It is good to keep in mind the lateral thrust we have been discussing, so that the vang will be operated with restraint.

The off-center vang (A in the diagram) pulls directly downward on the boom, but with this arrangement the vang must be relocated and readjusted as the boom is pulled in or slacked off. Usually three or four location points on the side deck are necessary, with the points being either directly under the vang's point of attachment to the boom or somewhat farther forward. When the vang is rigged in this manner, there is no need to rig a preventer to guard against an accidental jibe, *unless* the boat is rolling or heeling and apt to dip the end of her boom in a sea. In such a case, there is a possibility of breaking the boom, so a preventer, running from the outer end of the boom to the foredeck (as illustrated), should be rigged. Some offshore racers have *antitripping reef points* (also illustrated) to raise up the end of the boom and help prevent such an accident. Even use of the flattening reef can help raise the end of the boom slightly. Some boats carry their off-center vangs attached to a slide on the genoa track, but this should not be done unless the track is bolted or fastened very securely, because the vang exerts a tremendous upward

An off-center vang, rigged to the side deck, requires adjustments as the boom is pulled in or slacked off. The blooper visible under the boom is the author's "secret weapon" in nonspinnaker PHRF races. (Rip Henderson photo)

and sometimes slightly lateral pull. Some lifeline stanchions have strong securing straps at their base (see Figure 3-2), and these are convenient for the vang's attachment when the stanchions are through-bolted to the deck, as they should be.

Mainsheet travelers were described and illustrated in Chapter 4 (Figure 4-12). The mainsheet lead should be kept on the boat's centerline or perhaps even slightly to weather of the centerline in light airs. But the lead, which slides on the traveler track, should be eased to leeward slightly as the wind increases. The traveler acts like the vang in removing excess twist and somewhat flattening the draft. Both the vang and the traveler also tighten the leech. It should not be overtightened when beating; however, tightening the leech is nearly always beneficial in downwind sailing, especially when the luff is well slacked to increase and move aft the sail's draft. Very wide travelers should be slightly curved to follow the arc of the boom so that the traveler can be adjusted for wind changes without adjusting the mainsheet when sailing close-hauled (see Figure 6-16).

Sometimes there is a slight problem in attaching the

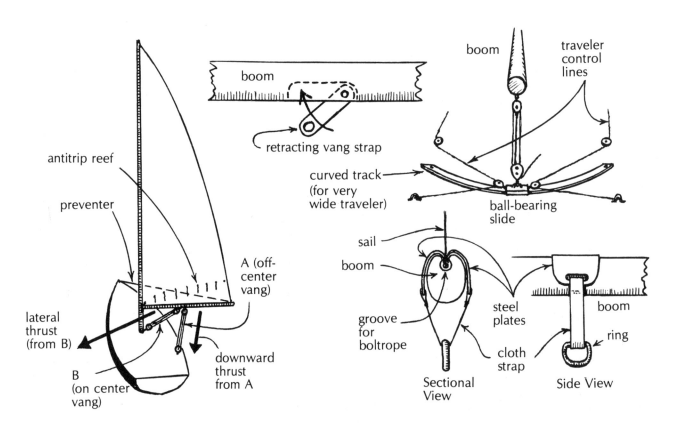

Figure 6-16. VANG AND TRAVELER

vang to a roller-reefing boom. If the sail's foot is attached to the boom with slides on a track, a strap can be inserted between the sail and the boom, but if the foot is attached to the boom by a boltrope fitting into a boom groove, the problem becomes more difficult. Some boats have a swaged ball on the vang that fits into a keyhole slot on the underside of an aluminum boom, but this is usually not strong enough when used on a large, offshore racer. Alternatives are a vang with a claw ring (see Figure 4-12) or a slit cut in the sail's foot just above the boom for a strap, when the vang is of the off-center type. When the vang is rigged on center, a pivoting strap that retracts into a boom slot is sometimes used (Figure 6-16). Obviously, the metal strap is retracted when the boom is turned while roller-reefing. A simple alternative for a wooden boom is a small hole drilled through the boom near its top. A copper tube can be driven through the hole to prevent water from leaking into the boom. Then a removable nylon rope for securing the vang is passed through the tube. Another innovation is the use of two curved steel plates that fit into a grooved boom, as shown in Figure 6-16.

Most top racing sailors realize the importance of proper vang and traveler adjustments, but in some cases there is a tendency for former skippers of small boats with bendy rigs to overdo these adjustments when sailing racing-cruisers with nonflexible rigs, because pulling the boom down can overtighten the leech when the top of the mast will not bend aft. In light airs when sailing close-hauled, the vang should be used sparingly. Also, vang tension should be moderate when the boom is heavy except in a fresh breeze. With a large, overlapping headsail, the vang should not be so tight nor the traveler setting so wide that the bottom of the jib slot is closed or seriously constricted. The larger the mainsail in relation to the jib area, the greater the importance of proper vang adjustment. Vang tension becomes increasingly important as the wind increases and swings aft. When quarter reaching and running, the vang tension can help prevent yawing and rolling, because without the vang, the sail's head twists so far forward that its pulling force can work to windward of the boat's centerline, even though the foot pulls to leeward (see Figure 6-17).

TRIM AND TWIST TOGETHER

Trim and twist have been discussed separately, but here I'd like to say more about how they work together and a little more about how they affect the slot between the jib and the main. Properly shaping the slot with adjustments that control twist and trim is probably most dif-

A cabintop mainsheet traveler just forward of the companionway. This type usually needs the sheet boom blocks spread apart fore and aft to prevent the boom from bending. (Sally Henderson photo)

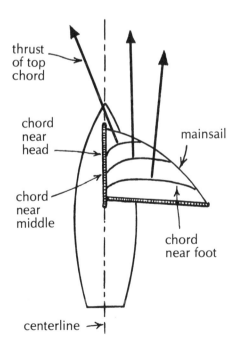

Figure 6-17. SAIL TWIST WHEN RUNNING

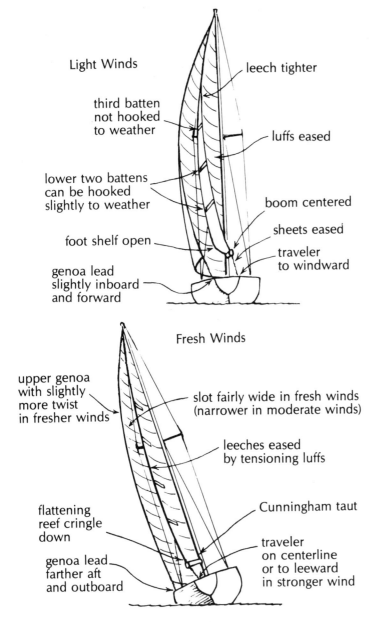

Light Winds

leech tighter

third batten
not hooked
to weather

luffs eased

lower two battens
can be hooked
slightly to weather

boom centered

sheets eased

foot shelf open

traveler
to windward

genoa lead
slightly inboard
and forward

Fresh Winds

upper genoa
with slightly
more twist
in fresher winds

slot fairly wide in fresh winds
(narrower in moderate winds)

leeches eased
by tensioning luffs

flattening
reef cringle
down

Cunningham taut

genoa lead
farther aft
and outboard

traveler
on centerline
or to leeward
in stronger wind

Figure 6-18. TWIST AND TRIM
(From *Better Sailing*)

chance of working together. Careful monitoring of the speedometer, of course, should give you some indication of proper adjustment. A number of leading sailmakers now advocate moving the jib lead quite far forward, but this can be overdone when it causes the leech to hook inboard and jam the slot.

It is much easier to control proper adjustment of the slot when the boat is sailing close-hauled. Figure 6-18 shows approximately what the slot should look like when beating in light and also in fresh winds. There is considerably more twist and draft in the sails in light weather. This is accomplished by moving the sheet leads inboard and easing luff tension. A major reason for greater twist in light airs is to prevent the top of the sails from stalling as a result of being overtrimmed. The airflow is less apt to stay attached to the sail when the wind is light. The drawing of the top boat shows the traveler moved slightly to windward, but the sheet is well eased so that the main twists and the boom is on the boat's centerline (the boom should seldom if ever be to windward of the centerline). Ordinarily, this adjustment would slack the leech, but this is kept tight by slacking the luff and adjusting the leech line. The lower part of the sail can be allowed to hook to weather slightly in the interest of achieving a full-draft curve. An indication of the hook can be obtained by looking at the battens from the stern. The batten just above the sail's middle should not be allowed any hook to weather. Another way to judge the main's draft and trim is to tie a streamer, or leech telltale, to that batten pocket. The telltale should stream straight aft and not turn under the lee side of the sail, which would indicate that the flow is not attached. The flow might be reattached by easing the sheet and/or increasing the twist slightly.

We can see that the leech of the jib on the upper boat in Figure 6-18 follows the leech curve of the twisted main. This is accomplished by trimming the sail inboard, while moving the lead forward counteracts too much twist. If the boat lacks an inboard track for the jib, the jib lead is slightly farther aft. This keeps the slot approximately uniform in width but makes it a trifle too wide. One way of overcoming this problem is with a *Barber-haul,* a line running from the clew or sheet (between the clew and lead block) to an inboard winch. It would give the same effect as moving the lead slightly inboard.

The lower boat (in Figure 6-18), sailing in a fresher breeze, has a uniform slot, but there is much less twist to the sails. The main boom is well to leeward of the centerline, the jib is trimmed to the rail to keep the slot open, and sails are flattened with luff tension and a flattening reef. The genoa is led farther aft to keep the slot

ficult when reaching without a spinnaker. There is little you can do to control the twist of a boomless headsail when reaching except to use a jib with a high clew (a reaching jib) and/or move the lead block forward. Even so, the jib will twist far too much when reaching and fail to work efficiently with a well-vanged mainsail. When this is the case, especially if the boat is masthead-rigged, it may be worth compromising some of the mainsail's efficiency by easing the vang a bit in order to give the two sails greater shape conformance and thus a better open aloft. In a fresher breeze, the lead would be still farther aft. The main's leech is eased not only by tensioning the luff but also by slacking the leech line. This trim position keeps the battens angled slightly to leeward of a line parallel to the boat's centerline.

ORDERING SAILS

When ordering new sails, it is best to give the sailmaker all information even remotely related to the shape, size, and cut of each sail. With mainsails, the most vital measurements are, of course, the mast and boom lengths. If the boat does not have a rating certificate showing luff and foot lengths, the sailmaker should take these measurements, but this is impossible when the boat and the sail loft are a long distance apart. Luff and foot measurements are nearly always marked by black bands, described earlier. Spar measurements for sailmaking purposes should be made between the inside edges of the black bands (between the top of the bottom band and the bottom of the top band on the mast, and between the after side of the mast and the forward edge of the after band on the boom). If the spars are not banded before the sail is made, the boat owner must decide what luff and foot measurements will give him the most speed for the least rating. He may prefer, as most owners do, that the sailmaker use the standard sailplan drawn by the boat's designer. However, if the winds usually are light in the racing area, the owner may wish slightly longer luff and foot lengths, with the bands placed at the very ends of the spars. He also might want to have the corners of the sails come almost to the bands for maximum sail size and adjust edge tension entirely with a Cunningham and a flattening reef (rather than with a downhaul and an outhaul). On the other hand, if the racing area winds usually are heavy or the boat is somewhat tender, the owner may decide to decrease the rating with a slightly smaller mainsail. At any rate, if the spars are not banded before the sail is made, they should be banded after the sail is made, for maximum rating benefit. More is said about measurement rules in the next chapter.

When taking luff and foot measurements for the sailmaker, use a steel tape stretched taut, and give the maximum measurement. Do not try to allow for sail stretch. This is the sailmaker's job, and, of course, stretch allowance will depend on the cloth finish, weight, edging material, and the sail's cut. It is very important that the sailmaker know the exact locations of the tack and clew fittings. If possible, these should be positioned so that the luff and the foot make straight lines when those edges are stretched taut. In other words, the outhaul and gooseneck fitting pins that pass through the clew and tack grommets should not be too low or too high off the boom, nor should the tack pin be too close or too far away from the mast. If the pins are located so that the luff and foot cannot be stretched to make straight lines from head to tack and from tack to clew, the fittings should be moved or changed. But if this is impossible, the sailmaker should know the exact pin locations. When boats have roller reefing that is not inside the mast, the tack pin usually must be set far abaft the mast's sail track. In this case, the sailmaker must cut the sail to compensate or secure the sail slides with a jackline or *relieving line* (a short line running along the lower luff that holds the lower slides a short distance away from the luff).

Other information that will be helpful to the sailmaker includes: how you tune your boat's rig, whether or not the mast will be absolutely straight, how taut the jibstay will be carried, and the amount of mast rake; hull form, beam, displacement, and stiffness; jib overlap; description of other sails that will be carried simultaneously with the new sail; traveler length and lead positions; typical racing weather conditions; wave conditions; whether emphasis should be placed on upwind or downwind sailing; a description of the existing sail inventory; how much the new sail will be used for racing or cruising; whether the sail will be unbent or left bent to its boom; any unusual sailing habits or characteristics of the skipper, crew, or boat. If the boat has been measured, a copy of her rating certificate should be sent to the sailmaker. He should have a copy of her hull plans as well as her sailplan, if these are available. Most sailmakers have standard sailplans of stock boats. Of course, there should be ample communication by mail and telephone, or, preferably, visits between the sailmaker and the buyer. Sails are expensive, so it is worthwhile to be thorough in supplying the sailmaker with pertinent information.

SOME PRACTICAL CONSIDERATIONS

Following is a list of miscellaneous suggestions about sails.

1. Lower battens should be stiff but slightly flexible at the inner end, while the upper batten should be flexible, especially at the inner end.

2. When roller reefing is provided, the bottom batten should be horizontal so that it can be rolled around the boom without bending. It is sometimes desirable to have two or three grommets put in the leech of the sail at the

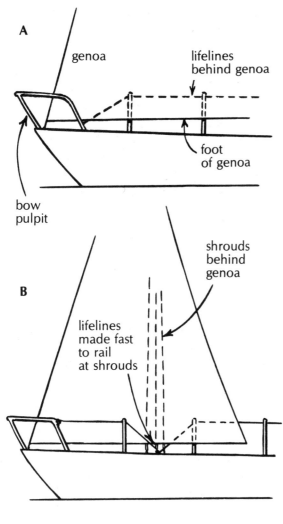

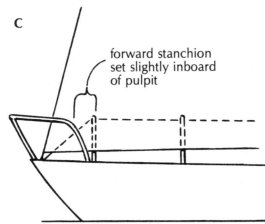

Figure 6-19. LIFELINES AND RAIL-TRIMMED GENOA

most probable reefed-clew locations so that a line can be rove through to facilitate pulling back on the leech and thereby prevent wrinkles at the foot. Various reefing methods and techniques are discussed in Chapter 9.

3. Some sailmakers use small, lightweight shackles to secure the sail slides to the sail. These are strong and dependable, and, when they are of the proper type, do not chafe the sail.

4. When mainsails are small, it is generally desirable that they be unbent from their booms when not in use. If possible, try to fold them so that the creases run fore and aft. When mainsails are too large to fold, it is best to leave them bent and furled or faked down (accordion-folded) on top of the boom. Be sure to cover the sail with a loose-fitting (for ventilation) sail cover to protect against sun rot, bird droppings, and industrial smog.

5. Jibs or other sails that must be stuffed into bags should be hoisted at least 15 minutes or more before the start of a race so that the wrinkles and creases have a chance to smooth out.

6. Use a strong main topping lift leading to the masthead. A prestretched Dacron rope lift can be led over a block at the masthead and then down to the base of the mast, and it will not badly chafe the mainsail leech. A wire lift, however, should be dead-ended aloft, because it can soon fatigue when run over a small sheave aloft, and it can chafe the mast when it runs down to the deck. When attached aloft, the wire lift can have a rope tail just above the boom and be adjustable at the boom. If the wire chafes the leech, the lift can be held away with a piece of shock cord (elastic cord) running through a block on the backstay and down to a cleat on or near the deck. The shock cord should be long enough to allow slacking off when the boom is broad off.

7. An excessive roach on the mainsail (or mizzen) is the least penalized sail area, but it is hard to control. Large roaches often cause the leech area to fall forward, forming a hard ridge just forward of the battens. Extra tension on the vang to tighten the leech can help correct this fault.

8. Leech lines have already been mentioned, but more should be said about them. They are most important in battenless jibs to stop violent leech flutter, but leech lines also are needed in mainsails to help shape these sails by deepening the draft curves in light airs, as discussed earlier. There are various ways to secure a leech line. Some have small plastic cleats, but for most jibs that are not used in very heavy weather, Velcro tape simplifies adjustment. Many heavy-weather jib leech lines are too light. Leech flutter can not only harm boat speed but also damage the leech in a blow. Adjust the leech line no tighter than necessary to stop the flutter,

though, because it may cause the leech to curl inboard and disturb the airflow around the sail.

9. Even if mainsail luff tension is controlled with a Cunningham, it is a good idea to have a sliding gooseneck, which allows a little luff adjustment with a downhaul. This rig prevents a large crease in the sail above the tack that results from extensive use of the Cunningham. It also allows the boom to be raised when reefing, sometimes eliminating the need to slack the halyard when shallow reefing.

10. An efficient outhaul adjustment is a must for racing. The worm screw type with a handle at the end of the boom is very powerful and satisfactory, but it has one drawback in that it cannot be adjusted while the boom is broad off. The outhaul that uses blocks and cleats mounted near the middle of the boom should not be used with roller reefing, because in this case, the boom should be smooth so it will be harmless to the sail when a reef is rolled in. An effective outhaul is the type that has a wire that runs through the boom and winds up on an internal reel. It is operated by a removable crank handle at the forward end of the boom.

11. A problem with low-cut genoas on racing-cruisers is the interference of lifelines with the foot of the sail. The problem is most difficult when the genoa is close-hauled and trimmed to a rail track. Three solutions are suggested in Figure 6-19. Setting the forward stanchion slightly inboard of the pulpit to allow a gap through which the jib can pass (Figure 6-19(C)) is the safest solution, and it may be the only one allowed by local racing rules. When the genoa is trimmed inside the lifelines on a beat, of course, there is no problem, although the foot will ride up over the lifelines or bow pulpit when the sheets are eased for reaching. It is a good idea to have the foot reinforced to guard against chafe where it touches the pulpit and lifelines. If the genoa trims to the rail, it is wise to bend the forward stanchions slightly inboard (up to 10 degrees), but when the close-hauled genoa trims to the deck, the stanchions might be bent slightly outboard.

12. Most genoas are very sensitive to lead adjustments. A change of a few inches in the lead's position can make a significant difference in performance. Most genoa leads are on tracks running almost fore and aft, and they should be set in accordance with advice given earlier. Remember that moving the lead forward tightens the leech, which is advisable when reaching and when beating in light winds. Moving the lead aft tends to slacken the leech, and this is done when beating in fresher winds. Many genoas seem to perform best in moderate winds when the foot lies against the shrouds and the upper leech is six inches or so away from the spreader tips. Put a band of tape around each spreader exactly six inches inboard of the tip in order to have a guide for judging the distance of the sail from the tip. Once optimum lead positions are ascertained, they should be marked with a waterproof marker. These marks should be made for all sails and different strengths of wind. If this cannot be done, proper positions should be marked in a notebook. Measure the holes for lead settings on each side of the boat to see that they match perfectly, because they don't always correspond.

13. If there are a lot of cleats and winches on your mast and your boat has no baby stay, rig an antifouling line running from a point about six feet up the mast to an eye in the deck or cabin trunk about four feet forward of the mast. This will help prevent the jib from fouling on mast fittings when coming about.

14. When headsail luff foil systems are used, nets should be rigged between the lifelines and the rail forward to keep the hankless headsails from washing overboard. Hankless sails remaining on deck are usually left in long, zippered sausage bags. Heavy-weather storm jibs should be hanked to stays, so when the jibstay is a luff foil, there should be an inner stay (removable on a sloop) for a hank-on storm staysail. A less desirable alternative is to have grommets put in a storm jib that is intended for a luff foil so that it can be secured to the foil with lashings.

7/ Rules, Measurement, and Racing

Some of the most commonly used handicap measurement rules are very complex and often confusing to many owners of newly acquired racing-cruisers, especially to racing novices or former skippers of one-design classes. The rules discussion in this chapter is not to provide a detailed study but to explain in the simplest way the main points and basic principles.

Two of the most important handicap-rating rules for American racing-cruisers are the previously mentioned MORC (Midget Ocean Racing Club) rule and the IOR (International Offshore Rule). These systems, however, are not nearly as popular as the one used by the PHRF (Performance Handicap Racing Fleet), which has almost 80 fleets in 30 states. In the United States, more than 20,000 boats race under the PHRF, as opposed to only about 2,000 racers in IOR and about 1,500 in MORC. A relatively new and extremely complex method of handicapping is the Measurement Handicap System, but, as of 1982, only about 500 boats had MHS certificates.

These are the principal rules used in the United States,

although there are certain local, simplified measurement rules for more informal racing, such as the Off Soundings Club Rule (used mostly on Long Island Sound) and the FORA (Florida Ocean Racing Association) Rule. Then, too, there is the USYRU, United States Yacht Racing Union (formerly North American Yacht Racing Union) simplified measurement rule, which is intended "for use in informal fun races as might be held afternoons or evenings by an individual yacht club with a miscellaneous fleet of cruising boats."

Chapters 2 and 3 discussed the various dimensions and characteristics of a yacht that affect speed. Some of the most important and readily measurable of these are the sailing length, or L measurement (the effective LWL when the boat is underway and heeled), sail area, displacement (or hull depth), beam, draft, stability, freeboard, rig, and propeller (size, type, and location). The more complex measurement rules — MORC, IOR, and MHS — take into consideration most of these speed-affecting factors.

Again, the most fundamental measure of a boat's

speed is her sailing length, because the square root of this measurement is her approximate, easily attained top speed (at a speed-length ratio of 1.0), when sailing full and by in moderate winds. Sail area is equally important, because this is the driving or motivating force, and displacement or hull depth with beam, considered as resistance, can be thought of as the bulk or weight to be moved. In the various measurement formulas, sail area (SA) is expressed as a square root because this is a surface or square measurement. Displacement (disp. or D) expressed as volume or cubic measurement, is shown in the formulas as a cube root. In other words, the rated lengths of racing-cruisers of different sizes vary with the square root of their sail area and the cube root of their displacement.

Most measurement rating formulas give a rated length in feet, which is then applied to time allowance tables to obtain the actual handicap time for a particular race. This is discussed later. Yachts assigned a rating under the rules mentioned in this chapter must be measured by official measurers approved by the race- or rule-sponsoring organization or club.

The common designations for sail area measurements are illustrated in Figure 7-1. These are essentially the same for all the rules mentioned, but there are slight variations in the definitions of some measurement limits. Thus, the exact wording should be taken from the particular rule in use. The P designation is the mainsail (or P miz for mizzen) luff length, B is the mainsail (or B miz for mizzen) foot length, P_2 or I is the height of the foretriangle, J is the base of the foretriangle, and LL is the jib luff length. An LP measurement, as explained in the last chapter, is a perpendicular from the jib luff to the clew (Figure 6-8). Black-banding spars was also described in the last chapter. The rules state that these bands must have accompanying stoppers (to prevent pulling the sails beyond the bands) or halyard markers (to show when the head of the sail has reached the bottom of the upper black band).

When a halyard is marked (painted bands usually are required) to indicate hoist limit, be sure the top of the sail's headboard is no lower than the bottom of the black band, so that the sail can be hoisted to the greatest height for light-air sailing and so that maximum distance is allowed for luff adjustment. If judging the headboard and band alignment from the deck, remember that perspective can make it appear that the headboard is aligned properly when it is several inches lower than the band. Try to check the alignment from aloft, at the same level as the band, or else from a location some distance away from your boat when the halyard is marked to indicate full hoist.

John Wright, the USYRU's chief measurer, using a level to check a mast measurement on the author's Ohlson 38. (Sally Henderson photo)

USYRU'S SIMPLIFIED RULE

The USYRU's simplified rule, which often is still referred to as the NAYRU rule (even though the latter organization is now the USYRU), is seldom used. Nevertheless, it is a good rule to start with, since it is the least complex of the measurement rules used in the United States. The basic formula is

$$0.15 \left[\frac{\text{LWL} \times \sqrt{\text{S}}}{\text{G}} + \text{LWL} + \sqrt{\text{S}} \right] \times \text{K} .$$

LWL is load waterline length and S is sail area. K is a combination of factors considering propeller type, keel configuration, and age of the boat. Prop factors are 0.99 for feathering or folding types, 0.97 for a solid, two-bladed prop, and 0.95 for a solid three-bladed prop. Keel factors are 1.00 for a configuration that separates the rudder from the keel and .098 for a continuous keel with rudder attached. The age factor is 1.00

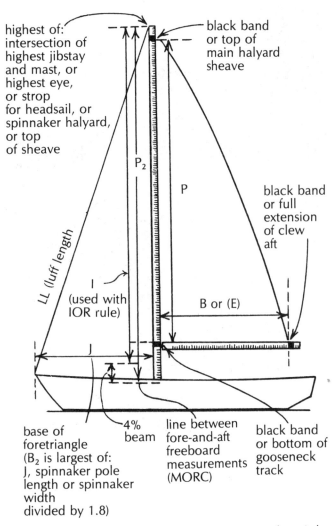

highest of:
intersection of
highest jibstay
and mast, or
highest eye,
or strop
for headsail, or
spinnaker halyard,
or top
of sheave

black band
or top of
main halyard
sheave

P_2

P

LL (luff length)

I
(used with
IOR rule)

black band
or full
extension
of clew
aft

B or (E)

J

base of
foretriangle
(B_2 is largest of:
J, spinnaker pole
length or spinnaker
width
divided by 1.8)

4%
beam

line between
fore-and-aft
freeboard
measurements
(MORC)

black band
or bottom of
gooseneck
track

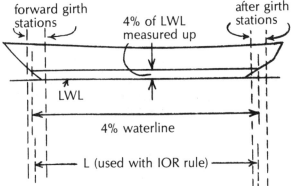

forward girth
stations

4% of LWL
measured up

after girth
stations

LWL

4% waterline

L (used with IOR rule)

NOTE: Exact wording of designations should be taken from the rule in use.

Figure 7-1. SIMPLIFIED MEASUREMENT DESIGNATIONS

– 0.01 (age – 3), with a maximum of 1.00 and a minimum of 0.95. G in the formula is

$$0.5\sqrt{[(RT)^2 - 0.2d] \times BWL}$$

where d is maximum draft and BWL is maximum beam at the waterline. RT stands for rolling time, and it is an approximation of displacement derived from artifically rolling the boat in smooth water and timing her period of roll with a stopwatch.

S in the basic formula is the sum of the areas of the foretriangle, mainsail, and mizzen (if any). One interesting feature of the rule is that there are special allowances when skippers wish to race under working sails. If neither an overlapping jib nor a spinnaker is used, the foretriangle is rated 0.5(Lf x J), and if either overlapping jib or spinnaker is used, the foretriangle is rated 0.75(Lf x J). When both overlapping jib and spinnaker are used, the rating is 1.00(Lf x J). Lf is luff length and J is the base of the foretriangle (see Figure 7-1). A jibheaded mainsail is rated 0.4(foot x hoist).

Exact particulars of this rule and of the other handicapping systems presented in this chapter obviously should be taken from the latest official publications of the rules, which are available from the USYRU, Box 209, Newport, Rhode Island 02840. The USYRU simplified method has been reasonably satisfactory for informal racing, but it has several weaknesses, including a rather inaccurate measure of sailing length and displacement.

THE MIDGET OCEAN RACING CLUB RULE

The Midget Ocean Racing Club (MORC), founded in 1954, was inspired by the Junior Offshore Group (JOG), a British club devoted to racing small boats offshore. Like the British group, the MORC incorporates safety regulations into its measurement rule. These safety measures were discussed in Chapters 3 and 4. Although the rule was intended for boats smaller than 24 feet LOA, in 1958 the maximum length limit was increased to just under 30 feet.

The handicap part of the MORC rule was based on the CCA rule in use in 1954. When the MORC rule was first developed by designer William Shaw with the help of Olin Stephens, the CCA rule was tried on a number of boats below 24 feet LOA, and it was found that this rule favored abnormally heavy boats with very large sail areas, and, of course, small boats are relatively deeper and beamier than large boats. Thus the CCA rule, then extant, was modified (by adjusting the rule constants) to suit the smaller boats.

Like the old CCA rule, the MORC uses the *base boat* concept for handicapping. Through careful study and observation of various racing-cruiser types, a base boat, or imaginary ideal boat, is conceived. Theoretically, the base boat is a fast, seaworthy, and generally wholesome type, and its dimensions serve as a standard of comparison with those of the boat being measured. When the measured dimensions (or other measured characteristics) tending to increase speed are greater than those of the base boat, the differences increase the handicap rating, but when the dimensions tending to increase speed are less than those of the base boat, the differences reduce the rating.

The MORC rule takes into account length, draft, sail area, and ballast, which, of course, are helpful to speed; it also takes into account displacement and the propeller, which cause drag and reduce speed. There is separate treatment for beam and freeboard, which can be harmful to speed through head resistance, wetted-surface drag, and windage, but which are often helpful to speed through their effects on the boat's stability. The various parameters are measured carefully by an official measurer, and displacement is determined by weighing the boat, or, in certain circumstances, by calculating the weight from lines drawings.

The current MORC measurement formula (effective February 1, 1980) is

$$.875L(1 + BMCR + DRCR + DISCR + FBCR + SACR + BALCR + LBCR + PROP + PEN).$$

L in the formula stands for the rated length and it approximates the boat's sailing length. The various letter groups in the formula are as follows: BMCR, beam correction; DRCR, draft correction; DISCR, displacement correction; FBCR, freeboard correction; SACR, sail area correction; BALCR, ballast correction; LBCR, live ballast correction; PROP, propeller correction; and PEN, equipment penalties. L is .7(4 percent WL) + .3 (LWLR) + TC. The 4 percent WL is the measurement of a waterline 4 percent of the LWL measured up from the waterline (see Figures 7-1 and 7-2). LWLR stands for "load waterline rated," and it may include some extra length when a particularly thick rudder extends abaft the load waterline. TC represents a transom correction, which is one-tenth of the transom width.

Entire details of the rule will not be covered here, but an example of a measurement correction is as follows: DRCR = 0.10(ΔDR). ΔDR is a draft deviation, which is (DRR − DB)/DB, where DB, which stands for base

draft, is .186L. DRR is the rated draft. This is simply DR (draft) for a keel yacht, but for a keel-centerboard yacht, it is DR + CBA(S)/(1.67L), where CBA(S) stands for "exposed projected area of one side of centerboard." DRR for a centerboard yacht is 0.9DRM (see Figure 7-2 for DRM).

The other dimension corrections are treated in a similar way, with a base dimension established and a deviation, which is the measured dimension minus the base divided by the base. These deviations form a part of the correction formulas. For example, ballast deviation (ΔBAL) is (BAL − BBAL)/BBAL (when ballast is greater than or equal to a third of the boat's displacement). BBAL stands for base ballast, and it is $(0.552L)^3$ in pounds, where L is in feet. The ballast correction formula is $0.08(\Delta$BAL) + 0.08(ΔBAL)^2. (Incidentally, the ballast measurement (BAL) recognizes that lead is more effective ballast than iron, for the formula multiplies iron-keel weight by .92.)

Since initial stability, which gives a boat power to carry her sail, is an important factor, the MORC rule considers initial stability not only with the ballast correction but also with beam measurements. There is a correction for waterline beam, and also a live ballast correction that takes into account maximum beam (BMX) and the effect of crew weight on deck near the rail. The correction formula is $0.08(\Delta$BMX) + 0.267(ΔBMX)^2, and the base maximum beam is 0.375L.

Sail area correction is half the sail area deviation (ΔS), which is the rated sail area, minus the base sail area (BSA), divided by BSA. RSA is equal to the sum of the rated areas of the main, foretriangle, and mizzen (if there is one), plus .076 times the square of the rated height of the rig. The foretriangle is rated at $0.617P_2$ x B_2, which means it is rated at 61.7 percent of the height of the foretriangle times its base (since 100 percent of a triangle's area is half its base times its altitude). There is no penalty for jib overlap up to 170 percent of J, and there is now a progressive credit for less overlap down to 155 percent. The mainsail's area is rated at 0.363(P x B) + ASPM. This means 36.3 percent of the base times the altitude, plus an aspect-ratio penalty when the P measurement is greater than 2.4B.

The proper correction is −10.PF(PS/L)^2, where PS is propeller diameter and PF is propeller factor. There are various factors that take into account two- and three-bladed props and the type of blade (feathering, folding, or solid). The factors vary from 0.75 for a folding prop to 4.5 for a solid prop with three blades.

The equipment penalties (PEN in the basic formula) are for headstay luff systems, grooved headfoils or

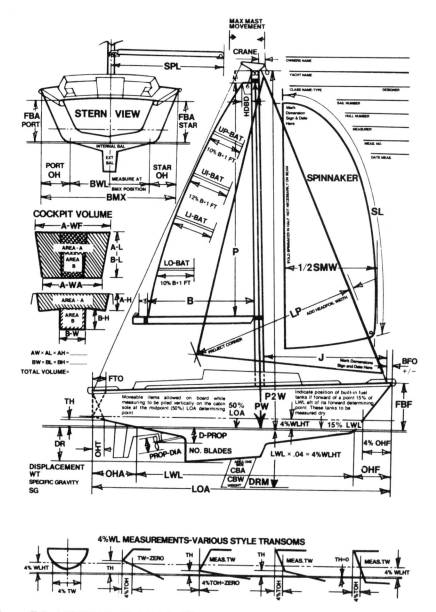

Figure 7-2. MORC FIELD MEASUREMENT WORKSHEET DIAGRAM, 1979 RULE

similar luff support systems, and extra backstays. For each penalty, .005 is added to PEN.

The MORC rule has been successful in that it has stimulated keen racing in reasonably seaworthy boats. By and large, the rule has encouraged short-ended, dinghy-type boats, and many of them sacrifice looks for speed. Still, they are fast and sporty (if sometimes a bit tricky to sail), and they usually are quite roomy for their length. In addition to the MORC measurement rule, there is the MORC/PR rule, in which boats under 30 feet overall can compete against each other without measurement. Their ratings are assigned according to actual performance as observed by experienced handicappers. This approach does not encourage any particular kind of boat, but attempts to rate equitably all different types. MORC also has a development rule for boats up to 22 feet LOA, whereby racing is done on a boat-for-boat basis. These craft must be designed to certain dimensions and specifications, and the system tends to accentuate the development of speed at some sacrifice to other qualities.

Complete information about MORC can be obtained by writing the MORC International Offices, 21330 Center Ridge Road, Cleveland, Ohio 44116.

INTERNATIONAL OFFSHORE RULE

From 1934 until 1970, the dominant handicap rule for the larger American yachts in formal offshore races was the CCA (Cruising Club of America) rule, the base-boat system that inspired the MORC. Beginning in 1970, however, the CCA was replaced by the International Offshore Rule (IOR), which was a kind of compromise between the CCA and the British RORC (Royal Ocean Racing Club) rule, with a few features from other rules. The IOR was adopted for the primary purpose of allowing the fairest possible competition between ocean-racing yachts from different countries in international competition. Acceptance of the IOR by all the major yachting nations allowed boats all over the world to be designed to the same rule, which theoretically ensured that no race participant would enjoy any special advantage.

The IOR turned out to be more of a development rule than one for handicapping fairly a broad spectrum of designs, and the rule does favor certain types of boats. Those yachts not designed to the IOR seldom have a good chance of beating those that have been designed to it, and, unless given an age allowance, even boats conforming to the rule tend to become obsolete for racing relatively quickly. One benefit of a development rule, however, is that it constantly improves racing performance of boats favored by the rule, although often at the expense of other desirable design characteristics.

The basic IOR formula for measured rating (MR) is:

$$MR = \left[\frac{0.13L\sqrt{SC}}{\sqrt{BD}} + 0.25L + 0.2SC + DC + FC \right] \times DLF$$

L is rated length; B, rated beam; D, rated depth; SC, sail area value; DC, draft correction; FC, freeboard correction; and DLF, displacement length factor. The yacht's final rating (R) is:

$$R = MR \times EPF \times CGF \times MAF \times SMF \times LRP \times CBF,$$

where EPF is engine and propeller factor; CGF, center of gravity factor; MAF, movable appendage factor; SMF, spar material factor; LRP, low rigging penalty; and CBF, centerboard factor.

After a look at the IOR book, which is packed with lengthy formulas, it is hard to realize that the rule is based on a rather simple premise. The fundamental part of the MR factor is moving force, which is length times the square root of sail area, divided by the bulk to be moved. This concept is similar to the theory behind

some of the older rules, such as the Universal and the later Storm Trysail Club rules, although these systems use the cube root of displacement as the measure of bulk and the IOR uses the square root of beam times depth to approximate bulk. As Olin Stephens, one of the founders of the IOR, explained, "The square root of midsection area will bear a constant relation to cube root of displacement as long as the prismatic coefficient is held constant." Of course, the prismatics of boats vary, but the IOR reasons that the variation in the type of yacht racing under the rule will not be significant, and using beam times depth, instead of displacement, saves the expense and trouble of weighing yachts. Naturally, there is much more to the IOR than the above basic principle, but the rest of the rule amounts to numerous refinements and less significant factors that affect speed.

Under the IOR, the determination of L, which approximates sailing length, is similar to the RORC method of measuring distance between points established forward and aft by girth measurements related to beam. Rated length is length between the forward and after girth stations (LBG), minus a forward overhang component (FOC), minus an after overhang component corrected (AOCC). Girths (distances measured around the hull with the measuring tape held vertical) are taken at four different stations. These are the forward girth station (FGS), where the girth is equal to one-half of B; the forward inner girth station (FIGS), where the girth is equal to three-quarters of B; the after girth station (AGS), where the girth is equal to three-quarters of B; and the after inner girth station (AIGS), where the girth is equal to seven-eighths of B, plus the GD, if any, used at AGS. GD is the girth difference when an after girth of 0.75B in length cannot be placed on the yacht or cuts the transom. In this case, a girth is taken as far aft as possible and its position is recorded as AGS. The length of this girth is measured and the difference between its length and 0.75B is recorded as GD. Examples of girth stations are shown in Figures 7-1 and 7-3.

The formula for the forward overhang component is

$$FOC = \frac{GSDF(FF - 0.3B + 0.15BF)}{0.125B + FF - FFI - 0.15(BFI - BF) + 0.5GDFI}.$$

GSDF is girth station difference forward; FF is freeboard forward; FFI is freeboard forward inner; BFI is beam forward inner; BF is beam forward; and GDFI is girth difference forward inner. Those measurements with the word *inner* are made at the inner girth station.

The formula for AOC is complicated, so it will not be

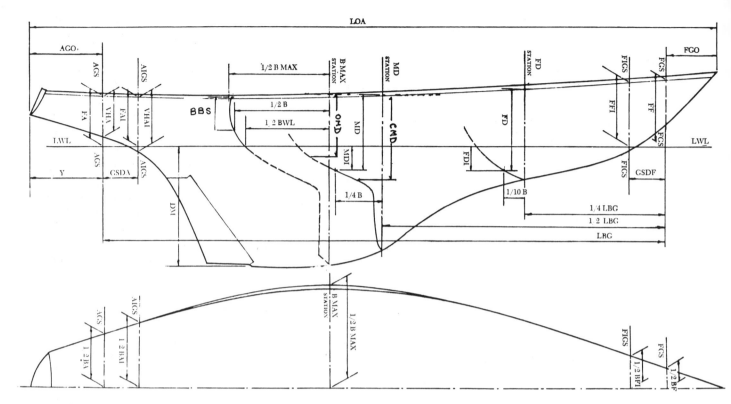

Figure 7-3. IOR HULL MEASUREMENTS

given here. For the sake of this rating rule discussion, it should be sufficient to say that the formula attempts to position the after end of L in such a way that it is reasonably fair to boats with different types of sterns. Under the RORC rule, the AOC had encouraged the development of boats with narrow, "pinched-in" sterns in order to reduce the rated length while maintaining a long actual sailing length. Even many of the early IOR boats had narrow sterns, but the latest AOC in the IOR has encouraged much fuller sterns and more buoyancy aft. Unfortunately, however, many of these boats have very fine bows, and the lack of hull balance, together with considerable depth of hull forward in some cases, has aggravated steering problems in some heavy-weather conditions.

B, rated beam, is a most important measurement, not only because it is a part of the basic MR formula, but also because it plays a part in many of the other measurements, as we have seen with the location of the girth stations. The determination of B requires a BMAX (beam maximum) measurement, which is the greatest beam exclusive of extraneous features such as rubbing strakes. Then B is measured in the BMAX station at a

point one-sixth of BMAX, below a point determined by a sheer correction just below the sheerline.

D, rated depth, considers the immersed depth of the hull proper, and the formula is

$$D = 1.3MDIA + 0.9FDIC + 0.055(3FOC - AOCC) + \frac{L + 10 \text{ ft.}}{30}.$$

MDIA is midship depth immersed adjusted, and FDIC is forward depth immersed corrected. A mid depth station, MDS, is established at half of the LBG, and a forward depth station at a quarter of LBG. At the MDS, three depths are measured: CMDI, center mid depth immersed, measured 0.125B from the centerline; MD, mid depth, measured 0.25B from the centerline; and OMD, outer mid depth, offset .375B from the centerline. The forward depth station has only one depth measurement, which is 0.10B from the centerline.

Draft and several other measurements are considered in relation to a base. DB, base draft, is determined from the formula: 0.146L + 2.0 feet. The difference between rated draft, RD (which takes into account measured draft, DM; centerboard extension, CD; and BD), and the base is DD, the draft difference, and this may be either positive or negative. When negative or zero, the

$$DD = 0.04L \left(\frac{RD}{DB} - 1.0 \right).$$

but when positive, the

$$DD = 0.07L \left(\frac{RD}{DB} - 1.0 \right).$$

There is a centerboard factor, CBF, for boats with centerboards or drop keels. It is

$$CBF = 0.95 + \frac{L}{150 \, (DM + CMD1)}.$$

Freeboard also has a base: FB = 0.057L + 1.20 feet. If the measured freeboard, FM, exceeds the base, the freeboard correction, FC, equals 0.15(FB – FM), but if FM is less than FB, FC = 0.25(FB – FM).

The DLF, displacement length factor, at the end of the MR formula, is

$$DLF = 1.0 + 5.7 \, (BDR - 1.0)^{1.75}$$

where BDR is a base displacement ratio. Displacement is derived from beam and depth amidships.

In the final rating formula, EPF, engine and propeller factor, is derived from the formula EPF = 1 – (EMF + DF), where EMF, engine moment factor, is

$$\frac{0.1EM}{L^2 \times B \times D}.$$

Engine moment, EM, is engine weight times its distance from the middle of LBG. The moment is considered because of its effect on the boat's pitching characteristics. Weight concentrated in the boat's middle normally lessens her tendency to hobbyhorse. The P part of the factor has to do with the prop drag, which depends on such matters as prop size, location, shaft length, whether the blades are movable, and whether there is a propeller aperture. Propeller factors, PF, entered in a propeller drag factor formula, vary from 0.475 for a small, in-aperture, folding or feathering

prop, to 2.05 for a solid prop out of aperture with exposed shaft. The Drag Factor, DF, formula is

$$DF = PF \left(\frac{PDC}{DB} \right)^{\frac{1}{2}} \times \frac{PS}{L}$$

where PDC is propeller depth corrected and PS is propeller size.

CGF, center of gravity factor, has to do with the boat's stability. This indication of her sail-carrying power is found with an inclining test. The test involves artificially heeling the boat with weights suspended known distances from her centerline and measuring the angle of heel to evaluate her righting moment, RM. Inclining was also done under the CCA rule, and Figure 7-4 explains how it was done. The method shown is somewhat different under the present IOR, but the CCA method is easy to comprehend and easy to carry out without special equipment. It is a good test for determining mast and rigging size (see Chapter 5).

As we can see in Figure 7-4, the boat is inclined with jerry cans of water (or any other weight) at the end of a boom suspended horizontally at right angles to the topsides amidships (the spinnaker pole can be used). Angles of heel are measured for two different weights (on one side of the boat and then on the other), so two jerry cans are shown. When one can is suspended, one weight is provided, and when both cans are suspended, a second weight is provided.

Figure 7-4 shows the pendulum deflection in a bucket of water. The IOR formulas, from which CGF is derived, involve pendulum deflections, PD, but the measuring procedure does away with a bucket on the cabin sole, because the present IOR requires that no one (including the measurer) be on board when the yacht is inclined. The "readings" are now done on what the IOR calls a "manometer," a kind of clinometer or level. The accompanying photograph shows the manometer used by John Wright, the chief measurer for the USYRU. Water is put into a reservoir and plastic tube, and it seeks its level on each side of the boat. Pencil lines on a linoleum marking pad record the water-level changes and thus the angle of heel. The device is clamped to the boat's stern pulpit.

After the righting moment is found and corrected, it is used in the formula

$$\frac{0.97L \times (BWL)^3}{RMC}$$

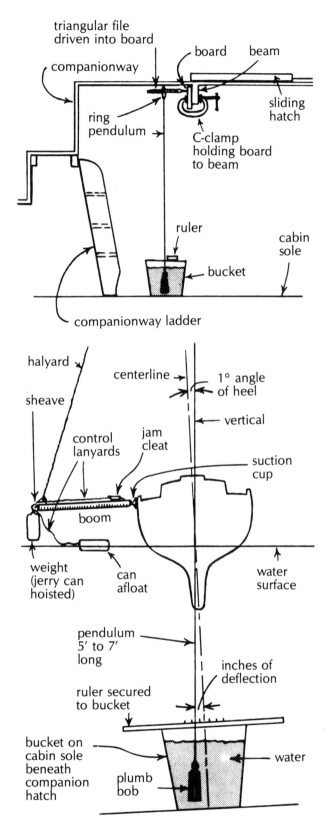

Figure 7-4. INCLINING

to produce a tenderness ratio, TR. If the TR is less than 35.0,

$$CGF = \frac{2.2}{TR - 5.1} + 0.8877,$$

but if TR is greater than 35.0, then

$$CGF = 0.0064TR + 0.7440.$$

The movable appendage factor, MAF, considers only what might be called offbeat underwater parts, such as trim tabs and bilgeboards. The factor does not apply to normal rudders, centerboards, or drop keels. It is also true that only spars built of unconventional materials are affected by the spar material factor, SMF. Masts and booms (with the exception of the spinnaker pole) built entirely or partly of materials other than aluminum, steel, or fiberglass are awarded an SMF of 1.03. The low rig penalty, LRP, is for yachts that save weight aloft and reduce spreader length with rigging attached to the mast below a point 25 percent of IG, height of the genoa halyard.

The last factor in the final rating formula is the CBF, centerboard factor, and this obviously applies to boats with centerboards and also to those with drop keels.

$$CBF = 0.95 + \frac{L}{150(DM + CMDI)},$$

where DM is measured draft and CMDI is center mid depth immersed.

Rated sail area is derived from the areas of the individual sails, combined and corrected. The IOR rule book has about 14 pages of details that should be studied before sails are ordered and the yacht is measured. The rated area of a jibheaded mainsail is 0.35(EC x PC) + 0.2EC(PC - 2E). This means the main's rated area amounts to 70 percent of its measured area (the square footage using the foot and hoist measurements). The last term in the formula has to do with the aspect ratio. It permits an unpenalized ratio up to 2:1, but there is an increasing penalty above that figure. The rated sail area of the foretriangle, RSAF, is

$$0.5IC \times JC\left[1 + 1.1\left(\frac{LP - JC}{LP}\right)\right] + 0.125JC(IC - 2JC).$$

This area is rated at 100 percent, and the aspect-ratio

John Wright's manometer secured to the stern pulpit of the author's boat. The water reservoir is on the right, the marking block is on the left. Note the inexpensive backstay adjuster, which consists of a plain turnbuckle with two shower-curtain rings. (Sally Henderson photo)

penalty is similar to that of the main. There is a jib-overlap penalty that increases gradually when the overlap exceeds 150 percent of J. The IOR recognizes that the mainsail's efficiency is affected by its mast, and this is reflected in its method of rating sail area. The jib is rated 100 percent and the main 70 percent. As a result, there has been a resurgence over the past few years of the fractional rig.

In order to reduce the cost of racing, there are certain limits on the number of sails a boat rating under 45 feet may carry on board during a race.

What has been under discussion is the most recent Mark III version of the IOR. There is also the Mark IIIA part of the rule, which provides age allowances for some of the older yachts. This is done to help correct inequities in handicapping and to extend the racing life of the older designs. To be eligible for age benefits under IIIA, a yacht must have a hull date of December 1980 or earlier. Yachts with hull dates of December 1972 or earlier are in Division 1; those with hull dates January 1973 through December 1975, inclusive, are in Division 2; and those with hull dates January 1976 and later are in Division 3. Benefits are applied to the displacement length factor, DLF, in the measured rating formula. Naturally, Division 1 boats get the greatest age allowance, while Division 2 boats get the next greatest allowance. For yachts of certain ages there are also rig allowances that affect the rated sail area.

The IOR rule book is available from the USYRU, Box 209, Newport, Rhode Island 02840. Yacht owners must pay particular attention to the instructions on how to prepare their boats for measurement.

MEASUREMENT HANDICAP SYSTEM

The latest and undoubtedly the most scientific rating rule is the Measurement Handicap System, MHS. This was devised, after years of research involving extensive model testing and computer studies, for the purpose of equitably handicapping many different types of racing-cruisers and allowing them to remain competitive on a continuing basis. With the MHS, the emphasis is on true handicapping rather than on design development. Research for the rule was initiated as a velocity prediction program (VPP) at the Massachusetts Institute of Technology, and it soon became known as the H. Irving Pratt Ocean Race Handicapping Project. Later the program was taken over by the USYRU and administered by a committee that includes some of the top American designers.

The VPP is based on a proven method of predicting the speed of merchant or naval ships, in which the calculation of propeller thrust is considered in relation to hull drag, which is figured from the towing of models in a testing tank. For a sailboat, of course, the thrust from sails must be calculated, and hull drag must be figured at different angles of heel and leeway; the wind's force (and direction) must be considered in relation to the boat's speed and her point of sailing. Thus, it is obvious that, compared with the velocity prediction of a power-driven ship, predicting a sailboat's speed is extremely complex.

The measurement of a yacht for the MHS is also complex, for it involves the entire shape of the hull rather than measurements at specific points, as in the IOR and

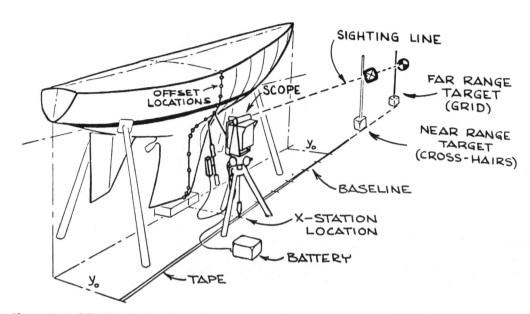

Figure 7-5. SCHEMATIC ARRANGEMENT FOR MEASURING WITH PROTOTYPE HULL MEASURING DEVICE (From a "Summary of the H. Irving Pratt Ocean Race Handicapping Project" by Joseph E. Kerwin and John N. Newman, in *The Fourth Chesapeake Sailing Race Symposium,* 1979, courtesy The Society of Naval Architects and Marine Engineers)

other rules. Taking the whole shape into account avoids the distortion of hull lines by the designer for the purpose of creating a boat with optimal measurements. This makes it very difficult if not impossible for him to "beat the rule." Measurements can be taken from lines plans of the boat when the drawings are complete and in agreement with the IOR measurements, in which case the information is processed through a digitizer.

Field measurements, for yachts without complete lines plans and an IOR rating, are made with an electromechanical device that sometimes is referred to as the "black box." This device is set up at a number of stations along the hull while the boat is out of water and blocked-up level. A retractable Kevlar string wound on a spring-loaded spool on the box is touched to the hull surface at about 20 or 30 offset locations along approximately 15 vertical stations (representing hull sections) on each side of the boat. Figure 7-5 shows how this is done. Although the hull measuring device illustrated is the prototype, and newer types do away with the scope and sighting targets, the illustration explains the principle involved. The offset locations are not precisely spaced as are sections on a lines plan, so that designers cannot exploit areas between definite locations. Measurements are tape-recorded and then fed into a computer, which produces a visual facsimile of the hull lines.

As mentioned, the VPP was based on extensive tank testing. This was done with a series of hull forms systematically modified to evaluate the effect of the important parameters on speed. The model-testing tank at Delft, Holland, was used to test a *geosim* (geometrically similar) family of models derived from the Standfast 43, a typical ocean-racer of the mid-1970s. The basic parameters were altered systematically to produce 405 different but related hypothetical designs. Later models of differing designs, including some popular stock boats, were tested to confirm or correct conclusions drawn from the results of the geosim model tests. The speed of each of these boats was predicted not just for one condition of sailing but for a variety of conditions. As a result, there is a kind of matrix system of rating whereby handicaps are based on different wind velocities and points of sailing. In addition, considerations have been made for the effect of crew weight and reduction of sail in fresh winds.

The formulas resulting from the VPP are very complex and probably incomprehensible to anyone but a student of higher mathematics, but here is an example of the all-important formula for sailing length. It is:

$$L = .3194(LSM1 + LSM2 + LSM4)$$

where LSM1 (Second Moment Length 1) is for the yacht

in sailing trim floating upright, LSM2 is for the yacht in sailing trim floating with 2 degrees heel, and LSM4 is for a deep flotation (LSM3 for 25 degrees heel has been removed from the latest version of L formula). The deep flotation shows the yacht's length in a partially sunk condition, and it takes into account the effect of bow and stern waves. The LSM formula involves integral calculus, and it is expressed as:

$$LSM = 4.35 \sqrt{\left[\frac{\int x^2 S^{\frac{1}{2}} dx}{\int S^{\frac{1}{2}} dx}\right] - \left[\frac{\int x S^{\frac{1}{2}} dx}{\int S^{\frac{1}{2}} dx}\right]^2}$$

S is an element of sectional area and X is length in the fore-and-aft direction. The formula accounts for the added sailing length due to overhangs and also the prismatic coefficient or fullness at the ends. The constant 4.35 brings the length close to the yacht's waterline length.

Aside from length, other parameters affecting hull drag that are considered by the MHS are displacement, a beam-depth ratio, wetted surface area, draft, sectional area of the hull, and propeller installation. Of course, air drag above the water is also considered. Stability is deduced by an inclining experiment as used by the IOR, although the righting moment is given for 2 degrees and higher angles of heel, including the limit of positive stability.

Sail and rig considerations are very similar to those of the IOR except for certain sail area calculations. Also, aerodynamic drag from the mast is taken into account by the MHS with a mast diameter measurement. The heeling and propulsive force of the sails for different wind velocities and points of sailing are calculated from lift and drag coefficients, which were determined by tests with both models and full-size boats.

An MHS measurement certificate does not produce a rated length in feet as is customary with most measurement rating rules; rather, it produces time allowances in decimal hours and seconds per mile. These allowances are for five wind strengths (8, 10, 12, 14, and 16 knots) and for various race courses. These courses are divided into three categories: B/R/R (Beat/Reach/Run), Circular Random, and Linear Random. B/R/R is equal distances of beating, reaching, and running; Circular Random is equal distances in every wind direction as though sailing around a perfectly round island with constant wind direction; and Linear Random is equal periods of *time* of wind from every direction. It is up to the race committee or class organization to decide which time allowance will be used. Their decision will be based

on the kind of course the boats will be sailing (point-to-point or round-the-buoys) and the expected wind strength. B/R/R is the most appropriate time allowance for the usual round-the-buoys course with a lot of windward work, while Linear Random is most appropriate for the average point-to-point race with minimal beating. Circular Random may be the most suitable average when one allowance is used for all races during the season. To find out how much time you get or must give to a competitor in a given race, subtract the time allowances of the two boats, and the result gives the seconds (or decimal hours) per mile that one boat gives to the other; then multiply this figure by the length of the race in miles.

Although the MHS has been criticized for favoring older, heavier boats, it has given a new lease on life to many boats that were considered completely outmoded for serious racing. Measurements for custom boats are expensive, but many stock boats are allowed relatively simple and inexpensive standard hull measurements. This means that when a stock hull is molded or otherwise built to close standards, only one hull need be measured (except for flotation measurements), and all sister boats can use the same measurements.

In addition to providing reasonably fair handicapping for all kinds of racing-cruisers, the MHS offers useful performance information. A rating certificate will give such estimates as the boat's range of positive stability and her optimum sailing angles for greatest V_{mg} (speed made good). For about $50 extra, the USYRU supplies a ''Performance Package,'' which gives additional information on stability and performance data, including *polar diagrams,* showing speed curves for all different points of sailing. An example is illustrated in Figure 7-6, which is the true-wind polar for my sloop, *Kelpie,* an Ohlson 38. The curves for five different wind strengths run from close-hauled at about 40 degrees from the true wind (in 8- and 10-knot winds) to 180 degrees (with the wind dead aft). It can be seen that the farther away a curve is from the center from which the angle lines radiate, the higher the boat speed. This gives the boat's optimum headings for fastest speed. The large boat shapes near the center simply indicate a point of sailing and show when the spinnaker is being carried, whereas the small black boats on either side of the 165-degree line show optimum heading angles when the boat is running.

The MHS will rate only dual-purpose boats, not racing machines. Very light boats and those with minimal accommodations cannot race under this system. Accommodations regulations and other details of the rule are available from the USYRU.

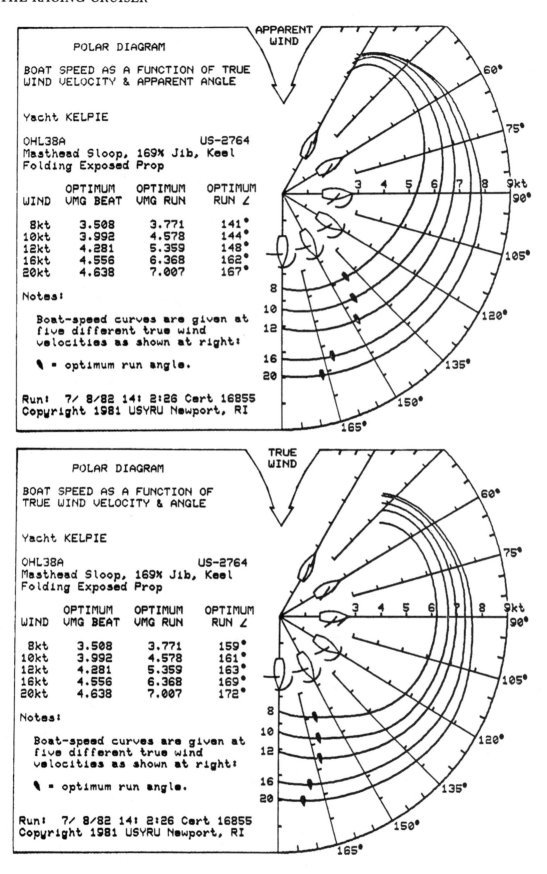

POLAR DIAGRAM

BOAT SPEED AS A FUNCTION OF TRUE
WIND VELOCITY & APPARENT ANGLE

Yacht KELPIE

OHL38A   US-2764
Masthead Sloop, 169% Jib, Keel
Folding Exposed Prop

| | OPTIMUM | OPTIMUM | OPTIMUM |
WIND	VMG BEAT	VMG RUN	RUN ∠
8kt	3.508	3.771	141°
10kt	3.992	4.578	144°
12kt	4.281	5.359	148°
16kt	4.556	6.368	162°
20kt	4.638	7.007	167°

Notes:

   Boat-speed curves are given at
   five different true wind
   velocities as shown at right:

   ◗ = optimum run angle.

Run: 7/ 8/82 14: 2:26 Cert 16855
Copyright 1981 USYRU Newport, RI

POLAR DIAGRAM

BOAT SPEED AS A FUNCTION OF
TRUE WIND VELOCITY & ANGLE

Yacht KELPIE

OHL38A   US-2764
Masthead Sloop, 169% Jib, Keel
Folding Exposed Prop

| | OPTIMUM | OPTIMUM | OPTIMUM |
WIND	VMG BEAT	VMG RUN	RUN ∠
8kt	3.508	3.771	159°
10kt	3.992	4.578	161°
12kt	4.281	5.359	163°
16kt	4.556	6.368	169°
20kt	4.638	7.007	172°

Notes:

   Boat-speed curves are given at
   five different true wind
   velocities as shown at right:

   ◗ = optimum run angle.

Run: 7/ 8/82 14: 2:26 Cert 16855
Copyright 1981 USYRU Newport, RI

Figure 7-6. KELPIE'S POLAR DIAGRAMS

PERFORMANCE HANDICAP RACING FLEET

By far the most popular rating method is the PHRF (Performance Handicap Racing Fleet) system, which handicaps a boat according to her observed performance, rather than having her measurements applied to a rating rule. This method is similar to the previously mentioned MORC/PR rule, because it uses the judgment of experienced handicappers to assign ratings. These handicaps are intended to reflect boat performance only and not the skipper's ability. The primary reasons for the PHRF's popularity are its simplicity, ease with which a rating may be obtained, emphasis on pure handicapping rather than design development, and the fact that it usually works well for stock boats.

The PHRF, which was started many years ago on the West Coast, was originally called the Pacific Handicap Racing Fleet. Now the system has spread to all parts of the country, and race results from every sailing area can be studied and evaluated for more accurate and uniform ratings. Sister boats, however, are not expected to have identical ratings nationwide, because handicappers from each area consider local sea and wind conditions. Nevertheless, sisters should rate closely, and all of them within one area should have the same rating, provided they are standard boats with headsails of similar size.

Handicappers assume that all boats are in racing condition, and no special credit is given for gear that happens to retard speed, such as solid propellers. It is assumed that the boat to be rated has a folding prop or retractable outboard motor, that the genoa LP is a maximum 155 percent of the J measurement, that the spinnaker girth is 180 percent of J, that the spinnaker-pole length is equal to J, and that the boat is in racing condition with a clean bottom and good sails. No credit is given for small headsails, but when a jib's LP exceeds 155 percent or a spinnaker pole is oversize, the boat is moderately penalized. No measurements are required unless it is necessary to determine the amount of jib overlap or the spinnaker and pole sizes. A good feature of PHRF is that there is a nonspinnaker division in which spinnakers (but not boomed-out jibs or headsails carried wing-and-wing) are forbidden. This allows relatively easy racing with a small crew.

Ratings under the PHRF, like those under MHS, are time allowances, and they are in seconds per mile. The difference between the ratings of two boats is the number of seconds the faster boat gives to the slower one for each mile of the race. Unlike a handicap system that provides rated lengths in feet and where low ratings are desirable, the PHRF and MHS provide ratings that treat boats with the highest numbers most favorably. A sample of PHRF ratings is given in the Appendix.

Ratings are adjusted by 3-second or 6-second (per mile) increments when boats are modified. Examples of recommended adjustments are: a 6-second penalty for NE (no engine), a 3-second credit for IB (inboard auxiliary on a small yacht), a 3-second penalty for OB (outboard auxiliary on yachts with standard inboards), a 3-second penalty for each 10 percent increase of J for OP (spinnaker-pole length over 100 percent of J), a 3-second penalty for each 10 percent of J for OS (spinnaker girth over 180 percent of J), a 3-second penalty for each 5 percent of J for BS (bowsprit, where J is increased over standard), a 3-second penalty for each 5 percent increase of J for TM (mast taller than class standard), a 3-second credit for each 5 percent decrease of J for SM (mast shorter than class standard), a 6-second credit for SD (shoal-draft version of standard), and a 6-second credit for CB (centerboard version of standard). When a yacht is radically modified, it must be considered a custom yacht.

The PHRF is intended for monohull boats at least 20 feet long overall, and they must have approved cruising accommodations with enclosed cabins. As with other handicap systems, the PHRF deals with safety, and boats racing under the rule must be self-righting and have watertight integrity. There are also minimum safety equipment requirements, which include such items as distress flares, horseshoe lifering with drogue, safety harnesses, radio receiver, tools (including a hacksaw), and a radar reflector. Equipment lists and other details of the rule are available from your local PHRF organization or the USYRU, which has become involved with the PHRF and its administration.

TIME ALLOWANCE TABLES

When a yacht has a rated length (in feet), it is applied to time allowance tables to obtain the handicap for a particular race. These allowances can either be *time-on-time* (based on the elapsed time of the yacht) or *time-on-distance* (based on the length of the race course). The latter system is almost always used for monohulls racing in American waters. Standard allowances and those used for IOR racing in the U.S. are the USYRU tables, one of which is shown in the Appendix. It is taken from the booklet entitled *Time Allowance Tables,* published by the USYRU. These tables, originated and used continuously since 1908, are based on the assumption that, considering the average summer winds experienced while racing over a triangular course, the rate at which boats draw apart approximates 0.6 of the time differences between the boats when their speeds are equal to the square roots of their ratings. As stated in the preface of *Time Allowance Tables,* the allowance per mile between yachts of different ratings is:

$$\frac{2160}{\sqrt{r}} - \frac{2160}{\sqrt{R}}$$

(R is the larger yacht's rating and r the smaller yacht's rating.) The figure 2160 is the number of seconds in one hour multiplied by 0.6.

To illustrate how the allowance tables work, let us suppose a boat rating 16 feet races a boat rating 25 feet over a one-mile course. At a speed-to-rated-length ratio of 1.0, the 16-foot boat makes four knots (the square root of 16) and the 25-foot boat makes five knots (the square root of 25). It takes the 16-footer 900 seconds to cover the mile and the 25-footer 720 seconds. Subtracting the difference of seconds per mile and multiplying by .6, we arrive at 108. *Time Allowance Tables* gives the allowance for one nautical mile in seconds and decimals. If we look up in the tables the allowance for a 16-foot rating and a 25-foot rating, and then subtract the two allowances, we also arrive at the 108 figure, which is the seconds per mile that the 25-foot boat gives to the 16-footer. The usual race, of course, is much farther than one mile, so the allowance must be multiplied by the number of miles in the race course.

In the standard USYRU time allowance tables (1 and 3), the figures show in seconds or decimal hours the allowances that yachts ranging between the ratings of 10.0 and 99.9 receive from a yacht rating 100 feet (formerly 150 feet) sailing over one nautical mile. The Fishing Bay Yacht Club of Virginia, however, has devised a handy set of tables (derived from the standard USYRU tables), that assume that the scratch boat (having zero time allowance) is always a hypothetical entry with a rating of 30 feet. Pages from these tables are reproduced in the Appendix. With a standard time allowance table, a yacht's allowance is subtracted from her elapsed time (actual time over the course) to obtain the corrected time, and the yacht with the best corrected time wins the race. With the Fishing Bay Yacht Club (FBYC) tables, this procedure is the same for yachts rating under 30 feet, but for ratings *over* 30 feet, the time allowances are *added* to their elapsed times. In the FBYC tables, time allowances for ratings from 15 to 44.9 feet are calculated for races ranging from 10 to 32 miles long. Thus, for races within this distance range, the allowance of each entry may be read directly from the tables. These tables can not only simplify time allowance calculations for the race committee, but they enable the skipper to learn quickly how much time he

gives to or receives from another yacht. By timing his own and a competitor's rounding of a mark of known distance from the start, the skipper or navigator can make one simple subtraction (or addition, if one of the yachts rates above 30 feet) to determine his boat's corrected-time position during the race or at the finish. This should help eliminate the complaints occasionally heard from one-design sailors that they object to handicap racing because they have to "wait for the Monday morning newspaper to read the results of Sunday's race."

The latest USYRU time allowance publications not only give allowances in seconds per mile (Tables 1 and 2) but also in decimal hours (Tables 3 and 4). These latter tables save time for the race committee, but they require the use of a decimal clock. When a committee uses the decimal system, it is often confusing to sailors who think of time in terms of hours, minutes, and seconds. However, the USYRU booklets contain handy tables that convert decimal hours to minutes and seconds.

When the course is upwind, the time allowances favor the large, high-rated boats; but when the course is downwind, the smaller boats are favored. To compensate for this, the race committee may use an assumed course length greater or less than the actual length of the course, when the wind direction or some other factor favors boats of one size range. An assumed course length shorter than actual reduces handicaps and hence favors the larger boats, while an assumed course length longer than actual tends to favor the smaller boats. Some local fleets are now experimenting with varying the .6 factor, depending on the point of sailing of each leg.

If an assumed course length is used, the distance is often stated in the race circular in areas of prevailing winds. In areas of unpredictable winds, contestants might be notified at the start by signals explained in the circular and given by the committee boat. MORC has its own time allowance, which is based on the USYRU tables.

SOME GENERAL THOUGHTS ON HANDICAP RULES

There never has been and never will be a perfect handicap rule. The main reason for this is that racing conditions are variable and constantly changing. For example, a drop in wind strength may favor the smaller boats early in a race, but if the wind drops after the big boats finish, the small boats will be penalized. On the other hand, the breeze may fill in after the large racers finish, allowing the small fry to save their time. Even if we disregard the element of luck, there are imperfections in the leading handicap rules. MORC has been criticized because it is relatively easy to design a boat to beat the rule, so the rate of obsolescence is faster than it should be. The IOR suffers from the same problem with its system of measurements to specific points. Furthermore, it seems ridiculous to have a complex rule that needs an arbitrary factor such as age allowance to make it fair. Certainly, it is not logical to assume that every new boat is faster than one that is older.

The big problems with PHRF are that it can inadvertently penalize skipper ability in some cases, and rating a custom boat often involves too much guesswork. The major fault of the MHS is that it is very complex, requiring elaborate measurements and expense for custom boats and sometimes a lot of work for race committees.

Despite these faults and criticisms, handicapping is the most effective it has ever been, and there is a rule for every kind of racing. In most cases, boats may race under two or three rules; if they are not happy with one system, they can switch to another. On the bright side of the current systems, the IOR and MORC fill the need for development rules, and they offer reasonably fair handicapping of certain boat types for international racing. PHRF fills the need for a simple, inexpensive system of handicapping all types of boats in a manner that is normally fair, especially for popular stock designs. When inequities do exist under the PHRF, the ratings tend to become fairer in time. The MHS offers an ultrascientific rule that yields very accurate handicapping for multipurpose boats on a continuing basis. No one need fear that his rating will become less favorable because he wins races. Although the rule is complicated, the method of measuring hulls is superior, avoiding specific measurement points, and the MHS method is even being considered for use under the IOR. Of course, measurements are obtained easily from standard hulls. When the system of choosing different ratings according to various wind strengths and points of sailing is too onerous for race committees, they may decide to use one arbitrary wind strength for the whole season and perhaps a Circular Random course for all races. Doing so, however, would allow luck to play a greater part.

In selecting a cruising boat to race or preparing a boat for measurement, most owners naturally are interested in obtaining the most favorable rating possible. However, they should realize that if the rating rule under which the new boat will race is at all accurate (and most rating rules are quite accurate), *the more favorable the rating, the slower the speed.* In other words, drastic reductions in rated length will make the boat slower.

Some owners spend a great deal of time and money in an effort to lower their rating materially, but in most cases when the rating is lowered, boat performance suffers, and the time and money would have been better spent on tuning and practice. Of course, minor rating improvements, or at least the best possible rating for a given speed potential, can be gained by making such legitimate measurement preparations as black-banding the spars and advantageously loading, ballasting, and trimming the hull.

Most calculations in rated length are carried out to four decimal places, but the assigned rating is usually resolved to the nearest tenth of a foot. Thus, .05 of a foot will resolve to .1, but .049 will be .0. The entire range from .95 through 1.049 will be counted as 1 foot of rating, yet there is almost a tenth of a foot between the extremes of the range. This near-tenth-of-a-foot amounts to a free means of making the boat go faster. As an example of this, a boat with a rating of 24.9530 could have as much as 11.37 square feet of area added to her mainsail, which would increase her rating to 25.0485. With or without the added sail area, however, her resolved rating would be 25.0. Of course it pays to get the most sail area for a given rating — one reason why some of the leading sailmakers offer computer programming services. These services are usually available at low cost, whether or not sails are ordered.

For optimum rated sail area, be sure that the LPs of light headsails are no longer than the number 1 genoa's LP, that there is no penalty for excessive batten length, that you are not penalized for excessive roach, and that the spinnaker pole is no longer than J.

Under most rules it may help to add some deeply located inside ballast in locales where strong winds prevail, especially when the boat is tender. Furthermore, it is usually true that keeping the ballast as far forward as allowed under the measurement rules is helpful to the boat's rating. The reason for this is that a slight bow-down trim can produce an optimal LWL for rating purposes, and the flotation plane often minimizes stability, which is beneficial to the inclining test, in the wedge-shaped hull (see Figure 7-7). Also, under the IOR, the bow-down trim may improve rated depth, but one has to be careful not to aggravate any tendency to root. And in some small boats with only moderate buoyancy aft, a certain amount of ballast may be needed forward to counteract crew weight in the cockpit.

There are various theories about whether or not it helps to install a folding propeller, but there is agreement that a folding prop is well worth its charge in rating when it is exposed. A solid prop that can hide

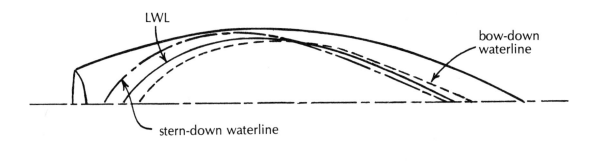

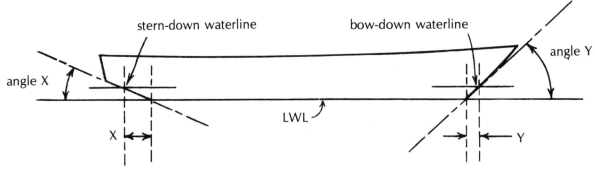

Since angle X is more acute than angle Y, distance X is greater than distance Y.

Figure 7-7. EFFECT OF TRIM ON STABILITY AND LWL

behind a keel or skeg may not cause excessive drag, but fixed blades fully exposed to the water flow can slow the boat noticeably in certain conditions. I have many times seen boat speed dramatically improve after a switch from a solid to a folding prop.

There are three possible types of potentially competitive boats for handicap racing: (1) the very fast boat with an unfavorable rating, (2) the smart, fairly fast boat with a moderate rating, and (3) the slow boat with a favorable rating. It is possible to have a slow boat with an unfavorable rating, but it is rare to have a fast boat with a very favorable rating for any length of time (without the rule's being changed, the rating's being changed, or the boat's being barred from racing under the rule). The most desirable type is either (1) or (2). The most important considerations for racing should be boat performance and speed, no matter what the handicap rule. The second consideration should be the general wholesomeness of the type. Some extreme designs may enjoy temporary advantages before rule loopholes are closed, but for long-range racing enjoyment and safety, the boat should be wholesome, fast but thoroughly seaworthy, comfortable, and soundly designed and constructed.

USYRU RACING RULES

Nearly all formal races in this country use the USYRU racing rules (see Chapter 1) or, to be technically correct, the International Yacht Racing Rules as adopted by the United States Yacht Racing Union. These are not rating measurement rules, but rules for race conduct, management, and right-of-way. Certain parts of these rules concerning signals, starting lines, and other aspects of race conduct were discussed in Chapter 1, but what has not been discussed is the essential matter of right-of-way. Only the basic principles are presented here. As said in Chapter 1, a copy of the current USYRU rules should be carried on every racing boat, and these rules (especially the parts dealing with right-of-way) should be learned and studied periodically to refresh the memory. Obviously, when a large group of racing boats congregate at the starting line or a turning mark, there is real danger of collisions and accidents if even one skipper does not know the right-of-way rules. Furthermore, damage can be extensive when large, heavy racing-cruisers collide. Part I, "Definitions," and Part IV, "Right of Way Rules" — "Rights and Obligations

When Yachts Meet" of the 1981-84 USYRU rules are included in the Appendix.

The novice racing skipper should first familiarize himself with the racing terms definitions given in Part I of the USYRU rules and then learn Rules 31 through 46 in Part IV (see the Appendix).

Essentially, the rules are as follows: When boats on opposite tacks converge, the one on the starboard tack has the right-of-way. The three exceptions to this rule are when a premature starter returns to the starting line on the starboard tack to restart, when a mark toucher (see Rule 52) returns to reround the mark on the starboard tack, and at a downwind mark when the inside boat on the port tack with a proper overlap has the right-of-way over an outside starboard-tack boat.

When boats on the same tack converge, the windward boat keeps clear.

The boat clear astern must keep clear of the boat clear ahead. "A yacht is *clear astern* of another when her hull and equipment, in normal position, are abaft an imaginary line projected abeam from the aftermost point of the other's hull and equipment, in normal position. The other yacht is *clear ahead*." Two yachts overlap if neither is clear astern.

"A yacht which establishes an overlap to leeward from clear astern shall allow the windward yacht ample room and opportunity to keep clear." During the existence of that overlap, the leeward yacht may not sail above her proper course.

Right-of-way yachts are prohibited from balking or preventing yachts over which they have the right-of-way from keeping clear. This is explained in Rule 35.

When on a free leg (not a windward leg) after starting, the windward yacht may not bear off below her proper course when she is within three lengths of either a leeward boat or one clear astern that is steering a course to pass to leeward. However, after starting, the leeward boat or one clear ahead may luff (alter course toward the wind until head-to-wind) as she pleases, except that the leeward boat may not sail above her proper course while the overlap exists if the helmsman of the windward yacht has been abreast or forward of the mainmast of the leeward yacht. This is referred to as the "mast abeam" position. It is illustrated in Figure 7-8. Before the start, boats are allowed to luff, but they must do so slowly. There are some fine distinctions between luffing before the starting signal has been made, luffing after the starting signal but before the boat has crossed the starting line, and luffing after the starting signal after the starting line has been crossed. These distinctions might seem minor, but they should be studied carefully in the USYRU rules (see the Appendix). Some

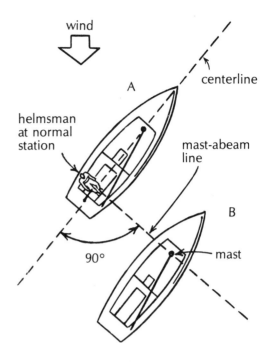

Boat A, passing to windward of boat B, has just reached the mast-abeam position. Prior to reaching this position, A could have been luffed by B, but now B has lost her luffing rights.

Figure 7-8. MAST ABEAM

of the important aspects of luffing are discussed in Chapter 8.

When tacking or jibing, a boat must keep clear of a yacht "on a tack" (a boat that is not tacking or jibing).

When boats are overlapped rounding or passing a turning mark, the outside boat must give the inside boat room to round or pass it, except in several cases, such as an outside starboard-tack boat converging on the mark with an inside port-tacker at the end of a beat, or when boats are *barging* at the start (barging situations often develop at the start, and these are discussed in the next chapter in relation to starting techniques). A boat clear astern may not establish an overlap and be entitled to room when the boat clear ahead is within two of her own lengths of the mark. However, a boat may tack between the mark and another boat within two lengths of the mark and thereafter claim room.

When safe pilotage requires one of two close-hauled boats on the same tack to make a substantial alteration in course to clear an obstruction (defined in Part I of the USYRU rules), and if she intends to tack, but cannot tack without colliding with the other boat, she must hail the other boat for room to tack.

The preceding is a condensed and simplified version of the right-of-way principles. Exact wording should be taken from the USYRU rules.

A yacht can protest another for racing-rule infringements. The protesting yacht should fly a red flag (mentioned in Chapter 1); an attempt should be made to inform the yacht protested that a protest will be lodged; and the protest should be delivered to the race committee as soon as possible after the finish. Exact protest procedure can be obtained from the USYRU rules or the race circular or instructions. A hearing is held by the race committee or a protest committee, and one (or both) of the parties involved in the protest may be disqualified. Decisions of the race or protest committee may be appealed for final determination to the USYRU Appeals Committee when there is a question involving solely the interpretation of the rules. Results of appeals are published by the USYRU in a book entitled *Decisions of the Appeals Committee*. The serious racing skipper should acquire and study this book. It may be obtained from the USYRU, Box 209, Newport, RI 02840.

8/ Starting Technique

This section on starting is intended chiefly for sailors who are beginning to race, but it is also useful for small-boat racing skippers beginning to race large boats. There is a definite difference between starting in a lightweight dinghy and starting in a large, relatively heavy, slower turning, and more elaborately rigged racing-cruiser. Chapter 1 presented the basic mechanics of starting — the signals, time, setting and slanting the line — but here the discussion covers the attempt to maneuver a boat at optimum starting speed into one of the best positions as the starting signal is given.

The time just before the start is often the most nerve-racking part of the race. Even the most casual-appearing skipper usually is nervous. If he isn't, the chances are that he is not one of the best starters. The reason for tension and keyed-up emotions at the start is that many boats are fighting for a few top starting positions, and every competent skipper realizes that he is at a disadvantage unless he starts at one of those positions. Races can be won or lost at the start of a short race for small, one-design boats. The start is not that crucial for

a variety of racing-cruiser types sailing a long course, but the skipper of a handicap racer might find that the difference between a good and a bad start would be the equivalent of a change in his rating by almost a foot in an average round-the-buoys race.

In the opinion of many experts, the following are the main considerations for obtaining good starts, listed in order of importance:

1. Acquiring freedom to go where you want immediately after the start (in order to follow the best course strategy).

2. Obtaining clear wind immediately after the start.

3. Being positioned, with right-of-way, at the *favored end* of the starting line at the starting signal.

4. Being close to or at the line with full way as the starting signal is made.

The first consideration will depend, of course, on the overall race plan or strategy. This results from observation and prediction of wind, current, wave conditions, and other factors. These are discussed in Chapter 10.

Clear wind, listed second, is freedom from disturbed

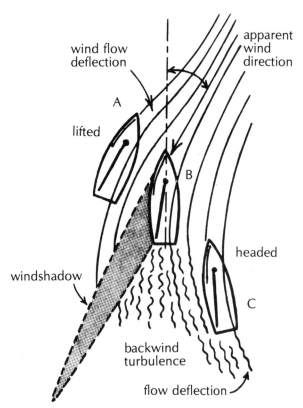

Figure 8-1. BACKWIND AND WINDSHADOW

air in the form of windshadow and especially backwind. In large racing fleets, the "dirty" or disturbed wind in the starting area can have a devastating effect on boat performance. Sails not only make turbulence but also cause a partial absence of wind in their blanketing zone (windshadow), and they bend or deflect the wind at the region ahead of the luff and especially behind the leech. This is shown by the boats beating to windward in Figure 8-1. Boat B's windshadow is the shaded region directly to leeward of the apparent wind. The wind flow is deflected by B so that A is sailing in a lift or favoring wind slant, while boat C is sailing in a header or heading deflection. Successful starts depend very much on the skipper's awareness and understanding of the behavior of disturbed wind.

The third starting consideration recommends that the boat making a good start have the right-of-way. With a windward start, this means starting on the starboard tack and being clear to leeward (not converging with right-of-way boats to leeward). Occasionally, it might pay to make a port-tack start — when, for example, you are making a port-tack approach and the rest of the fleet is late getting to the line, or there is a gap in the group of starboard-tackers through which you can pass to cross the starting line. Usually, in large fleets, a port-tack start is too risky. A rule of thumb is that if you can easi-

ly fetch the mark (or committee boat) while on the starboard tack, you should make a starboard-tack start.

The third consideration also recommends being at the favored end of the line. This means being at the end that is the shortest "sailing distance" to the first turning mark of the course. If the start is downwind, the shortest sailing distance is usually the shortest actual distance, but if the start is to windward (the usual closed-course start), the shortest sailing distance includes tacking, and this is *not always* the shortest actual distance. One end of the line is favored when the line is slanted away from the perpendicular to the *rhumb-line course* (direct, straight-line course) to the first mark when starting downwind, or when the line is slanted away from the perpendicular to the wind direction with a windward start. (This was discussed in Chapter 1.)

Figure 8-2 illustrates how a windward starting line's slant or angle to the wind makes one end favored. Before boats A and B cross the line, the leeward end of the line is favored. After they cross the line, the wind shifts, causing the windward end to be favored. A simple way of determining the favored end just before the start is illustrated by boat C. She is luffing head-to-wind near the middle of the line, and her bow is pointing closer to the leeward than to the windward end of the line, indicating the leeward end is favored at that time. If her bow were pointing nearer to the windward end while she lay head-to-wind, the windward end would be favored. Figure 8-2 shows that a start at the favored end can put a boat far ahead of a competitor starting at the line's opposite end when the wind holds steady. It also shows that a wind shift can quickly change the situation.

The fourth consideration for good starting is obvious. The closer the starting boat is to the line and the faster she is moving, the sooner she will cross the line. However, this is less important than the other considerations. In the interest of reaching the proper side of the course in the quickest time, or in getting clean air, it may pay to make a slow or late start. Generally, boat speed at the start will depend on the size and weight of the boat. Large, heavy boats should have ample headway at all times, because they are relatively slow to accelerate, and they usually need greater speed for best maneuverability and steering control, compared with light-displacement, daggerboard dinghies that can "turn on a dime."

THE WINDWARD START

Windward starts are the ones most frequently encountered when racing over a closed course, and, as said in Chapter 1, the race committee always tries to set the

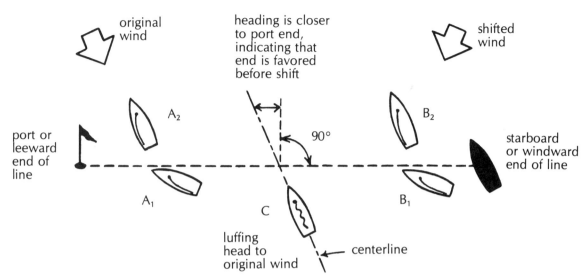

Figure 8-2. FAVORED END OF THE STARTING LINE

line approximately square to the wind. Of course, the committee attempts to position the line with respect to the wind so that neither end is favored and all starting points anywhere along the line are equally attractive. This is the perfect starting line, but, unfortunately, it is an ideal that seldom is achieved, because the wind rarely holds absolutely steady. A last-minute shift usually favors, if only slightly, one end or the other.

All starts are either one or some combination of five types: (1) the timed start, (2) running the line, (3) sitting on the line, (4) dipping, and (5) barging. These are illustrated in Figure 8-3, which shows how the basic types are commonly used when the windward or starboard end of the line is favored and also when the port or leeward end is favored. Many starting situations require a combination of two or more types, such as when a timed start is combined with a sitting or no-headway start, as shown by C + B when the leeward end is favored.

There are several variations of timing a start. In Figure 8-3, situation 2 (leeward end favored), boat B "runs the line" or reaches along the line while the time is taken with a stopwatch as she sails from one end to the other or from one end to the line's middle. It is then known how long it will take for her to get from the middle back to the favored end, after allowing for the time it takes to turn, or, in the case of C + B, after allowing for the boat to pick up speed after way has been lost.

A popular timing method is known as the Vanderbilt system, illustrated in Figure 8-3, situation 1. Boat A crosses the starting line headed away from the first turning mark, 2 minutes and 20 seconds before the starting signal near the location on the line where the start will

be made. It is estimated that the boat can be jibed around in 14 seconds, so this is added to the 2:20 time remaining (until the start), which makes 2:34. This figure is divided in half to give 1:17. The helmsman then steers the boat on a steady course away from the line until there is 1:17 remaining. Then he jibes around to head back for the selected starting spot. After taking 14 seconds to jibe, the boat is allowed 1:03 to return to the line. She should reach it as the starting signal is made, provided there is no current, the wind is steady, and there is no interference from other boats. The boat does not have to cross the starting line headed the wrong way (away from the first mark) at exactly 2:20 before the start. She can cross any time around 2 or 3 minutes (or a greater or lesser time) before the starting signal. It is only necessary that the time remaining be added to the time allowed for jibing or tacking. This figure then is divided by two, which gives the proper time remaining at which the turn should be made. The courses for this kind of start should be, as nearly as possible, beam reaches so that boat speed will be the same leaving as approaching the line.

The Vanderbilt system works well when only a few boats are racing, but today's starts are usually crowded, and the interference of other boats (or, if not of the boats themselves, their disturbed air) nearly always upsets any starting method that relies on precise timing. For all practical purposes, most effective timed starts in crowded fleets result from practice in judging and controlling the boat's speed and from close observation of competitors and the anticipation of their maneuvers. In a crowded fleet it is often wise to begin following a tentative Vanderbilt plan, but if a crowd begins to form in

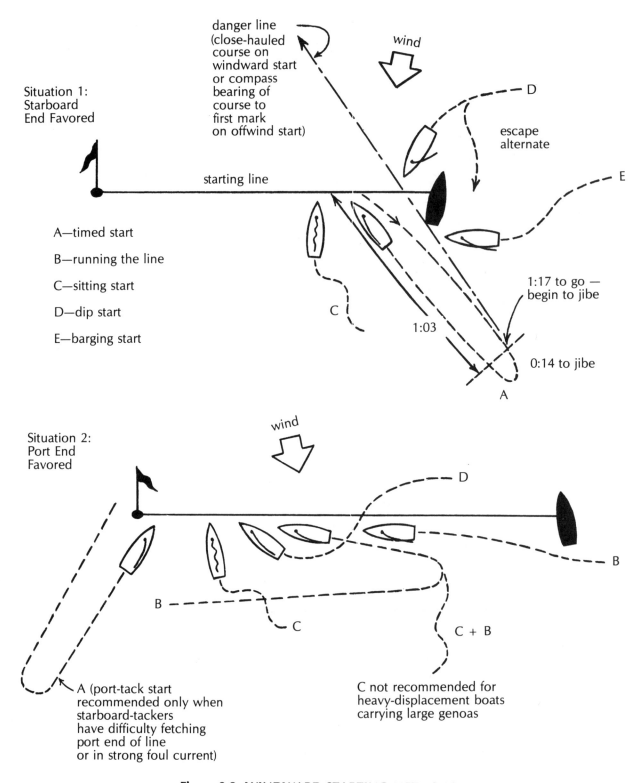

Situation 1:
Starboard
End Favored

danger line
(close-hauled
course on
windward start
or compass
bearing of
course to
first mark
on offwind start)

wind

D

escape
alternate

E

starting line

A—timed start

B—running the line

C—sitting start

D—dip start

E—barging start

C

1:03

1:17 to go —
begin to jibe

0:14 to jibe

A

Situation 2:
Port End
Favored

wind

D

B

B

C

C + B

A (port-tack start
recommended only when
starboard-tackers
have difficulty fetching
port end of line
or in strong foul current)

C not recommended for
heavy-displacement boats
carrying large genoas

Figure 8-3. WINDWARD STARTING METHODS

your selected starting area, make your turn early in order to allow for interference. If that interference never materializes, then your boat's speed can be killed by slacking sheets or sailing a crooked or slightly weaving course.

Running the line, as shown by boat B in Figure 8-3, is the most commonly used start for large racing-cruisers when the leeward end of the line is favored. Although this is not a true timing method, a certain amount of timing is involved with most starting methods. The skipper or helmsman should be informed continually of the time remaining, especially just before the starting signal. In the case of boat B, the skipper should know how long it takes her to reach along the line from one end to the other so that he can best judge when to begin running the line in order to arrive at the selected starting point at gunfire (as the starting signal is made). When the line is crowded, it is wise to begin running the line early to allow for course alterations, and if you find that you are arriving at the starting spot too early, you can slack sheets to reduce speed. The danger in this starting method is that boats to leeward have the right-of-way, and the line-runner could be forced over the line prematurely. For this reason, the run should be made a safe distance to leeward of the line and a careful lookout should be kept for converging boats to leeward.

A popular start for small dinghies is the sitting start (boat C in Figure 8-3). Since small, light-displacement boats can pick up speed or accelerate very rapidly, it is common practice among some small-boat skippers to stay very close to the selected starting spot, keeping very little way on their boats by luffing or slacking sheets. Then, a few seconds before gunfire, they bear off, trim in, and are off with the starting signal. This seldom works with large racing-cruisers because they are relatively slow to pick up speed. When a heavy-displacement boat tries a sitting start, she will more than likely end up a "sitting duck." She is also in a very vulnerable position with boats to leeward, because, before starting, a leeward boat, even if she is behind the mast-abeam position (see Figure 7-8), may luff a windward boat, provided the latter is given the opportunity to keep clear and the luffing is done slowly. However, before her starting signal, the leeward boat behind the mast-abeam position cannot luff above a close-hauled course (see Rule 40). Rule 38.2 (luffing *after* starting) does not allow an overlapped boat to leeward to sail above her proper course while the overlap exists, *if at any time during its existence* the windward boat was ahead of the mast-abeam position, but there is no proper course before the starting signal. The leeward boat forward of "mast abeam" can luff slowly, higher than close-

hauled, even if she had been abaft the mast line (mast-abeam position) when the overlap began. Thus the heavy line-sitter is particularly vulnerable to leeward boats.

The size of the headsails carried on many racing-cruisers is another consideration with line-sitting and being dependent on quick maneuvering and acceleration. A large masthead genoa cannot be tacked or trimmed in as quickly as the jib on a small one-design boat. Furthermore, the genoa with great overlap can get caught aback when the boat is killing way by luffing head-to-wind. However, when there is plenty of open water around the boat, usually several minutes before the start, a large boat can use a modified sitting method (provided some headway is retained) when this method is combined with line-running or a timed start, as shown by C + B in Figure 8-3.

An early, cautious port-tack approach, as illustrated in situation 2 by B or C + B (or farther up the line when the windward end is favored), is an effective means of maneuvering into the desired position for the final starboard-tack charge for the starting line. The early approach on the port tack usually allows maximum room to maneuver in relatively clear air. If the starboard-tackers are late in arriving at the line, the port-tack boat can come about ahead of them, but if they are early, the port-tacker might find a hole or gap astern of the first group of starboard-tack boats through which she can pass to tack. A port-tacker doesn't have the course-altering restrictions of a starboard-tacker (see Rule 34).

The dip start (shown by boats D in the illustration) can be very dangerous, but there are one or two occasions when the method can be effective. As can be seen in the illustration, the dip-starter stays on the wrong side of the line until just before the start, at which time she dips back across to the correct side of the line at or near the desired starting location. The principal danger in this kind of start is in not being able to find a space or hole into which to dip. Obviously, the dipper has no rights over boats to leeward. This kind of start might be effective when there is a strong current with the wind that causes most conventional starters to be late in reaching the line.

A commonly used dip start for small boats is shown in situation 1, where the windward end is favored and the committee boat is at that end. In this case, there is often a small, semiprotected area into which a small boat can dip, but this is not always true for a big boat. The large boat cannot maneuver as quickly and needs more space than a small one. The large boat might attempt a dip method, however, if she leaves an escape opening, as shown by D (alternate) in situation 1. In this case, D maneuvers some distance to weather of the committee boat, and when it appears that the starting fleet will be late, she dips. If there is no room, she jibes over while still to weather of the committee boat and makes a barging start similar to the start of boat E.

One of the most commonly used and overused starts is the barging start (boat E). Before beginning to race, and especially before attempting a barging start, the novice skipper should thoroughly acquaint himself with the antibarging rule (USYRU Rule 42.4). This is an important exception to the rule that requires an outside overlapped boat to give room to an inside boat at a mark of the course (see Rule 42). When the windward end of the line is favored, and a boat approaches the mark at that end to windward of the starboard-tack, close-hauled course (or compass bearing of the first mark on an offwind start), as illustrated by the dot-dash line in Figure 8-3, she is said to be barging, and she cannot claim room from an overlapped leeward boat. Before the starting signal, the leeward boat may slowly luff above her close-hauled course if she is forward of the mast line, but after the starting signal before crossing the line, the leeward boat may not deprive the windward boat of room by sailing above her close-hauled course (or by heading above the first mark on an offwind start). However, if she is near enough to the starting-line mark, she may be able, while holding a proper close-hauled course (or a course to the first mark on an offwind start), to prevent an overlapped windward boat from squeezing in on the correct side of the mark. Of course, after crossing the line, normal luffing rights after starting (Rule 38) become effective.

Barging is legal if there is room to leeward of the barger, but when there is no room, the barger must kill way or circle to wait for a gap between the mark and the boats to leeward of the mark. Barging starts are risky when the windward end of the line is crowded, but the method can be effective: (1) when there are not many boats, (2) in light airs, when it is wise to stay near the line and approach it on a fast reach, and (3) when it is desired for strategy purposes to get to the right-hand side of the course in the quickest time. It is common practice to barge on leeward (offwind) starts also. In this case, the danger line (shown in Figure 8-3) is the course from the windward end of the line to the first mark.

On a crowded, well-set, windward starting line (set nearly square to the wind), boats will be fairly distributed along the line from one end to the other. Leeward boats, especially the one farthest to leeward, will be at a disadvantage if the correct course lies to the right-hand side of the race course. However, if the correct course is to port, the leeward boats (especially the one farthest to leeward) will benefit in two ways: by being closer to the correct side of the course, and by having clear wind yet the capability of backwinding windward competitors. A standard technique for obtaining clear wind is illustrated by boat A in the line's middle in Figure 8-4. Boat A slowly luffs boat B, to windward of her, in order to widen her starting space and to move farther to windward of C. Before losing too much headway, A bears off onto her proper course, and her skipper hopes she is mostly clear of C's backwind. Boat D has an ideal start *if* a lifting shift is expected or if she is especially close-winded and can work to weather of B's backwind. However, D would be hurt by a header and would have to tack at the first opportunity.

The boats farthest to windward have an advantage in that they are not boxed in or trapped by windward boats. Thus, they can soon tack to clear their wind. If the correct strategic course lies to starboard, they can come about and hold on the port tack. But if the correct course lies to port, a windward boat can take a short *hitch* (*board* or tack) for wind-clearing purposes, but then return immediately to the starboard tack, as shown by boat E in Figure 8-4. Boat F, farthest to leeward, should have the theoretical advantage over all boats to windward when clear wind is the only consideration, but a heading shift could prevent her from fetching the leeward end of the line, while a lifting shift would cause her to lose sailing distance on her windward competitors.

It is the safest policy not to aim for the starting spot farthest to leeward or windward, because of this windshift risk in the former case, and because, at the most windward spot, there is danger that a wind shift or a competitor's luff will put you in a barging position. If the committee boat happens to be at the leeward end, the most leeward boat has the added danger of being trapped in the "coffin corner," as described in Chapter 1 (Figure 1-7). A leeward starter sailing into this trap ought to jibe around and attempt a port-tack start behind or through a gap in the starboard-tackers. On crowded lines, safe yet advantageous starting spots are often found in the vicinity of a sixth of the line's distance, or slightly less, from either end, depending on which side is correct for the course strategy and which end is the most favored when considering minimum sailing distance to the first mark.

LEEWARD STARTS

Most race committees will try to set a windward starting line, but on a point-to-point course, it is not always

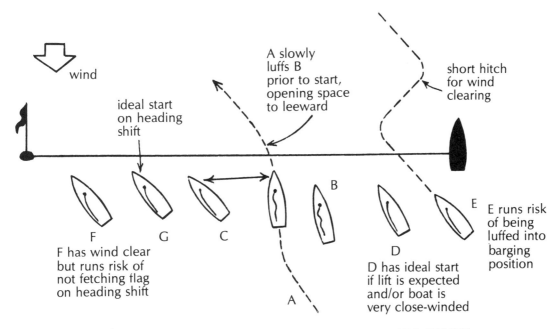

Figure 8-4. OBTAINING CLEAR AIR ON WINDWARD STARTS

possible to start dead to windward. Thus, the skipper of a racing-cruiser who will compete in distance races can expect more than a few leeward or offwind starts.

The most serious wind disturbance is caused by backwind on the windward start, but on downwind starts, the effects of blanketing gain in relative importance. As said in Chapter 1, the race committee usually gives the reaching starting line a considerable slant away from the perpendicular to the rhumb-line course, with the leeward end being set closer than the windward end to its first mark. This is an attempt to spread boats evenly along the line. If the line were set square to the rhumb-line course, boats would jam at the windward end in order to avoid windshadows and at the same time to blanket their leeward competitors. However, if the line is slanted sufficiently, the leeward boats will be slightly ahead of the windshadows of competitors getting equally good starts to windward. An important point concerning windshadows is that they lie directly to leeward of the *apparent* wind. Since boats move slowly in light air, the windshadows often lie farther forward in light winds than in heavy winds — but not always.

Figure 8-5 shows examples of two boats — high-performance, displacement racing-cruisers — with one sailing above and the other below a beam reach. Approximate but typical speed curves, similar to those shown in the polar diagram in Figure 7-6, are labeled on the right-hand side of the diagram. They show relative speeds on all points of sailing in light and heavy breezes.

Under the low-sailing boat, the light-air windshadow lies slightly forward of the heavy-air windshadow, as might be expected, but the opposite is true with the close-reaching boat. This is the case because optimum speeds lie above the beam reach in light winds but below the beam reach in heavy winds, and also because the apparent wind results from the relativity of boat speed to true wind speed. Some dinghy sailors new to racing-cruisers might not fully appreciate that a displacement boat, unlike a boat that planes easily, often has her heavy-air windshadow ahead of her light-air shadow. Of course, a close scrutiny of wind indicators will be most helpful in this matter.

When starting at the leeward end of the line on a reaching start, the skipper should be sure he is ahead of the windshadow of boats to windward, and that his course will be one of optimum speed or at least in a farther-off-the-wind and divergent direction, to avoid being blanketed. Of course, windward starters should try to blanket boats to leeward provided they don't become engaged in costly luffing matches.

The speed curves in Figure 8-5 suggest that, on a near beam reaching start, a course slightly higher than a beam reach should be favored in light airs, but one slightly lower than the beam reach should be favored in heavy winds. Light- and heavy-wind reaching starts are shown in Figure 8-6. In light winds, when the line is slanted adequately toward the first mark, boat A, starting at the line's leeward end, will probably pull ahead of

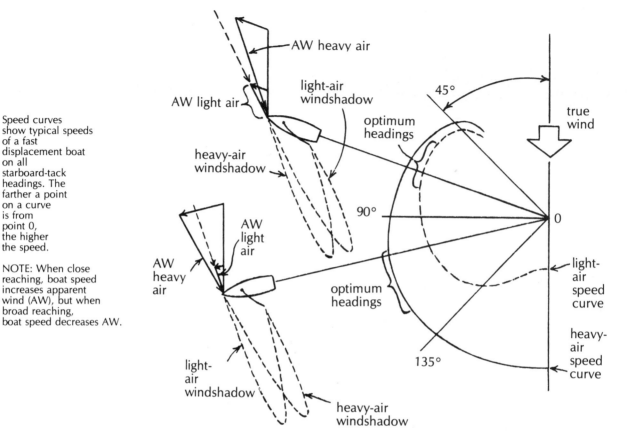

Speed curves show typical speeds of a fast displacement boat on all starboard-tack headings. The farther a point on a curve is from point 0, the higher the speed.

NOTE: When close reaching, boat speed increases apparent wind (AW), but when broad reaching, boat speed decreases AW.

Figure 8-5. SPEED CURVES AND WINDSHADOWS

B starting at the other end, provided wind and current are the same for both and that boat speeds are the same on identical points of sailing. In heavy winds, however, the opposite is the case. The odds are that boat B at the windward end will take the start and soon put A in her windshadow, especially if the line is not slanted adequately. Also, B will have a slightly better chance to set her spinnaker than will A. Before the start, wind conditions at both ends of the line should be observed carefully. If the windward end is near a shore, there might be a partial lee or disturbed area near that end. When the wind is light and particularly if the current is foul (against you), *stay close to the line*. However, if the wind is light but the current fair, keep a good distance directly upcurrent of the line to avoid being swept by or over the line in case the breeze dies. Under such conditions, the anchor should be rigged and available for instant use.

An important consideration for handicap racers on any kind of start is relative boat performance due to variations in size and design. We will talk about this in more detail when we discuss tactics, but suffice it to say that before the start, the competition should be "sized up." Obviously, it would be unwise to start slightly to windward and behind a very close-winded competitor that could work across your bow on a windward start. It would also be unwise to start just ahead and to leeward of a larger, faster boat that would soon pass to windward, giving you a devastating dose of bad air. This risk must be weighed carefully before making a leeward-end reaching start in a small boat.

On near beam reaching starts, the Vanderbilt start often works well, because speed sailing away from the line should be nearly equal to the speed sailing back to the line. However, on downwind as well as upwind starts, some allowance in timing must be made for maneuvering to avoid other boats when the line is crowded.

Since broad reaching and running starts involve carrying the spinnaker, the time of setting and the manner of carrying this sail are the critical factors. More often than not on reaching starts, it is best to delay setting the spinnaker until immediately after the start. This is especially true for less experienced skippers. The delay allows maximum freedom to maneuver and the ability to luff competitors carrying spinnakers. Often a well-timed, leeward-end start, when the wind is not too far aft, allows the boat carrying a large jib to luff and completely collapse the 'chutes of her rivals to windward. Of course, the boat carrying her jib should have her spinnaker rigged and ready to break out or set at a moment's notice.

Consideration of course strategy is important with downwind starting, even though the first turning mark can be fetched. A straight rhumb-line course seldom is the fastest one, because a boat should be sailed, whenever possible, on her fastest points of sailing in the regions of most favorable current and wind. Thus, it is also important on a leeward start to avoid getting "boxed in" at the wrong end of the line. Think in terms of having freedom to go where you want to go immediately after starting. If the first leg of the course is a long, close reach, it will probably pay to start to leeward, bear off slightly, and foot rather than pinch up. The footing boat to leeward will profit by a lifting shift, which will enable her to ease sheets for more speed. She will profit by a significant heading shift because this will put the windward boats farther behind her. More is said of this in the discussion of strategy in Chapter 10.

Following is a list of preparations and suggestions for starting for the beginner:

1. Arrive at the starting area at least a half hour before the start for your class.

2. Observe the wind, weather, current, and the starts of classes ahead of yours. Check the current at the buoy end of the line.

3. Study the race circular and current tables, lay out the course on the chart, and write down the compass direction of each rhumb-line course.

4. Size up the competition. Determine your most dangerous competitors, consider the performance characteristics of rival boats, try to estimate where they will start, and observe what sails they are carrying.

5. Set your own sails early, to smooth out wrinkles and make the proper adjustments. Rig telltales and wind indicators. Locate and lay out all gear that will be needed.

6. Plan the overall course strategy. Let this be the first consideration in planning the start.

7. Try to determine where there will be the cleanest air. Observe where boats are bunched in classes starting ahead of yours.

8. Luff head-to-wind to determine the favored end. Note your heading on the compass. Then luff up five minutes or so later and note the compass heading to

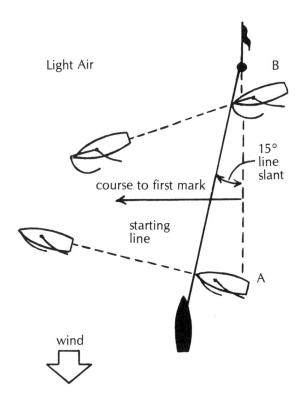

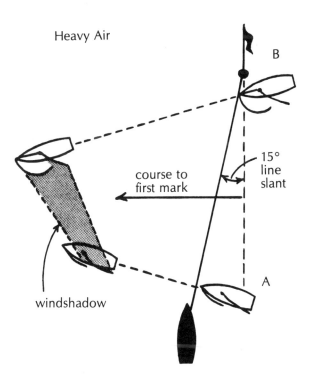

Figure 8-6. REACHING STARTS

determine whether the wind has shifted. Keep track of the shifts.

9. Run the line and take your time from one end to the other.

10. Be informed of the time continually. Especially just before the starting signal, a timer should call out time remaining to the helmsman, and another crewmember should watch the signals.

11. Start on the starboard tack unless there is an obvious advantage in a port-tack start.

12. Be very cautious with a barging or dip start, and always look for boats to leeward. Check the race circular to see that there is no *five-minute rule* or some variation of it. This is an occasionally used special rule that forbids crossing the line or its extensions after the preparatory signal.

13. In most cases, during a windward start, don't try for the extreme end of the line but aim for spots a few boat lengths closer to the line's middle.

14. With large, heavy boats, especially, keep ample headway for best maneuverability and starting speed.

15. If you are late for the start, bear off and crack sheets for maximum speed.

16. If you are a little early, pinch *slightly,* let the sails luff, or sail a crooked, weaving course. In small boats, the jib sometimes is backed to kill way, but this can be risky for a large boat with a large genoa. In this case, it is better to slack the main to kill way. Try to trim in and pick up speed well before the starting signal.

17. Favor the timed or modified timed start with a large, heavy boat, especially with reaching starts or when the line is not overly crowded.

18. Consider an early port-tack approach when there is bunching at the windward end during a windward start.

19. If using the Vanderbilt system, turn slightly sooner than you normally would when the starting area is congested.

20. Never get far away from the starting area, and in light airs stay close to the line.

21. Be very cautious of current in light air. Stay up-current of the line and have the anchor ready for instant use.

22. In most cases, avoid the middle of a line on a windward start, because one end is usually favored and there is a chance of becoming trapped or boxed-in at the middle.

23. When starting to windward on a crowded line, try to open up space by luffing the boat slowly to windward and working away from the boat to leeward.

24. If a boat slightly ahead and to leeward luffs up a great deal and you are moving fast, consider reaching off under her stern at top speed.

25. Auxiliary engines must be shut off before the preparatory signal, but in light airs be sure to utilize your legally allowed engine time to maneuver into the most advantageous position.

26. On downwind starts, try to blanket competitors, but avoid luffing matches. Have the spinnaker ready to set, but when reaching, it is the safest policy to delay the set until immediately after the start.

27. Always have a crewmember looking out for boats that may be blocked from view by the genoa. On a big boat, just before starting, have him stationed in the bow pulpit so that he can sight down the starting line to be sure you are not over the line early.

9/ Sailing Technique

Since it is assumed that the reader is familiar with the fundamentals of sailing and boat handling, this chapter will try to emphasize some of the finer and most important points pertaining to racing helmsmanship and sail handling. Although some sailors feel that seamanship occasionally must be compromised to win a race, and it is true that there sometimes is a fine line between risky sailing and optimum performance, this book follows the philosophy that sound, safe, and efficient sailing techniques not only are the most prudent but nearly always produce the most speed.

HELMSMANSHIP

Let's consider the helm itself. A well-balanced boat with a light, sensitive, and responsive helm encourages good helmsmanship. On the other hand, a poorly balanced boat with a heavy helm that lacks "feel" seldom can be sailed up to her optimum to windward or downwind. A boat that "steers like a truck" may be sailed like one.

Helm response and feel will depend on such matters as helm balance; size, type, and location of the rudder; hull size, weight, and shape; mechanical advantage of the wheel, or length of the tiller, and so forth. We have already talked about balance, certain aspects of wheel-versus-tiller steering, and rudder design. It should be sufficient to state that the following conditions should be met to encourage the best helmsmanship:

1. Most boats should have a *slight* weather helm when beating in moderate breezes at optimum angles of heel. As a general rule, boats with rudders attached to their keels should carry more weather helm than boats with rudders separated from their keels. However, the helm should never be so unbalanced that it stalls the rudder on a beat, and, of course, this should be avoided whenever possible on any point of sailing. Semibalanced spade rudders should have very little weather helm, and a lee helm should never be tolerated. It should only be necessary for the helmsman to push *or* pull the helm (depending on which side of the boat he is occupying), but not to *both* push *and* pull the helm when beating in

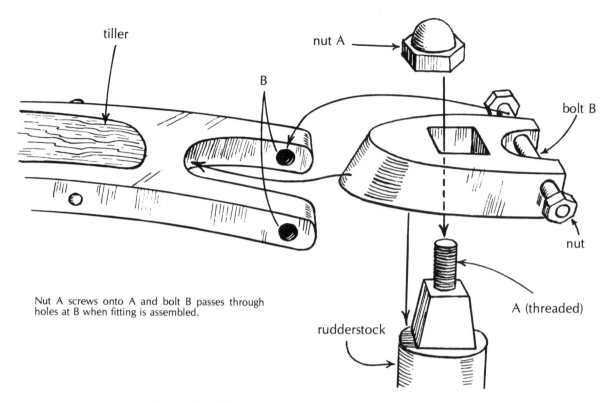

Nut A screws onto A and bolt B passes through holes at B when fitting is assembled.

Figure 9-1. TILLER–RUDDERSTOCK CONNECTION

A generous-sized wheel allows the helms-man to sit to one side, where he can see the jib. The main's flattening reef and the roller on the baby stay allow the jib to slide around it easily during a tack. (From Sail and Power, *Third Edition)*

A tiller extension folded back when not in use. The lines on the tiller are attached to the jibsheet and shock cord for self-steering.

smooth waters. Corrections for imperfect balance have been discussed.

2. Small rudders and long tillers make the helm light and easy to handle, but when this is overdone, the rudder tends to stall easily, and steering control and quick response are sacrificed. Conversely, large rudders and short tillers make a heavy but effective helm. Obviously, there must be a happy medium. Instant helm response is needed when sailing downwind in heavy seas with a spinnaker set. For this reason the rudder should be well aft, the tiller should be located where it will not be obstructed, and a wheel should not have too much mechanical advantage (perhaps three-fourths to one full turn from rudder on-center to hard over for a small yacht, as shown in Figure 4-8).

3. Helm mechanisms (gears, cable sheaves, etc.) should be well lubricated for smooth operation, and "play," or looseness, in the tiller should not be tolerated. Figure 9-1 illustrates an effective tiller-rudderstock connection. A square hole through the tiller fits over the square end of the rudderstock. There is a short threaded section with a nut (A in the diagram) just above the squared part of the stock. The squared section is tapered so that when looseness develops in the connection, nut A may be tightened to force the tiller farther down on the stock to eliminate the play. The helmsman should take care, however, to see that the assembly is such that tightening the nut will not draw the entire rudder upward so that it binds or rubs against the hull or fairing piece between the rudder's head and the hull. Many tillers of the type illustrated are fitted

with a bolt and nut, shown at location B, to tighten or control the vertical motion of the tiller handle. This should be kept tight also. It is always wise to inspect the rudder carefully each time the boat is hauled or slipped to see that the rudder has not warped and that there is no binding of the rudderstock, jamming in the hard-over position, or excessive play at the gudgeons. A loose tiller or a binding rudder not only may be unsafe but also can be damaging to optimum helmsmanship.

Different kinds of boats require slightly different helm techniques when beating to windward. The most effective technique can be determined only after complete familiarity with one's boat and considerable practice and experience racing in various conditions of wind and sea. With some boats, it pays to foot off slightly or sail full and by, to gain speed and lessen leeway. With other boats, however, it may be best to pinch up slightly to gain distance to windward if the costs in leeway and speed are not too great. The important considerations when beating, regardless of the amount of leeway, are the boat's actual course and her speed, which shows her speed made good (Vmg), or her actual progress dead to windward. Some boats respond well to the feathering technique (pinching up sharply in the puffs to reduce heel and gain distance to windward), but others do not. A slow, easy action on the helm is most suitable for some boats, but others react well to a quicker response to headers and lifts. You must get to know your own boat.

In general, when the forefoot is deep and sharp and there is ample draft and lateral plane, the boat might be sailed very close to the wind, provided she has an efficient sailplan. On the other hand, a boat with a full entrance and soft (shallow) forefoot, with below-normal draft, generally should be sailed full and by. Heavy keel boats with deep, narrow hulls that make large waves at high speeds should be pointed high in good winds. Beamy centerboarders usually should not be pinched, at least to the extent that they make considerable leeway, because this causes great forward resistance, especially in a seaway. In smooth water, however, some centerboarders with deep, high-aspect-ratio, dagger-type boards can point very high when they have sufficient speed. Any boat with a very short board or keel is apt to make leeway at slow speeds, particularly after tacking or in light airs with motorboat swells, so they should never be pinched at those times. Heavy boats with long keels and large rudders should be sailed with a gentle, easy helm action, whereas light fin-keelers can be turned much more quickly. The former type should be tacked slowly and allowed to forereach a good distance in some cases, but, comparatively speaking, the latter might almost be slammed about in a moderate wind with smooth water.

Regardless of boat type, beating almost always involves some sort of a weaving, up-and-down helm action when attempting to avoid the rougher waves, conforming to changes of wind velocities and brief shifts, and also when alternately prodding the wind to gain distance upwind and then bearing away to pick up speed when the boat begins to slow. When the wind is fresh, puffy, and shifting rapidly, the helmsman who anticipates and responds instantly to each fluctuation in the wind can gain considerable distance to windward over the relatively steady helmsman who turns the boat slowly to meet only the more definite fluctuations — *provided* the boat can tolerate the quick helm treatment.

The best windward helmsmen, whether or not they are fully aware of it, make use of nearly all their senses. They *watch* the luff telltales and the luffs of sails (especially the jib) for lifting or fluttering, *watch* the fluctuations of wind indicators, *watch* the waves and puffs on the water, *watch* for changes in jibstay sag, *feel* the liveliness of the boat, *feel* the changes in pressure on the helm, *feel* the changes of wind direction and velocity on the face and neck, *feel and see* any changes in angle of heel, *listen* to leech flutters and the rattle of sail slides indicating a fluttering luff, *listen* to the sound of breaking seas, *listen* to the splash of the bow wave, and even *listen* to the rush of water along the rail and the hiss of the quarter wave. It is especially important that the racing-cruiser helmsman develop his senses and not rely merely on vision, because distance racing often involves sailing at night and occasionally in fog.

In this age of scientific gadgetry, the sailor has not been neglected. Computers figure optimum headings, sensors measure pressure on the sails, and apparent-water indicators monitor flow around the keel. In the interest of simplicity and economy, however, I am not in favor of overloading a boat with expensive gadgets. Furthermore, they can distract a helmsman from giving his full attention to steering. Sailor-builder-designer Bill Luders recently wrote me: "On a well-organized boat, I am sure instrumentation helps, but when the helmsman tries to do too much, he often loses his concentration and doesn't sail the boat as well as he should."

The most basic instruments needed are a good speedometer, apparent-wind indicator, and anemometer. These are not essential, but they are particularly helpful at night and on long-distance races when no competitors are in sight. The anemometer measures the velocity of the apparent wind, and it is most useful in determining what sails to carry and when to change sail. The transducer assembly is usually at the masthead, where wind speeds normally will be higher than at the deck level. Wind strength indicated on the dial depends on the heading of the boat, and the apparent wind, obviously, is much stronger when beating than when running.

Wind direction, of course, can be shown with telltales and simple masthead flies, such as the excellent Windex (see accompanying photo), but electronic indicators with dials at a low level easily readable from the cockpit save the helmsman from getting a crick in his neck from glancing up constantly at the masthead. Especially useful are the devices, such as those made by Kenyon, that have a close-hauled indicator expanding the scale between 0 and 45 degrees for easy reading when beating to windward (see Figure 9-2). Wind-direction indicators are necessary to obtain the full value from the apparent-wind polar diagram supplied by a designer or the MHS (see Figure 7-6).

A good speedometer is of value not only to the helmsman but also to sail trimmers. There are a number of different types of underwater transducers, such as strain-gauge wands, impellers, Pitot tubes, and even a system that detects changes in water temperature. The kind I prefer, however, is the paddlewheel type of impeller, such as the one made by Signet, because of its accuracy combined with economy, low drag, and resistance to catching seaweed. It also generates its own electricity and thus needs no battery. One disadvantage is that the paddlewheel is sensitive to marine growth, but the impeller can be withdrawn into the boat for cleaning without much difficulty.

Dials for the instruments generally are mounted on the after side of the cabin trunk or above the compan-

Wind direction can be determined with the masthead-mounted Windex. Some models are available with masthead lights. (Courtesy Davis Instruments Corporation)

Kenyon apparent-wind indicator   close-hauled indicator

(Courtesy Kenyon Marine)

ionway. The dials should be illuminated at night with dim red lights, since red light does not inhibit night vision.

Another instrument particularly valuable for sailing at night is the inclinometer, an inexpensive, simple device made of either a rigid plumb bob or a ball in an oil-filled, curved, glass tube. It gives the boat's angle of heel. All boats have heeling angles that cannot be exceeded without harm to their speed. These vary with different boats and sea conditions, and the critical angles must be learned by monitoring the speedometer carefully.

An important consideration for the racing helmsman in some popular yachting areas is a technique for sailing in motorboat swells. There is a plethora of boats under power during the weekends, and they can cause a very confused sea. Whenever possible, it is best, especially in light airs, to take a course that avoids frequently traveled powerboat tracks. It would be helpful if there were an educational program to inform powerboat owners of the harm they can do to a racing fleet through disturbance not only of the water but also of the wind. Of course, sailboat skippers cannot expect complete absence of interference, but they have the right to expect a displacement motorboat passing close by to slow down and pass astern. Nearly all racing yachts now fly racing or class flags on their backstays and bow pulpits, so it is not difficult to recognize when a sailboat is participating in a formal race.

beta light

beta light

counterbalance

shroud

distance apart gives apparent wind angle

Figure 9-2. WIND-DIRECTION INDICATORS
(From *Better Sailing*)

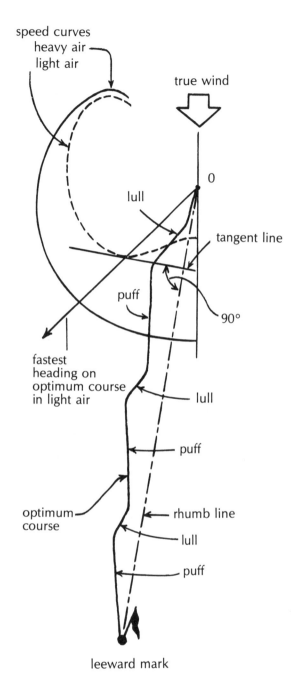

speed curves
heavy air
light air

true wind

0

lull

tangent line

puff

90°

fastest
heading on
optimum course
in light air

lull

puff

optimum
course

rhumb line

lull

puff

leeward mark

NOTE: The fastest light-air heading for the rhumb-line course is found by drawing a line from point 0 (the course beginning) through the point where the tangent line touches the light-air speed curve.

Figure 9-3. DOWNWIND STEERING

Sailing in a seaway, especially a confused sea, is a technique that can be learned only through practice. In general, the boat should be sailed full and by and should be worked to weather only in the relatively smooth spots. In good breezes, however, it often pays to luff into a steep sea to gain distance to windward and then to bear off quickly to gain speed as the wave passes under the hull. Sails should be cut full and held securely against slatting. Sheets must be alternately eased in and out when pitching in powerboat swells, in order to damp the waves' jolting effect and to allow for the sudden changes in apparent wind caused by the pitching. Lightweight drifter-type jibs are good in light airs, because they fill out quickly after collapsing in confused seas.

Masthead wind indicators can be a great aid when the water is not too rough, but they often are useless in a confused seaway because of their oscillations when the boat rolls and pitches. Indicators with heavy counterbalance weights may behave better in such conditions with their weights lightened or removed. Before crossing a particularly sizable powerboat wake, it is a good idea (when it fits in with the strategy) to tack just before reaching the disturbed wind and water. The slap of the waves under the counter can be helpful. Of course, in light airs and confused seas, the boat should be heeled slightly to leeward and allowed to foot with eased sheets. Heavy-displacement boats with large sail areas often have the advantage in these conditions, because they have the momentum to carry through a rough patch of water if they are kept moving.

When sailing downwind, it seldom pays to run off dead before the wind except in heavy winds. The skipper should try to determine and utilize those points of sailing that give optimum speeds at various wind velocities. Generally, the lighter the wind, the higher the boat should be sailed. This can be seen clearly by studying the polar diagram in Figure 7-6. Optimum points of sailing can be used by "working" the boat to leeward, or, in other words, using the technique of bearing off in puffs and heading higher in lulls. This method of steering downwind is illustrated in Figure 9-3, which relates the weaving course to light- and heavy-air speed curves. As mentioned before, the farther any point on a curve is from the central point 0, the faster the speed.

It can be seen that optimum speeds are on considerably higher points of sailing in light airs than in heavy winds, especially when the wind is well aft. Thus, the weaving course illustrated is faster than the rhumb-line course, because advantage is being taken of variations in wind velocity. If the wind is gradually freshening, it may help initially to stay high of the rhumb-line course, and, conversely, if the wind is growing lighter, it may help to stay low initially so that later you can sail higher as the wind lightens. When the wind is shifty, it may pay, in addition to working to leeward, to "tack downwind," a method of broad reaching on an optimum point of sailing on one tack, then jibing over, and broad reaching on the other tack. We shall discuss this in the next chapter when we talk about strategy. Spinnaker helmsmanship is discussed later.

TACKING TECHNIQUE

On American racing-cruisers, the large genoa jib is still the most commonly used headsail for beating in all but the lightest and heaviest winds. Thus, proper handling of the genoa is a must in developing an efficient tacking technique. The difference between good and poor handling of this sail when coming about can mean a difference of many boat lengths in distance gained to windward.

If the boat is of medium size or larger, the crew should be organized so that one man is stationed forward just prior to tacking in order to help the genoa around the mast when the boat is head to wind. Two men are stationed at the large sheet winch that will be taking in the genoa on the new tack. One of these men will be the *cranker* (one who turns the winch handle) and the other will be a *tailer* (one who pulls and keeps tension on the tail of the sheet while it is being cranked in). Another crewmember — perhaps the helmsman on a small racing-cruiser — slacks off the genoa sheet on the boat's opposite side just before she is turned into the wind.

It is important that the man slacking the sheet not do it too fast or too suddenly, because this can kill the boat's momentum. In most cases, the sheet should be eased when the boat is head-to-wind or nearly so. At this point, the man stationed forward quickly gathers in the foot of the sail, pulling it forward so that it will clear the shrouds and mast. As the boat turns through the eye of the wind, the jib blows through the space between the mast and the jibstay. The tailer at the leeward winch has perhaps two or three turns on the winch with the sheet, and he begins pulling in the sheet, hand over hand, as quickly as possible while the man forward comes aft to help by pulling aft on the clew of the genoa. This is a very critical point in the tacking maneuver, because if the tailer can gather in the sheet fast enough before the sail begins to fill, he can save a great deal of time that would have to be spent slowly cranking in the sail. When the jib fills, the tailer quickly flips more turns

around the winch. The cranker quickly inserts the handle and begins to crank by turning the handle all the way around in circles until he tires. Then he ratchets with a back-and-forth motion or, with a two-speed winch, reverses direction, turning the handle in complete circles the opposite way, until he runs out of steam, and then ratchets for the last few inches of trim. Some winchers put the handle in the winch while the sheet is being pulled in hand over hand (before cranking is begun). This saves the time of inserting the handle, but it means the line can slip on the winch unless extra turns are put on the winch initially or cranking is halted temporarily to put on extra wraps. The latter alternative wastes time, and if too many wraps are put on initially, the turns are apt to override, which will ruin the tack completely.

The helmsman can be a great help to the jib trimmers by bearing away fast after passing through the wind's eye so that the jib can blow through the slot with its leech clear of the spreaders. Then the helmsman can momentarily reverse the helm to slow the turning speed and thereafter turn slowly in order to facilitate rapid trimming. This is illustrated in Figure 9-4. Exact helm technique will vary with individual boats. Large, heavy boats should be allowed to forereach by turning slowly in order to gain distance to windward, but small, light-displacement boats should be turned more quickly because they lose speed faster. Regardless of boat type, however, the basic principle illustrated in Figure 9-4 should nearly always be used. As the boat is turned toward the wind, the apparent wind draws farther aft (relative to the true wind) as a result of the loss of speed and the side wind created by the boat's turning. This is one reason it is important not to cast off the jibsheet until nearly head-to-wind. When tacking a light-air, doublehead rig, it helps to cast off the staysail sheet when beyond head-to-wind. The backed staysail will help turn the boat and allow the jib topsail to slide quickly around the staysail.

The apparent wind is also quite far aft just after the boat completes the tack but before she picks up speed. For this reason it is important not to sheet the jib in as flat as it is normally carried to windward until the boat gains full headway. Also, the mainsheet should be eased temporarily at this time. If there is a crewmember assigned to slacking the jibsheet at the beginning of the tacking operation, he may next switch over to slacking the main. Mainsheet slacking is often neglected on racing-cruisers, but the practice can be effective on small boats. In one respect this should be even more effective on a large boat, which takes longer to accelerate. The person who slacks the jib, however, should see that

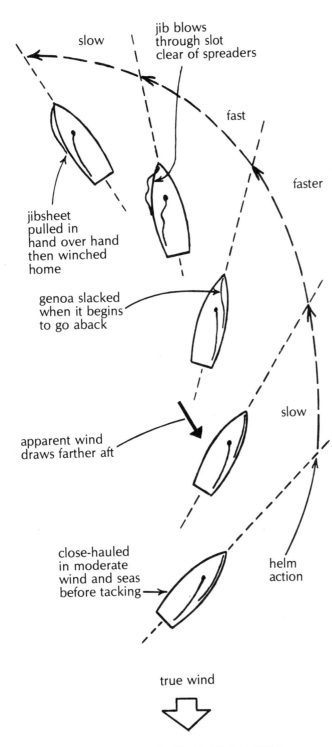

slow

jib blows
through slot
clear of spreaders

fast

faster

jibsheet
pulled in
hand over hand
then winched
home

genoa slacked
when it begins
to go aback

slow

apparent wind
draws farther aft

close-hauled
in moderate
wind and seas
before tacking

helm
action

true wind

Figure 9-4. TACKING TECHNIQUE

the jibsheet is entirely clear before he leaves it. There is nothing that can ruin a good tack faster than having the windward sheet foul or jam in its lead block.

Good, free-turning shroud rollers (*thin* tubes of wood, metal, or plastic that fit over the lower part of the outboard shrouds) can prevent chafe and help speed up tacking, because they reduce the friction caused by the genoa and its sheet dragging across the shrouds. Be sure that the jibsheet shackle is not a kind that will foul on the shrouds and be sure it cannot come open when the sail is thrashing violently. In a fresh breeze, it is a good idea to lash the shackles closed. Some sailors (including myself) prefer to tie their jibsheets to the sail with bowlines, mainly to prevent a flogging shackle from hitting anyone. Bowlines are effective knots that will not jam and can be removed quickly, but if they are used in a fresh breeze, be sure the sheet is heavy enough, because a bowline can reduce the strength of a line by almost 50 percent. A tied-on sheet obviously is beneficial in light airs, because it eliminates the weight of a shackle, and the sheet can be light, despite the fact that its strength is reduced by knotting.

SHORTENING DOWN AND CHANGING SAILS

For optimum racing performance, boats should have their sailplan and area matched to the strength of wind. Obviously, in light airs the greatest possible area and the lightest-weight headsails will be carried. In moderate winds, large but heavier jibs are carried. When it really breezes up, sail should be reduced to prevent excessive heeling or broaching-to when running. If weather helm becomes excessive, or the lee rail becomes buried, it is definitely time to shorten sail. Of course, on a short leg during a race, this might be too costly if the sail-reducing operation is slow. Thus it might pay to slack off the main temporarily and let it luff temporarily until rounding the turning mark, if the next leg provides a better opportunity to alter the sailplan.

Shifting jibs is simplified and little time is wasted with a double-groove luff foil. The main advantage of this system is that it is not necessary to lower one sail before its replacement is hoisted (when there are two halyards), but luff foils are not without problems. The boltrope can jam in its groove and the original jib can stick to its replacement when the sails are wet. Jamming can be alleviated by using multiple feeders, made with a special feeder ring or two lashed below the standard feeder box (see Figure 5-3), and if necessary having a crewmember help the sail into the feeder. When sails stick together, it helps to get air between them by slacking the sheet of the

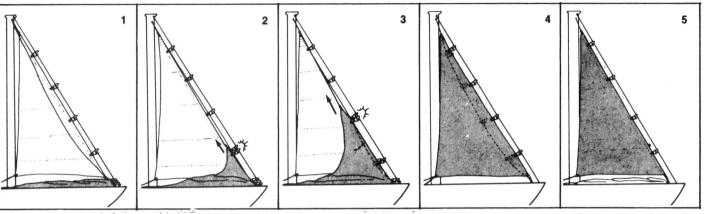

Figure 9-5. HOIST-RELEASE JIB HANK   (Courtesy Nicro Corporation)

leeward jib and perhaps luffing a bit. Another problem is that the luff is partly detached when the sail is raised or lowered, so it is helpful if the inboard jib can be hoisted or doused. This might be arranged by coming about just before a sail change is made. Nets or a network of light lines should connect the forward lifelines to the rail so that lowered sails will not slide overboard.

When your boat has a conventional, hanked-on jib, it can be changed most efficiently when beating by hanking on the replacement jib beneath the standing jib, laying out its foot along the windward rail, tying (or snapping) on the windward sheet, and then coming about slowly. While the boat is head-to-wind, the standing jib is lowered and its hanks are unsnapped as it comes down. The halyard is transferred quickly (if there is only one), and the replacement jib is hoisted quickly as the boat fills away on the new tack. With practice, this method is remarkably quick. Changing jibs while sailing downwind usually is not difficult, because the spinnaker can be hoisted, and a "baldheaded" sail change seldom is necessary.

Not long ago, a "hoist-release" jib hank was developed by Nicro Fico, enabling the lowered, hanked-on replacement jib to be hoisted without first lowering the standing jib. When the replacement is hoisted, its top hank strikes and releases the bottom hank of the standing jib, then releases the next hank, and so on up the jib, which falls free of the headstay (see Figure 9-5). I have not used this system, so I can't vouch for its efficiency, but it sounds like a good idea. It is most desirable to have hank-on jibs for shorthanded cruising and for offshore work where extremely heavy weather might be expected, because a hankless jib is more difficult to control and it can jam or escape its luff groove in a real blow.

Jibs can be reefed, but this method of shortening down is not entirely satisfactory. It works best with moderate-size jibs of heavy material with adequate reinforcement to take the strain at the leech cringle and at the reefed clew. The method is most satisfactory when off the wind, because the eased sheet lessens strain on the sail's leech, and there is no risk of shaking out the rolled-up bunt when tacking.

Distance races usually require frequent headsail changes with the number 2 or number 3 genoa or a doublehead rig when it begins to blow. At sea or in rough waters, a high-cut jib should be used so that its foot will not scoop up the leeward bow wave. However, in short, round-the-buoys races, it is often too costly to take the time to change jibs when it breezes up in the middle of the race. Thus, many skippers prefer to leave up the number 1 genoa and reef the main. Shortening sail this way can be very effective, because the boat will lose little if any speed during the reefing operation, and the sail's TCE will be moved forward to help correct for extra weather helm caused by excessive heeling. The drawbacks of the method are that the large genoa might scoop up seas, and the sail is difficult to handle in a blow, especially if the winches are undersize and when frequent tacking is anticipated. Also, keep in mind that when the main halyard has a rope tail, the reefed sail is supported by the strength of the wire-to-rope linkage. Sailmakers and others have argued that wire-to-rope splices are nearly as strong as the wire itself, and this may be so when the splice is made properly, but you don't always know how it was made. I saw a wire-to-rope splice pull apart inside the mast on a chartered boat, so I prefer an all-wire halyard even if it requires a reel winch, which must be handled very carefully.

Most racing-cruisers today use the so-called jiffy

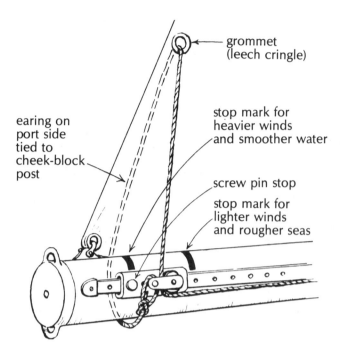

earing on port side tied to cheek-block post

grommet (leech cringle)

stop mark for heavier winds and smoother water

screw pin stop

stop mark for lighter winds and rougher seas

Figure 9-6. JIFFY REEFING

method of reefing. This is a simplified version of old-fashioned "points" reefing, made possible by relatively short booms and modern, nonstretch sailcloth. Normally, a single clew *earing* (reefing line) is attached to one side of the boom near its after end and then led up through a leech cringle and back down to the opposite side of the boom. The earing is then led through a cheek block, then forward to a winch on the boom or mast. Sometimes the earing is rigged to a slide on a track on one side of the boom, as shown in Figure 9-6. This arrangement permits fine adjustment of the earing and allows the cheek block to be slid aft in the event that roller reefing is also used. It also allows easy repositioning of the cheek block if two mainsails are used.

On a medium-size racing-cruiser, the normal reefing procedure is to set up the topping lift reasonably taut, slack the mainsheet, and slack the main halyard until the luff reefing *cringle* (grommet) reaches the tack, where the cringle is secured with a lashing or a special tack hook. Then the earing is winched in to bring the leech cringle down to the boom. After the halyard is tensioned properly, the sheet is trimmed back in. On short windward legs, the bunt can be left hanging down, but on long legs it should be rolled up and lashed. This is normally done with a few reef points or a long lacing line rove through eyelets in the sail. It is a good idea to add an extra lashing around the boom at the clew in case someone should inadvertently slack off the earing before the reef points have been untied, which could damage the sail easily if the topping lift is slack.

Roller reefing is not often used these days, but many of the older boats are fitted with this system of reducing

The clew of a jiffy-reefed main has an extra line passed through the grommet to prevent the sail from being torn if the reef earing is slacked before the reef points are released. (Rip Henderson photo)

sail. There is one advantage in the method, namely, that sail reduction theoretically is infinitely variable. Deep roller reefs usually produce a poor-setting sail with a droopy boom and wrinkled foot, but shallow roller reefs can be effective. If your boat has roller reefing and you want to change to jiffy reefing, you don't have to abandon the former. You can have both if you don't fasten bulky fittings to the boom. A track and sliding cheek block, which can be slid aft, can be fastened to the boom's after end (see Figure 9-6), and the earing's winch can be put on the mast or cabintop. If it is put on the mast, lead the earing through a block at the gooseneck, down to another block at the base of the mast, and up to the winch. On my boat, I occasionally jiffy-reef and then turn the boom a number of times to roll up the bunt. This ensures that the bunt will not fill with water in wet weather, but the procedure is troublesome because several sail slides must be removed, and the tack and clew must be lashed.

A special tack fitting that simplifies jiffy reefing. Two hooks on the fitting allow easy adjustment of the luff cringle on the leeward side. (Rip Henderson photo)

SPINNAKER TECHNIQUE

It is assumed that the reader is familiar with modern parachute spinnakers. Something was said about their construction and cloth in Chapter 6. To reiterate, the best all-purpose spinnaker is the radial-head or tri-radial spinnaker. The former may be the best for running, but the tri-radial is a little more versatile, because it allows slightly closer reaching by virtue of its radial clews, which lessen bias stretch. The star-cut spinnaker is not as popular as it was a few years ago. It is a limited, specialized sail, superior only for very close reaching and running in heavy weather. I would get a star-cut only after I had one or two all-purpose 'chutes and a half-ounce, light-air spinnaker.

One-design racers usually carry spherical-shaped spinnakers (roundish when viewed from the front or back), but racing-cruisers carry narrower 'chutes that are somewhat banana-shaped when viewed from the side (see Figure 9-7). The reason for this is that the leading handicap rules put a limit (without penalty) of 180 percent of J on spinnaker girth, thereby creating a sail with large shoulders and a rather straight waist. The banana shape is a poor one, especially in a breeze when there is too much area aloft. Racing sailors often are tempted to carry such 'chutes in heavy weather at considerable risk to boat control. There is a need for better spinnaker regulations, which would restrict the size and shape of 'chutes on offshore boats. In heavy weather when boats are broaching-to under spinnaker, it is better seamanship and sometimes makes the boat go faster to carry a "wung-out" jib (poled out on the side opposite the main) instead of the 'chute.

There are several fundamental rules for trimming the spinnaker. For the sake of speed, simplicity, and efficiency, it is a good plan to set the sail initially in accordance with these rules and then vary the trim to suit specific conditions. In other words, the fundamentals should be used, not as an inflexible dictum, but as a point of departure for subsequent fine adjustments. The rules are as follows: (1) The chord of the spinnaker should be almost parallel with the chord of the correctly trimmed mainsail (sailing between a beam reach and a dead run); (2) the pole should be more or less squared (at a 90-degree angle) to the apparent wind; (3) the pole should be level or cocked up slightly, and its inboard end should be at the highest position on the mast except in light airs; (4) the clew should be level with or only slightly lower than the tack; and (5) the halyard should be eased slightly in fresh winds.

The first rule is explained in Figure 9-8. This is probably the most basic preliminary consideration, although

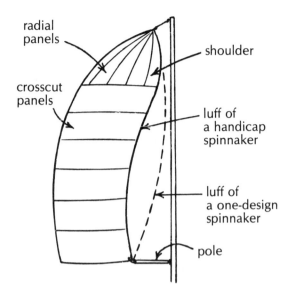

Figure 9-7. HANDICAP SPINNAKER

it should not be taken absolutely literally. When sailing lower than a beam reach and higher than a dead run, the spinnaker's chord should be aligned so that it is nearly parallel to the main boom when the mainsail is trimmed, to utilize optimum drag (as discussed in Chapter 6). Reciprocally, of course, the main boom can be adjusted to agree with a correctly positioned spinnaker chord. However, when sailing near a beam reach, take care that the spinnaker doesn't significantly backwind the mainsail.

The rule of keeping the pole squared to the apparent wind is a very good one, but it should not be hard and fast. A few experts advocate carrying the pole slightly farther forward in moderate winds because this allows maximum easing of the sheet and moves the 'chute forward away from the mainsail. It is true that when the wind and the pole are well aft, the chord of the spinnaker cannot be kept parallel to the mainsail's chord, and a narrow handicap 'chute may not be able to produce maximum drag acting in the direction in which the boat is moving. Of course, we want to use maximum

A Whitby 45 using a reaching strut to minimize compression on the spinnaker pole when it is guyed forward. The curling luff indicates the spinnaker is "on edge."

drag rather than lift when running (see "Sail Trim" in Chapter 6). If the pole is angled a little forward of being squared to the apparent wind, however, take care to see that the spinnaker is not blanketed by the main. This is especially important in light airs. For this reason and because the upper area of the 'chute may sag forward of being squared to the wind in light airs, some successful sailors prefer to oversquare the pole slightly (bring it a little farther aft) and also to heel the boat slightly to weather so gravity will help roll the 'chute out from behind the lee of the main. In heavy winds it helps to undersquare the pole (ease it farther forward) for better steering control, especially if the boat is tending to heel or take knockdowns to windward.

When the 'chute can be moved far enough from the mainsail in a moderate-to-fresh breeze, there may be space for a sizable spinnaker staysail. Some of the newer staysails are very tall, with a luff length up to 90 percent of full hoist. Carrying such a large sail without blanketing the spinnaker requires that the apparent wind be near the beam and that the pole be raised so that it is perpendicular to the jibstay, thereby getting the 'chute as far as possible from the staysail. A number 1 genoa or reacher might also be used in this manner, but a large staysail works better, because it is tacked down several feet abaft the stem, and this further separates it from the spinnaker. For a general-purpose staysail, a moderate-size sail, with perhaps 70 percent hoist (70 percent of the genoa's luff length), is a versatile sail that can be carried in varied conditions of wind strength and direction.

The spinnaker should be encouraged to lift in all but the lightest airs or very strong winds when steering control becomes a problem. So that the sail can be allowed maximum upward lift, the inboard end of the pole should be at its highest position on the pole track (attached to the forward side of the mast) when the strength of wind is sufficient to support the weight of the sail or keep it well lifted. In light airs, however, the wind will not have the strength to lift the sail, so the inboard end of the pole should be lowered. The pole should be kept level (horizontal when the boat is unheeled) to take advantage of the pole's full length, thereby keeping the spinnaker tack the maximum distance from the mast. There are several exceptions to the rule, however. In fresh winds, the pole's outboard end can be cocked up slightly to give the sail extra upward lift when the inboard end is at the top of its track, and to make the pole follow the same angle the guy creates with the deck to help equalize strains on the pole lift and downhaul (foreguy). In very strong winds, however, when the spinnaker has too much lift, it may

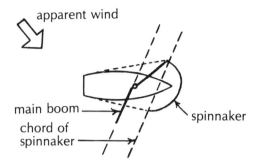

Figure 9-8. SPINNAKER CHORD POSITION

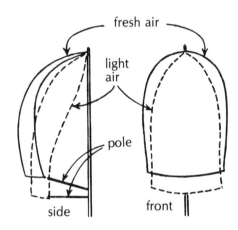

Figure 9-9. SPINNAKER DRAFT

pay to lower the outboard end of the pole below the level of the inboard end. This helps choke the sail and makes the angle of the guy exert a downward pull to equalize the extra upward pull of the lifting spinnaker. It might even help to rig a forward lead block, perhaps near the shrouds, for the guy to increase its downward pull.

The modern spinnaker's draft is controlled largely by the up-and-down position of the pole. Raising the pole and thus raising the sail's foot slacks the leeches, widens the shoulders, and flattens the draft; lowering the pole tightens the leeches and especially the luff, narrows the shoulders, and increases the cross-sectional curvature or luff-to-leech draft. This is one reason it is good to keep the pole low in light airs — to increase the spinnaker's draft. Generally, the foot should be raised when reaching in moderate winds and lowered when running in light airs. The effect on spinnaker shape of raising and lowering the foot is illustrated in Figure 9-9.

The pole should never be raised so much that the tack is considerably higher (no more than seven percent of the luff length higher) than the clew, because this will create a lopsided and less effective spinnaker shape. Using a lightweight sail and light sheets without shackles will permit the maximum amount of clew lift. Raising the main boom on its gooseneck track will increase the mainsail draft, which is desirable when running, and it will allow the spinnaker sheet passing under the boom to rise up, which in turn will let the 'chute's clew fly higher. When the 'chute's clew and leech are hooking inboard and backwinding the mainsail, it helps to lead the spinnaker sheet through a block at the end of the main boom, in the same way a high-cut reaching jib usually is led.

The spinnaker halyard should be eased a foot or more in fresh breezes to move the sail's head away from the mainsail. The amount of easing will depend primarily on the strength of wind. Usually, the halyard should not be eased when this lowers the head. There should be enough wind to make the head move almost horizontally away from the spinnaker halyard block. The head should be only slightly lower than the level of the block. Easing the sheet, guy, and halyard will move the entire spinnaker forward, which helps the sail avoid the main's blanket and moves the CE of the sailplan forward. This can be helpful to steering control while running, but if the spinnaker begins to oscillate, the halyard at least should be *two-blocked* (the sail should be hoisted all the way up). Furthermore, in a strong wind, the 'chute should be flattened with its sheet and the pole should be lowered for better control.

If the halyard can be eased enough on a reach, a large jib might be effectively carried simultaneously with the spinnaker. This is sometimes referred to as the *double slot,* where there is a slot between the spinnaker and the jib and also between the jib and the main. It requires a good breeze so that the halyard can be eased generously, perhaps two or three feet; the pole must be well lifted to flatten the 'chute and get its luff and leech to leeward; and the sheet's lead should be far aft. This sail combination is most effective on or just below a beam reach. When the wind is farther aft, a jib can interfere with the spinnaker, but when the breeze is sufficient to lift the 'chute, a spinnaker staysail can fill in the lower space efficiently. Usually, however, even this staysail will not draw effectively when the wind is on the stern. Lately, sailors have had some success with tall, narrow staysails (*tallboys* or *ribbon staysails*) tacked to the weather rail near the mid-foredeck, thus avoiding the mainsail's blanket while running. Such a sail might also be used effectively to damp rolling when the leech is brought in close to the mainmast, with the chord of the staysail aimed slightly forward at an angle of about 60 degrees to the boat's centerline.

When sailing in unsteady, shifty winds, the spinnaker's trim or the boat's heading must be changed constantly to meet the changes of wind direction and velocity. Most successful racers use a combination of changing course and trim. The helmsman bears off in the puffs and heads up in the lulls. And, of course, he bears off when headed and heads up slightly when the shift is lifting (coming from farther astern). He must be careful not to sail so high that the spinnaker luff begins to break; nor should he sail so low that the spinnaker becomes blanketed by the main. Either of these extremes can cause the sail to collapse completely.

At the same time, while the helmsman is making moderate course alterations, a competent crewmember should be playing the sheet. This man, the sheet trimmer, is as important as the helmsman. He should keep the spinnaker luff *on edge* (on the verge of luffing), and he is responsible primarily for preventing the 'chute from collapsing. The sheet should be kept eased until the luff begins to roll inward. A quick tug on the sheet can prevent the luff from breaking. The sheet trimmer should be stationed forward when reaching, perhaps near the main shrouds, so that he can see the spinnaker and watch a wind indicator at the same time. In light to moderate winds, he can put a turn or two of the sheet around its winch and then lead it forward. In heavy winds, a secondary trimmer can be stationed aft near the winch, while the primary trimmer stands forward, calls instructions to the secondary man, and pulls down on the sheet when the luff begins to curl. If the sheet is too far outboard for the primary trimmer to reach with his hand, he can use a *snatch line* or *tweaker* (a short line attached to the sheet for the purpose of pulling it in or down to prevent the luff from breaking).

It is important that the helmsman constantly refer to his wind indicators (telltales or especially the masthead indicator) in order to change course to keep the pole nearly square with the apparent wind. He can also accomplish this by adjusting the guy. Perhaps the greatest difference between cruising and racing with the spinnaker is the amount of pole and guy adjustment. On a cruiser, the guy is usually anchored or rarely adjusted, but on a racer, especially when the helmsman alters course only slightly, the guy is adjusted more frequently to keep the 'chute properly positioned to the apparent wind. Another adjustment that should be made frequently is the pole height. In general, the pole should go up on a reach and in puffs, but it should be lower when running and during lulls, in accordance with the draft alterations mentioned earlier.

To repeat, the lighter the breeze, the higher the

The British system of removing a cruising spinnaker utilizes a sliding sleeve called a Spee-Squeezer. An equivalent American system produced by North Sails is called a Snuffer, while a related method using rings connected with lines is called the Spinnaker Sally. (Roger M. Smith photo courtesy Parbury Henty and Co., Ltd.)

helmsman should steer when running with the spinnaker. The polar diagram shown in Figure 7-6 illustrates this point. When steering by the apparent wind and reading the direction from the dial of an electronic AWI (Apparent Wind Indicator), optimum headings would be still higher: 141 degrees in an 8-knot wind, 144 degrees in a 10-knot wind, 148 degrees in a 12-knot wind, 162 degrees in a 16-knot wind, and 167 degrees in a 20-knot wind. Of course, these headings are optimal for just one boat, but she is a fairly representative type of seaworthy racing-cruiser (an Ohlson 38), and her polar shows in a general way that it seldom is advisable to run far off the wind except in a breeze or stronger.

There are two basic means of setting the spinnaker: by stopping it or by setting it from a turtle or bag. The first method consists of rolling or bunching the leeches together and binding them at about two- or three-foot intervals from head to foot with weak cotton thread so that the entire sail resembles a long, thin sausage, usually with two thin legs (representing the stopped clews) at the bottom. The stopped sail is then hoisted, and the sail is broken out (the stops broken) by hauling aft on the sheet. Formerly, this was the accepted manner of setting a spinnaker, but the method is rarely used today except on large boats in heavy weather. It is usually faster and easier to set the sail from a turtle or bag.

A (Pole Set to Starboard)

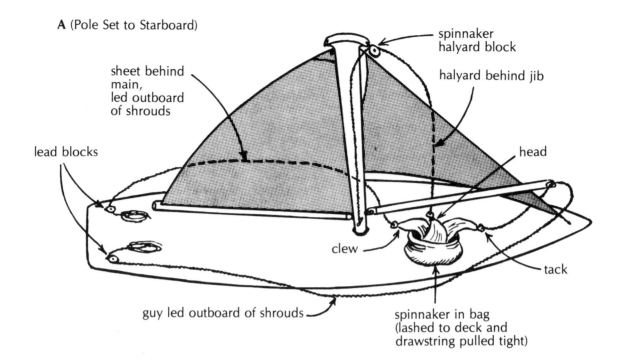

sheet behind
main,
led outboard
of shrouds

spinnaker
halyard block

halyard behind jib

head

lead blocks

clew

tack

guy led outboard of shrouds

spinnaker in bag
(lashed to deck and
drawstring pulled tight)

B (Pole to be Set to Port)

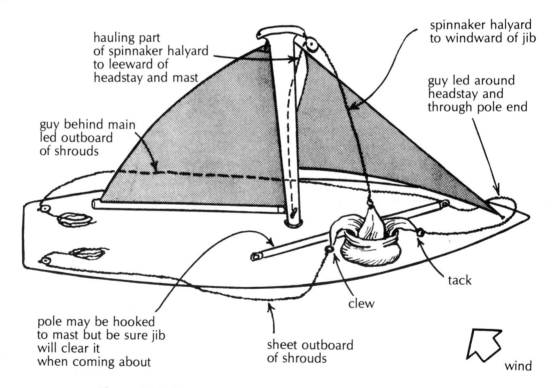

hauling part
of spinnaker halyard
to leeward of
headstay and mast

spinnaker halyard
to windward of jib

guy led around
headstay and
through pole end

guy behind main
led outboard
of shrouds

pole may be hooked
to mast but be sure jib
will clear it
when coming about

tack

clew

sheet outboard
of shrouds

wind

Figure 9-10. PREPARING THE 'CHUTE FOR HOISTING

There is little if any difference between setting from a turtle or a sailbag, because the bag is actually a kind of turtle. Almost the only difference is that the turtle (a spinnaker-setting container in the form of a specially designed bag, box, or bucket) is often secured forward of the jibstay, but when an ordinary sailbag is used instead of a turtle, the bag generally is secured abaft the jibstay on the foredeck just forward of the mast. This method of using the ordinary sailbag on the foredeck is very popular. It is shown in Figure 9-10.

Before preparing the spinnaker for setting, you must first determine which tack the boat will be on after rounding the windward turning mark when the boat is on the desired downwind heading. You may figure this mentally, or by watching boats that have rounded ahead of you, or by laying out the next course on the chart and drawing in the direction of the true wind. Figure 9-10 shows a boat approaching the turning mark on the starboard tack. It shows how the spinnaker is prepared for hoisting when the boat is to remain on the starboard tack after rounding, with the pole rigged to be carried on the starboard side (drawing A). It also shows how the 'chute is prepared when the boat will jibe onto the port tack after rounding, with her pole rigged to be carried on the port side (drawing B). The preparation shown in B would also be correct if the turning mark were to be left to starboard, requiring a tack at the mark, with the downwind course to be sailed on the port tack. Although the pole is lying on the deck in Figure 9-10(B), the inboard end of the pole may be hooked to the mast if the jib will clear easily when tacking. Obviously, the jibsheet must be led over the pole, and the pole lift cannot be rigged until after the tack.

The first step in preparing the 'chute for hoisting is to see that it is properly bagged or turtled. This requires that the leeches be folded, being sure they are not crossed, in order to prevent the sail from becoming twisted when it is hoisted. A recommended procedure is to dump the loose sail on a bunk down below where it is out of the way and protected from the wind, and then have a crewmember or two pull the two leeches together, starting at the head and working toward the foot. The two side-by-side leeches are neatly accordion-folded up to a short distance from the foot. Then the two clews are pulled apart, and the loose bulk of the sail is stuffed into the bag, followed by the folded leeches, but the three corners of the sail (the head and clews) are left hanging out of the bag. Next, the drawstring at the mouth of the bag is pulled taut and tied with a slipknot, and the bagged sail is taken to the foredeck, where it is secured to a deck eye or cleat with a lanyard made fast to the bag's bottom. After this, the three corners are

shackled or tied to their respective lines as shown in Figure 9-10. Another method of bagging the 'chute is to accordion-fold each leech separately and pack them in the bag on either side of the head. Either way ensures that the bagged sail is not twisted, but take care to hoist smartly and pull on the sheet promptly when hoisting to minimize the risk that the sail will spin and create a twist as its head goes aloft.

In the diagram the guy is led around the jibstay and the outboard end of the pole is hooked onto the guy. This is the way it is usually done. While the 'chute is being hoisted, the guy is pulled aft, and this hauls the tack of the sail close to the pole and then pulls the pole aft to its desired position. However, if you want to snap the pole onto the ring of the guy's swivel shackle (see Figure 9-11) in the interest of minimizing chafe on the guy (or for some other reason), the bag must be moved closer to the jibstay. The tack of the 'chute should then be carried around the stay, where it is secured to the guy shackle to which the pole is attached. Of course, the guy and sheet should be led aft outboard of the shrouds. These lines, together with the halyard, should be led over (not under or through) the lifelines up forward, but the sheet and guy usually must lead under the lifelines aft to reach their lead blocks.

Although the spinnaker sometimes is hoisted to windward of the jib on small racing boats, this is rarely done on a larger racing-cruiser, except perhaps in very light airs when the wind is well aft. The accepted practice is to hoist the 'chute to leeward of the jib, as illustrated. This prevents the sail from fouling on the jibstay, and it provides a lee for the 'chute behind the jib. Of course, it usually pays to drop the jib quickly after the spinnaker is hoisted, unless the wind is well forward and strong enough to allow a double-slot sail combination. Notice in Figure 9-10(A) that the halyard runs behind the jib. B's halyard will also be to leeward of the jib after she has jibed or tacked.

The pole lift and downhaul (foreguy) are not shown in Figure 9-10 for the sake of simplifying and clarifying the drawing, but these lines must be attached to the pole. Two popular ways of rigging the pole are shown in Figure 9-11. Arrangement A, with the lift and downhaul attached to the pole's middle, is the simplest and the most satisfactory method for small and even medium-size boats, but arrangement B, with a bridle and downhaul attached near the pole's end, is preferable on larger boats and when there is a great deal of strain on the pole. As said earlier, the pole lift should not be rigged in Figure 9-10(B) until after the jibe or tack has been completed so that the jib will not foul the lift.

On racing-cruisers, there are two different basic

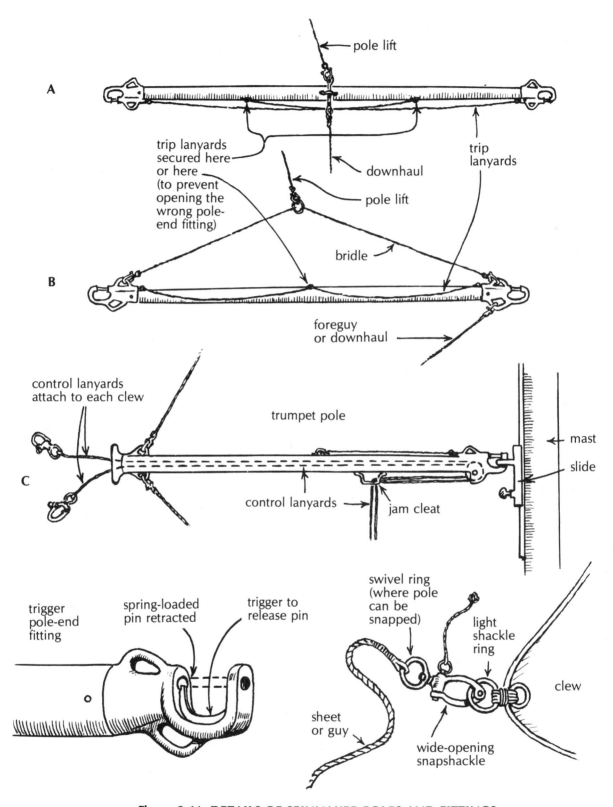

Figure 9-11. DETAILS OF SPINNAKER POLES AND FITTINGS

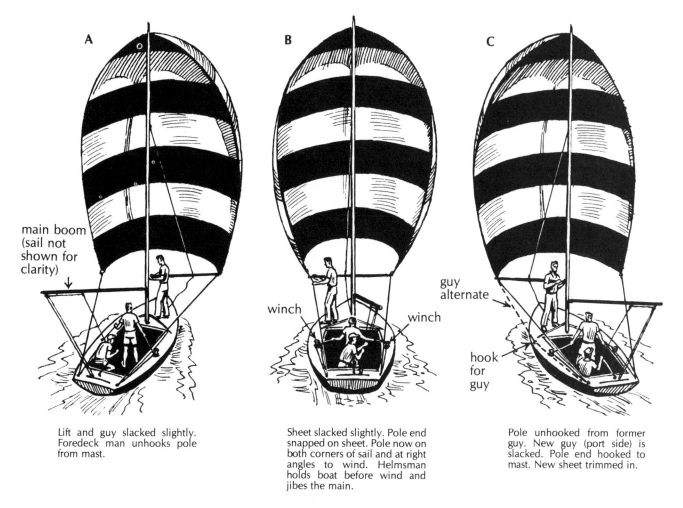

A

main boom (sail not shown for clarity) ↓

Lift and guy slacked slightly. Foredeck man unhooks pole from mast.

B

winch   winch

Sheet slacked slightly. Pole end snapped on sheet. Pole now on both corners of sail and at right angles to wind. Helmsman holds boat before wind and jibes the main.

C

guy alternate

hook for guy

Pole unhooked from former guy. New guy (port side) is slacked. Pole end hooked to mast. New sheet trimmed in.

Figure 9-12. END-FOR-END JIBE

methods used to jibe the 'chute: *end-for-ending the pole* and the *dip-pole jibe* (sometimes called the *freewheeling jibe*). The first method is illustrated in Figure 9-12. Of course, this requires a pole with similar fittings at each end, and matters are simplified when the lift and downhaul are rigged from the pole's middle, as shown in the illustration. The inboard end of the pole is unhooked from the mast and hooked onto the sheet (or shackle ring). At the midpoint of the jibe, the pole is not attached to the mast but to each clew of the 'chute or to the guy and sheet. The pole end that is attached to the former guy (the new sheet after jibing) or its shackle ring is then detached from the corner of the sail, and it is hooked onto the mast. Thus, where one end of the pole was connected to the mast on one tack, the other end is connected on the opposite tack.

Although the illustration shows only one man on the foredeck, larger boats may require another crewmember or more up forward to help handle the pole. Generally, however, it is best to use the least number of men forward who can do the job efficiently, in the interest of keeping excess weight off the foredeck. Furthermore, there should be ample crew in the cockpit for jibing the main and for the all-important jobs of handling the sheet and guy. The lines should be adjusted to keep the chord of the 'chute more or less square to the wind during the jibing operation, and the sheet should be trimmed promptly after jibing.

Figure 9-13 illustrates the principle of the dip-pole jibe. This method differs from end-for-ending in that the pole remains connected to the mast during the entire operation and the spinnaker clews are attached to the same pole-end fitting on each tack. Dip-poling usually requires that the inboard end of the pole be raised to its highest position on the mast so that the pole can be swung from one side of the boat to the other, with the

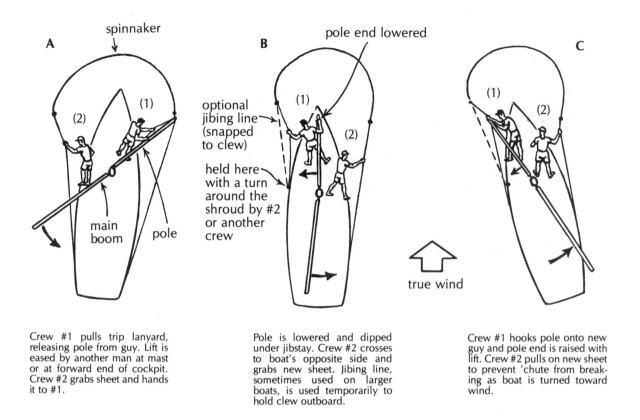

Crew #1 pulls trip lanyard, releasing pole from guy. Lift is eased by another man at mast or at forward end of cockpit. Crew #2 grabs sheet and hands it to #1.

Pole is lowered and dipped under jibstay. Crew #2 crosses to boat's opposite side and grabs new sheet. Jibing line, sometimes used on larger boats, is used temporarily to hold clew outboard.

Crew #1 hooks pole onto new guy and pole end is raised with lift. Crew #2 pulls on new sheet to prevent 'chute from breaking as boat is turned toward wind.

Figure 9-13. DIP-POLE JIBE FOR MEDIUM-SIZE RACING-CRUISERS

outboard end having clearance to swing under the jibstay. Figure 9-13 shows two men on the foredeck, but another might be needed on a large boat to control the pole lift. Of course, he would be stationed at the mast if the lift is cleated on the mast, or stationed at the forward end of the cockpit if the lift is controlled from the cockpit area. This man has an important duty to see that the pole is lowered at the right moment to pass under the jibstay without "beaning" a crewmember on the foredeck.

In step A of Figure 9-13, the pole is eased forward where crewmember number 1, the bow man, can reach the tripping lanyard (see Figure 9-11) and release the outboard pole end from the guy. Meanwhile, crewmember number 2 grabs the sheet and pulls it slightly forward and inboard. In step B, crew number 1 has helped the pole under the jibstay and has received the sheet (which will become the new guy) from crew number 2, who then crosses over to the opposite side of the boat, where he grabs the new sheet (former guy). It may be necessary for crew number 2 to help crew

number 1 attach the pole to the new guy before crossing over to the boat's other side. In fresh winds, it is a good idea to use a jibing line, as illustrated, to get enough slack in the guy for easy attachment. Whether or not number 1 will need help may depend on several factors, an important one being the design of the pole-end fitting. The trigger fitting shown in Figure 9-11 can greatly simplify the pole-to-guy attachment. The spring-loaded pin on a pole-end fitting should be facing upward, as shown in Figure 9-11(B), for quick release and connection of the guy, but some sailors feel that the pin should face down on the end-for-end jibe to facilitate hooking the pole to the mast. In step C of Figure 9-13, crew number 1 has hooked the pole to the guy, and number 2 pulls aft on the sheet, helping to keep the chord of the 'chute nearly square to the wind. The main should be slacked off slowly to prevent it from blanketing the 'chute before the pole has been guyed aft and the boat turned onto her new course.

On big boats in heavy weather, it is common practice to rig double sheets and guys (two lines from each clew) to facilitate dip-pole jibing. This method has several variations, but they are similar in principle. One variation is shown in Figure 9-14, method 1, a jibe from starboard to port tack. In step 1, the sheet, A, is taut while the extra sheet, C, is slack. When the pole is swung under the jibstay in step 2, the bight of the slack sheet, C, is carried forward (outside the shrouds) and attached to the pole end, and this line becomes the new guy in step 3. Meanwhile, old guy B (formerly carried slack while extra guy D took the strain) is now pulled taut and becomes the new sheet, while D is carried slack. With this method, the line with the aftermost lead block is used for the sheet, but the line with the lead block located farther forward becomes the guy. On some boats with narrow sterns, of course, the forwardmost sheet lead might be most beneficial, so sheet D would be used.

There is another variation sometimes referred to as the *lazy-guy* or *interim-guy* method, where the sheet and guy both use the aftermost leads and the extra guy is used only as an interim line to hold the spinnaker's clew that will become the tack on completing the jibe. By this method, line C takes the strain in step 1 (Figure 9-14, method 1) while A is slacked off and its bight carried forward to where it is hooked to the pole end (the same way C is rigged in step 2). After the jibe, A takes the strain again and C is slacked off.

Still another method of dip-poling is shown in Figure 9-14. This makes use of a *trumpet pole* (illustrated in Figure 9-11) or a similar type of pole with internal (or external) *controlling lanyards* or *outhaulers*. In step 1 (Figure 9-14, method 2), controlling lanyard F is slacked while G is hauled taut at the inboard end of the pole. (These lines run through the pole as shown in Figure 9-11.) The pole is then dipped and moved over to the 'chute's other clew.

Experienced sailors do not always agree on which basic jibing method is the most effective, but end-for-ending is the most appropriate for small or perhaps medium-size boats, when the lift and downhaul are rigged from the pole's middle, when jibing from one running course to another, and when the wind is not very strong. Dip-poling is more suitable on large boats, when the downhaul and pole lift are rigged to the pole's outboard end, when the pole-end fittings differ, when making a wide-turning jibe (jibing from a run to a reach or a reach to a reach), and when it is blowing hard.

The generally accepted means of handing or lowering the 'chute is first to hoist the jib (if it is not already up), then to guy the pole all the way forward, release the tack shackle, and let the tack fly off to leeward. The helmsman holds the boat on a somewhat downwind

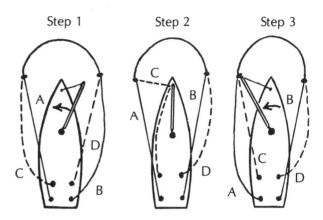

Method 1: Double Guys and Sheets

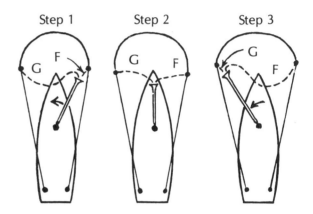

Method 2: Trumpet Pole or Outhauling

Figure 9-14. DOUBLE-LINE METHODS OF DIP-POLING

course if possible, to help blanket the sail. It is hauled down under the main by the leech and stuffed down the companionway. As the leech is hauled down, the foot is gathered in to keep the sail out of the water. The luff must be allowed to fly off to leeward so the sail cannot fill. In a very light breeze when on a dead run or nearly so, it can help to lower the spinnaker on the windward side by detaching the pole from the mast, sliding it aft, and hauling the 'chute in by its tack instead of its clew. If there is any strength in the wind, however, the sail should be handed in the lee of the jib. The man who lowers should always keep a turn of the halyard around a winch or cleat if the wind is fresh. When approaching a downwind turning mark, beginners often wait until the last minute to lower the 'chute, and sometimes they are carried beyond the mark. Try to approach the mark on a broad reach so that the spinnaker can be lowered early. If the mark is approached with the wind slightly forward of the quarter, the jib can be made to draw effectively, and this will permit an earlier handing of the 'chute.

A fairly recent development is the use of a *retrieving line* to hand a spinnaker. This is a line attached to a patch (sometimes called a *belly button*) located a little above the center of the sail. It is used to pull the sail down and onto the deck when the halyard is slacked. With this method, there is no need to release the tack, and the sail can be hauled down from the foredeck and stuffed into the forward hatch. This prevents the sail from descending in the vicinity of the jib winches and possibly interfering with quick trimming of the jib. The retrieving line should be kept on the leeward side of the 'chute.

Following is an abbreviated list of frequently encountered spinnaker difficulties with a few suggestions on prevention and/or remedies. These troubles can be minimized, of course, with careful planning and much practice.

1. Premature Filling

The 'chute fills before it is fully hoisted and cleated.

Cause

Failure to keep the 'chute completely blanketed while hoisting, or the twine breaking too soon when the sail is stopped.

Prevention

Keep the jib up while hoisting and steer off the wind. A Zip-R-Turtle can help. This is a substitute for stopping, and it consists of a zipper whose two halves are stitched about a foot apart up the sail's centerline, from the head to a point just above the foot. That part of the sail between the zipper's halves forms a tube that holds the "gathered" or bundled body of the sail after the two zipper halves have been closed. The zipper is opened by trimming the sheet. Most sailmakers can install the device and supply complete operating instructions. If the 'chute is stopped, consider using fairly heavy twine with a special breaking line rigged under the stops to break them. In strong winds, hoist the 'chute with a turn of its halyard around a winch.

Remedy

If the 'chute should fill prematurely while you are hoisting it, quickly put a turn of the halyard around the nearest cleat or winch, and tell the helmsman to bear off and blanket the sail at once.

2. Fouled Halyard

The spinnaker halyard wraps around the headstay aloft.

Cause

Some boats carry shackles at both ends of the halyard so that the 'chute can be hoisted with either end. When the halyard straddles the headstay as in Figure 9-10(A), the leeward end sometimes is carried forward to get it behind the jib when preparing the 'chute for hoisting. This will make the halyard wrap around the stay. It is the most usual cause of fouling.

Prevention

Carry the leeward end of the halyard around behind the leech of the jib before attaching it to the head of the 'chute, or carry the windward end of the halyard around the headstay, being sure that the spinnaker block swivels. It is a good idea to hook the halyard to the bow pulpit just before hoisting, but don't carry it there permanently, because it causes harmful windage when beating. Always look aloft to see that everything is clear before hoisting.

Remedy

Jibe onto the tack that reduces the halyard's wrap, and haul the 'chute down in the lee of the main. Normally, this would mean that, if the 'chute were set on the starboard tack, it should be handed on the port tack.

3. Chafed Halyard

Cause

When on the same tack for long periods, especially at sea in rough water or groundswell, the hauling part of the halyard to windward of the headstay is apt to chafe on the stay.

Prevention

Take the hauling part of the halyard to leeward of the stay. See that the spinnaker block is on a crane or bolt (see Figure 5-5) that holds it well clear of the headstay. Be sure to check the legal limits allowed by your handicap rule, however. (The MORC rule, for instance, does not allow a spinnaker halyard block to be mounted ahead of a point .012 x P_2 forward of the foreside of the mast.)

Remedy

If the halyard is badly chafed, it should be replaced. This can be done without going aloft by *marrying* the new halyard to the old one. The two halyards are sewn or heat-sealed together and taped end-to-end. Then the old halyard is pulled through its block, and this automatically reeves through the new halyard.

4. Hourglassed Spinnaker

A twist more or less halfway up the 'chute that prevents the sail's middle from filling. Above and below the twist, however, the sail fills out or balloons, and this makes it look like an hourglass.

Cause

Improper turtling or bagging or failure to hoist fast and spread the clews quickly.

Prevention

Be sure the leeches lie together when the sail is bagged, and be sure there is a swivel at the head of the sail. Hoist and trim fast. Have a crewmember help the sail out of the bag during the hoisting, and keep tension on the sheet and guy to spread the clews. Zip-R-Turtles can assist with this problem also.

Remedy

If the twist is not too far down from the head, it can very often be cleared by slacking the halyard slightly and giving it several quick jerks. This should cause the swivel to turn and the sail to untwist. It may also be helpful to yank down on the middle of the sail's foot. A twist near the bottom might be cleared in light airs by slacking the halyard slightly and interchanging the tack and clew under the lee of the jib, but don't try this in a strong wind. If neither of these methods works, the sail must be lowered to be cleared.

5. Headstay Wrap

This occurs when the middle part, or belly, of the sail wraps around the headstay.

Cause

The spinnaker is particularly vulnerable to wrapping in rough water and damp air when the sail collapses and lies against the headstay.

Prevention

Try to keep the 'chute full by paying close attention to helmsmanship (especially avoid sailing by the lee in light winds) and sheet trim. Also, be extra careful when jibing in a seaway. Be sure the jib is hoisted while handing or hoisting the 'chute. A foolproof way of preventing a wrap is to set a *spinnaker net* (a network of lines or cloth tapes hoisted in the foretriangle, as shown in Figure 9-15). Of course, a spinnaker net can be troublesome on a short race, so some boats carry two or three *antiwrap lines* (also illustrated in Figure 9-15). These are lines, usually of shock cord, that are rigged permanently from the mast to rings or slides on the headstay. When the jib is hoisted, its top hank carries the rings or slides aloft, thereby hoisting the lines out of the jib's way.

Remedy

There is not always a sure way to recover from a bad wrap. A few spinnakers have had to be cut away with a knife, but these were extreme cases. When the wrap first occurs, try jibing at once to move the wind that caused the wrap to the boat's other side, but hold a course before the wind. The sail may unwrap itself. If this doesn't work, the 'chute can be unwound by sailing by the lee and heading up sharply and then down sharply in a series of course changes, with each change reducing the wrap by one turn. The jib halyard should always be detached from the lowered jib when the 'chute is

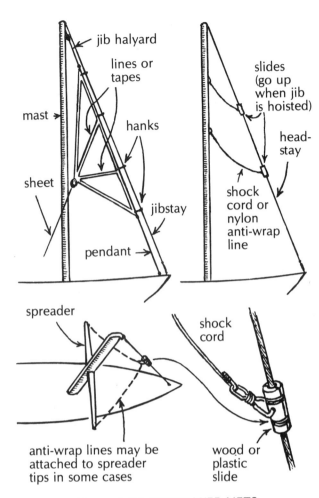

Figure 9-15. SPINNAKER NETS

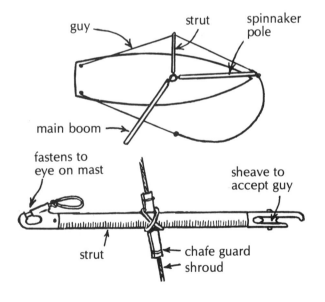

Figure 9-16. REACHING STRUT

hoisted, because the halyard could also get wrapped, and the sail could become pinched between the halyard and the stay. Also, the halyard might have to be used to send a man aloft in a bosun's chair to clear the wrap.

6. Breaking the Pole

Cause

(a) Improper rigging of the pole lift and downhaul (foreguy), (b) allowing the pole to strike or bear too hard against the headstay, (c) compression on the pole when beam reaching.

Prevention

The lift and guy should be rigged from the same position on the pole as shown in Figure 9-11, A or B. It is safer to use rig B in strong winds when there is great upward pressure from the lifting spinnaker. Try to equalize upward and downward pressures by raising or lowering the outboard end of the pole or changing the guy lead. Prevent the pole from bearing hard against the headstay by keeping sufficient tension on the guy. Use prestretched Dacron or in some cases wire for guys. Keeping the outboard end of the pole low will give the pole more resistance to breaking against the headstay. Pole compression results from the guy's pulling aft when the pole is guyed all the way forward. This problem can be solved by using a *reaching strut,* illustrated in Figure 9-16. The strut holds the guy away from the windward shrouds, thus preventing chafe, reducing the pole's pressure against the headstay, and reducing compression by increasing the angle between the pole and the guy.

Remedy

A broken pole must be replaced, but if the pole is only slightly damaged or cracked, a temporary repair can be made by binding wood splints tightly to each side of the pole at the damaged area.

7. Spinnaker Knockdown

This can occur to leeward or windward.

Cause

A windward knockdown occurring in a strong wind can be caused by guying the spinnaker too far aft while running, by slackening the sheet too much, and even by insufficient use of the main boom vang, which allows a bad twist at the head of the mainsail. Leeward knockdowns occurring in strong winds can be caused by trimming the sheet too flat while the pole is guyed forward and the boat is steered too high.

Prevention and Remedy

To avoid windward knockdowns, flatten the 'chute by trimming the sheet, guy the pole farther forward, and head up. To avoid leeward knockdowns, ease the sheet when the boat begins to heel and bear off to gain stability. If the boat begins to heel severely and broach-to, slack the spinnaker sheet all the way. Have a man standing by to slack the vang to prevent tripping on the main boom. If the spinnaker sheet becomes submerged so that it cannot be reached in a severe knockdown, ease the guy until the pole is against the headstay, and then release it so the line will run through the pole-end fitting and allow the 'chute to spill its wind.

8. Steering and Control Problems

Cause

(a) Carrying the chute in too much wind and/or in heavy seas, (b) poor spinnaker design, (c) rudder too far forward on a hull with a short keel, (d) extremely unbalanced hull that is fine forward and full aft.

Prevention

Flatten the 'chute by lowering the pole, overtrimming the sheet, and two-blocking the halyard. Use a small, flat spinnaker with narrow shoulders. Be sure the main boom is well vanged. Tillers give a quicker helm response than wheels, skegs help directional stability, and after-mounted rudders are beneficial to steering control. When there is a tendency to roll rhythmically or yaw, try to avoid violent rudder changes, because this only aggravates the tendency. Don't fight the helm but use an easy, minimal helm action. Keep crew weight aft.

Remedy

According to C.A. Marchaj, wind-tunnel tests have shown that steering by the lee may help (provided there is no tendency to knockdown or to collapse the 'chute from blanketing), but be sure to rig a preventer to avoid an accidental jibe. If the boat cannot be controlled, use a boomed-out jib instead of the spinnaker. Setting this sail is done most simply by setting the pole to windward, keeping the jib blanketed under the lee of the main, and outhauling the jib's clew to the outboard end of the pole.

9. Handing Difficulties

Cause

(a) Tack shackle jamming from wind pressure, (b) sheet getting away from the man tending it after the tack has been released, (c) halyard getting away from its tender, (d) the 'chute going overboard or blowing aft as it is being lowered.

Prevention

Consider using wide-opening snapshackles hinged near the apex to open a full 180 degrees on the guy and sheet (see Figure 9-11). Fit the shackle pull pins with strong, heavy lanyards. A few boats use a sacrificial rope ring at each clew so that the rope can be cut if the shackle cannot be opened. Another emergency solution is to uncleat the guy and let it run through the pole end.

If the sheet gets away from its tender after the tack is released, the 'chute will stream from the masthead like a flag. This is the reason I prefer to knot the end of the sheet, but only just prior to handing. Some sailors strongly oppose knotting the sheet, because it may not allow the sheet enough slack to spill the 'chute completely. However, when the sheet has adequate length (the rule of thumb is twice the overall length of the boat), a knot at the very end of the line jamming in the lead block should allow ample spillage. Knotting involves little risk if done just before lowering, when the 'chute is blanketed by the jib. In an emergency, the guy can be released, and it will run through the end of the pole.

As said before, the man who lowers the 'chute in a breeze should have a turn on the winch or cleat. He must watch the men handing the sail and lower no faster than they can take it in. The sail should be handed by one leech and the foot only to keep it from filling, and it should be smothered and stuffed below immediately. On yawls especially, the 'chute should not be allowed to blow aft, because it could descend on the mizzen. To avoid this, the helmsman should head off, if possible, until the sail is lowered. A retrieving line, described earlier, can be helpful.

Remedy

If the sheet escapes from its tender after the tack has been released, causing the 'chute to fly free from the masthead, then the best course of action is usually to run dead before the wind to lessen the apparent wind and to blanket the 'chute with the main. Then, perhaps a crewmember at the stem can hook the loose sheet with a boathook. If the 'chute goes overboard, haul it back aboard by one corner (the head, tack, or clew) only, because if the sail is pulled by two corners, it will fill with water, drag like a sea anchor, and probably tear.

A final thought on spinnakers: When there is more than one of these sails on board, the one most suited to the wind strength and point of sailing should be set. A lightweight running spinnaker should not be carried on a reach in a fresh breeze, nor should a heavy reaching 'chute be carried on a run in light airs. If wind conditions change, making the hoisted 'chute inappropriate while you are far from the leeward mark, the spinnaker probably should be changed. In light airs, it is not much of a problem to change from a heavy 'chute to a light one. The new 'chute (to be set) is properly turtled and attached at its usual hoisting location on the foredeck. A new sheet is bent and pretrimmed to about the same position as the sheet in use. The new 'chute's tack is carried forward to the headstay. The outboard end of the pole is lowered to within easy reach, and the pole is guyed forward. A man on the bow releases the hoisted 'chute's tack from the guy and then snaps on the new sail's tack. Meanwhile, a man at the mast is lowering the hoisted 'chute, while another man (or two) gathers it in. The halyard is quickly exchanged from one sail to the other, and the new 'chute is hoisted and trimmed.

If the boat has two spinnaker halyards, of course, the replacement 'chute may be hoisted before the standing one is lowered. This is done by hoisting the replacement to leeward but inside (to windward of) the sheet and clew of the standing 'chute. The replacement's tack is temporarily lashed to the jibstay or bow pulpit. After the sail is hoisted and trimmed behind the mainsail, the tack of the standing 'chute is released, and the guy snap-shackle is transferred to the replacement sail. After hav-

ing its tack released, the original sail blows aft behind the replacement 'chute, where it is gathered in as its halyard is slacked. Meanwhile, the temporary tack lashing has been released, the pole is squared, and the replacement sail is trimmed properly.

In heavy-air conditions when you are caught flying a light running 'chute, it may not be worth changing sails if the course can be nearly a dead run. When running, of course, the boat's speed is subtracted from the true wind speed to decrease apparent wind velocity. When reaching, however, the genoa can be hoisted and usually will draw effectively while the light 'chute is handed. In some cases, it may be helpful to sail with the genoa in lieu of the spinnaker, but if the boat speed drops, the heavy 'chute can be hoisted in the usual manner under the lee of the jib.

CREW ORGANIZATION

Duties assigned to the crew, such as winching, tacking and jibing, and setting, handing, and reefing sails, have already been discussed, but a few words should be said about how the skipper organizes his crew for the greatest effectiveness and racing efficiency. Of course, the number of crew and their job specialties vary with the boat size, the rig, and the length of the race. The smallest MORC boats sailing short races over simplified courses can be sailed with a crew of three. It is even possible to race these boats singlehanded with certain modifications to the running rigging, such as leading the halyards, pole lift, and pole downhaul back to the cockpit. However, for maximum racing efficiency, most small, sloop-rigged racing-cruisers should carry a crew of four. Slightly larger boats will normally need a crew of five racing round the buoys, and a crew of six for night races and when a boat has more than one mast, especially when racing in fresh winds. Boats in the 40-to-50-foot range might need a crew of from six to 10, depending on the rig and the race length. The larger and more complicated the rig, the more crew will be required, and distance races involving night sailing require a sizable crew to combat fatigue. On most overnight races a boat should have sufficient crew to permit half the members to sleep below while the other half handles the boat and stands watch on deck. It should not be necessary to rouse the watch below for normal maneuvers and sail changes, except in emergencies.

The racing crew may be divided into two groups: the foredeck, those members who often work forward of the mainmast and whose primary duties are to handle the spinnaker and other headsails; and the after guard, those members concentrated in or near the cockpit area. Of course, most of the crew have primary and secondary jobs, and in some cases their position might shift from forward to aft, or vice versa, such as when more crew are needed on the foredeck in heavy weather to jibe or hand the spinnaker. On most medium-size boats, the after guard might consist of the skipper, who is not only in command but also is the principal tactician and helmsman; one or two winch men, crankers who supply the speed and power for winch operation; a sheet trimmer, who specializes in fine adjustments and continually plays the sheets; and a navigator, who obviously has a key role in offshore races. On round-the-buoys races, the navigator often doubles as a winch tailer, tactician, or even relief helmsman if he has the "tiller touch." His navigational duties on a short race may be as follows: time the start; lay out the courses (draw the courses on the chart and figure the headings in degrees or points); keep the skipper informed of the location of rounding marks, other competitors, and time or distance to the lay line (fetch line); figure handicaps; and, when visibility is poor, keep an approximate *dead reckoning* position (a position derived from recording the course and speed over a known period of time). On most races, a skilled sheet trimmer is probably an even greater asset than a good navigator, especially on a spinnaker leg in light airs. It is important to have the trimmer playing the sheets constantly. A common mistake made by inexperienced trimmers is to uncleat the sheet before trimming, which wastes valuable time. The sheet should be trimmed and then uncleated and recleated.

The foredeck crew consists of a foredeck captain and one, two, or even more assistants, depending on the size of the boat. Small boats should have minimal crew forward (in many cases, only one man) so that the hull will remain properly trimmed. Only one man (usually the one in charge of the foredeck) should go forward to prepare the spinnaker for hoisting. The foredeck captain must be experienced in the handling of spinnakers, because it is his responsibility to carry out and/or direct the setting, positioning, jibing, changing, and handing of the 'chute. His assistants may include a mast man to handle halyards and/or the lift, and perhaps a bow man to help during jibes or at other hectic moments. Of course, these crewmembers are also responsible for setting and changing jibs and staysails. When beating to windward, the foredeckers usually man the windward or leeward rail (depending on the strength of wind) nearly amidships to help effect the proper angle of heel. Normally, on all but very small boats, at least one of these men will be needed forward to help the jib around the mast when tacking.

Additional skills and specialties are needed on distance races. An important specialist is the cook, who often is not required to stand regular watches. It is also advisable that other crewmembers have special aptitudes in or knowledge of weather prediction, medicine or first aid, mechanics, electronics, marlinspike seamanship, and sail repair. Of course, the navigator needs to be a specialist in celestial as well as radio navigation and dead reckoning when offshore, and there never can be too many competent helmsmen on a long-distance race.

Two-watch systems, requiring half the crew to be on duty while the other half is off, can comprise four-, five-, or six-hour watches. When four-hour periods are used, it becomes necessary to *dog,* or divide, one of the four hours in half, customarily from 1600 to 1800 and from 1800 to 2000, to alternate the assignment of watch periods to the crew each day. *Swedish systems* make use of five watches in a 24-hour period; this automatically alternates the watches every day. Two popular Swedish systems are as follows: 0200-0600, 0600-1200, 1200-1800, 1800-2200, 2200-0200; and 0000-0400, 0400-0800, 0800-1300, 1300-1900, 1900-2400. With the first method, watches are essentially six hours during daylight and four hours at night, but with the second method, watches are composed of four-, five-, and six-hour periods with the shorter watches tending to be at night. Occasionally, for the sake of boat-handling continuity, a rotating watch system is used. With this system, one man goes off watch and is replaced by a new man coming on watch every hour.

The ideal crew is almost impossible to find, because there simply are not enough highly skilled and experienced crew for every boat. Of course, it is very desirable to have the same crew team for every race, but most skippers are not so fortunate as to have every member a regular. Many skippers feel that it is better to sign on crewmembers who will be regular and dependable even if they lack experience. With time and patience, most enthusiastic greenhorns can be trained. Good sources of crew supply, for round-the-buoys races at least, are sailing program juniors and some women. More and more women are crewing, even on ocean races, and they are capable of handling almost any job, except perhaps one requiring brute strength, such as winching in a genoa jib in a heavy breeze. Another source of crew supply for racing-cruisers is small-boat racers. They are usually skilled and eager but not very regular because of their own racing schedule. Skippers of the larger ocean-racers can often obtain crew for special distance races from the skippers and crew of the smaller racing-cruisers that do not normally participate in ocean races.

Beyond what has been said, there can be no hard-and-fast rules for assigning jobs to the crew, because specific assignments will depend on individual skills and degrees of experience. The crewmember who does a particular job best should be given that job as his regular assignment. However, in practice sessions or some informal races, it is a good idea to trade off or switch jobs for the sake of developing a broader range of skills and greater versatility for emergency situations. Since racing a boat is a team operation, practice in boat and sail handling is of tremendous value. Most skippers of racing-cruisers do not hold practice sessions often enough.

Qualities to look for in a regular crew are: enthusiasm, a willingness to learn and a desire to excel, team spirit and the ability to get along with others, dependable availability, intelligence, and experience. These are listed in approximately the right order of importance.

In the long run, if the crew will be regular, it is probably better to sign on the person who has a strong desire to learn and win even if he is inexperienced, rather than have a crew of high intelligence and experience but half-hearted and lacking in competitive spirit. Of course, in distance ocean races, experience and all-around proficiency in seamanship become quite important. Other desirable qualities for the offshore sailor are perseverance, neatness, and resistance to seasickness. A good sense of humor is always an asset.

10/   Strategy and Tactics

A distinction must be made between strategy and tactics. Strategy is the general, overall plan for the race, taking into account wind, current, and waves but ignoring the presence of competitors. Tactics, however, is boat-vs.-boat competition, your plan of attack or defense with regard to the presence and proximity of other boats. Unless a race is very short and extremely crowded, strategy is usually of much greater importance to the outcome of the race than tactics. This is especially true with handicap racing because of the unequal speed of many boats. However, tactics are nearly always involved near the starting line, around turning marks, and whenever boats crowd together in round-the-buoys racing. Also, boat-vs.-boat tactics are involved when one or two competitors become more important than others, such as near the end of a race series.

WIND STRATEGY

As suggested in Chapter 8, it is always wise to plan, well before the start, the general course strategy based on observation and prediction of weather, current, and sea conditions. The start can be considered successful when the starter is free to pursue this strategy in the least amount of time after the starting signal. In most areas where currents are moderate, the strategy should be based primarily on weather expectations. The reasons for this are that wind strength dictates what sails are carried; wind direction and strength (together with current) indicate the location of rough and smooth water; wind strength can vary in different locations and at different times; and wind shifts can completely change the relative positions of boats with respect to sailing time to the finish. Of course, current is very important, but many races have been lost in areas of weak current by basing the strategy on current alone and not considering the more significant effects of changes in strength and direction of the wind. There are few racing areas in the U.S. where winds, regardless of their direction, are absolutely consistent and steady.

It might be convenient to consider that there are three types of wind shifts: (1) *general,* where the wind shifts about the same amount over the entire racing area; (2)

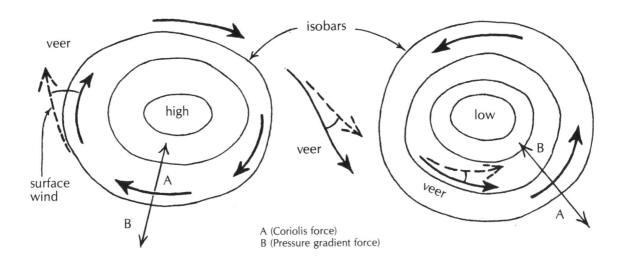

veer

isobars

surface wind

veer

high

veer

low

B

A

veer

B

A

A (Coriolis force)
B (Pressure gradient force)

Figure 10-1. VEERING OF NORMAL GUSTS

oscillating, when the wind shifts back and forth, varying in behavior from one location to the next within the racing area; and (3) *bending shifts,* when the wind flow is distorted or bent near shore by the geography and topography of the land.

Weather-system winds to a great extent result from the movement and location of highs and lows (high or low barometric pressure). In the Northern Hemisphere, winds swing around a high in a clockwise, outward direction, but they move counterclockwise and inward around a low. The general flow of air moves from a high to a nearby low. When a low passes to the south of you, it produces backing winds (shifting counterclockwise). On the East Coast there is often a lengthy period of wet, sometimes stormy weather (the wet northeaster). A low passing to the north, however, brings a strong veering (clockwise) shift. Compared with lows, highs move much more slowly, and their winds are often light in the summertime. When a high passes to the south, the wind backs. There are occasions, however, when an approaching high will bring a light northerly that will die (when the center of the high passes directly over you) and the wind will often fill in from the south after the high has passed. A calm may also result when a high passing to the south is opposed by an easterly sea breeze. When a high passes to the north, the wind will veer. Frontal passages (either warm or cold) nearly always produce veering winds.

Land-sea breezes are due to differences in temperature of the land and water. In midmorning of a hot spring or summer day, the land heats much faster than the water, causing the air over the land to rise. This leaves a partial void into which the cooler air over the

water is sucked. Thus, a sea breeze is created. The sea breeze may begin in the late morning but usually reaches its highest velocity in the midafternoon. At night, however, when the land has cooled but water temperatures have changed very little, the thermal activity is reversed, and there is a breeze off the land. This wind often reaches its peak early in the morning before dawn and continues until it subsides gradually in the early hours of daylight. The strength of a land-sea breeze depends on temperature, clearness of the weather, character of the land (fields, plains, and beaches heat up faster than wooded areas), and the strength of the prevailing or dominating wind system. The land-sea breeze may cause a shift in the dominating weather-system wind, such as when an East Coast southerly is influenced by a sea breeze to create a southeaster. Then, again, the weather-system wind may be calmed or increased when it is opposed or reinforced by the land-sea breeze.

Oscillating shifts may be caused on calm days by small, isolated thermals along an irregular shore directly exposed to the sun. These thermals are similar to bubbles or cells of heated air that break away periodically and rise from the ground, allowing the air to drift into the void beneath the bubble. This may cause periodic shifts over small, local areas near shore. Isolated oscillating shifts often occur on windy days when the air is vertically unstable, with a cool wind flowing over irregularly heated land, such as during the typical East Coast northwester. In these conditions, the winds are gusty when the cool, strong wind aloft drops down to the surface. Puffs in themselves cause oscillating shifts, because the increase in wind velocity causes the ap-

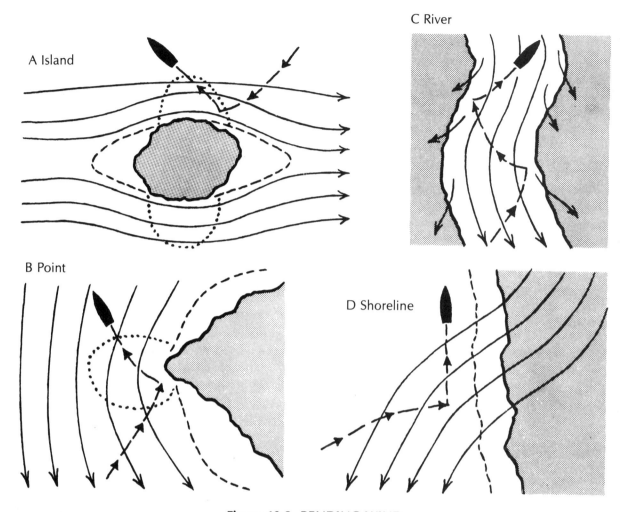

Figure 10-2. BENDING WIND

parent wind to draw farther aft. Some gusts are cat's-paws, which radiate or fan out slightly from the center. In addition, gusts descending from the strong winds aloft are slowed less by surface friction, and this normally makes them veer. The wind aloft closely follows the direction of the isobars, because there is a balance between *pressure gradient force,* the tendency of the air to flow directly into a low or out of a high, and the *Coriolis force,* the deflection of air motion (to the right in the Northern Hemisphere) due to the earth's rotation. At the surface, however, the Coriolis force is less strong because of the decreased wind velocity, and this causes the wind to angle (about 10 degrees over water) into a low or out of a high (see Figure 10-1). Thus, boats normally are lifted by gusts of this type on the starboard tack but are headed on the port tack. The English meteorologist and small-boat sailor Alan Watts gives a complete and more technical explanation of the phenomenon in his book *Wind and Sailing Boats.*

The remaining wind shift is the bending shift, caused by the geography and topography of the land. Examples of how the surface winds can be affected by the land are illustrated in Figure 10-2. A bent wind, sometimes called a shore slant when the bend is favorable, is not a true shift but an apparent one. Although the general, overall wind appears to change its direction when a boat sails into a bend, the change of direction is only a result of the distorted flow lines near shore. Four typical situations are shown in Figure 10-2. The long arrows show the flow lines, the areas enclosed by dotted lines show the approximate regions of fast wind speed, and the areas enclosed by dashed lines indicate slow wind speed, from the effects of either blanket or rebound. The wind bends in order to pass around islands or peninsulas, as shown in situations A and B, and it tends to be channeled down a river, as in situation C, or to follow the axis of a long body of water. When the wind blows obliquely across a fairly regular shoreline, the bend is such that the flow lines tend to cross the shore at right angles, but then they bend to follow the water's axis a short distance offshore (situation D). Sailors can take advantage of the bending flow lines when beating, often by tacking close to the shore toward the center of the wind's rotation but avoiding the lee of the land, as suggested by the broken-arrow courses of the boats in the diagram. Although it often pays to tack almost immediately on prolonged headers of the general or oscillating type, it nearly always pays to sail well into a wind bend header before tacking. Of course, bent winds are affected by such factors as the altitude of the shore, gaps along the shore through which the wind can funnel, thermal conditions, and the dominance of weather-system winds.

Wind shifts and variations of wind strength are difficult to predict. The study of a recent weather map can be helpful, and the racing skipper should listen to a good marine weather broadcast before, and also during, every race. Especially useful are the Weather Bureau's continuous VHF broadcasts on FM 162.55, 162.40, and 163.27 MHz. It is important to have some idea of the general weather pattern (the location of highs, lows, fronts), and good broadcasts give the strength, direction, and probable shifting of the general winds, the likelihood of thunderstorms, and so forth.

The longer the race, the greater the significance of general weather forecasts. In short races, sailors are concerned with weather in a very limited area over a limited period of time, and weather reports are not so detailed as to cover small, specific localities. Furthermore, meteorologists seldom can predict with any accuracy the exact time of a weather change. The round-the-buoys sailor should be informed of the general weather picture, but he must also draw on his local knowledge and use his powers of observation to attempt a prediction of weather in his locality. He should keep records of local weather behavior and learn the influence of local geography on the wind through thermal activity and wind bending. He should also observe the general characteristics of each directional wind in his region (for instance, that a northwester is puffy and shifty, or that a southerly is fairly steady, or that a northerly may die).

Careful, continual observation can help in predicting weather changes. Among the visual signs of wind changes are: wind streaks on the water; the activity of smoke and flags; the movement of lower clouds and distant sailboats. Certain clouds, such as high-altitude cirrocumulus (mackerel sky), altostratus, and altocumulus, can warn of approaching fronts, while cumulonimbus (thunderheads) can warn of an imminent

thunderstorm of either the frontal or the isolated air-mass type. Cumulus clouds can predict fair weather and perhaps the presence of sea breeze or other thermal wind activity. As said before, fronts should produce veering winds, but an approaching, isolated, counter-clockwise-moving storm passing to the south should produce backing winds. A fluctuating barometer can be helpful in predicting these shifts and the usual increase in wind velocity associated with the approach and passage of a front or low. A falling glass will announce the approach of these disturbances, and the glass will rise rapidly and indicate that the wind will further increase temporarily after the passage of a cold front.

Wind changes can even be influenced by tide. The wind tends to come up (freshen) and go down with the tide. This has been recognized for a long time by many experienced sailors, but I've never heard an entirely satisfactory explanation of the phenomenon. Meteorologist Alan Watts offers as a possible explanation that the wind increase may be due to the "flattening of the surroundings," but he admits that "the reason is obscure." Nevertheless, the wind often will begin to freshen at the start of the flood tide but slacken at the start of the ebb, and this also can herald a wind shift.

Although the time and the extent of a wind shift are difficult to predict, we can try to place our boat in the right location to receive maximum benefit or the least harm from any shift. As pointed out many years ago by John Trevor and Harold Calahan (in their book *Wind and Tide in Yacht Racing*) and by Dr. Manfred Curry, the gains from being in an advantageous location during a wind shift can be enormous. Below is a list of general rules that usually hold true when beating in shifty winds.

1. *Tack on prolonged or significant headers.* On oscillating wind shifts, small boats should tack almost immediately, but racing-cruisers should not tack with very rapid oscillations, especially in light airs, because of the time and way lost when tacking. All boats should sail well into a wind bend before tacking, but all boats usually should tack at once on a severe, heading, general shift.

2. *When sailing toward an expected header, foot (don't point), but point toward an expected lift unless there is a possibility of overstanding.* The boat that foots out but sags to leeward of a competitor gains in a heading shift, because this puts the competitor behind in the footing boat's wake. When the shift is lifting, however, the boat behind but to windward decreases the distance she is behind and increases her distance to windward. In a distance race when nearly fetching the mark, it usually pays to foot, because the odds are that

there will be a general wind shift sooner or later. A header will put the footing boat ahead, and a significant lift may allow her to fetch, while the boat that has pointed will be behind on the header and will have overstood on the significant lift.

3. *When the windward mark lies dead to windward, tack toward the heading side of the course.* Sail toward the expected header, to the right side of the course when expecting veering winds or to the left side of the course when expecting backing winds. The antithetical corollary to this rule is: Don't sail toward a general shift that is expected to lift. This can be seen by studying Figure 10-3. Notice that a boat on the lifted side of the course (to the left of the rhumb line on a veering shift) has a much greater distance to sail than one on the headed side of the course experiencing the same shift. The reason for this is that the headed boat may come about and fetch (or nearly fetch) the mark on the opposite tack, while the lifted boat cannot fetch on either tack. The amount the headed boat gains over the lifted one will depend on the time and degree of shifting (see rule 5).

4. *When the mark lies nearly dead to windward and the wind's shifting is entirely unpredictable, keep as close to the rhumb-line course as is consistent with nonexcessive tacking.* The reasoning behind this rule is that no matter which way the wind shifts, the boat near the rhumb line cannot lose drastically. Since she will lose some ground if she sails into a lifting shift, the first tack should be toward the most probable header. When the general shifting is completely unpredictable and neither tack is favored by favorable current, seas, bending winds, or thermal winds, the port tack usually should be taken first because, more often than not, a general shift will veer rather than back in normal, fair weather (in the Northern Hemisphere).

5. *Distance from the rhumb line should be minimal when the shift is expected to be major or early, but greater when the shift is expected to be minor or late.* This is a corollary of rule 4, and it is explained in Figure 10-3.

6. *When the mark definitely does not lie dead to windward, take the close tack until the opposite tack is definitely closer.* The *close tack* may be defined as the tack that allows you to head closest to the windward mark when sailing close-hauled, whereas the *far tack* is the opposite tack. The reasoning behind this rule is that almost any shift will favor a boat on the close tack by allowing her to fetch or nearly fetch the mark on a lifting shift, but in a severe heading shift, she can come about and come close to fetching on the opposite tack. On the other hand, the boat taking the far tack first is

hurt by a lift, because this will put the mark almost dead to windward, while a header usually will mean that she has overstood and wasted time on her initial tack. This is explained in Figure 10-4. Almost the only exception to this rule is when a boat on the far tack sails into a slight, early header that just allows her to fetch on the opposite tack. This is illustrated by the dashed course lines in Figure 10-4.

7. *Don't sail out to the lay line until close to the windward mark.* The reason for this is that any wind shift can be harmful to a boat on the *lay line* — the line on which a boat can fetch the windward mark (also called fetch line). When she is aimed for the mark on this line, a lifting shift means that she has overstood, while a heading shift means that her tacking angle is less than 90 degrees (assuming the boat can "sail square" or sail a course that is 45 degrees from the true wind). An important exception to this rule is that it pays to keep to one side of the course when sailing in very light airs, because thermal winds occur frequently near a shore, and also because excessive tacking, required to stay near the rhumb line, can be very costly in light airs.

8. *Consider tacking when on port tack during puffs and when on starboard tack during lulls in normal, vertically unstable winds.* This rule, based on the previously mentioned principle that normal gusts tend to veer (see Figure 10-1), might be considered a corollary to rule 1. Both of these rules are more appropriate for small, light-displacement boats. However, under certain circumstances, it can be useful for a small racing-cruiser to tack during prolonged gusts, lulls, or oscillating shifts. Often a gusting header on the port tack will not appear to be a header because of the neutralizing effect of the increased wind velocity tending to draw the apparent wind aft. However, on the opposite tack, the wind veer and the normal puff lift can reinforce each other to create a significant lift. The same principle applies to lulls when on the starboard tack.

9. *In light airs, work into the nearest wind streak regardless of which way it will shift. When expecting a new general shifted wind, try to stay with the old wind as long as possible, but at the same time, work toward the direction of the expected new breeze. Don't tack in a calm spot.* When sailing in light airs, you are concerned primarily with keeping the boat moving even if it is not in the direction closest to the next mark, partly because a moving boat creates her own apparent wind. Also, you are concerned with staying in the most breeze, the last of a dying breeze, and in being the first to reach a new breeze. This latter principle also applies to the calm before a storm. You can often take advantage of the light breeze that is sucked into a thunderstorm in order

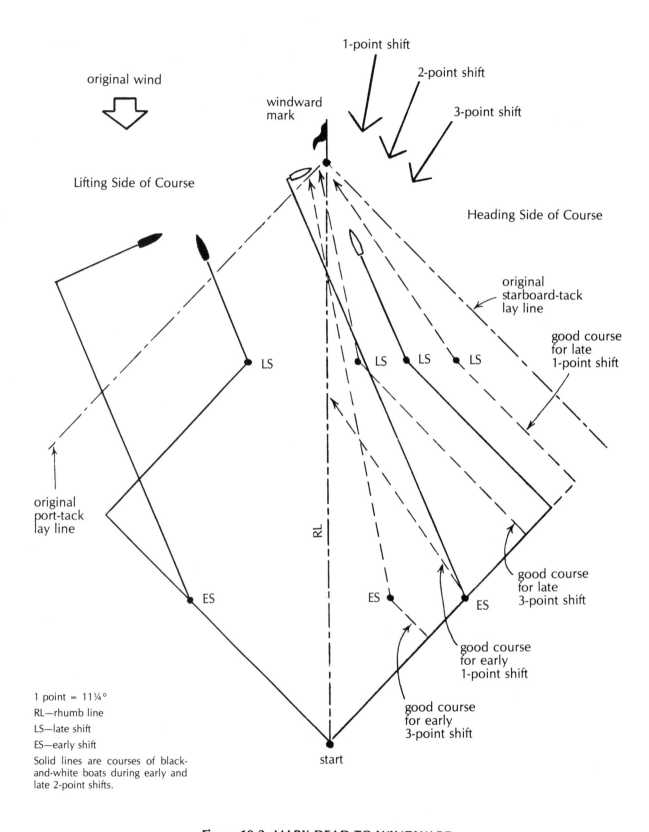

original wind

Lifting Side of Course

windward
mark

1-point shift

2-point shift

3-point shift

Heading Side of Course

original
starboard-tack
lay line

good course
for late
1-point shift

LS   LS   LS   LS

original
port-tack
lay line

good course
for late
3-point shift

ES   ES   ES

good course
for early
1-point shift

good course
for early
3-point shift

1 point = 11¼°
RL—rhumb line
LS—late shift
ES—early shift
Solid lines are courses of black-
and-white boats during early and
late 2-point shifts.

RL

start

Figure 10-3. MARK DEAD TO WINDWARD

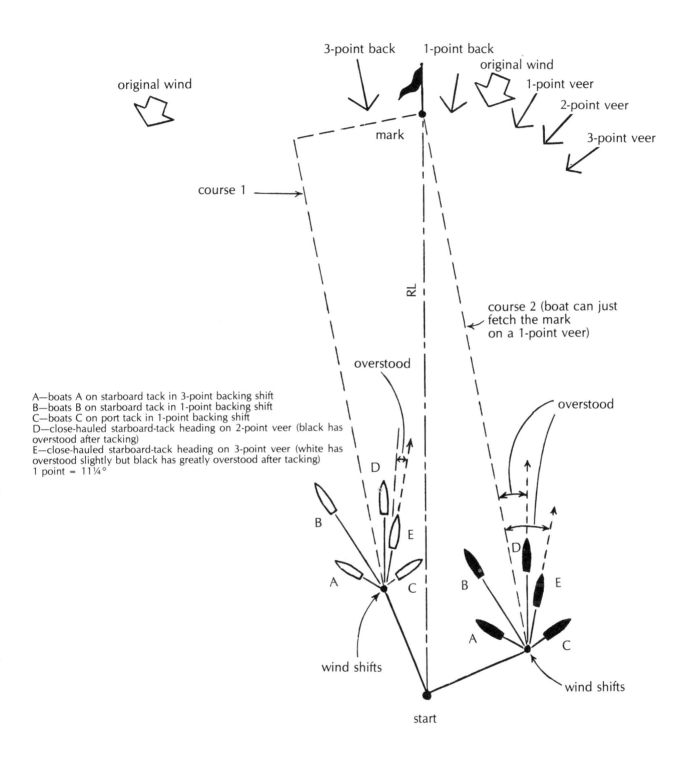

3-point back   1-point back

original wind

original wind
1-point veer
2-point veer
3-point veer

mark

course 1

RL

course 2 (boat can just
fetch the mark
on a 1-point veer)

overstood

overstood

A—boats A on starboard tack in 3-point backing shift
B—boats B on starboard tack in 1-point backing shift
C—boats C on port tack in 1-point backing shift
D—close-hauled starboard-tack heading on 2-point veer (black has
overstood after tacking)
E—close-hauled starboard-tack heading on 3-point veer (white has
overstood slightly but black has greatly overstood after tacking)
1 point = 11¼°

B

D

E

A   C

B   D

E

A   C

wind shifts

wind shifts

start

Course 1 is longer than course
2 (exception to the close-tack
rule)

White boats are ahead of black
boats

Figure 10-4. MARK DEFINITELY NOT DEAD TO WINDWARD

SITUATION	CONDITION	RULE	PARTICULAR EXCEPTION	GENERAL EXCEPTIONS
Mark dead to windward	severe general shift expected (direction fairly certain)	keep to heading side of course, don't go far from rhumb line	late shift (it can pay to cross rhumb line slightly to lifting side if shift will be late)	if current, smooth water, wind bending, thermals, greater wind strength, or placement of competitors justifies other course
	slight general shift expected (direction fairly certain)	keep to heading side of course, sail farther from rhumb line initially, especially on late shift	when shifting is uncertain it is risky to sail much farther than halfway to lay line	
	oscillating and/or gusty wind	tack toward next probable header, tack on definite prolonged headers	you are tacking too often and boat is slow in stays	
	shifting unknown	tack toward most probable header, don't go far from rhumb line, if no thermal or bending wind, keep to right of rhumb line	in light airs (avoid tacking and keep to one side of course — in the most wind)	
Mark definitely not dead to windward	shifting unknown or oscillating	take close tack to the mark first, tack on headers	you are sailing beyond the point where opposite tack is closer	
	close tack will take you into a header	take close tack to the mark first, tack on headers	on a very slight header it may pay not to tack	
	close tack will take you into minor lift	don't take close tack first; take short tack toward heading side	you can almost fetch on close tack	
	close tack will take you into major lift	take close tack	if shift will be late and not extreme, keep on heading side near rhumb line	

Figure 10-5. CHART FOR BEATING IN SHIFTY WINDS

to sail toward the storm and be one of the first boats to get the shift and strong winds. Since thunderstorm winds can be dangerous, this must be done cautiously with sheets ready to run and sails ready to be lowered at a moment's notice. If the storm is an ominous frontal type, sails should be shortened or lowered early.

10. *In bending winds, sail well into the bend before tacking, and in most cases head for shore toward the center of the wind's rotation, but be careful to avoid the land's blanket.* This has already been discussed and illustrated in Figure 10-2. One further suggestion is that it will be helpful to plot the estimated wind bend on a chart so that you can plan your course to take maximum advantage of the shift.

Of course, as with any rules, there may be exceptions to any of the 10 wind-shift rules. They must be considered along with other factors, such as the presence of other competitors, disturbed wind, and the current. The racing sailor must be flexible, keep an open mind, and look at the whole picture, taking into account every influencing factor.

At times, it may seem that to be successful the skipper needs a computer to interpret all the available data. In an attempt to simplify slightly the complicated matter of choosing the correct course on a beat, especially in shifty, nonbending winds, the chart in Figure 10-5 gives the two possible general situations (the mark dead to windward or definitely not dead to windward), the particular wind-shift conditions, the appropriate rule, the particular exceptions, and the general exceptions.

Many of the strategic principles for beating in shifting winds also apply to sailing downwind. As mentioned in Chapter 9, it often pays to tack downwind in order to avoid sailing with the wind dead aft. Figure 10-6, which uses the same speed curves as in Figure 9-3, illustrates the advantage of tacking downwind in light airs. Boat B, sailing with the true wind on her quarter, has about a third of A's distance to the leeward mark farther to sail, but B sails almost twice as fast. This is partly due to the fact that all of A's speed is subtracted from the true wind speed, whereas only part of B's speed is subtracted. Thus, A is sailing in less apparent wind than B. However, it does not help to tack downwind to any great extent in heavy winds in a displacement boat, because the boat cannot be pushed appreciably above her hull speed. Of course, speed curves will vary with individual boats, but those illustrated are approximations of a fast, nonplaning racing-cruiser. (Obviously, a planing boat should be sailed high enough to allow planing.)

General rules for sailing downwind in shifty winds are as follows:

1. *Tack downwind in light airs, and avoid sailing*

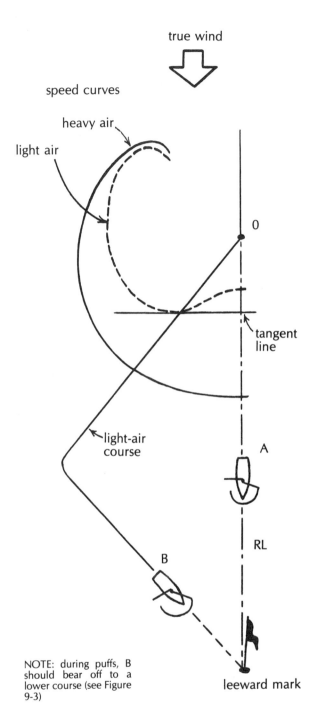

NOTE: during puffs, B should bear off to a lower course (see Figure 9-3)

Figure 10-6. TACKING DOWNWIND

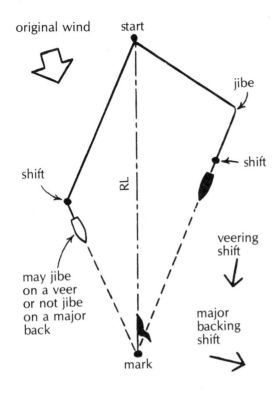

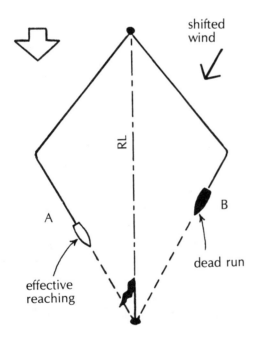

Figure 10-7. DOWNWIND STRATEGY IN SHIFTY WINDS

with the wind dead aft. This is especially true if the current is favorable because of the low apparent wind strength. The exceptions to this rule are in heavy-wind sailing and when the boat is tending to heel to leeward.

2. *Bear off in gusts and head up in lulls.* This was discussed in Chapter 9.

3. *When the mark does not lie dead to leeward, take the close tack first.* This is the same principle as in rule 6 for upwind sailing. A boat with her spinnaker set, bound for a mark not quite dead to leeward, should be put on her optimum downwind heading (perhaps with the wind slightly abaft her quarter if the air is light), and she should start out on the tack that brings her closest to the mark. If the wind shifts so that it is blowing from dead astern, the boat can jibe and approach the mark on an efficient sailing angle on the opposite tack. If the wind shifts the opposite way, however, with the wind much farther ahead (more on the beam), the boat may bear off and come close to or make the mark on a good sailing angle without jibing. The boat taking the far tack first, on the other hand, will either have a greater distance to sail to the mark when the wind shifts one way, or she will be caught with the wind almost dead aft when the shift is in the opposite direction. This is explained in Figure 10-7.

4. *When the leeward mark lies dead to leeward, sail away from the direction of the expected shift.* This is also explained in Figure 10-7. Boat A sails away from the direction of the expected shift. When the shift occurs, she has the wind dead aft, but she may jibe and approach the mark at an efficient sailing angle. Boat B, however, becomes caught with the wind dead aft. She cannot jibe onto either tack and head directly for the mark on an efficient point of sailing.

Of course, these rules are also subject to exceptions due to the influence of current, wind bend, and the whereabouts of other competitors.

CURRENT STRATEGY

In most yachting areas, current is sufficiently strong to be a very important factor in racing. It often is difficult to decide whether the overall strategy should be based primarily on the wind or on the current. Of course, wind and current strategy often coincide, but when they conflict, the choice between the two should be influenced by such considerations as the strength of the current in the racing area, strength of the wind, direction of flow, time of maximum flow and slack water, regions of greatest velocity, the degree of weather certainty, predictability of wind shifts, character of the wind (gusty, shifty, bending, or light and fluky), and effect of wind on the current. Obviously, if the current is weak in the racing area, strategy based on the current should not be emphasized as much as it would be if the flow were of greater strength. Also, current strategy gains importance in light, steady winds. A greater emphasis should be put on current strategy when the flow is adverse rather than favorable, partly because of the longer exposure to the current when it is against you. Current should be a minor consideration when it is slack while sailing a short leg, but great consideration should be given to being in or away from the location where the flow will begin to change first. If the weather is very unpredictable, it may be useful to emphasize current strategy, especially if the flow is strong. It will nearly always help to tack toward shore, beating against a current, when wind bending or shore thermals can be utilized. In offshore races that are beyond coastal currents or in areas of favorable current where the depth of water is fairly uniform, it usually is worth putting the emphasis on wind strategy. Wind may have a considerable effect on current, because it can affect the strength and direction of flow and time of changing.

Fortunately, current is a lot more predictable than wind. Of great assistance to racing skippers are the *Tidal Current Tables* (for Atlantic and Pacific Coasts of North America) published by the U.S. Department of Commerce. These tables are published every year and can be obtained from almost any good yachting-supply store, the National Ocean Survey and its sales agents, or the U.S. Government Printing Office. The tables give the direction, velocity, and time of maximum current from numerous coastal stations. It is not wise, however, to rely always on the exact figures in the tables, because certain conditions of the wind and weather can cause inaccuracies. Current flow should continually be checked visually during a race by watching the leaning of tall buoys, the wakes of crab or lobster pots, wakes of channel markers or fish stakes, boats and especially ships at anchor (which lie to the current rather than the wind), and by keeping track of the boat's lateral movement (excluding leeway) with bearings when crossing a current. In very light airs, it often pays to ease a light anchor over the side when in shallow water to check movement made good or lost over the bottom. It may help at certain times to make a slight course alteration in the interest of passing close to a buoy or other stationary object to "read" or interpret the flow.

Basic rules for sailing in current are as follows:

1. *Stay in shoal water and out of channels when the current is foul, but stay in channels and in deep water when the current is fair.* Friction over the bottom tends to slow the current, so it flows faster in deep water and in channels than over shoals.

2. *It can be beneficial to stay offshore in deep water initially when the current first changes from fair to foul, and, conversely, to stay inshore in shoal water initially when the flow changes from foul to fair.* The reason for this is that the current changes first in shallow waters, where it has the least momentum. Thus, it is usually wise to stay in shallow water when the change is favorable until the flow changes in deep water. When the change is adverse, however, it is usually wise to stay in deep water until the current becomes slack in that location in order to benefit from the favorable flow for the greatest length of time.

3. *When crossing a current at or nearly at right angles to the flow, allowance must be made for its lateral push by heading slightly above or upcurrent of the rhumbline course.* This is an obvious rule, but current is often misinterpreted, and sometimes the rule is not observed at all. The current's lateral push can be estimated by noting the velocity and direction of the flow in the current tables and by visually judging the flow past turning marks, crab pots, and so forth. Also, the boat's lateral movement can be judged by utilizing a range, such as the next turning mark lined up against an object on shore. A boat's proper heading can be determined by drawing a simple vector diagram when the boat's speed and the current's speed and direction are known. For example, if the boat were making two knots in a northerly direction and the current were flowing two knots toward the west, the boat should be headed northeast to counteract the current's lateral push. A table to figure the heading necessary to compensate for a lateral current appears in the annual publication *Eldridge Tide and Pilot Book.*

4. *Whenever possible, plan your course to take advantage of a lee bow current.* There are times when a close-hauled course can be planned to angle the direction of flow against the lee bow. This will naturally set the boat to windward and be advantageous when competitors are sailing in a current of *differing* direction that angles the flow against their windward bows. It can help to tack into the mouth of a river to pick up a lee bow current. This is illustrated in Figure 10-8, which shows a boat tacking toward the river for lee-bow benefits in situation A, but five hours later in situation B (based on actual current studies of the area), the current at the river's mouth has changed so that it is on the windward bow. Therefore, in this case, it would be wrong to tack inshore. Situation C, Figure 10-8, shows the part that a strong lee-bow current can play in light airs. Although the port-tack boat is headed close to the

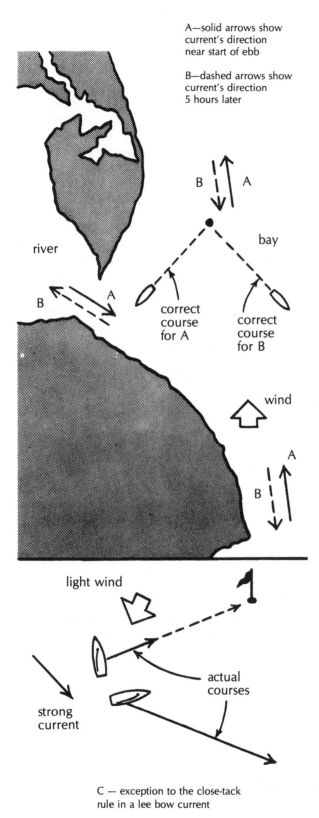

A—solid arrows show
current's direction
near start of ebb

B—dashed arrows show
current's direction
5 hours later

river

bay

correct
course
for A

correct
course
for B

wind

light wind

actual
courses

strong
current

C — exception to the close-tack
rule in a lee bow current

Figure 10-8. LEE BOW CURRENT

windward mark, she is swept away from the mark, while the starboard-tack boat taking the far tack (heading away from the mark) is swept directly to the mark so that she can round it without tacking. Taking an extra tack can be disastrous in very light air. Also, there is a danger that the port-tack boat will overstand or understand. There are occasions when a boat working to windward will head almost directly into an adverse current, and the question arises as to whether or not it is wise to pinch up slightly in order to bring the current on the lee bow. Except, perhaps, when pinching to fetch a mark without tacking, it does not pay to pinch when the boat's speed is noticeably lessened. The often-misunderstood "lee-bow effect" is not a result of added hydrodynamic lift; it is merely the vectorial movement of the boat in the direction toward which the current is flowing. The distance to windward gained by a boat pinching (with the current on her lee bow) over a boat footing (with the same current on her windward bow) will be the same as if the two boats were sailing on identical courses during the same period of time in no current. The direction of flow can be obtained at current stations from the tables. For some areas, detailed current charts are published.

5. *Consider the benefits or detriments of the accelerated current past a point of land and the possible eddy behind the point.* Current often speeds up when it flows past a point or through the constricted area between two opposite points in a river or bay when there is a Venturi force. Also, there is often a relatively weak countercurrent close to shore behind (under the current-sheltered side of) the point. Obviously, it pays to avoid the eddy or accelerated current when it is adverse but to sail into it when it is favorable, provided this plan does not oppose other important strategic considerations.

6. *Watch for tiderips and stay on their favorable side.* Tiderips are streaks of ruffled water agitated by the friction of two opposing currents, or a slow and a fast current moving in the same direction. Of course, it is beneficial to keep on the most favorable side of a rip. Although it is sometimes difficult to tell which side is favorable, this usually can be determined by noting the water's depth, the time of the current's changing from the tables, and the direction of flow from the tables or a current chart, and also by comparing the speeds of boats on both sides of the rip.

COMPETITION TACTICS

As previously mentioned, there should be a slightly different emphasis on competition (boat-vs.-boat) tactics in large-boat, handicap racing compared with small class-boat or one-design racing, because big and little boats should be handled differently and the performance characteristics of handicap racers are often dissimilar. Below is a list of general tactical rules, noting differences between large- and small-boat tactics:

1. *In most cases, loose-cover your most serious competition.* Loose-covering means that you keep yourself in a relatively advantageous tactical position with respect to the competition. This is a defensive technique that can be used when you are ahead of or at least even with the competitor. The main objective of the defense is, in most cases, to stay between your competitor and the next mark of the course, so that he will not receive any special benefits from wind or current that you will not receive. An exception exists when you are directly to leeward of the windward mark and your competitor is dead to leeward of you. In this position, any wind shift theoretically will benefit your competitor, as a lift will shorten the windward distance between the two boats, and a header will shorten the distance between the leading boat and the other one.

2. *Do not use tight-covering tactics unless match-racing or unless you must beat a particular rival to win a series.* *Tight-covering* means that the leading boat stays close to her competitor so that the competitor is blanketed or backwinded. Of course, the boat being covered tries to break away by tacking, jibing, or other maneuvering to get her wind clear. These tactics often develop into luffing matches or *tacking duels* (where the covered boat takes many rapid tacks or feigns tacking in order to break away from her cover, while the covering boat tries to stay on top of her competitor). However, all this maneuvering is very costly with respect to the rest of the competition in a fleet race. It is especially important when handicap-racing large boats not to become preoccupied with one competitor, except under the special circumstances of match racing or the consideration of series standings.

3. *Make every attempt to clear your wind when you are covered, and try to break into the covering boat's zone of wind deflection when it is favorable to you.* If you are being covered, you must try to break the cover or at least take the tack of least wind interference when beating. When to leeward, you may be able to dodge your competitor's windshadow by bearing off and footing. Or, if you are to windward, you may be able to pinch clear of your competitor's backwind. The approximate area of relative wind disturbance is illustrated in Figure 10-9. Although neither boat, A or B, is hurting the other (because B is ahead of A's backwind and A is ahead of B's windshadow), B is helping A because of

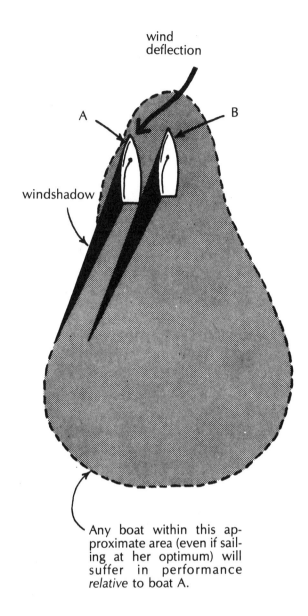

wind deflection

A   B

windshadow

Any boat within this approximate area (even if sailing at her optimum) will suffer in performance *relative* to boat A.

NOTE: boat B is not being hurt by boat A, but A is being helped by B

Figure 10-9. RELATIVE DISTURBANCE OF THE WIND

the wind deflection or bend that allows A to sail in a lift. Thus, if A were being covered by B, and A succeeded in breaking through B's blanket fairly close aboard, the leeward boat would have the advantage of the wind deflection. If A were slightly farther astern in B's blanket, she might be able to come about and clear B's windshadow on the opposite tack. Be sure to study the wind indicators when judging the direction of windshadows. Never follow closely behind another boat, because of the adverse effect of wind deflection, backwind, and wake.

4. *When covering on a beat, try to force your competitor into making a strategic mistake by allowing him to split tacks with you when his tack will take him toward the lay line, toward a general lifting shift on the far tack from the mark, or into a region of less wind or worse current.* If you have a competitor covered effectively, consider letting him escape by splitting tacks with you when his tack will take him into harmful conditions of wind or current. Remember that he will be hurt by a future lifting shift, by almost all shifts when on the far tack from the mark, and by any shift on the lay line. (See rules 3, 6, and 7 for beating in shifty winds.) If you are close to the mark, however, and your competitor will not be hurt by splitting tacks, keep him covered and carry him to the lay line.

5. *If ahead and to leeward of a competitor, foot for a header but pinch for a lift.* This principle has been explained in rule 3 for beating in shifty winds. It usually is best for the boat behind and to windward to pinch slightly if she is close-winded or else to tack for the sake of clearing her wind.

6. *When converging with another boat on opposite tacks, bear off and pass under her stern if your boat is comparatively heavy and slow, but consider tacking under the other's lee bow when your boat is comparatively fast and lively.* It is a common practice in small-boat racing to tack under a rival's lee bow in the so-called *safe leeward position* in order to backwind the rival and/or to profit by wind deflection. However, this can be dangerous in a large, heavy handicap racer, because the tacking boat's lack of acceleration and the other's momentum may allow the windward boat to forge ahead to the point where she can blanket the boat that has just tacked. Whether or not you should tack under a rival's lee bow depends on the speed of your boat in stays, how fast she will pick up speed, and the relative size of the boats. (Obviously, it would be foolish to tack under a larger, faster boat that is bound to "run over" you.) Furthermore, the strategic situation must be considered. You don't want to tack under a lee bow if you are close to and will be headed for the lay line.

Remember that crossing under the stern will allow you subsequent maneuvering freedom.

7. *On a beat, consider consolidating your position with a short tack that will place you dead ahead of a rival who is far behind but slightly to windward of you, if that rival is outperforming you to windward as a result of having a better wind.* This tactic is effective when covering a rival, but it is usually not advisable unless the other boat is in a better wind. In racing-cruisers, avoid extra tacks in very light airs, and don't tack ahead of a much larger, faster boat.

8. *On a reaching leg, plan your course so you will be on an optimal point of sailing during the latter part of the leg.* This usually means sailing low initially and then sailing higher near the end of the leg. It is important that a boat be on an optimal point of sailing as she approaches the turning mark and converges with competitors. An exception to this rule might be in the case where it is necessary to sail high initially in order to carry a spinnaker at the end of the leg, when the next leg is a course that requires the use of a spinnaker. This is especially true for a large boat with an inexperienced crew, since setting the 'chute may take time.

9. *In most cases, approach a windward mark to be left to port on the starboard tack, but consider approaching a mark to be left to starboard on the port tack.* When leaving the mark to port, it is important to have the right-of-way when converging on the mark with other boats. However, when leaving the mark to starboard, a boat approaching on the port tack slightly above the lay line usually can beat a converging starboard-tack rival around the mark for the simple reason that the starboard-tacker must come about to round the mark. This is especially true with large, heavy boats that are slow in stays.

10. *When rounding a mark, don't turn so fast that you kill way; sail closest to the mark after nearly completing the turn; and, if strategy allows, avoid tacking as you round.* A sharp turn, especially in a large, heavy boat, will kill her way. It is best to make a wide approach so that an easy turn will bring you close to the mark after you have rounded it. This is done to backwind following competitors and to avoid disturbed air from rivals ahead of you. If turning onto a windward leg, try to avoid tacking immediately (unless an instant tack is necessary for strategic purposes), because a tack made while rounding kills headway more than if the boat were allowed to pick up full speed before coming about. Also, the delay in tacking gives the crew time to clear up spinnaker gear that could cause entanglements when tacking.

11. *In most cases, try for the inside position when*

rounding a mark, and try to maneuver into a position where you can backwind or blanket your nearby competition. This means that you hold high when turning onto a windward leg, and that you keep directly to windward of competitors when turning onto a downwind leg. It is usually best to be on the inside at the mark when rounding, but be careful not to establish your overlap when closer than two boat lengths from the mark (see Chapter 7 and USYRU Rule 42.3).

12. *At the finish, try to be on the starboard tack, head for the close end of the line, and finish between your competition and the committee boat.* It is advisable to have the right-of-way when converging on the finish line with other boats. When the line is not exactly square to the last leg of the course, head for the line's end that is closest to you. In the case of a "photo finish" with a competitor, it may help you if you finish between the competitor and the committee boat.

These rules incorporate the main competition tactical principles used on the course and when rounding buoys. Starting tactics were dealt with in Chapter 8. As final advice on tactics, remember to look at the overall strategic picture before involving yourself in boat-for-boat tactics, stay clear of trouble by avoiding congestions of boats, try to anticipate conditions that could lead to collisions or entanglements, learn the racing rules, and never gamble by splitting with your main competition unless you feel certain the odds are in your favor.

A big difference between class-boat racing and handicap racing is variations in boat performance. In class-boat racing, it is important for the skipper to size up his competition by considering the human element, such as whether or not a rival skipper likes to pinch his boat or sail her full and by, whether or not another skipper is inclined to luff a boat passing him to windward, whether another skipper will fight for an inside position at the mark. A handicap skipper must consider the human element also, but he must learn the performance characteristics of his rivals' boats. These characteristics can affect his tactical judgment in several ways. When a competitor is very close-winded, it might be a mistake to start to windward of her or to attempt to pass her to windward. If a rival's boat is slowed by choppy head seas, you might be able to escape her cover by tacking offshore into a chop, especially when the current is against the wind. When your boat is a centerboarder, you might be able to elude a deep-keel covering boat by heading for shoal water. If your rival has a soft forefoot or a shallow keel and falls off the wind after tacking, you might profit by a brief tacking duel to escape her cover. When your boat has a short fin and spade rudder, you may be able to outmaneuver a competitor with a long keel and a more forward rudder, when starting or rounding buoys. If your boat is heavy, you may be able to tack sooner than a light competitor to fetch the windward mark, by relying on your ability to luff and forereach around the mark.

These are just a few examples of how it can help to size up the boats of your racing rivals. The anomaly of handicap racing is that sister boats sometimes do not have close races, but boats of entirely different lines, even based on opposite design concepts (but with similar ratings), often engage in extremely close boat-for-boat racing. But this is just another intriguing aspect of the sport of competition in racing-cruisers.

Appendixes

Part 1 — Definitions

When a term defined in Part 1 is used in its defined sense it is printed in *italic* type. All preambles and definitions rank as rules.

Racing — A yacht is *racing* from her preparatory signal until she has either *finished* and cleared the finishing line and finishing *marks* or retired, or until the race has been *postponed, abandoned, cancelled,* or a general recall has been signalled, except that in match or team races, the sailing instructions may prescribe that a yacht is *racing* from any specified time before the preparatory signal.

Starting — A yacht *starts* when, after fulfulling her penalty obligations, if any, under rule 51.1(c), (Sailing the Course), and after her starting signal, any part of her hull, crew or equipment first crosses the starting line in the direction of the course to the first *mark.*

Finishing — A yacht *finishes* when any part of her hull, or of her crew or equipment in normal position, crosses the finishing line from the direction of the course from the last *mark,* after fulfilling her penalty obligations, if any, under rule 52.2, (Touching a Mark).

Luffing — Altering course towards the wind.

Tacking — A yacht is *tacking* from the moment she is beyond head to wind until she has *borne away,* when beating to windward, to a *close-hauled* course; when not beating to windward, to the course on which her mainsail has filled.

Bearing Away — Altering course away from the wind until a yacht begins to *gybe.*

Gybing — A yacht begins to *gybe* at the moment when, with the wind aft, the foot of her mainsail crosses her centre line, and completes the *gybe* when the mainsail has filled on the other *tack.*

Close-hauled — A yacht is *close-hauled* when sailing by the wind as close as she can lie with advantage in working to windward.

Clear Astern and *Clear Ahead; Overlap* — A yacht is *clear astern* of another when her hull and equipement in normal position are abaft an imaginary line projected abeam from the aftermost point of the other's hull and equipment in normal position. The other yacht is *clear ahead.*

The yachts *overlap* when neither is *clear astern;* or when, although one is *clear astern,* an intervening yacht *overlaps* both of them.

The terms *clear astern, clear ahead* and *overlap* apply to yachts on opposite *tacks* only when they are subject to rule 42, (Rounding or Passing Marks and Obstructions).

Leeward and *Windward* — The *leeward* side of a yacht is that on which she is, or, when head to wind, was, carrying her mainsail. The opposite side is the *windward* side.

When neither of two yachts on the same *tack* is *clear astern,* the one on the *leeward* side of the other is the *leeward yacht.* The other is the *windward yacht.*

Proper Course — A *proper course* is any course which a yacht might sail after the starting signal, in the absence of the other yacht or yachts affected, to *finish* as quickly as possible. The course sailed before *luffing* or *bearing away* is presumably, but not necessarily, that yacht's *proper course.* There is no *proper course* before the starting signal.

Mark — A *mark* is any object specified in the sailing instructions which a yacht must round or pass on a required side.

Every ordinary part of a *mark* ranks as part of it, including a flag, flagpole, boom or hoisted boat, but excluding ground tackle and any object either accidentally or temporarily attached to the *mark.*

Obstruction — An *obstruction* is any object, including a vessel under way, large enough to require a yacht, when more than one overall length away from it, to make a substantial alteration of course to pass on one side or the other, or any object which can be passed on one side only, including a buoy when the yacht in question cannot safely pass between it and the shoal or object which it marks.

Postponement — A *postponed* race is one which is not started at its scheduled time and which can be sailed at any time the race committee may decide.

Abandonment — An *abandoned* race is one which the race committee declares void at any time after the starting signal, and which can be re-sailed at its discretion.

Cancellation — A *cancelled* race is one which the race committee decides will not be sailed thereafter.

Part IV — Right of Way Rules

RIGHTS AND OBLIGATIONS WHEN YACHTS MEET

The rules of Part IV do not apply in any way to a vessel which is neither intending to *race* nor *racing;* such vessel shall be treated in accordance with the International Regulations for Preventing Collisions at Sea or Government Right of Way Rules applicable to the area concerned.

The rules of Part IV apply only between yachts which either are intending to *race* or are *racing* in the same or different races, and, except when rule 3.2(b)(xxviii), (Race Continues After Sunset), applies, replace the International Regulations for Preventing Collisions at Sea or Government Right of Way Rules applicable to the area concerned, from the time a yacht intending to *race* begins to sail about in the vicinity of the starting line until she has either *finished* or retired and has left the vicinity of the course.

SECTION A — OBLIGATIONS AND PENALTIES

31 Disqualification

31.1 A yacht may be disqualified or otherwise penalised for infringing a rule of Part IV only when the infringement occurs while she is *racing,* whether or not a collision results.

31.2 A yacht may be disqualified before or after she is *racing* for seriously hindering a yacht which is *racing,* or for infringing the sailing instructions.

32 Avoiding Collisions

A right-of-way yacht which fails to make a reasonable attempt to avoid a collision resulting in serious damage may be disqualified as well as the other yacht.

33 Rule Infringement

33.1 ACCEPTING PENALTY
A yacht which realises she has infringed a racing rule or a sailing instruction is under an obligation either to retire promptly or to exonerate herself by accepting an alternative penalty when so prescribed in the sailing instructions, but when she does not retire or exonerate herself and persists in *racing,* other yachts shall continue to accord her such rights as she has under the rules of Part IV.

33.2 CONTACT BETWEEN YACHTS RACING
When there is contact between the hulls, equipment or crew of two yachts, both shall be disqualified or otherwise penalised unless:

either

(a) one of the yachts retires in acknowledgement of the infringement, or exonerates herself by accepting an alternative penalty when so prescribed in the sailing instructions,

or

(b) one or both of these yachts acts in accordance with rule 68, (Protests by Yachts).

33.3 WAIVING RULE 33.2
A race committee acting under rule 33.2 may waive the requirements of the rule when it is satisfied that the contact was minor and unavoidable.

34   Hailing

34.1   Except when *luffing* under rule 38.1, (Luffing and Sailing above a Proper Course after Starting), a right-of-way yacht which does not hail before or when making an alteration of course which may not be foreseen by the other yacht may be disqualified as well as the yacht required to keep clear when a collision resulting in serious damage occurs.

34.2   A yacht which hails when claiming the establishment or termination of an *overlap* or insufficiency of room at a *mark* or *obstruction* thereby helps to support her claim for the purposes of rule 42, (Rounding or Passing Marks and Obstructions).

SECTION B — PRINCIPAL RIGHT OF WAY RULES AND THEIR LIMITATIONS

These rules apply except when over-ridden by a rule in Section C.

35   Limitations on Altering Course

When one yacht is required to keep clear of another, the right-of-way yacht shall not so alter course as to prevent the other yacht from keeping clear; or so as to obstruct her while she is keeping clear, except:

(a)   to the extent permitted by rule 38.1, (Same Tack, Luffing and Sailing above a Proper Course after Starting), and

(b)   when assuming a *proper course:*
either

(i)   to *start,* unless subject to rule 40, (Same Tack Luffing before Starting), or to the second part of rule 44.1(b), (Returning to Start),
or

(ii)   when rounding a *mark.*

36   Opposite Tacks — Basic Rule

A *port-tack* yacht shall keep clear of a *starboard-tack* yacht.

37   Same Tack — Basic Rules

37.1   WHEN OVERLAPPED
A *windward yacht* shall keep clear of a *leeward yacht.*

37.2   WHEN NOT OVERLAPPED
A yacht *clear astern* shall keep clear of a yacht *clear ahead.*

37.3   TRANSITIONAL
A yacht which establishes an *overlap* to *leeward* from *clear astern* shall allow the *windward yacht* ample room and opportunity to keep clear.

38   Same Tack — Luffing and Sailing above a Proper Course after Starting

38.1   LUFFING RIGHTS
After she has *started* and cleared the starting line, a yacht *clear ahead* or a *leeward yacht* may *luff* as she pleases, subject to the *proper course* limitations of this rule.

38.2   PROPER COURSE LIMITATIONS
A *leeward yacht* shall not sail above her *proper course* while an *overlap* exists, if when the *overlap* began or, at any time during its existence, the helmsman of the *windward yacht* (when sighting abeam from his normal station and sailing no higher than the *leeward yacht)* has been abreast or forward of the mainmast of the *leeward yacht.*

38.3   OVERLAP LIMITATIONS
For the purpose of rule 38 only: An *overlap* does not exist unless the yachts are clearly within two overall lengths of the longer yacht; and an *overlap* which exists between two yachts when the leading yacht *starts,* or when one or both of them completes a *tack* or *gybe,* shall be regarded as a new *overlap* beginning at that time.

38.4   HAILING TO STOP OR PREVENT A LUFF
When there is doubt, the *leeward yacht* may assume that she has the right to *luff* unless the helmsman of the *windward yacht* has hailed "Mast Abeam", or words to that effect. The *leeward yacht* shall be governed by such hail, and, when she deems it improper, her only remedy is to protest.

38.5   CURTAILING A LUFF
The *windward yacht* shall not cause a *luff* to be curtailed because of her proximity to the *leeward yacht* unless an *obstruction,* a third yacht or other object restricts her ability to respond.

38.6   LUFFING TWO OR MORE YACHTS
A yacht shall not *luff* unless she has the right to *luff* all yachts which would be affected by her *luff,* in which case they shall all respond even when an intervening yacht or yachts would not otherwise have the right to *luff.*

39   Same Tack — Sailing below a Proper Course after Starting

A yacht which is on a free leg of the course shall not sail below her *proper course* when she is clearly within three of her overall lengths of either a *leeward yacht* or a yacht *clear astern* which is steering a course to pass to *leeward.*

40   Same Tack — Luffing before Starting

Before a right-of-way yacht has *started* and cleared the starting line, any *luff* on her part which causes another yacht to have to alter course to avoid a collision shall be carried out slowly and in such a way as to give a *windward yacht* room and opportunity to keep clear. However, the *leeward yacht* shall not so *luff* above a *close-hauled* course, unless the helmsman of the *windward yacht* (sighting abeam from his normal station) is abaft the mainmast of the *leeward yacht.* Rules 38.4, (Hailing to Stop or Prevent a Luff); 38.5, (Curtailing a Luff); and 38.6, (Luffing Two or more Yachts), also apply.

41 Changing Tacks — Tacking and Gybing

41.1 BASIC RULE
A yacht which is either *tacking* or *gybing* shall keep clear of a yacht *on a tack.*

41.2 TRANSITIONAL
A yacht shall neither *tack* nor *gybe* into a position which will give her right of way unless she does so far enough from a yacht *on a tack* to enable this yacht to keep clear without having to begin to alter her course until after the *tack* or *gybe* has been completed.

41.3 ONUS
A yacht which *tacks* or *gybes* has the onus of satisfying the race committee that she completed her *tack* or *gybe* in accordance with rule 41.2.

41.4 WHEN SIMULTANEOUS
When two yachts are both *tacking* or both *gybing* at the same time, the one on the other's port side shall keep clear.

SECTION C — RULES WHICH APPLY AT MARKS AND OBSTRUCTIONS AND OTHER EXCEPTIONS TO THE RULES OF SECTION B

When a rule of this section applies, to the extent to which it explicitly provides rights and obligations, it over-rides any conflicting rule of Section B, Principal Right of Way Rules and their Limitations, except rule 35, (Limitations on Altering Course).

42 Rounding or Passing Marks and Obstructions

42.1 ROOM AT MARKS AND OBSTRUCTONS WHEN OVERLAPPED
When yachts are about to round or pass a *mark,* other than a starting *mark* surrounded by navigable water, on the same required side or an *obstruction* on the same side:

(a) An outside yacht shall give each yacht *overlapping* her on the inside, room to round or pass the *mark* or *obstruction,* except as provided in rules 42.1(c), 42.1(d) and 42.4, (At a Starting Mark Surrounded by Navigable Water).
Room includes room for an *overlapping* yacht to *tack* or *gybe* when either is an integral part of the rounding or passing manoeuvre.

(b) When an inside yacht of two or more *overlapped* yachts either on opposite *tacks,* or on the same *tack* without *luffing* rights, will have to *gybe* in order most directly to assume a *proper course* to the next *mark,* she shall *gybe* at the first reasonable opportunity.

(c) When two yachts on opposite *tacks* are on a beat or when one of them will have to *tack* either to round the *mark* or to avoid the *obstruction,* as between each other rule 42.1(a) shall not apply and they are subject to rules 36, (Opposite Tacks — Basic Rule). and 41, (Changing Tacks — Tacking and Gybing).

(d) An outside *leeward yacht* with luffing rights may take an inside yacht to windward of a *mark* provided that she hails to that effect and begins to *luff* before she is within two of her overall lengths of the *mark* and provided that she also passes to windward of it.

42.2 CLEAR ASTERN AND CLEAR AHEAD IN THE VICINITY OF MARKS AND OBSTRUCTIONS
When yachts are about to round or pass a *mark,* other than a starting *mark* surrounded by navigable water, on the same required side or an *obstruction* on the same side:

(a) A yacht *clear astern* shall keep clear in anticipation of and during the rounding or passing manoeuvre when the yacht *clear ahead* remains on the same *tack* or *gybes.*

(b) A yacht *clear ahead* which *tacks* to round a *mark* is subject to rule 41, (Changing Tacks — Tacking and Gybing), but a yacht *clear astern* shall not *luff* above *close-hauled* so as to prevent the yacht *clear ahead* from *tacking.*

42.3 LIMITATIONS ON ESTABLISHING AND MAIN—TAINING AN OVERLAP IN THE VICINITY OF MARKS AND OBSTRUCTIONS

(a) When a yacht *clear astern* establishes an inside *overlap* she shall be entitled to room under rule 42.1(a), (Room at Marks and Obstructions when Overlapped), only when the yacht *clear ahead:*

(i) is able to give the required room and

(ii) is outside two of her overall lengths of the *mark* or *obstruction,* except when one of the yachts has completed a *tack* within two overall lengths of the *mark* or *obstruction,* or when the *obstruction* is a continuing one as provided in rule 42.3(f).

(b) A yacht *clear ahead* shall be under no obligation to give room to a yacht *clear astern* before an *overlap* is established.

(c) When an outside yacht is *overlapped* at the time she comes within two of her overall lengths of a *mark* or an *obstruction,* she shall continue to be bound by rule 42.1(a), (Room at Marks and Obstructions when Overlapped), to give room as required even though the *overlap* is thereafter broken.

(d) A yacht which claims an inside *overlap* has the onus of satisfying the race committee that the *overlap* was established in proper time.

(e) An outside yacht which claims to have broken an *overlap* has the onus of satisfying the race committee that she became *clear ahead* when she was more than two of her overall lengths from the *mark* or *obstruction.*

(f) A yacht *clear astern* may establish an *overlap* between the yacht *clear ahead* and a continuing *obstruction,* such as a shoal or the shore or another vessel, only when at that time there is room for her to pass between them in safety.

42.4 AT A STARTING MARK SURROUNDED BY NAVIGABLE WATER

"Anti-Barging" Rule

When approaching the starting line to *start,* a *leeward yacht* shall be under no obligation to give any *windward yacht* room to pass to leeward of a starting *mark* surrounded by navigable water; but, after the starting signal, a *leeward yacht* shall not deprive a *windward yacht* of room at such a *mark* by sailing either above the compass bearing of the course to the first *mark* or above *close-hauled.*

43 Close-Hauled, Hailing for Room to Tack at Obstructions

43.1 HAILING

When two *close-hauled* yachts are on the same *tack* and safe pilotage requires the yacht *clear ahead* or the *leeward yacht* to make a substantial alteration of course to clear an *obstruction,* and when she intends to *tack,* but cannot *tack* without colliding with the other yacht, she shall hail the other yacht for room to *tack* and clear the other yacht, but she shall not hail and *tack* simultaneously.

43.2 RESPONDING

The hailed yacht at the earliest possible moment after the hail shall:

either:

(a) *tack,* in which case the hailing yacht shall begin to *tack,* either

    (i) before the hailed yacht has completed her *tack,* or

    (ii) when she cannot then *tack* without colliding with the hailed yacht, immediately she is able to *tack* and clear her;

or

(b) reply "You *tack*", or words to that effect, when in her opinion she can keep clear without *tacking* or after postponing her *tack.*
In this case:

    (i) the hailing yacht shall immediately tack and

    (ii) the hailed yacht shall keep clear.

    (iii) The onus of satisfying the race committee that she kept clear shall lie on the hailed yacht which replied "You *tack*".

43.3 LIMITATION ON RIGHT TO ROOM TO TACK WHEN THE OBSTRUCTION IS ALSO A MARK

(a) When the hailed yacht can fetch an *obstruction* which is also a *mark,* the hailing yacht shall not be entitled room to *tack* and clear the hailed yacht and the hailed yacht shall immediately so inform the hailing yacht.

(b) If, thereafter, the hailing yacht again hails for room to *tack* and clear the hailed yacht, the hailed

yacht shall, at the earliest possible moment after the hail, give the hailing yacht the required room. After receiving room, the hailing yacht shall either retire immediately or exonerate herself by accepting an alternative penalty when so prescribed in the sailing instructions.

(c) When, after having refused to respond to a hail under rule 43.3(a), the hailed yacht fails to fetch, she shall retire immediately, or exonerate herself by accepting an alternative penalty when so prescribed in the sailing instructions.

44 Returning to Start

44.1 (a) After the starting signal is made, a premature starter returning to *start,* or a yacht working into position from the course side of the starting line or its extensions, shall keep clear of all yachts which are *starting* or have *started* correctly, until she is wholly on the pre-start side of the starting line or its extensions.

(b) Thereafter, she shall be accorded the rights under the rules of Part IV of a yacht which is *starting* correctly; but when she thereby acquires right of way over another yacht which is *starting* correctly, she shall allow that yacht ample room and opportunity to keep clear.

44.2 A premature starter while continuing to sail the course and until it is obvious that she is returning to *start,* shall be accorded the rights under the rules of Part IV of a yacht which has *started.*

45 Re-rounding after Touching a Mark

45.1 A yacht which has touched a *mark,* and is exonerating herself in accordance with rule 52.2, (Touching a Mark), shall keep clear of all other yachts which are about to round or pass it or have rounded or passed it correctly, until she has rounded it completely and has cleared it and is on a *proper course* to the next *mark.*

45.2 A yacht which has touched a *mark* while continuing to sail the course and until it is obvious that she is returning to round it completely in accordance with rule 52.2, (Touching a Mark), shall be accorded rights under the rules of Part IV.

46 Anchored, Aground, Capsized or Person Overboard

46.1 A yacht under way shall keep clear of another yacht *racing* which is anchored, aground, capsized or rescuing a person overboard. Of two anchored yachts, the one which anchored later shall keep clear, except that a yacht which is dragging shall keep clear of one which is not.

46.2 A yacht anchored or aground shall indicate the fact to any yacht which may be in danger of fouling her. Unless the size of the yachts or the weather conditions make some other signal necessary, a hail is sufficient indication.

46.3 A yacht shall not be penalised for fouling a yacht in distress which she is attempting to assist or a yacht which goes aground or capsizes immediately ahead of her.

Appendix B: INTERNATIONAL OFFSHORE RULE (IOR) MEASUREMENT SYMBOLS

ALPHABETICAL INDEX OF SYMBOLS IN THE RULE

AW, BW, CW, DW	Inclining weights
AWD, BWD, etc.	Weight distances
APD, BPD, etc.	Pendulum deflections
ARM, BRM, etc.	Righting moments one degree

Symbol		*Symbol*	
ACG1	AOCG factor	CMD	Center mid depth
ACG2	AOCG factor	CMDI	Ditto immersed
AGO	After girth overhang	D	Rated depth
AGS	After girth station	DB	Base draft
AGSL	Aft girth slope	DC	Draft correction
AIGS	After inner girth station	DD	Draft difference
AOC	Aft overhang component	DF	Propeller drag factor
AOCC	AOC corrected	DLF	Displacement length factor
AOCG	AOC girth	DLFA	Ditto Mk IIIA
AOCP	AOC profile	DM	Draft measured
APB	Aperture width bottom	DMT	Draft measured total
APH	Aperture height	DSPL	Displacement
APSL	Aft profile slope	E	Foot of mainsail
APT	Aperture width top	EB	Distance between masts
B	Rated beam	EBC	Ditto corrected
BA	Beam aft	EC	Foot of mainsail corrected
BAS	Boom above sheer line	EDL	Strut drive length
BADS	Ditto schooner foresail	EDC	Strut drive clearance
BADX	Ditto	EF	Foot of foresail
BADY	Ditto mizzen	EFC	Ditto corrected
BAI	Beam aft inner	EM	Engine moment
BAL	Sheet limit main boom	EMF	Engine moment factor
BALF	Ditto schooner foresail	EPF	Engine and propeller factor
BALY	Ditto mizzen	ESC	Exposed shaft clearance
BBS	B below sheer line	ESD	Exposed shaft depth
BCOR	BWL corrected	ESL	Exposed shaft length
BD	Boom depth main	EW	Engine weight
BDF	Ditto foresail	EWD	Engine weight distance
BDY	Ditto mizzen	EY	Foot of mizzen
BDR	Base displacement ratio	EYC	Ditto corrected
BF	Beam forward	FA	Freeboard aft
BFI	Beam forward inner	FAI	Freeboard aft inner
BHA	Buttock height aft	FB	Base freeboard
BHAI	Buttock height aft inner	FBI	Freeboard base of I
BLP	Batten leech penalty	FC	Freeboard correction
BLPS	Ditto foresail	FD	Forward depth
BLPY	Ditto mizzen	FDI	Ditto immersed
BL 1–5	Mainsail battens	FDIC	Ditto corrected
BS 1–5	Foresail battens	FDS	Forward depth station
BSC	Beam sheer correction	FF	Freeboard forward
BMAX	Beam maximum	FFD	Freeboard at FDS
BY 1–5	Mizzen battens	FFI	Freeboard forward inner
BWL	Beam waterline	FGO	Forward girth overhang
BWL 1	Ditto calculated	FGS	Forward girth station
CBDA, B	Centerboard CG drop	FIGS	Forward inner girth station
CBLD	Centerboard CG lateral	FM	Freeboard measured
CBF	Ditto factor	FMD	Freeboard at MDS
CBFA	Ditto Mk IIIA	FOC	Forward overhang component
CCF	} Curvature corrections at depth stations	FJ	Freeboard at fore end of J
CCM		FSP	Forestay perpendicular
CCC		G	Gaff length
CCO		GD	Girth difference

Symbol	
CD	Centerboard extension
CGF	Center of gravity factor
CGFA	Ditto Mk IIA
GO	Forestay outrigger
GSDA	Girth station difference aft
GSDF	Ditto forward
GY	Mizzen gaff
H	Hoist of gaff mainsail
HB	Headboard of mainsail
HBF	Ditto foresail
HBS	Ditto spinnaker
HBY	Ditto mizzen
HC	Gaff hoist corrected
HF	Hoist of gaff foresail
HFC	Ditto corrected
HGLA	Half girth length aft
HGLI	Ditto aft inner
HY	Hoist of gaff mizzen
HYC	Ditto corrected
I	Height of foretriangle
IC	Ditto corrected
IG	Height of Genoa halyard
IS	Height of schooner mainmast
ISP	Height of spinnaker halyard
IY	Height of mizzen mast
J	Base of foretriangle
JC	Ditto corrected
L	Rated length
LBG	Length between girths
LBGC	Ditto corrected
LL	Luff limit of spinnaker
LLA	Limit of length aft
LOA	Length overall
LP	Longest perpendicular
LPG	Ditto of jibs
LPIS	Ditto of inner jib
LRP	Low rigging penalty
MACG	Movable appendage CG
MACO	Movable appendage off CL
MAF	Movable appendage factor
MAW	Movable appendage weight
MAXJL	Maximum jib luff length
MD	Midship depth
MDI	Midship depth immersed
MDIA	Ditto adjusted
MDS	Mid depth station
MR	Measured Rating
MRA	Ditto Mk IIIA
MSA	Measured sail area
MSAT	Ditto of topsail
MSATF	Ditto of foretopsail
MW	Mast width
OF	Schooner foresail overlap
OMD	Outer mid depth
OMDI	Ditto immersed
P	Mainsail hoist
PC	Mainsail hoist corrected
PBW	Propeller blade width
PD	Propeller depth
PDC	Propeller depth corrected
PDT	Propeller depth below sheer
PL	Pendulum length

Symbol	
GDFI	Girth difference forward inner
GF	Foresail gaff
GLAI	Girth length aft inner
PRD	Propeller diameter
PRDC	Propeller diameter corrected
PS	Propeller size
PSF	Foresail hoist schooners
PSFC	Ditto corrected
PY	Mizzen hoist
PYC	Ditto corrected
R	Rating
RA	Rating Mk IIIA
RD	Rated draft
RM	Righting moment
RMC	Ditto corrected
RSA	Rated sail area
RSAB	RSA between masts schooners
RSAC	RSA combined abaft masts
RSAF	RSA foretriangle
RSAG	RSA schooner foresail
RSAK	RSA mizzen staysail
RSAL	RSA low limit
RSAM	RSA mainsail
RSAT	Total rated sail area
RSAY	RSA mizzen
RSBS 1–6	Rated sheer below sheer
S 1–3	Sides of mules and topsails
SATC	Sail area total correction
SBMAX	Length bow to BMAX
SBWF	Length BMAX to BWL Station Forward
SBWA	Ditto aft
SC	Sail area value
SCA	Ditto Mk IIIA
SCF	Sail correction factor
SDM	Length bow to draft station
SF	Spinnaker foot length
SL	Ditto luff/leech length
SMG	Ditto mid girth length
SMW	Ditto maximum width
SFJ	Length bow to FJ
SHR	Sail/hull ratio
SMF	Spar material factor
SPD	Length bow to PD station
SPS	Spinnaker pole height
SPIN	Spinnaker rated area
SPL	Spinnaker pole length
S	Square root RSAT or SPIN
ST 1–3	Propeller struts
SV	Screening value
TR	Tenderness ratio
TCI	Trim correction to I
VHA	Vertical height aft
VHAI	Vertical height aft inner
W	Calculated heeling weight
WCBA, B	Centerboard weights
WCBC	Centerboard weight total
Y	Distance AGS to LLA
YSAC	Combined RSA mizzen sails
YSD	Mizzen staysail depth
YSF	Mizzen staysail foot
YSMG	Mizzen staysail mid girth

Suffix S on freeboards FFS, FAS etc. Indicates standard or measured ashore
Suffix M on freeboards FFM, FAM etc. Indicates measured afloat
Suffix A on sail areas or rating, RSATA, RA Indicates Mk. IIIA

APSLC	Aft profile slope corrected	FBM 1	Freeboard at BMAX
BAPSL	Base aft profile slope	WLH (1-5)	Trial WL heights
MGM	Mainsail girth (mid)	TWL (1-5)	Trial WL beams
MGU	Mainsail girth (upper)	VSW	Vertical spacing

Appendix C: MIDGET OCEAN RACING CLUB (MORC) MEASUREMENT SYMBOLS

LOA	Length Overall	OHT	Overhang Transom
OHF	Overhang Forward	LWL	Load Waterline
OHA	Overhang Aft	BBM	Base Beam
BMX	Beam Maximum	BM	Beam Measured
BWL	Beam Waterline	DRR	Draft Rated
DR	Draft	DB	Draft Base
FBF	Freeboard Forward	BFB	Base Freeboard
FBA	Freeboard Aft	FBM	Freeboard Measured
P	Mainsail Hoist	SAB	Sail Area Base
B	Foot of Main	Rated B	Rated Foot of Main
HDBD	Headboard	MAX HDBD	Maximum Headboard
UP-BAT	Upper Batten	MAX END BAT	Maximum UP & LO Battens
UI-BAT	Upper Intermediate Batten	MAX INT BAT	Maximum Intermediate Battens
LO-BAT	Lower Batten	MIN MN AREA	Minimum Mainsail Area
P_2W	Foretriangle Height to waterline	RAMN	Rated Mainsail Area
P_2	Foretriangle Height Calculated	RATED P_2	Rated Foretriangle Height
J/B_2	Foretriangle Base Calculated	GENOA %	Genoa LP% of Foretriangle Base
SL	Spinnaker Luff	MAX SL	Maximum Spinnaker Luff
SPL	Spinnaker Pole Length	RATED $J(B_2)$	Rated Foretriangle Base
SMW	Spinnaker Maximum Width	J-SMW	Cal. J based on SMW/1.8
LP	Luff Perpendicular	J-LP	Cal. J from Max. LP/1.7
BFO	Bow Foretriangle Overhang + or −	RAFT	Rated Sail Area Foretriangle
FTO	Forward Transom Overhang	RSAT	Rated Sail Area Total
WT	Weight	DISB	Displacement Base
LKWT	Lead Keel Weight	DISP	Volume Displacement
IKWT	Iron Keel Weight	DISM	Displacement Measured
IBW	Inside Ballast Weight	ECBW	Excess Centerboard Weight
ESW	Excess Stores Weight	IWT	Iron Weight Total
CBW	Centerboard Weight	IWT + LKWT	Iron Keel Wt + Lead Keel Wt
CBA(s)	Max. Exposed CB Area	BBDR	Base Ballast Displ. Ratio
SG	Specific Gravity	BDR	Ballast Displacement Ratio
PS	Prop Size	DBMX	Delta Beam Max
DPROP	Propeller Depth	L	Rated Length
PF	Propeller Factor	BMCR	Beam Correction
TYPE	Folding, Feathering, Solid	DRCR	Draft Correction
C/L	Centerline	FBCR	Freeboard Correction
STRUT	Strut	SACR	Sail Area Correction
4% OHF	4% Overhang Forward	DISCR	Displacement Correction
4% OHA	4% Overhang Aft	I	Iron Ballast Correction
4% WL	4% Waterline	COR L	Corrected Length
TW	Transom Width	STF	Stability Factor
TH	Transom Height	PROP	Propeller Correction
C/VOL	Cockpit Volume		

Appendix D: MEASUREMENT HANDICAP SYSTEM (MHS) SYMBOLS

AMS 1	Area Maximum Section		EDMY	Effective Diameter Mizzenmast
AMS 2	Area Maximum Section Attenuated for Depth		EHM	Effective Height of Mainmast
APB	Aperture Width Bottom		EHMY	Effective Height Mizzenmast
APH	Aperture Height		FA_{ior}	Freeboard Aft according to IOR
APT	Aperture Width Top		FBAV	Freeboard Average
ATEK	Section Area at Trailing Edge of Keel		FF_{ior}	Forward Freeboard according to IOR
B	Effective Beam		GW	Gear Weight
BAD_{ior}	BAD according to IOR		I_{ior}	I according to IOR
BRR	Beat, Reach, and Run		IOR	International Offshore Rule
BTR	Beam Depth Ratio		IY_{ior}	Height of Mizzenmast according to IOR
CBSA	Section Area at Centerboard Trailing Edge		KCDA	Keel Centerboard Depth Adjustment
CGW	Crew and Gear Weight		L	Sailing Length
CGWL	Longitudinal Center of Gravity of Crew and Gear Weight		L_{ior}	Length according to IOR
			LPP	Lines Processing Program
CGWV	Vertical Center of Gravity Crew and Gear Weight		LR	Linear Random
CR	Circular Random		LSM	Second Moment Length
CRI	Committee for Review and Inspection		LSM0 LSM1, LSM2, LSM3, LSM4	Second Moment Lengths in various conditions
CW	Crew Weight			
D	Reduced Draft		MDL 1	Maximum Longitudinal Dimension of Mainmast
DHK	Draft of Hull and Fixed Keel		MDL 2	Longitudinal Dimension of Mainmast at Head
DHKA	Draft of Keel and Hull Adjusted		MDT 1	Maximum Transverse Dimension of Mainmast
DISP	Weight of Yacht in Sailing Trim		MDT 2	Transverse Dimension of Mainmast at Head
$DSPL_{ior}$	DSPL according to IOR		P_{ior}	P according to IOR
ECE	Effective Centerboard Extension		PHD 1	Folding Propeller Hub Diameter
ECM	Extension of Centerboard Measured below Hull or Keel		PHD 2	Feathering Propeller Hub Diameter
			PHL	Folding Propeller Hub Length
ECMA	ECM Adjusted for Keel or Hull Shape above Centerboard		PIPA	Propeller Installation Projected Area
EDM	Effective Diameter Mainmast		PRD	Propeller Diameter
EDMB	Base Effective Mainmast Diameter		PSA	Propeller Shaft Angle
EDMC	Effective Diameter of Mainmast Corrected		PSD	Propeller Shaft Diameter

PSL	Propeller Shaft Length	SHD	Strut Hub Diameter
R_{ior}	R according to IOR	SHL	Strut Hub Length
RMC_{ior}	RMC according to IOR	T	Effective Hull Depth
RM0	Righting Moment per Degree in Measurement Trim at 2° Heel	TL	Tapered Length of Mainmast
RM2	Righting Moment per Degree in Sailing Trim at 2° Heel	TLY	Tapered Length of Mizzenmast
		VPP	Velocity Prediction Program
RM3	Righting Moment per Degree in Sailing Trim at 25° Heel	WS	Wetted Surface

Appendix E: COMPARISON OF RATINGS, MHS VS. PHRF, ON CHESAPEAKE BAY

BOAT	1882 RATING (secs/mile)	
	MHS	PHRF
Alberg 37	293	162
Albin Nimbus 42	230	96
C&C 27	315	186
C&C 30	290	174
C&C 33	273	273
C&C 34 keel	268	144
C&C 35	242	126
C&C 38	249	120
C&C 39	226	150
Cal 29	304	174
Cal 40	253	114
Cal 9.2	279	156
Carter 3/4	266	150
Chance 30/30	285	168
Ericson 32-2	299	174
Ericson 37	258	120
Ericson 39	244	108
Evelyn 26	298	168
Gulfstar 40	248	114
Heritage 1 Ton	237	114
Islander 40	210	81
Luders 44	261	138
Morgan 38	276	132
Morgan 41 cb	260	120
New York 40	214	96
Ohlson 38	282	138
Pearson 36	253	132
Ranger 28	297	177
Santana 30	298	174
Santana 35	233	120
Tartan 30	304	168
Tartan 34	302	174
Viking 33	256	
Whitby 45	220	96

NOTE: Chesapeake MHS ratings are shown as 380 subtracted from Circular Random, 10 knot wind.

Appendix F: CONVERSION TABLE, USYRU TIME ALLOWANCES

CONVERSION TABLE - MINUTES AND SECONDS TO DECIMAL HOURS

MINUTES

00 - .0	01 - .0	02 - .0	03 - .0	04 - .0	05 - .0
06 - .1	07 - .1	08 - .1	09 - .1	10 - .1	11 - .1
12 - .2	13 - .2	14 - .2	15 - .2	16 - .2	17 - .2
18 - .3	19 - .3	20 - .3	21 - .3	22 - .3	23 - .3
24 - .4	25 - .4	26 - .4	27 - .4	28 - .4	29 - .4
30 - .5	31 - .5	32 - .5	33 - .5	34 - .5	35 - .5
36 - .6	37 - .6	38 - .6	39 - .6	40 - .6	41 - .6
42 - .7	43 - .7	44 - .7	45 - .7	46 - .7	47 - .7
48 - .8	49 - .8	50 - .8	51 - .8	52 - .8	53 - .8
54 - .9	55 - .9	56 - .9	57 - .9	58 - .9	59 - .9

SECONDS

00	01	02	03	04	05
00 - .0000	00 - .0167	00 - .0333	00 - .0500	00 - .0667	00 - .0833
01 - .0003	01 - .0169	01 - .0336	01 - .0503	01 - .0669	01 - .0836
02 - .0006	02 - .0172	02 - .0339	02 - .0506	02 - .0672	02 - .0839
03 - .0008	03 - .0175	03 - .0342	03 - .0508	03 - .0675	03 - .0842
04 - .0011	04 - .0178	04 - .0344	04 - .0511	04 - .0678	04 - .0844
05 - .0014	05 - .0181	05 - .0347	05 - .0514	05 - .0681	05 - .0847
06 - .0017	06 - .0183	06 - .0350	06 - .0517	06 - .0683	06 - .0850
07 - .0019	07 - .0186	07 - .0353	07 - .0519	07 - .0686	07 - .0853
08 - .0022	08 - .0189	08 - .0356	08 - .0522	08 - .0689	08 - .0856
09 - .0025	09 - .0192	09 - .0358	09 - .0525	09 - .0692	09 - .0858
10 - .0028	10 - .0194	10 - .0361	10 - .0528	10 - .0694	10 - .0861
11 - .0031	11 - .0197	11 - .0364	11 - .0531	11 - .0697	11 - .0864
12 - .0033	12 - .0200	12 - .0367	12 - .0533	12 - .0700	12 - .0867
13 - .0036	13 - .0203	13 - .0369	13 - .0536	13 - .0703	13 - .0869
14 - .0039	14 - .0206	14 - .0372	14 - .0539	14 - .0706	14 - .0872
15 - .0042	15 - .0208	15 - .0375	15 - .0542	15 - .0708	15 - .0875
16 - .0044	16 - .0211	16 - .0378	16 - .0544	16 - .0711	16 - .0878
17 - .0047	17 - .0214	17 - .0381	17 - .0547	17 - .0714	17 - .0881
18 - .0050	18 - .0217	18 - .0383	18 - .0550	18 - .0717	18 - .0883
19 - .0053	19 - .0219	19 - .0386	19 - .0553	19 - .0719	19 - .0886
20 - .0056	20 - .0222	20 - .0389	20 - .0556	20 - .0722	20 - .0889
21 - .0058	21 - .0225	21 - .0392	21 - .0558	21 - .0725	21 - .0892
22 - .0061	22 - .0228	22 - .0394	22 - .0561	22 - .0728	22 - .0894
23 - .0064	23 - .0231	23 - .0397	23 - .0564	23 - .0731	23 - .0897
24 - .0067	24 - .0233	24 - .0400	24 - .0567	24 - .0733	24 - .0900
25 - .0069	25 - .0236	25 - .0403	25 - .0569	25 - .0736	25 - .0903
26 - .0072	26 - .0239	26 - .0406	26 - .0572	26 - .0739	26 - .0906
27 - .0075	27 - .0242	27 - .0408	27 - .0575	27 - .0742	27 - .0908
28 - .0078	28 - .0244	28 - .0411	28 - .0578	28 - .0744	28 - .0911
29 - .0081	29 - .0247	29 - .0414	29 - .0581	29 - .0747	29 - .0914
30 - .0083	30 - .0250	30 - .0417	30 - .0583	30 - .0750	30 - .0917
31 - .0086	31 - .0253	31 - .0419	31 - .0586	31 - .0753	31 - .0919
32 - .0089	32 - .0256	32 - .0422	32 - .0589	32 - .0756	32 - .0922
33 - .0092	33 - .0258	33 - .0425	33 - .0592	33 - .0758	33 - .0925
34 - .0094	34 - .0261	34 - .0428	34 - .0594	34 - .0761	34 - .0928
35 - .0097	35 - .0264	35 - .0431	35 - .0597	35 - .0764	35 - .0931
36 - .0100	36 - .0267	36 - .0433	36 - .0600	36 - .0767	36 - .0933
37 - .0103	37 - .0269	37 - .0436	37 - .0603	37 - .0769	37 - .0936
38 - .0106	38 - .0272	38 - .0439	38 - .0606	38 - .0772	38 - .0939
39 - .0108	39 - .0275	39 - .0442	39 - .0608	39 - .0775	39 - .0942
40 - .0111	40 - .0278	40 - .0444	40 - .0611	40 - .0778	40 - .0944
41 - .0114	41 - .0281	41 - .0447	41 - .0614	41 - .0781	41 - .0947
42 - .0117	42 - .0283	42 - .0450	42 - .0617	42 - .0783	42 - .0950
43 - .0119	43 - .0286	43 - .0453	43 - .0619	43 - .0786	43 - .0953
44 - .0122	44 - .0289	44 - .0456	44 - .0622	44 - .0789	44 - .0956
45 - .0125	45 - .0292	45 - .0458	45 - .0625	45 - .0792	45 - .0958
46 - .0128	46 - .0294	46 - .0461	46 - .0628	46 - .0794	46 - .0961
47 - .0131	47 - .0297	47 - .0464	47 - .0631	47 - .0797	47 - .0964
48 - .0133	48 - .0300	48 - .0467	48 - .0633	48 - .0800	48 - .0967
49 - .0136	49 - .0303	49 - .0469	49 - .0636	49 - .0803	49 - .0969
50 - .0139	50 - .0306	50 - .0472	50 - .0639	50 - .0806	50 - .0972
51 - .0142	51 - .0308	51 - .0475	51 - .0642	51 - .0808	51 - .0975
52 - .0144	52 - .0311	52 - .0478	52 - .0644	52 - .0811	52 - .0978
53 - .0147	53 - .0314	53 - .0481	53 - .0647	53 - .0814	53 - .0981
54 - .0150	54 - .0317	54 - .0483	54 - .0650	54 - .0817	54 - .0983
55 - .0153	55 - .0319	55 - .0486	55 - .0653	55 - .0819	55 - .0986
56 - .0156	56 - .0322	56 - .0488	56 - .0656	56 - .0822	56 - .0989
57 - .0158	57 - .0325	57 - .0491	57 - .0658	57 - .0825	57 - .0992
58 - .0161	58 - .0328	58 - .0494	58 - .0661	58 - .0828	58 - .0994
59 - .0164	59 - .0331	59 - .0497	59 - .0664	59 - .0831	59 - .0997

Appendix G: FISHING BAY YACHT CLUB TIME ALLOWANCE TABLES

Based on Scratch Yacht of 30.0' Rating

The calculation of time allowances and corrected times for Cruising Class races has long been an onerous burden to all race committees. When this work has had to be done under adverse conditions, or the committees have lacked experience, the accuracy of the results, as well as the delays in posting them, have sometimes been justly criticized.

In search for "a better way," these Tables have been devised by the Fishing Bay Yacht Club to reduce the calculations required of the race committee to an absolute minimum.

The time allowance for each entry in a race of a given distance may be read directly from these tables and requires no calculation whatever. The 15' to 44.9' range of ratings with columns for races of 10 miles to 32 miles in length, cover 98 percent of the cases in most Chesapeake Bay Yacht Racing Association races.

These tables are derived from the standard USYRU Time Allowance Tables, and the differentials between corrected times of yachts, as determined from these tables, is always identical with those obtained by other methods of calculation.

A unique feature is the assumption that *the "scratch yacht" is always a hypothetical entry with a rating of 30.0'.* This requires a slight change of thinking in the application of time allowances for entries rating above 30.0', in that time allowances for such entries must be *added* to elapsed time, instead of subtracted.

The advantages provided by these tables are:

a. Subtraction of the scratch yacht's allowance from that of each yacht is eliminated.

b. Multiplication of allowance by distance for each yacht is eliminated.

c. It is unnecessary to wait until the entries are complete to determine the scratch yacht. Consequently, the time allowances for each yacht for the race can be taken directly from the tables as soon as the entry form comes in. Thus, much of the committee's work may be done ashore before the start of the race.

d. "Scratch sheets" listing yachts and time allowances can be more readily prepared in advance for distribution to skippers before the start.

e. Selection of the scratch yacht in the center of the range of ratings covered by these tables reduces the magnitude of the numbers to be dealt with, thus reducing chances for error and speeding up the committee's work.

The only special precaution required is to remember that time allowances for yachts rating *Over* 30.0' must be *Added* to their elapsed time to determine their corrected time.

For races longer or shorter than those covered by the tables, time allowances may still be determined readily from those given in the tables by addition or subtraction. For example, the time allowance of any yacht in a 41-mile race is her allowance for 30 miles *plus* her allowance for 11 miles. Similarly, the time allowance of any yacht in an eight-mile race is her allowance for 18 miles *less* her allowance for 10 miles.

These tables will also be most useful to the skipper who wants to know quickly, "how much time" another yacht must give him, or "how much time" he must give to another yacht. One simple subtraction (or, if one of the yachts rates above 30.0', an addition) gives the answer. By timing his own and the other yachts' roundings of an intermediate mark of known distance from the start, a skipper can easily determine his corrected time position in the race at any such mark of the course.

EXAMPLES

1. In a 20-Mile Race
   YACHT "A" — Rating 21.2'
   Time Allowance — taken from the 20-mile column of the tables = (−) 24:55

Elapsed Time for Yacht "A" was	4:36:59
SUBTRACTING (rating below 30.0') Time Allowance	(−) 24:55
Corrected Time =	4:12:04

   YACHT "B" — Rating 31.5'
   Time Allowance — taken from the 20-mile column of the tables = (+) 03:10

Elapsed Time for Yacht "B" was	4:04:16
ADDING (rating above 30.0') Time Allowance	(+) 03:10
Corrected Time =	4:07:26

2. How much time must a yacht rating 25.4' give to one rating 22.3' in a 15-mile race?
   From the 15-mile column in the tables:

The Time Allowance for a rating of 22.3' =	(−)	15:46
and for a rating of 25.4' =	(−)	08:33

   Since both yachts rate below 30.0' —
   Answer is the **DIFFERENCE** = 07:13

3. How much time must a yacht rating 35.6' give to one rating 30.5' in a 20-mile race?
   From the 20-mile column in the tables:

The Time Allowance for a rating of 35.6' =	(+)	10:47
and for a rating of 30.5' =	(+)	01:05

   Since both yachts rate above 30.0' —
   Answer is the **DIFFERENCE** = 09:42

4. How much time must a yacht rating 31.3' give to one rating 21.1' in an 18-mile race?
   From the 18-mile column in the tables:

The Time Allowance for a rating of 31.3' =	(+)	02:29
and for a rating of 21.1' =	(−)	22:46

   Since one yacht rates above 30.0' and the other rates below 30.0' —
   Answer is the **SUM** = 25:15

When one yacht rates *above* the scratch yacht rating of 30.0' (zero time allowance) and the other rates *below*, the time allowance of the larger yacht is (+), while that of the smaller is (−). The difference between the two is equal to the numerical total of these two time allowances, added without regard to sign.

Rating	Sec/Mi	10 Mi	11 Mi	12 Mi	13 Mi	14 Mi	15 Mi	16 Mi	17 Mi	18 Mi	19 Mi	20 Mi	Rating
15.0	163.35	27-14	29-57	32-40	35-24	38-07	40-50	43-34	46-17	49-00	51-44	54-27	15.0
15.1	161.49	26-55	29-36	32-18	34-59	37-41	40-22	43-04	45-45	48-27	51-08	53-50	15.1
15.2	159.65	26-36	29-16	31-56	34-35	37-15	39-55	42-34	45-14	47-54	50-33	53-13	15.2
15.3	157.83	26-18	28-56	31-34	34-12	36-50	39-27	42-05	44-43	47-21	49-59	52-37	15.3
15.4	156.03	26-00	28-36	31-12	33-48	36-24	39-00	41-36	44-12	46-49	49-25	52-01	15.4
15.5	154.26	25-43	28-17	30-51	33-25	35-60	38-34	41-08	43-42	46-17	48-51	51-25	15.5
15.6	152.50	25-25	27-57	30-30	33-02	35-35	38-08	40-40	43-12	45-45	48-17	50-50	15.6
15.7	150.76	25-08	27-38	30-09	32-40	35-11	37-41	40-12	42-43	45-14	47-44	50-15	15.7
15.8	149.03	24-50	27-19	29-48	32-17	34-46	37-15	39-44	42-14	44-43	47-12	49-41	15.8
15.9	147.31	24-33	27-00	29-28	31-55	34-22	36-50	39-17	41-44	44-12	46-39	49-06	15.9
16.0	145.64	24-16	26-42	29-08	31-33	33-59	36-25	38-50	41-16	43-42	46-07	48-33	16.0
16.1	143.97	23-60	26-24	28-48	31-12	33-36	35-60	38-24	40-47	43-11	45-35	47-59	16.1
16.2	142.31	23-43	26-05	28-28	30-50	33-12	35-35	37-57	40-19	42-42	45-04	47-26	16.2
16.3	140.66	23-27	25-47	28-08	30-29	32-49	35-10	37-31	39-51	42-12	44-33	46-53	16.3
16.4	139.02	23-10	25-29	27-48	30-07	32-26	34-45	37-04	39-23	41-42	44-01	46-20	16.4
16.5	137.39	22-54	25-11	27-29	29-46	32-03	34-21	36-38	38-56	41-13	43-30	45-48	16.5
16.6	135.79	22-38	24-54	27-09	29-25	31-41	33-57	36-13	38-28	40-44	43-00	45-16	16.6
16.7	134.21	22-22	24-36	26-51	29-05	31-19	33-33	35-47	38-02	40-16	42-30	44-44	16.7
16.8	132.64	22-06	24-19	26-32	28-44	30-57	33-10	35-22	37-35	39-48	42-00	44-13	16.8
16.9	131.08	21-51	24-02	26-13	28-24	30-35	32-46	34-57	37-08	39-19	41-30	43-42	16.9
17.0	129.52	21-35	23-45	25-54	28-04	30-13	32-23	34-32	36-42	38-51	41-01	43-10	17.0
17.1	127.99	21-20	23-28	25-36	27-44	29-52	31-60	34-08	36-16	38-24	40-32	42-40	17.1
17.2	126.47	21-05	23-11	25-18	27-24	29-31	31-37	33-44	35-50	37-56	40-03	42-09	17.2
17.3	124.96	20-50	22-55	24-60	27-04	29-09	31-14	33-19	35-24	37-29	39-34	41-39	17.3
17.4	123.46	20-35	22-38	24-42	26-45	28-48	30-52	32-55	34-59	37-02	39-06	41-09	17.4
17.5	121.97	20-20	22-22	24-24	26-26	28-28	30-30	32-32	34-33	36-35	38-37	40-39	17.5
17.6	120.50	20-05	22-05	24-06	26-06	28-07	30-08	32-08	34-08	36-09	38-09	40-10	17.6
17.7	119.04	19-50	21-49	23-48	25-48	27-47	29-46	31-45	33-44	35-43	37-42	39-41	17.7
17.8	117.60	19-36	21-34	23-31	25-29	27-26	29-24	31-22	33-19	35-17	37-14	39-12	17.8
17.9	116.17	19-22	21-18	23-14	25-10	27-06	29-03	30-59	32-55	34-51	36-47	38-43	17.9
18.0	114.75	19-08	21-02	22-57	24-52	26-47	28-41	30-36	32-31	34-26	36-20	38-15	18.0
18.1	113.33	18-53	20-47	22-40	24-33	26-27	28-20	30-13	32-07	33-60	35-53	37-47	18.1
18.2	111.93	18-39	20-31	22-23	24-15	26-07	27-59	29-51	31-43	33-35	35-27	37-19	18.2
18.3	110.54	18-25	20-16	22-06	23-57	25-48	27-38	29-29	31-19	33-10	35-00	36-51	18.3
18.4	109.17	18-12	20-01	21-50	23-39	25-28	27-18	29-07	30-56	32-45	34-34	36-23	18.4
18.5	107.83	17-58	19-46	21-34	23-22	25-10	26-57	28-45	30-33	32-21	34-09	35-57	18.5
18.6	106.48	17-45	19-31	21-18	23-04	24-51	26-37	28-24	30-10	31-57	33-43	35-30	18.6
18.7	105.14	17-31	19-17	21-02	22-47	24-32	26-17	28-02	29-47	31-33	33-18	35-03	18.7
18.8	103.82	17-18	19-02	20-46	22-30	24-13	25-57	27-41	29-25	31-09	32-53	34-36	18.8
18.9	102.50	17-05	18-47	20-30	22-12	23-55	25-38	27-20	29-02	30-45	32-27	34-10	18.9
19.0	101.19	16-52	18-33	20-14	21-55	23-37	25-18	26-59	28-40	30-21	32-03	33-44	19.0
19.1	099.89	16-39	18-19	19-59	21-39	23-18	24-58	26-38	28-18	29-58	31-38	33-18	19.1
19.2	098.60	16-26	18-05	19-43	21-22	23-00	24-39	26-18	27-56	29-35	31-13	32-52	19.2
19.3	097.32	16-13	17-51	19-28	21-05	22-42	24-20	25-57	27-34	29-12	30-49	32-26	19.3
19.4	096.05	16-00	17-37	19-13	20-49	22-25	24-01	25-37	27-13	28-49	30-25	32-01	19.4
19.5	094.78	15-48	17-23	18-57	20-32	22-07	23-42	25-16	26-51	28-26	30-01	31-36	19.5
19.6	093.53	15-35	17-09	18-42	20-16	21-49	23-23	24-56	26-30	28-04	29-37	31-11	19.6
19.7	092.29	15-23	16-55	18-27	19-60	21-32	23-04	24-37	26-09	27-41	29-14	30-46	19.7
19.8	091.06	15-11	16-42	18-13	19-44	21-15	22-46	24-17	25-48	27-19	28-50	30-21	19.8
19.9	089.84	14-58	16-28	17-58	19-28	20-58	22-28	23-57	25-27	26-57	28-27	29-57	19.9
Rating	Sec/Mi	10 Mi	11 Mi	12 Mi	13 Mi	14 Mi	15 Mi	16 Mi	17 Mi	18 Mi	19 Mi	20 Mi	Rating

SUBTRACT time allowances on this page from Elapsed Time

Rating	21 Mi	22 Mi	23 Mi	24 Mi	25 Mi	26 Mi	27 Mi	28 Mi	29 Mi	30 Mi	31 Mi	32 Mi	Rating
15.0	57-10	59-54	62-37	65-20	68-04	70-47	73-30	76-14	78-57	81-41	84-24	87-07	15.0
15.1	56-31	59-13	61-54	64-36	67-17	69-59	72-40	75-22	78-03	80-45	83-26	86-08	15.1
15.2	55-53	58-32	61-12	63-52	66-31	69-11	71-51	74-30	77-10	79-50	82-29	85-09	15.2
15.3	55-14	57-52	60-30	63-08	65-46	68-24	71-01	73-39	76-17	78-55	81-33	84-11	15.3
15.4	54-37	57-13	59-49	62-25	65-01	67-37	70-13	72-49	75-25	78-01	80-37	83-13	15.4
15.5	53-59	56-34	59-08	61-42	64-17	66-51	69-25	71-59	74-34	77-08	79-42	82-16	15.5
15.6	53-23	55-55	58-27	61-00	63-32	66-05	68-38	71-10	73-42	76-15	78-47	81-20	15.6
15.7	52-46	55-17	57-47	60-18	62-49	65-20	67-51	70-21	72-52	75-23	77-54	80-24	15.7
15.8	52-10	54-39	57-08	59-37	62-06	64-35	67-04	69-33	72-02	74-31	76-60	79-29	15.8
15.9	51-33	54-01	56-28	58-55	61-23	63-50	66-17	68-45	71-12	73-39	76-07	78-34	15.9
16.0	50-58	53-24	55-50	58-15	60-41	63-07	65-32	67-58	70-24	72-49	75-15	77-40	16.0
16.1	50-23	52-47	55-11	57-35	59-59	62-23	64-47	67-11	69-35	71-59	74-23	76-47	16.1
16.2	49-48	52-11	54-33	56-55	59-18	61-40	64-02	66-25	68-47	71-09	73-32	75-54	16.2
16.3	49-14	51-35	53-55	56-16	58-36	60-57	63-18	65-38	67-59	70-20	72-40	75-01	16.3
16.4	48-39	50-58	53-17	55-36	57-56	60-15	62-34	64-53	67-12	69-31	71-50	74-09	16.4
16.5	48-05	50-23	52-40	54-57	57-15	59-32	61-50	64-07	66-24	68-42	70-59	73-16	16.5
16.6	47-32	49-47	52-03	54-19	56-35	58-51	61-06	63-22	65-38	67-54	70-09	72-25	16.6
16.7	46-58	49-13	51-27	53-41	55-55	58-09	60-24	62-38	64-52	67-06	69-20	71-35	16.7
16.8	46-25	48-38	50-51	53-03	55-16	57-29	59-41	61-54	64-07	66-19	68-32	70-44	16.8
16.9	45-53	48-04	50-15	52-26	54-37	56-48	58-59	61-10	63-21	65-32	67-43	69-55	16.9
17.0	45-20	47-29	49-39	51-48	53-58	56-08	58-17	60-27	62-36	64-46	66-55	69-05	17.0
17.1	44-48	46-56	49-04	51-12	53-20	55-28	57-36	59-44	61-52	63-60	66-08	68-16	17.1
17.2	44-16	46-22	48-29	50-35	52-42	54-48	56-55	59-01	61-08	63-14	65-21	67-27	17.2
17.3	43-44	45-49	47-54	49-59	52-04	54-09	56-14	58-19	60-24	62-29	64-34	66-39	17.3
17.4	43-13	45-16	47-20	49-23	51-26	53-30	55-33	57-37	59-40	61-44	63-47	65-51	17.4
17.5	42-41	44-43	46-45	48-47	50-49	52-51	54-53	56-55	58-57	60-59	63-01	65-03	17.5
17.6	42-11	44-11	46-11	48-12	50-12	52-13	54-14	56-14	58-14	60-15	62-15	64-16	17.6
17.7	41-40	43-39	45-38	47-37	49-36	51-35	53-34	55-33	57-32	59-31	61-30	63-29	17.7
17.8	41-10	43-07	45-05	47-02	49-00	50-58	52-55	54-53	56-50	58-48	60-46	62-43	17.8
17.9	40-40	42-36	44-32	46-28	48-24	50-20	52-17	54-13	56-09	58-05	60-01	61-57	17.9
18.0	40-10	42-05	43-59	45-54	47-49	49-44	51-38	53-33	55-28	57-23	59-17	61-12	18.0
18.1	39-40	41-33	43-27	45-20	47-13	49-07	50-60	52-53	54-47	56-40	58-33	60-27	18.1
18.2	39-11	41-02	42-54	44-46	46-38	48-30	50-22	52-14	54-06	55-58	57-50	59-42	18.2
18.3	38-41	40-32	42-22	44-13	46-03	47-54	49-45	51-35	53-26	55-16	57-07	58-57	18.3
18.4	38-13	40-02	41-51	43-40	45-29	47-18	49-08	50-57	52-46	54-35	56-24	58-13	18.4
18.5	37-44	39-32	41-20	43-08	44-56	46-44	48-31	50-19	52-07	53-55	55-43	57-31	18.5
18.6	37-16	39-03	40-49	42-36	44-22	46-08	47-55	49-41	51-28	53-14	55-01	56-47	18.6
18.7	36-48	38-33	40-18	42-03	43-48	45-34	47-19	49-04	50-49	52-34	54-19	56-04	18.7
18.8	36-20	38-04	39-48	41-32	43-15	44-59	46-43	48-27	50-11	51-55	53-38	55-22	18.8
18.9	35-53	37-35	39-17	41-00	42-42	44-25	46-08	47-50	49-32	51-15	52-57	54-40	18.9
19.0	35-25	37-06	38-47	40-29	42-10	43-51	45-32	47-13	48-54	50-36	52-17	53-58	19.0
19.1	34-58	36-38	38-17	39-57	41-37	43-17	44-57	46-37	48-17	49-57	51-37	53-16	19.1
19.2	34-31	36-09	37-48	39-26	41-05	42-44	44-22	46-01	47-39	49-18	50-57	52-35	19.2
19.3	34-04	35-41	37-18	38-56	40-33	42-10	43-48	45-25	47-02	48-40	50-17	51-54	19.3
19.4	33-37	35-13	36-49	38-25	40-01	41-37	43-13	44-49	46-25	48-02	49-38	51-14	19.4
19.5	33-10	34-45	36-20	37-55	39-29	41-04	42-39	44-14	45-49	47-23	48-58	50-33	19.5
19.6	32-44	34-18	35-51	37-25	38-58	40-32	42-05	43-39	45-12	46-46	48-19	49-53	19.6
19.7	32-18	33-50	35-23	36-55	38-27	39-60	41-32	43-04	44-36	46-09	47-41	49-13	19.7
19.8	31-52	33-23	34-54	36-25	37-56	39-28	40-59	42-30	44-01	45-32	47-03	48-34	19.8
19.9	31-27	32-56	34-26	35-56	37-26	38-56	40-26	41-56	43-25	44-55	46-25	47-55	19.9
Rating	21 Mi	22 Mi	23 Mi	24 Mi	25 Mi	26 Mi	27 Mi	28 Mi	29 Mi	30 Mi	31 Mi	32 Mi	Rating

SUBTRACT time allowances on this page from Elapsed Time

Rating	Sec/Mi	10 Mi	11 Mi	12 Mi	13 Mi	14 Mi	15 Mi	16 Mi	17 Mi	18 Mi	19 Mi	20 Mi	Rating
20.0	088.62	14-46	16-15	17-43	19-12	20-41	22-09	23-38	25-07	26-35	28-04	29-32	20.0
20.1	087.42	14-34	16-02	17-29	18-56	20-24	21-51	23-19	24-46	26-14	27-41	29-08	20.1
20.2	086.24	14-22	15-49	17-15	18-41	20-07	21-34	22-60	24-26	25-52	27-19	28-45	20.2
20.3	085.05	14-11	15-36	17-01	18-26	19-51	21-16	22-41	24-06	25-31	26-56	28-21	20.3
20.4	083.87	13-59	15-23	16-46	18-10	19-34	20-58	22-22	23-46	25-10	26-33	27-57	20.4
20.5	082.71	13-47	15-10	16-33	17-55	19-18	20-41	22-03	23-26	24-49	26-11	27-34	20.5
20.6	081.54	13-35	14-57	16-18	17-40	19-02	20-23	21-45	23-06	24-28	25-49	27-11	20.6
20.7	080.39	13-24	14-44	16-05	17-25	18-45	20-06	21-26	22-47	24-07	25-27	26-48	20.7
20.8	079.25	13-12	14-32	15-51	17-10	18-29	19-49	21-08	22-27	23-47	25-06	26-25	20.8
20.9	078.11	13-01	14-19	15-37	16-55	18-14	19-32	20-50	22-08	23-26	24-44	26-02	20.9
21.0	076.98	12-50	14-07	15-24	16-41	17-58	19-15	20-32	21-49	23-06	24-23	25-40	21.0
21.1	075.87	12-39	13-55	15-10	16-26	17-42	18-58	20-14	21-30	22-46	24-02	25-17	21.1
21.2	074.76	12-28	13-42	14-57	16-12	17-27	18-41	19-56	21-11	22-26	23-40	24-55	21.2
21.3	073.65	12-17	13-30	14-44	15-57	17-11	18-25	19-38	20-52	22-06	23-19	24-33	21.3
21.4	072.56	12-06	13-18	14-31	15-43	16-56	18-08	19-21	20-33	21-46	22-59	24-11	21.4
21.5	071.48	11-55	13-06	14-18	15-29	16-41	17-52	19-04	20-15	21-27	22-38	23-50	21.5
21.6	070.40	11-44	12-54	14-05	15-15	16-26	17-36	18-46	19-57	21-07	22-18	23-28	21.6
21.7	069.33	11-33	12-43	13-52	15-01	16-11	17-20	18-29	19-39	20-48	21-57	23-07	21.7
21.8	068.26	11-23	12-31	13-39	14-47	15-56	17-04	18-12	19-20	20-29	21-37	22-45	21.8
21.9	067.20	11-12	12-19	13-26	14-34	15-41	16-48	17-55	19-02	20-10	21-17	22-24	21.9
22.0	066.15	11-02	12-08	13-14	14-20	15-26	16-32	17-38	18-45	19-51	20-57	22-03	22.0
22.1	065.10	10-51	11-56	13-01	14-06	15-11	16-17	17-22	18-27	19-32	20-37	21-42	22.1
22.2	064.07	10-41	11-45	12-49	13-53	14-57	16-01	17-05	18-09	19-13	20-17	21-21	22.2
22.3	063.04	10-30	11-33	12-36	13-39	14-43	15-46	16-49	17-52	18-55	19-58	21-01	22.3
22.4	062.02	10-20	11-22	12-24	13-26	14-28	15-30	16-32	17-34	18-36	19-38	20-40	22.4
22.5	061.00	10-10	11-11	12-12	13-13	14-14	15-15	16-16	17-17	18-18	19-19	20-20	22.5
22.6	059.99	09-60	10-60	11-60	12-60	13-60	14-60	15-60	16-60	17-60	18-60	19-60	22.6
22.7	058.99	09-50	10-49	11-48	12-47	13-46	14-45	15-44	16-43	17-42	18-41	19-40	22.7
22.8	058.00	09-40	10-38	11-36	12-34	13-32	14-30	15-28	16-26	17-24	18-22	19-20	22.8
22.9	057.01	09-30	10-27	11-24	12-21	13-18	14-15	15-12	16-09	17-06	18-03	19-00	22.9
23.0	056.03	09-20	10-16	11-12	12-08	13-04	14-00	14-56	15-53	16-49	17-45	18-41	23.0
23.1	055.06	09-11	10-06	11-01	11-56	12-51	13-46	14-41	15-36	16-31	17-26	18-21	23.1
23.2	054.09	09-01	09-55	10-49	11-43	12-37	13-31	14-25	15-20	16-14	17-08	18-02	23.2
23.3	053.13	08-51	09-44	10-38	11-31	12-24	13-17	14-10	15-03	15-56	16-49	17-43	23.3
23.4	052.17	08-42	09-34	10-26	11-18	12-10	13-03	13-55	14-47	15-39	16-31	17-23	23.4
23.5	051.22	08-32	09-23	10-15	11-06	11-57	12-48	13-39	14-31	15-22	16-13	17-04	23.5
23.6	050.27	08-23	09-13	10-03	10-53	11-44	12-34	13-24	14-15	15-05	15-55	16-45	23.6
23.7	049.33	08-13	09-03	09-52	10-41	11-31	12-20	13-09	13-59	14-48	15-37	16-27	23.7
23.8	048.40	08-04	08-52	09-41	10-29	11-18	12-06	12-54	13-43	14-31	15-20	16-08	23.8
23.9	047.48	07-55	08-42	09-30	10-17	11-05	11-52	12-40	13-27	14-15	15-02	15-50	23.9
24.0	046.55	07-45	08-32	09-19	10-05	10-52	11-38	12-25	13-11	13-58	14-44	15-31	24.0
24.1	045.64	07-36	08-22	09-08	09-53	10-39	11-25	12-10	12-56	13-42	14-27	15-13	24.1
24.2	044.73	07-27	08-12	08-57	09-41	10-26	11-11	11-56	12-40	13-25	14-10	14-55	24.2
24.3	043.82	07-18	08-02	08-46	09-30	10-13	10-57	11-41	12-25	13-09	13-53	14-36	24.3
24.4	042.92	07-09	07-52	08-35	09-18	10-01	10-44	11-27	12-10	12-53	13-35	14-18	24.4
24.5	042.03	07-00	07-42	08-24	09-06	09-48	10-30	11-12	11-54	12-37	13-19	14-01	24.5
24.6	041.14	06-51	07-33	08-14	08-55	09-36	10-17	10-58	11-39	12-21	13-02	13-43	24.6
24.7	040.26	06-43	07-23	08-03	08-43	09-24	10-04	10-44	11-24	12-05	12-45	13-25	24.7
24.8	039.38	06-34	07-13	07-53	08-32	09-11	09-51	10-30	11-09	11-49	12-28	13-08	24.8
24.9	038.51	06-25	07-04	07-42	08-21	08-59	09-38	10-16	10-55	11-33	12-12	12-50	24.9
Rating	Sec/Mi	10 Mi	11 Mi	12 Mi	13 Mi	14 Mi	15 Mi	16 Mi	17 Mi	18 Mi	19 Mi	20 Mi	Rating

SUBTRACT time allowances on this page from Elapsed Time

Rating	21 Mi	22 Mi	23 Mi	24 Mi	25 Mi	26 Mi	27 Mi	28 Mi	29 Mi	30 Mi	31 Mi	32 Mi	Rating
20.0	31-01	32-30	33-58	35-27	36-56	38-24	39-53	41-21	42-50	44-19	45-47	47-16	20.0
20.1	30-36	32-03	33-31	34-58	36-26	37-53	39-20	40-48	42-15	43-43	45-10	46-37	20.1
20.2	30-11	31-37	33-03	34-30	35-56	37-22	38-48	40-15	41-41	43-07	44-33	45-60	20.2
20.3	29-46	31-11	32-36	34-01	35-26	36-51	38-16	39-41	41-06	42-32	43-57	45-22	20.3
20.4	29-21	30-45	32-09	33-33	34-57	36-21	37-44	39-08	40-32	41-56	43-20	44-44	20.4
20.5	28-57	30-20	31-42	33-05	34-28	35-50	37-13	38-36	39-59	41-21	42-44	44-07	20.5
20.6	28-32	29-54	31-15	32-37	33-59	35-20	36-42	38-03	39-25	40-46	42-08	43-29	20.6
20.7	28-08	29-29	30-49	32-09	33-30	34-50	36-11	37-31	38-51	40-12	41-32	42-52	20.7
20.8	27-44	29-03	30-23	31-42	33-01	34-20	35-40	36-59	38-18	39-38	40-57	42-16	20.8
20.9	27-20	28-38	29-57	31-15	32-33	33-51	35-09	36-27	37-45	39-03	40-21	41-39	20.9
21.0	26-57	28-14	29-31	30-48	32-05	33-21	34-38	35-55	37-12	38-29	39-46	41-03	21.0
21.1	26-33	27-49	29-05	30-21	31-37	32-53	34-08	35-24	36-40	37-56	39-12	40-28	21.1
21.2	26-10	27-25	28-39	29-54	31-09	32-24	33-39	34-53	36-08	37-23	38-38	39-52	21.2
21.3	25-47	27-00	28-14	29-28	30-41	31-55	33-09	34-22	35-36	36-50	38-03	39-17	21.3
21.4	25-24	26-36	27-49	29-01	30-14	31-27	32-39	33-52	35-04	36-17	37-29	38-42	21.4
21.5	25-01	26-13	27-24	28-36	29-47	30-58	32-10	33-21	34-33	35-44	36-56	38-07	21.5
21.6	24-38	25-49	26-59	28-10	29-20	30-30	31-41	32-51	34-02	35-12	36-22	37-33	21.6
21.7	24-16	25-25	26-35	27-44	28-53	30-03	31-12	32-21	33-31	34-40	35-49	36-59	21.7
21.8	23-53	25-02	26-10	27-18	28-26	29-35	30-43	31-51	32-60	34-08	35-16	36-24	21.8
21.9	23-31	24-38	25-46	26-53	28-00	29-07	30-14	31-22	32-29	33-36	34-43	35-50	21.9
22.0	23-09	24-15	25-21	26-28	27-34	28-40	29-46	30-52	31-58	33-05	34-11	35-17	22.0
22.1	22-47	23-52	24-57	26-02	27-08	28-13	29-18	30-23	31-28	32-33	33-38	34-43	22.1
22.2	22-25	23-30	24-34	25-38	26-42	27-46	28-50	29-54	30-58	32-02	33-06	34-10	22.2
22.3	22-04	23-07	24-10	25-13	26-16	27-19	28-22	29-25	30-28	31-31	32-34	33-37	22.3
22.4	21-42	22-44	23-46	24-48	25-50	26-53	27-55	28-57	29-59	31-01	32-03	33-05	22.4
22.5	21-21	22-22	23-23	24-24	25-25	26-26	27-27	28-28	29-29	30-30	31-31	32-32	22.5
22.6	20-60	21-60	22-60	23-60	24-60	25-60	26-60	27-60	28-60	29-60	30-60	31-60	22.6
22.7	20-39	21-38	22-37	23-36	24-35	25-34	26-33	27-32	28-31	29-30	30-29	31-28	22.7
22.8	20-18	21-16	22-14	23-12	24-10	25-08	26-06	27-04	28-02	29-00	29-58	30-56	22.8
22.9	19-57	20-54	21-51	22-48	23-45	24-42	25-39	26-36	27-33	28-30	29-27	30-24	22.9
23.0	19-37	20-33	21-29	22-25	23-21	24-17	25-13	26-09	27-05	28-01	28-57	29-53	23.0
23.1	19-16	20-11	21-06	22-01	22-56	23-52	24-47	25-42	26-37	27-32	28-27	29-22	23.1
23.2	18-56	19-50	20-44	21-38	22-32	23-26	24-20	25-15	26-09	27-03	27-57	28-51	23.2
23.3	18-36	19-29	20-22	21-15	22-08	23-01	23-54	24-48	25-41	26-34	27-27	28-20	23.3
23.4	18-16	19-08	19-60	20-52	21-44	22-36	23-29	24-21	25-13	26-05	26-57	27-49	23.4
23.5	17-56	18-47	19-38	20-29	21-20	22-12	23-03	23-54	24-45	25-37	26-28	27-19	23.5
23.6	17-36	18-26	19-16	20-06	20-57	21-47	22-37	23-28	24-18	25-08	25-58	26-49	23.6
23.7	17-16	18-05	18-55	19-44	20-33	21-23	22-12	23-01	23-51	24-40	25-29	26-19	23.7
23.8	16-56	17-45	18-33	19-22	20-10	20-58	21-47	22-35	23-24	24-12	25-00	25-49	23.8
23.9	16-37	17-25	18-12	18-60	19-47	20-34	21-22	22-09	22-57	23-44	24-32	25-19	23.9
24.0	16-18	17-04	17-51	18-37	19-24	20-10	20-57	21-43	22-30	23-17	24-03	24-50	24.0
24.1	15-58	16-44	17-30	18-15	19-01	19-47	20-32	21-18	22-04	22-49	23-35	24-20	24.1
24.2	15-39	16-24	17-09	17-54	18-38	19-23	20-08	20-52	21-37	22-22	23-07	23-51	24.2
24.3	15-20	16-04	16-48	17-32	18-15	18-59	19-43	20-27	21-11	21-55	22-38	23-22	24.3
24.4	15-01	15-44	16-27	17-10	17-53	18-36	19-19	20-02	20-45	21-28	22-11	22-53	24.4
24.5	14-43	15-25	16-07	16-49	17-31	18-13	18-55	19-37	20-19	21-01	21-43	22-25	24.5
24.6	14-24	15-05	15-46	16-27	17-08	17-50	18-31	19-12	19-53	20-34	21-15	21-56	24.6
24.7	14-05	14-46	15-26	16-06	16-47	17-27	18-07	18-47	19-28	20-08	20-48	21-28	24.7
24.8	13-47	14-26	15-06	15-45	16-24	17-04	17-43	18-23	19-02	19-41	20-21	21-00	24.8
24.9	13-29	14-07	14-46	15-24	16-03	16-41	17-20	17-58	18-37	19-15	19-54	20-32	24.9
Rating	21 Mi	22 Mi	23 Mi	24 Mi	25 Mi	26 Mi	27 Mi	28 Mi	29 Mi	30 Mi	31 Mi	32 Mi	Rating

SUBTRACT time allowances on this page from Elapsed Time

Rating	Sec/Mi	10 Mi	11 Mi	12 Mi	13 Mi	14 Mi	15 Mi	16 Mi	17 Mi	18 Mi	19 Mi	20 Mi	Rating
25.0	037.65	06-17	06-54	07-32	08-09	08-47	09-25	10-02	10-40	11-18	11-55	12-33	25.0
25.1	036.78	06-08	06-45	07-21	07-58	08-35	09-12	09-48	10-25	11-02	11-39	12-16	25.1
25.2	035.92	05-59	06-35	07-11	07-47	08-23	08-59	09-35	10-11	10-47	11-22	11-58	25.2
25.3	035.07	05-51	06-26	07-01	07-36	08-11	08-46	09-21	09-56	10-31	11-06	11-41	25.3
25.4	034.23	05-42	06-17	06-51	07-25	07-59	08-33	09-08	09-42	10-16	10-50	11-25	25.4
25.5	033.39	05-34	06-07	06-41	07-14	07-47	08-21	08-54	09-28	10-01	10-34	11-08	25.5
25.6	032.55	05-26	05-58	06-31	07-03	07-36	08-08	08-41	09-13	09-46	10-18	10-51	25.6
25.7	031.72	05-17	05-49	06-21	06-52	07-24	07-56	08-27	08-59	09-31	10-03	10-34	25.7
25.8	030.89	05-09	05-40	06-11	06-42	07-12	07-43	08-14	08-45	09-16	09-47	10-18	25.8
25.9	030.07	05-01	05-31	06-01	06-31	07-01	07-31	08-01	08-31	09-01	09-31	10-01	25.9
26.0	029.25	04-53	05-22	05-51	06-20	06-50	07-19	07-48	08-17	08-47	09-16	09-45	26.0
26.1	028.44	04-44	05-13	05-41	06-10	06-38	07-07	07-35	08-03	08-32	09-00	09-29	26.1
26.2	027.63	04-36	05-04	05-32	05-59	06-27	06-54	07-22	07-50	08-17	08-45	09-13	26.2
26.3	026.82	04-28	04-55	05-22	05-49	06-15	06-42	07-09	07-36	08-03	08-30	08-56	26.3
26.4	026.02	04-20	04-46	05-12	05-38	06-04	06-30	06-56	07-22	07-48	08-14	08-40	26.4
26.5	025.23	04-12	04-38	05-03	05-28	05-53	06-18	06-44	07-09	07-34	07-59	08-25	26.5
26.6	024.44	04-04	04-29	04-53	05-18	05-42	06-07	06-31	06-55	07-20	07-44	08-09	26.6
26.7	023.66	03-57	04-20	04-44	05-08	05-31	05-55	06-19	06-42	07-06	07-30	07-53	26.7
26.8	022.88	03-49	04-12	04-35	04-57	05-20	05-43	06-06	06-29	06-52	07-15	07-38	26.8
26.9	022.10	03-41	04-03	04-25	04-47	05-09	05-32	05-54	06-16	06-38	06-60	07-22	26.9
27.0	021.33	03-33	03-55	04-16	04-37	04-59	05-20	05-41	06-03	06-24	06-45	07-07	27.0
27.1	020.56	03-26	03-46	04-07	04-27	04-48	05-08	05-29	05-50	06-10	06-31	06-51	27.1
27.2	019.79	03-18	03-38	03-57	04-17	04-37	04-57	05-17	05-36	05-56	06-16	06-36	27.2
27.3	019.03	03-10	03-29	03-48	04-07	04-26	04-45	05-04	05-23	05-43	06-02	06-21	27.3
27.4	018.27	03-03	03-21	03-39	03-57	04-16	04-34	04-52	05-11	05-29	05-47	06-05	27.4
27.5	017.52	02-55	03-13	03-30	03-48	04-05	04-23	04-40	04-58	05-15	05-33	05-50	27.5
27.6	016.78	02-48	03-05	03-21	03-38	03-55	04-12	04-28	04-45	05-02	05-19	05-36	27.6
27.7	016.04	02-40	02-56	03-12	03-29	03-45	04-01	04-17	04-33	04-49	05-05	05-21	27.7
27.8	015.30	02-33	02-48	03-04	03-19	03-34	03-50	04-05	04-20	04-35	04-51	05-06	27.8
27.9	014.57	02-26	02-40	02-55	03-09	03-24	03-39	03-53	04-08	04-22	04-37	04-51	27.9
28.0	013.84	02-18	02-32	02-46	02-60	03-14	03-28	03-41	03-55	04-09	04-23	04-37	28.0
28.1	013.11	02-11	02-24	02-37	02-50	03-04	03-17	03-30	03-43	03-56	04-09	04-22	28.1
28.2	012.39	02-04	02-16	02-29	02-41	02-53	03-06	03-18	03-31	03-43	03-55	04-08	28.2
28.3	011.67	01-57	02-08	02-20	02-32	02-43	02-55	03-07	03-18	03-30	03-42	03-53	28.3
28.4	010.95	01-50	02-00	02-11	02-22	02-33	02-44	02-55	03-06	03-17	03-28	03-39	28.4
28.5	010.24	01-42	01-53	02-03	02-13	02-23	02-34	02-44	02-54	03-04	03-15	03-25	28.5
28.6	009.53	01-35	01-45	01-54	02-04	02-13	02-23	02-32	02-42	02-52	03-01	03-11	28.6
28.7	008.82	01-28	01-37	01-46	01-55	02-03	02-12	02-21	02-30	02-39	02-48	02-56	28.7
28.8	008.12	01-21	01-29	01-37	01-46	01-54	02-02	02-10	02-18	02-26	02-34	02-42	28.8
28.9	007.43	01-14	01-22	01-29	01-37	01-44	01-51	01-59	02-06	02-14	02-21	02-29	28.9
29.0	006.74	01-07	01-14	01-21	01-28	01-34	01-41	01-48	01-55	02-01	02-08	02-15	29.0
29.1	006.05	01-00	01-07	01-13	01-19	01-25	01-31	01-37	01-43	01-49	01-55	02-01	29.1
29.2	005.37	00-54	00-59	01-04	01-10	01-15	01-21	01-26	01-31	01-37	01-42	01-47	29.2
29.3	004.68	00-47	00-51	00-56	01-01	01-06	01-10	01-15	01-20	01-24	01-29	01-34	29.3
29.4	004.00	00-40	00-44	00-48	00-52	00-56	01-00	01-04	01-08	01-12	01-16	01-20	29.4
29.5	003.33	00-33	00-37	00-40	00-43	00-47	00-50	00-53	00-57	00-60	01-03	01-07	29.5
29.6	002.66	00-27	00-29	00-32	00-35	00-37	00-40	00-43	00-45	00-48	00-51	00-53	29.6
29.7	001.99	00-20	00-22	00-24	00-26	00-28	00-30	00-32	00-34	00-36	00-38	00-40	29.7
29.8	001.32	00-13	00-15	00-16	00-17	00-18	00-20	00-21	00-22	00-24	00-25	00-26	29.8
29.9	000.66	00-07	00-07	00-08	00-09	00-09	00-10	00-11	00-11	00-12	00-13	00-13	29.9
Rating	Sec/Mi	10 Mi	11 Mi	12 Mi	13 Mi	14 Mi	15 Mi	16 Mi	17 Mi	18 Mi	19 Mi	20 Mi	Rating

SUBTRACT time allowances on this page from Elapsed Time

Rating	21 Mi	22 Mi	23 Mi	24 Mi	25 Mi	26 Mi	27 Mi	28 Mi	29 Mi	30 Mi	31 Mi	32 Mi	Rating
25.0	13-11	13-48	14-26	15-04	15-41	16-19	16-57	17-34	18-12	18-50	19-27	20-05	25.0
25.1	12-52	13-29	14-06	14-43	15-20	15-56	16-33	17-10	17-47	18-23	19-00	19-37	25.1
25.2	12-34	13-10	13-46	14-22	14-58	15-34	16-10	16-46	17-22	17-58	18-33	19-09	25.2
25.3	12-16	12-52	13-27	14-02	14-37	15-12	15-47	16-22	16-57	17-32	18-07	18-42	25.3
25.4	11-59	12-33	13-07	13-42	14-16	14-50	15-24	15-58	16-33	17-07	17-41	18-15	25.4
25.5	11-41	12-15	12-48	13-21	13-55	14-28	15-02	15-35	16-08	16-42	17-15	17-48	25.5
25.6	11-24	11-56	12-29	13-01	13-34	14-06	14-39	15-11	15-44	16-17	16-49	17-22	25.6
25.7	11-06	11-38	12-10	12-41	13-13	13-45	14-16	14-48	15-20	15-52	16-23	16-55	25.7
25.8	10-49	11-20	11-50	12-21	12-52	13-23	13-54	14-25	14-56	15-27	15-58	16-28	25.8
25.9	10-31	11-02	11-32	12-02	12-32	13-02	13-32	14-02	14-32	15-02	15-32	16-02	25.9
26.0	10-14	10-44	11-13	11-42	12-11	12-41	13-10	13-39	14-08	14-38	15-07	15-36	26.0
26.1	09-57	10-26	10-54	11-23	11-51	12-19	12-48	13-16	13-45	14-13	14-42	15-10	26.1
26.2	09-40	10-08	10-35	11-03	11-31	11-58	12-26	12-54	13-21	13-49	14-17	14-44	26.2
26.3	09-23	09-50	10-17	10-44	11-11	11-37	12-04	12-31	12-58	13-25	13-51	14-18	26.3
26.4	09-06	09-32	09-58	10-24	10-50	11-17	11-43	12-09	12-35	13-01	13-27	13-53	26.4
26.5	08-50	09-15	09-40	10-06	10-31	10-56	11-21	11-46	12-12	12-37	13-02	13-27	26.5
26.6	08-33	08-58	09-22	09-47	10-11	10-35	10-60	11-24	11-49	12-13	12-38	13-02	26.6
26.7	08-17	08-41	09-04	09-28	09-51	10-15	10-39	11-02	11-26	11-50	12-13	12-37	26.7
26.8	08-00	08-23	08-46	09-09	09-32	09-55	10-18	10-41	11-03	11-26	11-49	12-12	26.8
26.9	07-44	08-06	08-28	08-50	09-12	09-35	09-57	10-19	10-41	11-03	11-25	11-47	26.9
27.0	07-28	07-49	08-11	08-32	08-53	09-15	09-36	09-57	10-19	10-40	11-01	11-23	27.0
27.1	07-12	07-32	07-53	08-13	08-34	08-55	09-15	09-36	09-56	10-17	10-37	10-58	27.1
27.2	06-56	07-15	07-35	07-55	08-15	08-35	08-54	09-14	09-34	09-54	10-13	10-33	27.2
27.3	06-40	06-59	07-18	07-37	07-56	08-15	08-34	08-53	09-12	09-31	09-50	10-09	27.3
27.4	06-24	06-42	07-00	07-18	07-37	07-55	08-13	08-32	08-50	09-08	09-26	09-45	27.4
27.5	06-08	06-25	06-43	07-00	07-18	07-36	07-53	08-11	08-28	08-46	09-03	09-21	27.5
27.6	05-52	06-09	06-26	06-43	06-59	07-16	07-33	07-50	08-07	08-23	08-40	08-57	27.6
27.7	05-37	05-53	06-09	06-25	06-41	06-57	07-13	07-29	07-45	08-01	08-17	08-33	27.7
27.8	05-21	05-37	05-52	06-07	06-23	06-38	06-53	07-08	07-24	07-39	07-54	08-10	27.8
27.9	05-06	05-21	05-35	05-50	06-04	06-19	06-33	06-48	07-03	07-17	07-32	07-46	27.9
28.0	04-51	05-04	05-18	05-32	05-46	05-60	06-14	06-27	06-41	06-55	07-09	07-23	28.0
28.1	04-35	04-48	05-02	05-15	05-28	05-41	05-54	06-07	06-20	06-33	06-46	06-60	28.1
28.2	04-20	04-33	04-45	04-57	05-10	05-22	05-35	05-47	05-59	06-12	06-24	06-36	28.2
28.3	04-05	04-17	04-28	04-40	04-52	05-03	05-15	05-27	05-38	05-50	06-02	06-13	28.3
28.4	03-50	04-01	04-12	04-23	04-34	04-45	04-56	05-07	05-18	05-29	05-39	05-50	28.4
28.5	03-35	03-45	03-56	04-06	04-16	04-26	04-36	04-47	04-57	05-07	05-17	05-28	28.5
28.6	03-20	03-30	03-39	03-49	03-58	04-08	04-17	04-27	04-36	04-46	04-55	05-05	28.6
28.7	03-05	03-14	03-23	03-32	03-41	03-49	03-58	04-07	04-16	04-25	04-33	04-42	28.7
28.8	02-51	02-59	03-07	03-15	03-23	03-31	03-39	03-47	03-55	04-04	04-12	04-20	28.8
28.9	02-36	02-43	02-51	02-58	03-06	03-13	03-21	03-28	03-35	03-43	03-50	03-58	28.9
29.0	02-22	02-28	02-35	02-42	02-48	02-55	03-02	03-09	03-15	03-22	03-29	03-36	29.0
29.1	02-07	02-13	02-19	02-25	02-31	02-37	02-43	02-49	02-55	03-02	03-08	03-14	29.1
29.2	01-53	01-58	02-03	02-09	02-14	02-20	02-25	02-30	02-36	02-41	02-46	02-52	29.2
29.3	01-38	01-43	01-48	01-52	01-57	02-02	02-06	02-11	02-16	02-20	02-25	02-30	29.3
29.4	01-24	01-28	01-32	01-36	01-40	01-44	01-48	01-52	01-56	02-00	02-04	02-08	29.4
29.5	01-10	01-13	01-17	01-20	01-23	01-27	01-30	01-33	01-37	01-40	01-43	01-47	29.5
29.6	00-56	00-59	01-01	01-04	01-06	01-09	01-12	01-14	01-17	01-20	01-22	01-25	29.6
29.7	00-42	00-44	00-46	00-48	00-50	00-52	00-54	00-56	00-58	00-60	01-02	01-04	29.7
29.8	00-28	00-29	00-30	00-32	00-33	00-34	00-36	00-37	00-38	00-40	00-41	00-42	29.8
29.9	00-14	00-15	00-15	00-16	00-17	00-17	00-18	00-18	00-19	00-20	00-20	00-21	29.9
Rating	21 Mi	22 Mi	23 Mi	24 Mi	25 Mi	26 Mi	27 Mi	28 Mi	29 Mi	30 Mi	31 Mi	32 Mi	Rating

SUBTRACT time allowances on this page from Elapsed Time

Rating	Sec/Mi	10 Mi	11 Mi	12 Mi	13 Mi	14 Mi	15 Mi	16 Mi	17 Mi	18 Mi	19 Mi	20 Mi	Rating
30.0	000.00	00-00	00-00	00-00	00-00	00-00	00-00	00-00	00-00	00-00	00-00	00-00	30.0
30.1	000.66	00-07	00-07	00-08	00-09	00-09	00-10	00-11	00-11	00-12	00-13	00-13	30.1
30.2	001.30	00-13	00-14	00-16	00-17	00-18	00-20	00-21	00-22	00-23	00-25	00-26	30.2
30.3	001.95	00-20	00-21	00-23	00-25	00-27	00-29	00-31	00-33	00-35	00-37	00-39	30.3
30.4	002.60	00-26	00-29	00-31	00-34	00-36	00-39	00-42	00-44	00-47	00-49	00-52	30.4
30.5	003.25	00-32	00-36	00-39	00-42	00-45	00-49	00-52	00-55	00-59	01-02	01-05	30.5
30.6	003.89	00-39	00-43	00-47	00-51	00-54	00-58	01-02	01-06	01-10	01-14	01-18	30.6
30.7	004.52	00-45	00-50	00-54	00-59	01-03	01-08	01-12	01-17	01-21	01-26	01-30	30.7
30.8	005.15	00-51	00-57	01-02	01-07	01-12	01-17	01-22	01-28	01-33	01-38	01-43	30.8
30.9	005.77	00-58	01-03	01-09	01-15	01-21	01-27	01-32	01-38	01-44	01-50	01-55	30.9
31.0	006.39	01-04	01-10	01-17	01-23	01-29	01-36	01-42	01-49	01-55	02-01	02-08	31.0
31.1	007-02	01-10	01-17	01-24	01-31	01-38	01-45	01-52	01-59	02-06	02-13	02-20	31.1
31.2	007.64	01-16	01-24	01-32	01-39	01-47	01-55	02-02	02-10	02-18	02-25	02-33	31.2
31.3	008.26	01-23	01-31	01-39	01-47	01-56	02-04	02-12	02-20	02-29	02-37	02-45	31.3
31.4	008.89	01-29	01-38	01-47	01-56	02-04	02-13	02-22	02-31	02-40	02-49	02-58	31.4
31.5	009.50	01-35	01-44	01-54	02-03	02-13	02-23	02-32	02-41	02-51	03-00	03-10	31.5
31.6	010.11	01-41	01-51	02-01	02-11	02-22	02-32	02-42	02-52	03-02	03-12	03-22	31.6
31.7	010.72	01-47	01-58	02-09	02-19	02-30	02-41	02-51	03-02	03-13	03-24	03-34	31.7
31.8	011.32	01-53	02-05	02-16	02-27	02-38	02-50	03-01	03-12	03-24	03-35	03-46	31.8
31.9	011.92	01-59	02-11	02-23	02-35	02-47	02-59	03-11	03-23	03-35	03-46	03-58	31.9
32.0	012.52	02-05	02-18	02-30	02-43	02-55	03-08	03-20	03-33	03-45	03-58	04-10	32.0
32.1	013.12	02-11	02-24	02-37	02-51	03-04	03-17	03-30	03-43	03-56	04-09	04-22	32.1
32.2	013.71	02-17	02-31	02-45	02-58	03-12	03-26	03-39	03-53	04-07	04-20	04-34	32.2
32.3	014.30	02-23	02-37	02-52	03-06	03-20	03-35	03-49	04-03	04-17	04-32	04-46	32.3
32.4	014.89	02-29	02-44	02-59	03-14	03-28	03-43	03-58	04-13	04-28	04-43	04-58	32.4
32.5	015.48	02-35	02-50	03-06	03-21	03-37	03-52	04-08	04-23	04-39	04-54	05-10	32.5
32.6	016.06	02-41	02-57	03-13	03-29	03-45	04-01	04-17	04-33	04-49	05-05	05-21	32.6
32.7	016.64	02-46	03-03	03-20	03-36	03-53	04-10	04-26	04-43	04-60	05-16	05-33	32.7
32.8	017.21	02-52	03-09	03-27	03-44	04-01	04-18	04-35	04-53	05-10	05-27	05-44	32.8
32.9	017.78	02-58	03-16	03-33	03-51	04-09	04-27	04-44	05-02	05-20	05-38	05-56	32.9
33.0	018.35	03-03	03-22	03-40	03-59	04-17	04-35	04-54	05-12	05-30	05-49	06-07	33.0
33.1	018.92	03-09	03-28	03-47	04-06	04-25	04-44	05-03	05-22	05-41	05-59	06-18	33.1
33.2	019.49	03-15	03-34	03-54	04-13	04-33	04-52	05-12	05-31	05-51	06-10	06-30	33.2
33.3	020.05	03-20	03-41	04-01	04-21	04-41	05-01	05-21	05-41	06-01	06-21	06-41	33.3
33.4	020.61	03-26	03-47	04-07	04-28	04-49	05-09	05-30	05-50	06-11	06-32	06-52	33.4
33.5	021.17	03-32	03-53	04-14	04-35	04-56	05-18	05-39	05-60	06-21	06-42	07-03	33.5
33.6	021.73	03-37	03-59	04-21	04-42	05-04	05-26	05-48	06-09	06-31	06-53	07-15	33.6
33.7	022.28	03-43	04-05	04-27	04-50	05-12	05-34	05-56	06-19	06-41	07-03	07-26	33.7
33.8	022.83	03-48	04-11	04-34	04-57	05-20	05-42	06-05	06-28	06-51	07-14	07-37	33.8
33.9	023.37	03-54	04-17	04-40	05-04	05-27	05-51	06-14	06-37	07-01	07-24	07-47	33.9
34.0	023.91	03-59	04-23	04-47	05-11	05-35	05-59	06-23	06-46	07-10	07-34	07-58	34.0
34.1	024.46	04-05	04-29	04-54	05-18	05-42	06-07	06-31	06-56	07-20	07-45	08-09	34.1
34.2	025.00	04-10	04-35	05-00	05-25	05-50	06-15	06-40	07-05	07-30	07-55	08-20	34.2
34.3	025.54	04-15	04-41	05-06	05-32	05-58	06-23	06-49	07-14	07-40	08-05	08-31	34.3
34.4	026.08	04-21	04-47	05-13	05-39	06-05	06-31	06-57	07-23	07-49	08-15	08-42	34.4
34.5	026.62	04-26	04-53	05-19	05-46	06-13	06-39	07-06	07-33	07-59	08-26	08-52	34.5
34.6	027.15	04-32	04-59	05-26	05-53	06-20	06-47	07-14	07-42	08-09	08-36	09-03	34.6
34.7	027.68	04-37	05-04	05-32	05-60	06-27	06-55	07-23	07-51	08-18	08-46	09-14	34.7
34.8	028.21	04-42	05-10	05-39	06-07	06-35	07-03	07-31	07-60	08-28	08-56	09-24	34.8
34.9	028.72	04-47	05-16	05-45	06-13	06-42	07-11	07-39	08-08	08-37	09-06	09-34	34.9
Rating	Sec/Mi	10 Mi	11 Mi	12 Mi	13 Mi	14 Mi	15 Mi	16 Mi	17 Mi	18 Mi	19 Mi	20 Mi	Rating

ADD time allowances on this page to Elapsed Time

Rating	21 Mi	22 Mi	23 Mi	24 Mi	25 Mi	26 Mi	27 Mi	28 Mi	29 Mi	30 Mi	31 Mi	32 Mi	Rating
30.0	00-00	00-00	00-00	00-00	00-00	00-00	00-00	00-00	00-00	00-00	00-00	00-00	30.0
30.1	00-14	00-15	00-15	00-16	00-17	00-17	00-18	00-18	00-19	00-20	00-20	00-21	30.1
30.2	00-27	00-29	00-30	00-31	00-32	00-34	00-35	00-36	00-38	00-39	00-40	00-42	30.2
30.3	00-41	00-43	00-45	00-47	00-49	00-51	00-53	00-55	00-57	00-59	01-00	01-02	30.3
30.4	00-55	00-57	00-60	01-02	01-05	01-08	01-10	01-13	01-15	01-18	01-21	01-23	30.4
30.5	01-08	01-11	01-15	01-18	01-21	01-24	01-28	01-31	01-34	01-38	01-41	01-44	30.5
30.6	01-22	01-26	01-29	01-33	01-37	01-41	01-45	01-49	01-53	01-57	02-01	02-04	30.6
30.7	01-35	01-39	01-44	01-48	01-53	01-57	02-02	02-07	02-11	02-16	02-20	02-25	30.7
30.8	01-48	01-53	01-58	02-04	02-09	02-14	02-19	02-24	02-29	02-35	02-40	02-45	30.8
30.9	02-01	02-07	02-13	02-18	02-24	02-30	02-36	02-42	02-47	02-53	02-59	03-05	30.9
31.0	02-14	02-21	02-27	02-33	02-40	02-46	02-53	02-59	03-05	03-12	03-18	03-24	31.0
31.1	02-27	02-34	02-41	02-48	02-56	03-03	03-10	03-17	03-24	03-31	03-38	03-45	31.1
31.2	02-40	02-48	02-56	03-03	03-11	03-19	03-26	03-34	03-42	03-49	03-57	04-04	31.2
31.3	02-53	03-02	03-10	03-18	03-26	03-35	03-43	03-51	03-60	04-08	04-16	04-24	31.3
31.4	03-07	03-16	03-24	03-33	03-42	03-51	04-00	04-09	04-18	04-27	04-36	04-44	31.4
31.5	03-20	03-29	03-38	03-48	03-57	04-07	04-17	04-26	04-35	04-45	04-54	05-04	31.5
31.6	03-32	03-42	03-53	04-03	04-13	04-23	04-33	04-43	04-53	05-03	05-13	05-24	31.6
31.7	03-45	03-56	04-07	04-17	04-28	04-39	04-49	05-00	05-11	05-22	05-32	05-43	31.7
31.8	03-58	04-09	04-20	04-32	04-43	04-54	05-06	05-17	05-28	05-40	05-51	06-02	31.8
31.9	04-10	04-22	04-34	04-46	04-58	05-10	05-22	05-34	05-46	05-58	06-09	06-21	31.9
32.0	04-23	04-35	04-48	05-00	05-13	05-26	05-38	05-51	06-03	06-16	06-28	06-41	32.0
32.1	04-36	04-49	05-02	05-15	05-28	05-41	05-54	06-07	06-20	06-34	06-47	06-60	32.1
32.2	04-48	05-02	05-15	05-29	05-43	05-56	06-10	06-24	06-38	06-51	07-05	07-19	32.2
32.3	05-00	05-15	05-29	05-43	05-57	06-12	06-26	06-40	06-55	07-09	07-23	07-38	32.3
32.4	05-13	05-28	05-42	05-57	06-12	06-27	06-42	06-57	07-12	07-27	07-42	07-56	32.4
32.5	05-25	05-41	05-56	06-12	06-27	06-42	06-58	07-13	07-29	07-44	07-60	08-15	32.5
32.6	05-37	05-53	06-09	06-25	06-41	06-58	07-14	07-30	07-46	08-02	08-18	08-34	32.6
32.7	05-49	06-06	06-23	06-39	06-56	07-13	07-29	07-46	08-03	08-19	08-36	08-52	32.7
32.8	06-01	06-19	06-36	06-53	07-10	07-27	07-45	08-02	08-19	08-36	08-53	09-11	32.8
32.9	06-13	06-31	06-49	07-07	07-24	07-42	08-00	08-18	08-36	08-53	09-11	09-29	32.9
33.0	06-25	06-44	07-02	07-20	07-39	07-57	08-15	08-34	08-52	09-11	09-29	09-47	33.0
33.1	06-37	06-56	07-15	07-34	07-53	08-12	08-31	08-50	09-09	09-28	09-47	10-05	33.1
33.2	06-49	07-09	07-28	07-48	08-07	08-27	08-46	09-06	09-25	09-45	10-04	10-24	33.2
33.3	07-01	07-21	07-41	08-01	08-21	08-41	09-01	09-21	09-41	10-02	10-22	10-42	33.3
33.4	07-13	07-33	07-54	08-15	08-35	08-56	09-16	09-37	09-58	10-18	10-39	10-60	33.4
33.5	07-25	07-46	08-07	08-28	08-49	09-10	09-32	09-53	10-14	10-35	10-56	11-17	33.5
33.6	07-36	07-58	08-20	08-42	09-03	09-25	09-47	10-08	10-30	10-52	11-14	11-35	33.6
33.7	07-48	08-10	08-32	08-55	09-17	09-39	10-02	10-24	10-46	11-08	11-31	11-53	33.7
33.8	07-59	08-22	08-45	09-08	09-31	09-54	10-16	10-39	11-02	11-25	11-48	12-11	33.8
33.9	08-11	08-34	08-57	09-21	09-44	10-08	10-31	10-54	11-18	11-41	12-04	12-28	33.9
34.0	08-22	08-46	09-10	09-34	09-58	10-22	10-46	11-09	11-33	11-57	12-21	12-45	34.0
34.1	08-34	08-58	09-23	09-47	10-11	10-36	11-00	11-25	11-49	12-14	12-38	13-03	34.1
34.2	08-45	09-10	09-35	10-00	10-25	10-50	11-15	11-40	12-05	12-30	12-55	13-20	34.2
34.3	08-56	09-22	09-47	10-13	10-38	11-04	11-30	11-55	12-21	12-46	13-12	13-37	34.3
34.4	09-08	09-34	09-60	10-26	10-52	11-18	11-44	12-10	12-36	13-02	13-28	13-55	34.4
34.5	09-19	09-46	10-12	10-39	11-05	11-32	11-59	12-25	12-52	13-19	13-45	14-12	34.5
34.6	09-30	09-57	10-24	10-52	11-19	11-46	12-13	12-40	13-07	13-35	14-02	14-29	34.6
34.7	09-41	10-09	10-37	11-04	11-32	11-60	12-27	12-55	13-23	13-50	14-18	14-46	34.7
34.8	09-52	10-21	10-49	11-17	11-45	12-13	12-42	13-10	13-38	14-06	14-35	15-03	34.8
34.9	10-03	10-32	11-01	11-29	11-58	12-27	12-55	13-24	13-53	14-22	14-50	15-19	34.9
Rating	21 Mi	22 Mi	23 Mi	24 Mi	25 Mi	26 Mi	27 Mi	28 Mi	29 Mi	30 Mi	31 Mi	32 Mi	Rating

ADD time allowances on this page to Elapsed Time

Rating	Sec/Mi	10 Mi	11 Mi	12 Mi	13 Mi	14 Mi	15 Mi	16 Mi	17 Mi	18 Mi	19 Mi	20 Mi	Rating
35.0	029.24	04-52	05-22	05-51	06-20	06-49	07-19	07-48	08-17	08-46	09-16	09-45	35.0
35.1	029.76	04-58	05-27	05-57	06-27	06-57	07-26	07-56	08-26	08-56	09-25	09-55	35.1
35.2	030.28	05-03	05-33	06-03	06-34	07-04	07-34	08-04	08-35	09-05	09-35	10-06	35.2
35.3	030.80	05-08	05-39	06-10	06-40	07-11	07-42	08-13	08-44	09-14	09-45	10-16	35.3
35.4	031.32	05-13	05-45	06-16	06-47	07-18	07-50	08-21	08-52	09-24	09-55	10-26	35.4
35.5	031.83	05-18	05-50	06-22	06-54	07-26	07-57	08-29	09-01	09-33	10-05	10-37	35.5
35.6	032.35	05-23	05-56	06-28	07-01	07-33	08-05	08-38	09-10	09-42	10-15	10-47	35.6
35.7	032.85	05-29	06-01	06-34	07-07	07-40	08-13	08-46	09-18	09-51	10-24	10-57	35.7
35.8	033.36	05-34	06-07	06-40	07-14	07-47	08-20	08-54	09-27	10-00	10-34	11-07	35.8
35.9	033.86	05-39	06-12	06-46	07-20	07-54	08-28	09-02	09-36	10-09	10-43	11-17	35.9
36.0	034.36	05-44	06-18	06-52	07-27	08-01	08-35	09-10	09-44	10-18	10-53	11-27	36.0
36.1	034.86	05-49	06-23	06-58	07-33	08-08	08-43	09-18	09-53	10-27	11-02	11-37	36.1
36.2	035.36	05-54	06-29	07-04	07-40	08-15	08-50	09-26	10-01	10-36	11-12	11-47	36.2
36.3	035.85	05-59	06-34	07-10	07-46	08-22	08-58	09-34	10-09	10-45	11-21	11-57	36.3
36.4	036.34	06-03	06-40	07-16	07-52	08-29	09-05	09-41	10-18	10-54	11-30	12-07	36.4
36.5	036.84	06-08	06-45	07-22	07-59	08-36	09-13	09-49	10-26	11-03	11-40	12-17	36.5
36.6	037.33	06-13	06-51	07-28	08-05	08-43	09-20	09-57	10-35	11-12	11-49	12-27	36.6
36.7	037.81	06-18	06-56	07-34	08-12	08-49	09-27	10-05	10-43	11-21	11-58	12-36	36.7
36.8	038.29	06-23	07-01	07-39	08-18	08-56	09-34	10-13	10-51	11-29	12-08	12-46	36.8
36.9	038.77	06-28	07-06	07-45	08-24	09-03	09-42	10-20	10-59	11-38	12-17	12-55	36.9
37.0	039.25	06-32	07-12	07-51	08-30	09-09	09-49	10-28	11-07	11-47	12-26	13-05	37.0
37.1	039.73	06-37	07-17	07-57	08-36	09-16	09-56	10-36	11-15	11-55	12-35	13-15	37.1
37.2	040.21	06-42	07-22	08-03	08-43	09-23	10-03	10-43	11-24	12-04	12-44	13-24	37.2
37.3	040.69	06-47	07-28	08-08	08-49	09-30	10-10	10-51	11-32	12-12	12-53	13-34	37.3
37.4	041.17	06-52	07-33	08-14	08-55	09-36	10-18	10-59	11-40	12-21	13-02	13-43	37.4
37.5	041.64	06-56	07-38	08-20	09-01	09-43	10-25	11-06	11-48	12-30	13-11	13-53	37.5
37.6	042.10	07-01	07-43	08-25	09-07	09-49	10-32	11-14	11-56	12-38	13-20	14-02	37.6
37.7	042.57	07-06	07-48	08-31	09-13	09-56	10-39	11-21	12-04	12-46	13-29	14-11	37.7
37.8	043.04	07-10	07-53	08-36	09-20	10-03	10-46	11-29	12-12	12-55	13-38	14-21	37.8
37.9	043.50	07-15	07-59	08-42	09-26	10-09	10-53	11-36	12-20	13-03	13-47	14-30	37.9
38.0	043.96	07-20	08-04	08-48	09-31	10-15	10-59	11-43	12-27	13-11	13-55	14-39	38.0
38.1	044.42	07-24	08-09	08-53	09-37	10-22	11-06	11-51	12-35	13-20	14-04	14-48	38.1
38.2	044.88	07-29	08-14	08-59	09-43	10-28	11-13	11-58	12-43	13-28	14-13	14-58	38.2
38.3	045.33	07-33	08-19	09-04	09-49	10-35	11-20	12-05	12-51	13-36	14-21	15-07	38.3
38.4	045.79	07-38	08-24	09-09	09-55	10-41	11-27	12-13	12-58	13-44	14-30	15-16	38.4
38.5	046.24	07-42	08-29	09-15	10-01	10-47	11-34	12-20	13-06	13-52	14-39	15-25	38.5
38.6	046.70	07-47	08-34	09-20	10-07	10-54	11-41	12-27	13-14	14-01	14-47	15-34	38.6
38.7	047.16	07-52	08-39	09-26	10-13	11-00	11-47	12-35	13-22	14-09	14-56	15-43	38.7
38.8	047.60	07-56	08-44	09-31	10-19	11-06	11-54	12-42	13-29	14-17	15-04	15-52	38.8
38.9	048.04	08-00	08-48	09-36	10-24	11-13	12-01	12-49	13-37	14-25	15-13	16-01	38.9
39.0	048.48	08-05	08-53	09-42	10-30	11-19	12-07	12-56	13-44	14-33	15-21	16-10	39.0
39.1	048.92	08-09	08-58	09-47	10-36	11-25	12-14	13-03	13-52	14-41	15-29	16-18	39.1
39.2	049.36	08-14	09-03	09-52	10-42	11-31	12-20	13-10	13-59	14-48	15-38	16-27	39.2
39.3	049.81	08-18	09-08	09-58	10-48	11-37	12-27	13-17	14-07	14-57	15-46	16-36	39.3
39.4	050.25	08-23	09-13	10-03	10-53	11-44	12-34	13-24	14-14	15-05	15-55	16-45	39.4
39.5	050.69	08-27	09-18	10-08	10-59	11-50	12-40	13-31	14-22	15-12	16-03	16-54	39.5
39.6	051.12	08-31	09-22	10-13	11-05	11-56	12-47	13-38	14-29	15-20	16-11	17-02	39.6
39.7	051.55	08-35	09-27	10-19	11-10	12-02	12-53	13-45	14-36	15-28	16-19	17-11	39.7
39.8	051.98	08-40	09-32	10-24	11-16	12-08	12-60	13-52	14-44	15-36	16-28	17-20	39.8
39.9	052.40	08-44	09-36	10-29	11-21	12-14	13-06	13-58	14-51	15-43	16-36	17-28	39.9
Rating	Sec/Mi	10 Mi	11 Mi	12 Mi	13 Mi	14 Mi	15 Mi	16 Mi	17 Mi	18 Mi	19 Mi	20 Mi	Rating

ADD time allowances on this page to Elapsed Time

Rating	21 Mi	22 Mi	23 Mi	24 Mi	25 Mi	26 Mi	27 Mi	28 Mi	29 Mi	30 Mi	31 Mi	32 Mi	Rating
35.0	10-14	10-43	11-12	11-42	12-11	12-40	13-09	13-39	14-08	14-37	15-06	15-36	35.0
35.1	10-25	10-55	11-24	11-54	12-24	12-54	13-24	13-53	14-23	14-53	15-23	15-52	35.1
35.2	10-36	11-06	11-36	12-07	12-37	13-07	13-38	14-08	14-38	15-08	15-39	16-09	35.2
35.3	10-47	11-18	11-48	12-19	12-50	13-21	13-52	14-22	14-53	15-24	15-55	16-26	35.3
35.4	10-58	11-29	12-00	12-32	13-03	13-34	14-06	14-37	15-08	15-40	16-11	16-42	35.4
35.5	11-08	11-40	12-12	12-44	13-16	13-48	14-19	14-51	15-23	15-55	16-27	16-59	35.5
35.6	11-19	11-52	12-24	12-56	13-29	14-01	14-33	15-06	15-38	16-11	16-43	17-15	35.6
35.7	11-30	12-03	12-36	13-08	13-41	14-14	14-47	15-20	15-53	16-26	16-58	17-31	35.7
35.8	11-41	12-14	12-47	13-21	13-54	14-27	15-01	15-34	16-07	16-41	17-14	17-48	35.8
35.9	11-51	12-25	12-59	13-33	14-06	14-40	15-14	15-48	16-22	16-56	17-30	18-03	35.9
36.0	12-02	12-36	13-10	13-45	14-19	14-53	15-28	16-02	16-36	17-11	17-45	18-20	36.0
36.1	12-12	12-47	13-22	13-57	14-32	15-06	15-41	16-16	16-51	17-26	18-01	18-36	36.1
36.2	12-23	12-58	13-33	14-09	14-44	15-19	15-55	16-30	17-05	17-41	18-16	18-51	36.2
36.3	12-33	13-09	13-45	14-20	14-56	15-32	16-08	16-44	17-20	17-56	18-31	19-07	36.3
36.4	12-43	13-19	13-56	14-32	15-08	15-45	16-21	16-57	17-34	18-10	18-47	19-23	36.4
36.5	12-54	13-30	14-07	14-44	15-21	15-58	16-35	17-12	17-48	18-25	19-02	19-39	36.5
36.6	13-04	13-41	14-19	14-56	15-33	16-11	16-48	17-25	18-03	18-40	19-17	19-55	36.6
36.7	13-14	13-52	14-30	15-07	15-45	16-23	17-01	17-39	18-16	18-54	19-32	20-10	36.7
36.8	13-24	14-02	14-41	15-19	15-57	16-36	17-14	17-52	18-30	19-09	19-47	20-25	36.8
36.9	13-34	14-13	14-52	15-30	16-09	16-48	17-27	18-06	18-44	19-23	20-02	20-41	36.9
37.0	13-44	14-23	15-03	15-42	16-21	17-00	17-40	18-19	18-58	19-38	20-17	20-56	37.0
37.1	13-54	14-34	15-14	15-54	16-33	17-13	17-53	18-32	19-12	19-52	20-32	21-11	37.1
37.2	14-04	14-45	15-25	16-05	16-45	17-25	18-06	18-46	19-26	20-06	20-47	21-27	37.2
37.3	14-14	14-55	15-36	16-17	16-57	17-38	18-19	18-59	19-40	20-21	21-01	21-42	37.3
37.4	14-25	15-06	15-47	16-28	17-09	17-50	18-32	19-13	19-54	20-35	21-16	21-57	37.4
37.5	14-34	15-16	15-58	16-39	17-21	18-03	18-44	19-26	20-08	20-49	21-31	22-12	37.5
37.6	14-44	15-26	16-08	16-50	17-32	18-15	18-57	19-39	20-21	21-03	21-45	22-27	37.6
37.7	14-54	15-37	16-19	17-02	17-44	18-27	19-09	19-52	20-35	21-17	21-60	22-42	37.7
37.8	15-04	15-47	16-30	17-13	17-56	18-39	19-22	20-05	20-48	21-31	22-14	22-57	37.8
37.9	15-14	15-57	16-41	17-24	18-08	18-51	19-35	20-18	21-02	21-45	22-29	23-12	37.9
38.0	15-23	16-07	16-51	17-35	18-19	19-03	19-47	20-31	21-15	21-59	22-43	23-27	38.0
38.1	15-33	16-17	17-02	17-46	18-30	19-15	19-59	20-44	21-28	22-13	22-57	23-41	38.1
38.2	15-42	16-27	17-12	17-57	18-42	19-27	20-12	20-57	21-42	22-26	23-11	23-56	38.2
38.3	15-52	16-37	17-23	18-08	18-53	19-39	20-24	21-09	21-55	22-40	23-25	24-11	38.3
38.4	16-02	16-47	17-33	18-19	19-05	19-51	20-36	21-22	22-08	22-54	23-39	24-25	38.4
38.5	16-11	16-57	17-44	18-30	19-16	20-02	20-48	21-35	22-21	23-07	23-53	24-40	38.5
38.6	16-21	17-07	17-54	18-41	19-27	20-14	21-01	21-48	22-34	23-21	24-08	24-54	38.6
38.7	16-30	17-18	18-05	18-52	19-39	20-26	21-13	22-00	22-48	23-35	24-22	25-09	38.7
38.8	16-40	17-27	18-15	19-02	19-50	20-38	21-25	22-13	23-00	23-48	24-36	25-23	38.8
38.9	16-49	17-37	18-25	19-13	20-01	20-49	21-37	22-25	23-13	24-01	24-49	25-37	38.9
39.0	16-58	17-47	18-35	19-24	20-12	21-00	21-49	22-37	23-26	24-14	25-03	25-51	39.0
39.1	17-07	17-56	18-45	19-34	20-23	21-12	22-01	22-50	23-39	24-28	25-17	26-05	39.1
39.2	17-17	18-06	18-55	19-45	20-34	21-23	22-13	23-02	23-51	24-41	25-30	26-20	39.2
39.3	17-26	18-16	19-06	19-55	20-45	21-35	22-25	23-15	24-04	24-54	25-44	26-34	39.3
39.4	17-35	18-26	19-16	20-06	20-56	21-47	22-37	23-27	24-17	25-08	25-58	26-48	39.4
39.5	17-44	18-35	19-26	20-17	21-07	21-58	22-49	23-39	24-30	25-21	26-11	27-02	39.5
39.6	17-54	18-45	19-36	20-27	21-18	22-09	23-00	23-51	24-42	25-34	26-25	27-16	39.6
39.7	18-03	18-54	19-46	20-37	21-29	22-20	23-12	24-03	24-55	25-47	26-38	27-30	39.7
39.8	18-12	19-04	19-56	20-48	21-39	22-31	23-23	24-15	25-07	25-59	26-51	27-43	39.8
39.9	18-20	19-13	20-05	20-58	21-50	22-42	23-35	24-27	25-20	26-12	27-04	27-57	39.9
Rating	21 Mi	22 Mi	23 Mi	24 Mi	25 Mi	26 Mi	27 Mi	28 Mi	29 Mi	30 Mi	31 Mi	32 Mi	Rating

ADD time allowances on this page to Elapsed Time

Rating	Sec/Mi	10 Mi	11 Mi	12 Mi	13 Mi	14 Mi	15 Mi	16 Mi	17 Mi	18 Mi	19 Mi	20 Mi	Rating
40.0	052.82	08-48	09-41	10-34	11-27	12-19	13-12	14-05	14-58	15-51	16-44	17-36	40.0
40.1	053.25	08-53	09-46	10-39	11-32	12-26	13-19	14-12	15-05	15-59	16-52	17-45	40.1
40.2	053.68	08-57	09-50	10-44	11-38	12-32	13-25	14-19	15-13	16-06	16-60	17-54	40.2
40.3	054.12	09-01	09-55	10-49	11-44	12-38	13-32	14-26	15-20	16-14	17-08	18-02	40.3
40.4	054.54	09-05	09-60	10-54	11-49	12-44	13-38	14-33	15-27	16-22	17-16	18-11	40.4
40.5	054.96	09-10	10-05	10-60	11-54	12-49	13-44	14-39	15-34	16-29	17-24	18-19	40.5
40.6	055.38	09-14	10-09	11-05	11-60	12-55	13-51	14-46	15-41	16-37	17-32	18-28	40.6
40.7	055.79	09-18	10-14	11-09	12-05	13-01	13-57	14-53	15-48	16-44	17-40	18-36	40.7
40.8	056.20	09-22	10-18	11-14	12-11	13-07	14-03	14-59	15-55	16-52	17-48	18-44	40.8
40.9	056.61	09-26	10-23	11-19	12-16	13-13	14-09	15-06	16-02	16-59	17-56	18-52	40.9
41.0	057.02	09-30	10-27	11-24	12-21	13-18	14-15	15-12	16-09	17-06	18-03	19-00	41.0
41.1	057.44	09-34	10-32	11-29	12-27	13-24	14-22	15-19	16-16	17-14	18-11	19-09	41.1
41.2	057.85	09-38	10-36	11-34	12-32	13-30	14-28	15-26	16-23	17-21	18-19	19-17	41.2
41.3	058.26	09-43	10-41	11-39	12-37	13-36	14-34	15-32	16-30	17-29	18-27	19-25	41.3
41.4	058.66	09-47	10-45	11-44	12-43	13-41	14-40	15-39	16-37	17-36	18-35	19-33	41.4
41.5	059.07	09-51	10-50	11-49	12-48	13-47	14-46	15-45	16-44	17-43	18-42	19-41	41.5
41.6	059.48	09-55	10-54	11-54	12-53	13-53	14-52	15-52	16-51	17-51	18-50	19-50	41.6
41.7	059.88	09-59	10-59	11-59	12-58	13-58	14-58	15-58	16-58	17-58	18-58	19-58	41.7
41.8	060.27	10-03	11-03	12-03	13-03	14-04	15-04	16-04	17-05	18-05	19-05	20-05	41.8
41.9	060.67	10-07	11-07	12-08	13-09	14-09	15-10	16-11	17-11	18-12	19-13	20-13	41.9
42.0	061.07	10-11	11-12	12-13	13-14	14-15	15-16	16-17	17-18	18-19	19-20	20-21	42.0
42.1	061.47	10-15	11-16	12-18	13-19	14-21	15-22	16-24	17-25	18-26	19-28	20-29	42.1
42.2	061.87	10-19	11-21	12-22	13-24	14-26	15-28	16-30	17-32	18-34	19-36	20-37	42.2
42.3	062.26	10-23	11-25	12-27	13-29	14-32	15-34	16-36	17-38	18-41	19-43	20-45	42.3
42.4	062.65	10-26	11-29	12-32	13-34	14-37	15-40	16-42	17-45	18-48	19-50	20-53	42.4
42.5	063.04	10-30	11-33	12-36	13-39	14-43	15-46	16-49	17-52	18-55	19-58	21-01	42.5
42.6	063.43	10-34	11-38	12-41	13-45	14-48	15-51	16-55	17-58	19-02	20-05	21-09	42.6
42.7	063.81	10-38	11-42	12-46	13-50	14-53	15-57	17-01	18-05	19-09	20-12	21-16	42.7
42.8	064.20	10-42	11-46	12-50	13-55	14-59	16-03	17-07	18-11	19-16	20-20	21-24	42.8
42.9	064.58	10-46	11-50	12-55	13-60	15-04	16-09	17-13	18-18	19-22	20-27	21-32	42.9
43.0	064.96	10-50	11-55	12-60	14-04	15-09	16-14	17-19	18-24	19-29	20-34	21-39	43.0
43.1	065.34	10-53	11-59	13-04	14-09	15-15	16-20	17-25	18-31	19-36	20-41	21-47	43.1
43.2	065.72	10-57	12-03	13-09	14-14	15-20	16-26	17-32	18-37	19-43	20-49	21-54	43.2
43.3	066.10	11-01	12-07	13-13	14-19	15-25	16-32	17-38	18-44	19-50	20-56	22-02	43.3
43.4	066.48	11-05	12-11	13-18	14-24	15-31	16-37	17-44	18-50	19-57	21-03	22-10	43.4
43.5	066.86	11-09	12-15	13-22	14-29	15-36	16-43	17-50	18-57	20-03	21-10	22-17	43.5
43.6	067.24	11-12	12-20	13-27	14-34	15-41	16-49	17-56	19-03	20-10	21-18	22-25	43.6
43.7	067.62	11-16	12-24	13-31	14-39	15-47	16-54	18-02	19-10	20-17	21-25	22-32	43.7
43.8	067.99	11-20	12-28	13-36	14-44	15-52	16-60	18-08	19-16	20-24	21-32	22-40	43.8
43.9	068.35	11-23	12-32	13-40	14-49	15-57	17-05	18-14	19-22	20-30	21-39	22-47	43.9
44.0	068.72	11-27	12-36	13-45	14-53	16-02	17-11	18-20	19-28	20-37	21-46	22-54	44.0
44.1	069.09	11-31	12-40	13-49	14-58	16-07	17-16	18-25	19-35	20-44	21-53	23-02	44.1
44.2	069.46	11-35	12-44	13-54	15-03	16-12	17-22	18-31	19-41	20-50	21-60	23-09	44.2
44.3	069.83	11-38	12-48	13-58	15-08	16-18	17-27	18-37	19-47	20-57	22-07	23-17	44.3
44.4	070.20	11-42	12-52	14-02	15-13	16-23	17-33	18-43	19-53	21-04	22-14	23-24	44.4
44.5	070.57	11-46	12-56	14-07	15-17	16-28	17-39	18-49	19-60	21-10	22-21	23-31	44.5
44.6	070.93	11-49	13-00	14-11	15-22	16-33	17-44	18-55	20-06	21-17	22-28	23-39	44.6
44.7	071.29	11-53	13-04	14-15	15-27	16-38	17-49	19-01	20-12	21-23	22-35	23-46	44.7
44.8	071.65	11-56	13-08	14-20	15-31	16-43	17-55	19-06	20-18	21-30	22-41	23-53	44.8
44.9	072.01	12-00	13-12	14-24	15-36	16-48	18-00	19-12	20-24	21-36	22-48	24-00	44.9
Rating	Sec/Mi	10 Mi	11 Mi	12 Mi	13 Mi	14 Mi	15 Mi	16 Mi	17 Mi	18 Mi	19 Mi	20 Mi	Rating

ADD time allowances on this page to Elapsed Time

Rating	21 Mi	22 Mi	23 Mi	24 Mi	25 Mi	26 Mi	27 Mi	28 Mi	29 Mi	30 Mi	31 Mi	32 Mi	Rating
40.0	18-29	19-22	20-15	21-08	22-00	22-53	23-46	24-39	25-32	26-25	27-17	28-10	40.0
40.1	18-38	19-32	20-25	21-18	22-11	23-05	23-58	24-51	25-44	26-38	27-31	28-24	40.1
40.2	18-47	19-41	20-35	21-28	22-22	23-16	24-09	25-03	25-57	26-50	27-44	28-38	40.2
40.3	18-57	19-51	20-45	21-39	22-33	23-27	24-21	25-15	26-09	27-04	27-58	28-52	40.3
40.4	19-05	19-60	20-54	21-49	22-44	23-38	24-33	25-27	26-22	27-16	28-11	29-05	40.4
40.5	19-14	20-09	21-04	21-59	22-54	23-49	24-44	25-39	26-34	27-29	28-24	29-19	40.5
40.6	19-23	20-18	21-14	22-09	23-05	23-60	24-55	25-51	26-46	27-41	28-37	29-32	40.6
40.7	19-32	20-27	21-23	22-19	23-15	24-11	25-06	26-02	26-58	27-54	28-49	29-45	40.7
40.8	19-40	20-36	21-33	22-29	23-25	24-21	25-17	26-14	27-10	28-06	29-02	29-58	40.8
40.9	19-49	20-45	21-42	22-39	23-35	24-32	25-28	26-25	27-22	28-18	29-15	30-12	40.9
41.0	19-57	20-54	21-51	22-48	23-45	24-42	25-40	26-37	27-34	28-31	29-28	30-25	41.0
41.1	20-06	21-04	22-01	22-59	23-56	24-53	25-51	26-48	27-46	28-43	29-41	30-38	41.1
41.2	20-15	21-13	22-11	23-08	24-06	25-04	26-02	26-60	27-58	28-56	29-53	30-51	41.2
41.3	20-23	21-22	22-20	23-18	24-17	25-15	26-13	27-11	28-10	29-08	30-06	31-04	41.3
41.4	20-32	21-30	22-29	23-28	24-26	25-25	26-24	27-22	28-21	29-20	30-18	31-17	41.4
41.5	20-40	21-40	22-39	23-38	24-37	25-36	26-35	27-34	28-33	29-32	30-31	31-30	41.5
41.6	20-49	21-49	22-48	23-48	24-47	25-46	26-46	27-45	28-45	29-44	30-44	31-43	41.6
41.7	20-57	21-57	22-57	23-57	24-57	25-57	26-57	27-57	28-57	29-56	30-56	31-56	41.7
41.8	21-06	22-06	23-06	24-06	25-07	26-07	27-07	28-08	29-08	30-08	31-08	32-09	41.8
41.9	21-14	22-15	23-15	24-16	25-17	26-17	27-18	28-19	29-19	30-20	31-21	32-21	41.9
42.0	21-22	22-24	23-25	24-26	25-27	26-28	27-29	28-30	29-31	30-32	31-33	32-34	42.0
42.1	21-31	22-32	23-34	24-35	25-37	26-38	27-40	28-41	29-43	30-44	31-46	32-47	42.1
42.2	21-39	22-41	23-43	24-45	25-47	26-49	27-50	28-52	29-54	30-56	31-58	32-60	42.2
42.3	21-47	22-50	23-52	24-54	25-56	26-59	28-01	29-03	30-06	31-08	32-10	33-12	42.3
42.4	21-56	22-58	24-01	25-04	26-06	27-09	28-12	29-14	30-17	31-20	32-22	33-25	42.4
42.5	22-04	23-07	24-10	25-13	26-16	27-19	28-22	29-25	30-28	31-31	32-34	33-37	42.5
42.6	22-12	23-15	24-19	25-22	26-26	27-29	28-33	29-36	30-39	31-43	32-46	33-50	42.6
42.7	22-20	23-24	24-28	25-31	26-35	27-39	28-43	29-47	30-50	31-54	32-58	34-02	42.7
42.8	22-28	23-32	24-37	25-41	26-45	27-49	28-53	29-58	31-02	32-06	33-10	34-14	42.8
42.9	22-36	23-41	24-45	25-50	26-54	27-59	29-04	30-08	31-13	32-17	33-22	34-27	42.9
43.0	22-44	23-49	24-54	25-59	27-04	28-09	29-14	30-19	31-24	32-29	33-34	34-39	43.0
43.1	22-52	23-57	25-03	26-08	27-14	28-19	29-24	30-30	31-35	32-40	33-46	34-51	43.1
43.2	23-00	24-06	25-12	26-17	27-23	28-29	29-34	30-40	31-46	32-52	33-57	35-03	43.2
43.3	23-08	24-14	25-20	26-26	27-32	28-39	29-45	30-51	31-57	33-03	34-09	35-15	43.3
43.4	23-16	24-23	25-29	26-36	27-42	28-48	29-55	31-01	32-08	33-14	34-21	35-27	43.4
43.5	23-24	24-31	25-38	26-45	27-51	28-58	30-05	31-12	32-19	33-26	34-33	35-39	43.5
43.6	23-32	24-39	25-47	26-54	28-01	29-08	30-15	31-23	32-30	33-37	34-44	35-52	43.6
43.7	23-40	24-48	25-55	27-03	28-11	29-18	30-26	31-33	32-41	33-49	34-56	36-04	43.7
43.8	23-48	24-56	26-04	27-12	28-20	29-28	30-36	31-44	32-52	33-60	35-08	36-16	43.8
43.9	23-55	25-04	26-12	27-20	28-29	29-37	30-45	31-54	33-02	34-11	35-19	36-27	43.9
44.0	24-03	25-12	26-21	27-29	28-38	29-47	30-55	32-04	33-13	34-22	35-30	36-39	44.0
44.1	24-11	25-20	26-29	27-38	28-47	29-56	31-05	32-15	33-24	34-33	35-42	36-51	44.1
44.2	24-19	25-28	26-38	27-47	28-56	30-06	31-15	32-25	33-34	34-44	35-53	37-03	44.2
44.3	24-26	25-36	26-46	27-56	29-06	30-16	31-25	32-35	33-45	34-55	36-05	37-15	44.3
44.4	24-34	25-44	26-55	28-05	29-15	30-25	31-35	32-46	33-56	35-06	36-16	37-26	44.4
44.5	24-42	25-53	27-03	28-14	29-24	30-35	31-45	32-56	34-06	35-17	36-28	37-38	44.5
44.6	24-50	26-00	27-11	28-22	29-33	30-44	31-55	33-06	34-17	35-28	36-39	37-50	44.6
44.7	24-57	26-08	27-20	28-31	29-42	30-54	32-05	33-16	34-27	35-39	36-50	38-01	44.7
44.8	25-05	26-16	27-28	28-40	29-51	31-03	32-15	33-26	34-38	35-50	37-01	38-13	44.8
44.9	25-12	26-24	27-36	28-48	30-00	31-12	32-24	33-36	34-48	36-00	37-12	38-24	44.9
Rating	21 Mi	22 Mi	23 Mi	24 Mi	25 Mi	26 Mi	27 Mi	28 Mi	29 Mi	30 Mi	31 Mi	32 Mi	Rating

ADD time allowances on this page to Elapsed Time

Appendix H: OFFSHORE RACING COUNCIL (ORC) SAFETY REGULATIONS

1.0   PURPOSE AND USE

1.1   It is the purpose of these special regulations to establish uniform minimum equipment and accommodations standards for yachts racing under the International Offshore Rule and thereby to aid in promoting uniform offshore racing throughout the world.

1.2   These regulations do not replace, but rather supplement, the requirements of governmental authority, the Racing Rules and the International Offshore Rule. The attention of owners is called to restrictions in the rules on the location and movement of equipment.

1.3   The Offshore Racing Council strongly recommends the use of these special regulations by all organizations sponsoring races under the International Offshore Rule. Race Committees may select the category deemed most suitable for the type of race to be sailed. They are urged to depart from the regulations or modify or make exceptions thereto only when the most compelling circumstances so dictate.

2.0   OWNER'S RESPONSIBILITY

2.1   The safety of a yacht and her crew is the sole and inescapable responsibility of the owner, or owner's representative who must do his best to ensure that the yacht is fully found, thoroughly seaworthy and manned by an experienced crew who are physically fit to face bad weather. He must be satisfied as to the soundness of hull, spars, rigging, sails and all gear. He must ensure that all safety equipment is properly maintained and stowed and that the crew know where it is kept and how it is to be used.

2.2   Neither the establishment of these special regulations, their use by sponsoring organizations, nor the inspection of a yacht under these regulations in any way limits or reduces the complete and unlimited responsibility of the owner or owner's representative.

2.3   It is the sole and exclusive responsibility of each yacht to decide whether or not to start or continue to race.

3.0   INSPECTION

3.1   A yacht may be inspected at any time. If she does not comply with these special regulations her entry may be rejected, or she will be liable to disqualification or such other penalty as may be prescribed by the national authority or the sponsoring organization.

4.0   CATEGORIES OF OFFSHORE EVENTS

4.1   The International Offshore Rule is used to rate a wide variety of types and sizes of yachts in many types of races, ranging from long-distance ocean races sailed under adverse conditions to short-course day races sailed in protected waters. To provide for the differences in the standards of safety and accommodation required for such varying circumstances, four categories of races are established, as follows:

4.2   *Category 1 race.* Races of long distance and well offshore, where yachts must be completely self-sufficient for extended periods of time, capable of withstanding heavy storm and prepared to meet serious emergencies without the expectation of outside assistance.

4.3   *Category 2 race.* Races of extended duration along or not far removed from shorelines or in large unprotected bays or lakes, where a high degree of self-sufficiency is required of the yachts but with the reasonable probability that outside assistance could be called upon for aid in the event of serious emergencies.

4.4 *Category 3 race.* Races across open water, most of which is relatively protected or close to shorelines, including races for small yachts.

4.5 *Category 4 race.* Short races, close to shore in relatively warm or protected waters.

In the following lists, the star indicates that the item applies to the category in that column.

	RACE CATEGORY			
5.0 BASIC STANDARDS	**1**	**2**	**3**	**4**
5.1 All required equipment shall: *Function properly* *Be readily accessible* *Be of a type, size and capacity suitable and adequate for* *the intended use and size of the yacht*	●	●	●	●
5.2 *Yachts shall be self-righting (see IOR Part XII). They shall be strongly built, watertight, and, particularly with regard to hulls, decks and cabin trunks capable of withstanding solid water and knockdowns. They must be properly rigged and ballasted, be fully seaworthy and must meet the standards set forth herein. "Properly rigged" means (inter alia) that shrouds shall never be disconnected.*		●	●	●
5.3 *Inboard engine installation shall be such that the engine, when running, can be securely covered, and that the exhaust and fuel supply systems are securely installed and adequately protected from the effects of heavy weather. When an electric starter is the only provision for starting the engine, a separate battery shall be carried, the primary purpose of which is to start the engine.*	●	●	●	●
5.4 *Yacht equipment and fittings shall be securely fastened so as to remain in position should the yacht be capsized 180°.*	●	●	●	
5.5 *Yacht equipment and fittings shall be securely fastened.*				●
6.0 STRUCTURAL FEATURES				
6.1 *The hull, including deck, coach roof and all other parts, shall* form an integral, essentially watertight, unit and any openings in it shall be capable of being immediately secured to maintain this integrity (see 5.1). For example, running rigging or control lines shall not compromise this watertight unit. Centerboard and daggerboard trunks shall not open into the interior of the hull.	●	●	●	●
6.12 *Hatches.* No hatch forward of the BMAX station shall open inwards excepting ports having an area of less than 110 sq. in. (670cm²). Hatches shall be so arranged as to be above the water when the hull is heeled 90°. All hatches shall be permanently fitted so that they can be closed immediately and will remain firmly shut in a 180° capsize.	●	●	●	●
The main companionway hatch shall be fitted with a strong securing arrangement which shall be operable from above and below.	●	●	●	
6.13 *Companionways.* All blocking arrangements (washboards, hatch-boards, etc.) shall be capable of being secured in position with the hatch open or shut and shall be secured to the yacht by lanyard or other mechanical means to prevent their being lost overboard.	●	●	●	●
6.14 *Cockpit companionways,* if extended below main deck level, must be capable of being blocked off to the level of the main deck at the sheer line abreast the opening. When such blocking arrangements are in place this companionway (or hatch) shall continue to give access to the interior of the hull.	●	●	●	●
6.21 *Cockpits* shall be structurally strong, self-draining and permanently incorporated as an integral part of the hull. They must be essentially watertight, that is, all openings to the hull below the main deck level must be capable of being strongly and rigidly secured. Any bow, lateral, central or stern well will be considered as a cockpit for the purposes of 6.21, 6.22, 6.23 and 6.31.	●	●	●	●
6.22 *Cockpits opening aft to the sea.* The lower edge of the companionway shall not be below main	●	●	●	●

RACE CATEGORY 1 2 3 4

deck level as measured above. The openings shall not be less than 50% of max. cockpit depth multiplied by max. cockpit width. The requirement in 6.31 that cockpits must drain at all angles of heel, applies.

6.23   *Cockpit volume.*

6.23.1   Maximum volume of *all cockpits* below lowest coamings shall not exceed 6% L times B times FA. The cockpit sole must be at least 2% L above LWL.   [Cat: 1]

6.23.2   The maximum volume of *all cockpits* below lowest coamings shall not exceed 9% L times B times FA. The cockpit sole must be at least 2% L above LWL.   [Cat: 2, 3, 4]

6.31   *Cockpit drains*

6.31.1   *For yachts 21 feet rating and over.* Cockpit drains adequate to drain cockpits quickly but with a combined area (after allowance for screens, if attached) of not less than the equivalent of four ¾ in. (2cm) diameter drains. Yachts built before 1-1-72 must have drains with a combined area (after allowance for screens, if attached) of not less than the equivalent of two 1 in. (2.5cm) drains. Cockpits shall drain at all angles of heel.   [Cat: 1, 2, 3, 4]
    Yachts built before 1-1-77 may conform to 6.31.2 for races in Categories 3 and 4.

6.31.2   *For yachts under 21 feet rating.* Cockpit drains adequate to drain cockpits quickly but not less in combined area (after allowance for screens, if attached) than the equivalent of two 1 in. (2.5cm) diameter drains. Cockpits shall drain at all angles of heel.   [Cat: 1, 2, 3, 4]

6.4   *Storm covering* for all windows more than two square feet in area.   [Cat: 1, 2, 3]

6.51   *Sea cocks or valves* on all through-hull openings below LWL, except integral deck scuppers, shaft log, speed indicators, depth finders and the like, however a means of closing such openings, when necessary to do so, shall be provided.   [Cat: 1, 2, 3, 4]
    Does not apply in Category 4 races to yachts built before 1-1-76.

6.52   Soft wood plugs, tapered and of various sizes.   [Cat: 1, 2, 3, 4]

6.53   *Ballast and heavy equipment.* Inside ballast in a yacht shall be securely fastened in position. All other heavy internal fittings (such as batteries, stoves, gas bottles, tanks, engines, out-board motors, etc.) and anchors and chains (see 8.31 and 8.32) shall be securely fastened against a capsize.   [Cat: 1, 2, 3, 4]

6.54   *Sheet winches* shall be mounted in such a way that no operator is required to be substantially below deck.   [Cat: 1, 2, 3, 4]

6.6   LIFELINES, STANCHIONS AND PULPITS

6.61   *For all yachts*

6.61.1   *Life-line terminals.* A taut lanyard of synthetic rope may be used to secure life-lines, provided that when in position its length does not exceed 4 ins. (10cm).   [Cat: 1, 2, 3, 4]

6.61.2   *Stanchions shall* not be angled from the point of their attachment to the hull at more than ten degrees from vertical throughout their length.   [Cat: 1, 2, 3, 4]

6.61.3   *Overlapping pulpits.* Life-lines need not be affixed to the bow pulpit if they terminate at, or pass through, adequately braced stanchions 2 ft. (60cm) (18 ins. [45cm] for yachts under 21 ft. rating) above the working deck, set inside and overlapping the bow pulpit, provided that the gap between the upper life-line and the bow pulpit does not exceed 6 ins. (15cm).   [Cat: 1, 2, 3, 4]

6.61.4   *Pulpit and stanchion fixing.* Pulpits and stanchions shall be through-bolted or welded, and the bases thereof shall not be further inboard from the edge of the working deck than 5% of B max. or 6 ins. (15cm), whichever is greater. Stanchion bases shall not be situated outboard of the working deck.   [Cat: 1, 2, 3, 4]

6.62   *For yachts of 21 feet rating and over.*

	1	2	3	4

6.62.1 *Taut double life-lines,* with upper life-line of wire at a height of not less than 2 ft. (60cm) above the working deck, to be permanently supported at intervals of not more than 7 ft. (2.15m). When the cockpit opens aft to the sea, additional life-lines must be fitted so that no opening is greater in height than 22 ins. (56cm). **[1 ● 2 ● 3 ● 4 ●]**

6.62.2 *Pulpits.* Fixed bow pulpit (forward of headstay) and stern pulpit (unless life-lines are arranged as to adequately substitute for a stern pulpit). Lower life-lines need not extend through the bow pulpit. Upper rails of pulpits shall be at not less height above the working deck than upper life-lines. Upper rails in bow pulpits shall be securely closed while racing. **[1 ● 2 ● 3 ● 4 ●]**

Any lifeline attachment point will be considered as a stanchion in so far as its base shall not be situated outboard of the working deck.

6.63 *For yachts under 21 feet rating.*

6.63.1 *Taut single wire life-line,* at a height of not less than 18 ins. (45cm) above the working deck, to be permanently supported at intervals of not more than 7 ft. (2.15m). If the life-line is at any point more than 22 ins. (56cm) above the rail cap, a second intermediate life-line must be fitted. If the cockpit opens aft to the sea additional life-lines must be fitted so that no opening is greater in height than 22 ins. (56cm). **[1 ● 2 ● 3 ● 4 ●]**

6.63.2 *Pulpits.* Fixed bow pulpit and stern pulpit (unless life-lines are arranged as to adequately substitute for a stern pulpit). Lower life-lines need not extend through the bow pulpit. Upper rails of pulpits must be at no less height above the working deck than upper life-lines. Upper rails in bow pulpits shall be securely closed while racing. The bow pulpit may be fitted abaft the forestay with its bases secured at any points on deck, but a point on its upper rail must be within 16 ins. (40cm) of the forestay on which the foremost headsail is hanked. **[1 ● 2 ● 3 ● 4 ●]**

Any life-line attachment point will be considered as a stanchion so far as its base shall not be situated outboard of the working deck.

6.64 *Toe rails.* A toe-rail of not less than 1 in. (2.5cm) shall be permanently fitted around the deck forward of the mast, except in way of fittings. Location to be not further inboard from the edge of the working deck than one third of the local beam. **[1 ● 2 ● 3 ●]**

A third life-line (or second for yachts under 21 ft. rating) at a height of not less than 1 in. (2.5cm) or more than 2 ins. (5cm) above the working deck will be accepted in place of a toe-rail.

In yachts built before 1 January 1981 a toe-rail of ¾ in. (2cm) will be accepted.

7.0 ACCOMMODATIONS

7.11 *Toilet,* securely installed. **[1 ● 2 ●]**

7.12 *Toilet,* securely installed, or fitted bucket. **[3 ● 4 ●]**

7.2 *Bunks,* securely installed. **[1 ● 2 ● 3 ● 4 ●]**

7.31 *Cooking stove,* securely installed against a capsize with safe accessible fuel shutoff control capable of being safely operated in a seaway. **[1 ● 2 ●]**

7.32 *Cooking stove,* capable of being safely operated in a seaway. **[3 ●]**

7.41 *Galley facilities,* including sink. **[1 ● 2 ●]**

7.42 *Galley facilities.* **[3 ● 4 ●]**

7.51 *Water tanks,* securely installed and capable of dividing the water supply into at least two separate containers. **[1 ●]**

7.52 At least one securely installed water tank. **[3 ●]**

7.53 At least 2 gallons (9 litres) of water for emergency use carried in one or more separate containers. **[1 ● 2 ● 3 ●]**

	1	2	3	4
7.54 Suitable containers for water.			●	●
8.0 GENERAL EQUIPMENT				
8.1 *Fire extinguishers,* at least two, readily accessible in suitable and different parts of the boat.	●	●	●	●
8.21.1 *Bilge pumps,* at least two manually operated, securely fitted to the yacht's structure, one operable above, the other below deck. Each pump shall be operable with all cockpit seats, hatches and companionways shut.	●	●		
8.21.2 Each bilge pump shall be provided with permanently fitted discharge pipe(s) of sufficient capacity to accommodate simultaneously both pumps.	●	●		
8.21.3 No bilge pumps may discharge into a cockpit unless that cockpit opens aft to the sea. Bilge pumps shall not be connected to cockpit drains.	●	●	●	●
8.21.4 Unless permanently fitted, each bilge pump handle shall be provided with a lanyard or catch or similar device to prevent accidental loss.	●	●	●	
8.22 One manual bilge pump operable with all cockpit seats, hatches and companionways closed.			●	
8.23 One manual bilge pump.				●
8.24 Two buckets of stout construction each with at least 2 galls. (9 litres) capacity. Each bucket to have a lanyard.	●	●	●	●
8.31 *Anchors.* Two with cables except yachts rating under 21 feet, which shall carry at least one anchor and cable. Anchors and any chain shall be securely fastened in the position recorded on the Rating Certificate when not in use.	●	●	●	
8.32 One anchor and cable. Anchor(s) and any chain shall be securely fastened in the position recorded on the Rating Certificate when not in use.				●
8.41 *Flashlights,* one of which is suitable for signalling, water resistant, with spare batteries and bulbs.	●	●	●	
8.42 At least one flashlight, water resistant, with spare batteries and bulb.				●
8.5 *First aid kit* and manual.	●	●	●	●
8.6 *Foghorn.*	●	●	●	●
8.7 *Radar reflector.* If a radar reflector is octahedral it must have a minimum diagonal measurement of 18 ins. (46cm), or if not octahedral must have a documented 'equivalent echoing area' of not less than 10m².	●	●	●	●
8.8 *Set of international code flags* and international code book.	●			
8.9 *Shutoff valves* on all fuel tanks.	●	●	●	●
9.0 NAVIGATION EQUIPMENT				
9.1 *Compass,* marine type, properly installed and adjusted.	●	●	●	●
9.2 *Spare compass.*	●	●	●	
9.3 *Charts, light list and piloting equipment.*	●	●	●	
9.4 *Sextant, tables and accurate time piece.*	●			

	RACE CATEGORY			
	1	2	3	4
9.5 *Radio direction finder.*	●	●		
9.6 *Lead line or echo sounder.*	●	●	●	●
9.7 *Speedometer or distance measuring instrument.*	●	●	●	
9.8 *Navigation lights,* to be shown as required by the International Regulations for Preventing Collision at Sea, mounted so that they will not be masked by sails or the heeling of the yacht.	●	●	●	●

9.8   Yachts under 7m LOA shall comply with the regulations for those between 12m and 7m LOA (i.e. they shall exhibit sidelights and a sternlight).

10.0   EMERGENCY EQUIPMENT

	1	2	3	4
10.1 *Emergency navigation lights* and power source.	●	●	●	

10.21   *The following specifications for mandatory sails give maximum areas; smaller areas may well suit some yachts.*

	1	2	3	4
10.21.1 *One storm trysail* not larger than 0.175 P × E in area. It shall be sheeted independently of the boom and shall have neither a headboard nor battens and be of suitable strength for the purpose. The yacht's sail number and letter(s) shall be placed on both sides of the trysail in as large a size as is practicable.	●	●		
10.21.2 *One storm jib* of not more than 0.05 IG² in area, the luff of which does not exceed 0.65 IG, and of suitable strength for the purpose.	●	●		
10.21.3 *One heavy-weather jib* of suitable strength for the purpose with area not greater than 0.135 IG² and which does not contain reef points.	●	●		
10.22 One heavy-weather jib as in 10.21.3 (or heavy-weather sail in a boat with no forestay) and either: (a) a storm trysail as in 10.21.1 or (b) mainsail reefing equipment capable of reducing the effective luff to 60% P or less.			●	●
10.23 Any storm or heavy-weather jib if designed for a seastay or luff-groove device shall have an alternative method of attachment to the stay or a wire luff.	●	●	●	●
10.24 No mast shall have less than two halyards each capable of hoisting a sail.	●	●	●	●

10.3 *Emergency steering equipment*

	1	2	3	4
10.31 An emergency tiller capable of being fitted to the rudder stock.	●	●	●	
10.32 Crews must be aware of alternative methods of steering the yacht in any sea condition in the event of rudder failure. An inspector may require that this method be demonstrated.	●	●	●	●
10.4 *Tools and spare parts,* including adequate means to disconnect or sever the standing rigging from the hull in the case of need.	●	●	●	●
10.5 *Yacht's name* on miscellaneous buoyant equipment, such as life jackets, oars, cushions, etc. Portable sail number.	●	●	●	
10.61 *Marine radio transmitter and receiver.* If the regular antenna depends upon the mast, an emergency antenna must be provided.	●	●		

10.61   *Yachts fitted with VHF transceivers are recommended to install VHF* Channel 72 (156.625 MHz Simplex). This is an international ship-ship channel which, by "common use," could become an accepted yacht-yacht channel for all ocean racing yachts anywhere in the world.

	1	2	3	4
10.62 *Radio receiver* capable of receiving weather bulletins.	●	●	●	●

11.0 SAFETY EQUIPMENT

	RACE CATEGORY			
	1	2	3	4
11.1 *Life jackets,* one for each crew member.	●	●	●	●
11.2 *Whistles* attached to life jackets.	●	●	●	
11.3 *Safety belt* (harness type) one for each crew member.	●	●	●	

11.3 Each yacht may be required to demonstrate that two thirds of the crew can be adequately attached to strong points on the yacht.

	1	2	3	4
11.41 *Life raft(s)* capable of carrying the entire crew and meeting the following requirements:	●	●	●	

Must be carried on the working deck or in a special stowage opening immediately to the working deck containing the life-raft(s) only except that life-raft(s) packed in a valise and not exceeding 40 kg. may be securely stowed below deck adjacent to the companionway. Each raft shall be capable of being got to the lifelines within 15 seconds.

Must be designed and used solely for saving life at sea:

Must have at least two separate buoyancy compartments, each of which must be automatically inflatable; each raft must be capable of carrying its rated capacity with one compartment deflated:

Must have a canopy to cover the occupants:

Must have a valid annual certificate from the manufacturer or an approved servicing agent certifying that it has been inspected, that it complies with the above requirements and stating the official capacity of the raft which shall not be exceeded. The certificate, or a copy thereof, to be carried on board the yacht.

Must have the following equipment appropriately secured to each raft:

Sea anchor or drogue
1 Bellows, pump or other means for maintaining inflation of air chambers
1 Signalling light
3 Hand flares
1 Baler
1 Repair Kit
2 Paddles
1 Knife

	1	2	3	4
11.42 Provision for emergency water and rations to accompany raft.	●			
11.51 *Life ring(s),* at least one horseshoe type life ring equipped with a waterproof light and drogue within reach of the helmsman and ready for instant use.				●
11.52 At least one horseshoe-type life-ring equipped with a drogue and a self-igniting light having a duration of at least 45 minutes within reach of the helmsman and ready for instant use.	●	●	●	
11.53 At least one more horseshoe-type life-ring equipped with a whistle, dye marker, drogue, a self-igniting high-intensity water light, and a pole and flag. The pole shall be permanently extended and attached to the ring with 25 ft. (8m) of floating line and is to be of a length and so ballasted that the flag will fly at least 6 ft. (1.8m) off the water.	●	●		
11.61 *Distress signals* to be stowed in waterproof container(s), and meeting the following requirements for each category, as indicated:	●	●	●	●
11.62 Twelve red parachute flares.	●			
11.63 Four red parachute flares.			●	●
11.64 Four red hand flares.	●	●	●	●
11.65 Four white hand flares.	●	●	●	●
11.66 Two orange smoke day signals.	●	●	●	
11.7 *Heaving line* (50 ft. [16m] minimum length) readily accessible to cockpit.	●	●	●	●

Index